ADULT NONFICTION

814.54 D922m

Dunne, Dominick
Mansions of limbo

W9-ARD-402

8000234290

Dunne, D   814.54
                                D922m
The mansions of Limbo   c.1

WITHDRAWN

ADULT DEPARTMENT

1. Materials are not renewable.

2. Fine Schedule
   1-5 days overdue .... grace period, no fine
   6-10 days overdue .... 25¢ per item
   11-19 days overdue .... 75¢ per item
   20th day overdue .... $2.00 per item

3. Damage to materials beyond reasonable wear and all losses shall be paid for.

4. Each borrower is held responsible for all materials drawn on his card and for all fines accruing on the same.

FOND DU LAC PUBLIC LIBRARY
COUNTY EXTENSION DEPARTMENT
FOND DU LAC, WISCONSIN

THE MANSIONS OF LIMBO

THE MANSIONS OF LIMBO

DOMINICK DUNNE

CROWN PUBLISHERS, INC.

NEW YORK

All of the articles in this book were
previously published in *Vanity Fair.*

Copyright © 1991 by Dominick Dunne

All rights reserved. No part of this book may be reproduced or transmitted in any form
or by any means, electronic or mechanical, including photocopying, recording, or by
any information storage and retrieval system, without permission in writing
from the publisher.

Published by Crown Publishers, Inc.
201 East 50th Street
New York, New York 10022
Member of the Crown Publishing Group.

CROWN is a trademark of Crown Publishers, Inc.

Manufactured in the United States of America

Library of Congress Cataloging-in-Publication Data

Dunne, Dominick.
The mansions of limbo/Dominick Dunne.
        p.   cm.
        I. Title.
        PS3554.U492M36   1991
814′.54—dc20   91-6589
                        CIP
            ISBN 0-517-58385-2

        10   9   8   7   6   5

14.54
922m
: 1

To Tina Brown
who held out her hand,
with thanks and love

FOND DU LAC PUBLIC LIBRARY
COUNTY EXTENSION DEPARTMENT

CONTENTS

INTRODUCTION

YEARS AGO, reading a book whose title I no longer remember, I came across a sentence in which the words "the mansions of limbo" appeared. I was struck by those words. I loved the sound of them, and they have always stayed with me. In my Catholic youth, I learned that limbo was a blissful repository for the souls of infants who died before they were baptized, a community whose perfection was marred only by the fact that they were denied the sight of God. As I grew older, the meaning of limbo broadened to signify a state of privileged oblivion with a missing ingredient. When I began to put together the pieces from *Vanity Fair* that make up this collection, I tried to find a unifying factor in the kind of people and situations I write about, and the words that I read so long ago returned to me. However, I could never find the book in which I read them. Neither could scholarly friends or *Bartlett's Quotations* reveal their source. So I have simply usurped the words to make up the title of this book.

Not all, but most of the people I write about here soared in the decade of the eighties, a period in which the fortunes of the rich seemed limitless, and our information about them equally limitless. We knew, often with their cooperation, everything there was to know about them: how much money they were worth, how much they paid for their houses, their paintings, their curtains, their dresses, their centerpieces, and their parties. They acquired and acquired, and climbed and climbed. One man earned $550 million in a single year. The cost of another man's new house reached nearly $100 million. Perhaps it was bliss for them, but, certainly, it was bliss with a missing ingredient. Toward the end, some of the luminous figures went to jail for fiscal irregularities. The marriages of others began to disentangle. And a horrible new disease was killing the innocent in appalling numbers. Then the decade ended.

Has any other decade ever ended so promptly? On the twelfth

stroke of midnight on December 31, 1989, it was over, finished, done with, history. The sixties, as they will always be remembered, were reluctant to go. The sixties continued to dance to the music of time until the fourth year of the seventies, before allowing that patient decade to define itself. But people were sick of the eighties, sick of the criminal improprieties of Wall Street, sick of the obeisance to money while the homeless occupied more and more sidewalk space in our cities. People wanted the eighties to be finished. And yet, for as long as it lasted, there was a hilariously horrifying fascination in watching the people who overindulged in extravagance, especially the ones who fell so resoundingly from grace and favor. Twice I went to prisons, one in Lucca, Italy, the other in Bern, Switzerland, to interview financial figures whose life styles and careers had only recently blazed on the social and financial pages. In Venice an Australian heiress almost married a prince in an international social event, but the heiress was not really an heiress and the prince turned out to be a steward on Qantas Airlines, who eloped with his best man the night before the wedding. In Geneva I watched rich people, mad for instant heritage, stand on chairs and wildly overbid and overpay for the late Duchess of Windsor's jewels at an auction staged by Sotheby's in a circus atmosphere worthy of P. T. Barnum. Once I was the lone American on a sailing ship of English aristocrats and minor royals on a cruise through several tropical islands in the Caribbean, a nobleman's odyssey culminating in a bizarre costume ball on the sands of an island mansion where grand ladies wore tiaras and men adorned themselves with plumes, pearls, and white satin. On Lake Lugano, the beauty queen fifth wife of the man with the second largest art collection in the world, after that of the Queen of England, brought about the transfer of her husband's famed artworks from Switzerland to her native Spain in hopes of obtaining the title of duchess from the Spanish king. In New York, a great photographer, who recorded with acute precision the dark side of the netherworld as it has never been recorded before, took my picture only a short time before he died. In a Beverly Hills mansion, a film mogul and his wife were brutally slain gangland style, and, seven months later, their two handsome and privileged sons were arrested for the crime, after a massive spending spree with their new inheritance.

All the pieces do not fit into the pattern of the late decade. There are the eternal figures like the singer Phyllis McGuire, once the mistress of the gangster Sam Giancana, in her Las Vegas mansion, and the actress Jane Wyman, the only divorced wife of a United States president, who have defied time and continue to fascinate. There is Lady Kenmare, the chatelaine of a great house in the South of France, who flourished in international society in the thirties, forties, and fifties as the rumored murderess of her four husbands. And, finally, there is the beautiful and highly intelligent Queen Noor of Jordan, the American fourth wife of King Hussein, who sits on a precarious throne between Israel and Iraq during the war that will define the new decade.

Dominick Dunne
New York, 1991

THE MANSIONS
OF LIMBO

NIGHTMARE ON ELM DRIVE

ON A RECENT New York–to–Los Angeles trip on MGM Grand Air, that most luxurious of all coast-to-coast flights, I was chilled to the bone marrow during a brief encounter with a fellow passenger, a boy of perhaps fourteen, or fifteen, or maybe even sixteen, who lounged restlessly in a sprawled-out fashion, arms and legs akimbo, avidly reading racing-car magazines, chewing gum, and beating time to the music on his Walkman. Although I rarely engage in conversations with strangers on airplanes, I always have a certain curiosity to know who everyone is on MGM Grand Air, which I imagine is a bit like the Orient Express in its heyday. The young traveler in the swivel chair was returning to California after a sojourn in Europe. There were signals of affluence in his chat; the Concorde was mentioned. His carry-on luggage was expensive, filled with audiotapes, playing cards, and more magazines. During the meal, we talked. A week before, two rich and privileged young men named Lyle and Erik Menendez had been arrested for the brutal slaying of their parents in the family's $5 million mansion on Elm Drive, a sedate tree-lined street that is considered one of the most prestigious addresses in Beverly Hills. The tale in all its gory grimness was the cover story that week in *People* magazine, many copies of which were being read on the plane.

"Do you live in Beverly Hills?" I asked.

"Yes."

"Where?"

He told me the name of his street, which was every bit as prestigious as Elm Drive. I once lived in Beverly Hills and knew the terrain well. His home was in the same general area as the house where Kitty and Jose Menendez had been gunned down several months earlier in a fusillade of fourteen twelve-gauge shotgun blasts—five to the head and body of the father, nine to the face and body of the mother—that left them virtually unrecognizable as human beings, according to eyewitness reports. The slaying was so violent that it was assumed at first to have been of Mafia origins —a hit, or Mob rubout, as it was called, even in the *Wall Street Journal*. The arrest of the two handsome, athletic Menendez sons after so many months of investigation had shocked an unshockable community.

"Did you ever know the Menendez brothers?" I asked the teenager.

"No," he replied. They had gone to different schools. They were older. Lyle was twenty-two, Erik nineteen. In that age group, a few years makes an enormous difference.

"A terrible thing," I said.

"Yeah," he replied. "But I heard the father was pretty rough on those kids."

With that, our conversation was concluded.

Patricide is not an altogether new crime in the second echelon of Southland society. Nor is matricide. On March 24, 1983, twenty-year-old Michael Miller, the son of President Ronald Reagan's personal lawyer, Roy Miller, raped and clubbed to death his mother, Marguerite. In a minimally publicized trial, from which the media was barred, Miller was found guilty of first-degree murder but was acquitted of the rape charge, presumably on the technicality that the rape had occurred after his mother was dead. The judge then ruled that young Miller, who had been diagnosed as schizophrenic, was legally innocent of murder by reason of insanity. "Hallelujah," muttered Michael Miller after the verdict. He was sent to Patton State hospital, a mental institution in California.

On July 22, 1983, in a Sunset Boulevard mansion in Bel-Air, twenty-year-old Ricky Kyle shot his father, millionaire Henry Harrison Kyle, the president of Four Star International, a television-and-movie-production firm, in the back after awakening him in the middle of the night to tell him there was a prowler in the house. Several witnesses testified that Ricky had confided in them about a long-standing desire to kill his father, who was alleged to have been physically and mentally abusive to his son. The prosecution argued that Ricky was consumed with hatred for his father and greed for his fortune, and that, fearing that he was about to be disinherited, he plotted the ruse of the prowler. With the extraordinary leniency of the Southern California courts for first-time murderers, young Kyle was sentenced to five years for the slaying. Expressing dismay with the verdict, Ricky's mother told reporters she had hoped her son would be spared a prison term. "I think he has suffered enough," she said. Ricky agreed. "I feel like I don't deserve to go to prison," he said.

And then there were the Woodman brothers, Stewart and Neil, accused of hiring two assassins to gun down their rich parents in Brentwood. Tried separately, Stewart was convicted of first-degree murder. To escape the death penalty, he incriminated his brother. Neil's trial is about to start.

Further elaboration is not necessary: the point has been made. One other case, however, on a lesser social stratum but of equal importance, under the circumstances, should be mentioned: the Salvatierra murder, which received international attention. In 1986, Oscar Salvatierra, the Los Angeles–based executive of a newspaper called *Philippine News*, was shot while he was asleep in bed, after having received a death threat that was at first believed to be tied to the newspaper's opposition to former Philippine president Ferdinand Marcos. Later, Arnel Salvatierra, his seventeen-year-old son, admitted sending the letter and killing his father. In court, Arnel Salvatierra's lawyer convinced the jury that Arnel was the victim of a lifetime of physical and psychological abuse by his father. The lawyer, Leslie Abramson, who is considered to be the most brilliant Los Angeles defense lawyer for death-row cases, compared Arnel Salvatierra to the tragic Lisa Steinberg of New York, whose father, Joel Steinberg, had been convicted of murdering her after relentlessly abusing her. "What happens if the Lisa Steinbergs don't die?" Abramson asked the jury. "What happens if they get older, and if the cumulative effect of all these years of abuse finally drives them over the edge, and Lisa Steinberg pulls out a gun and kills Joel Steinberg?" Arnel Salvatierra, who had been charged with first-degree murder, was convicted of voluntary manslaughter and placed on probation.

This story is relevant to the Menendez case in that the same Leslie Abramson is one-half the team defending the affluent Menendez brothers. Her client is Erik Menendez, the younger brother. Gerald Chaleff, with whom she frequently teams, is representing Lyle. On an earlier burglary case involving the brothers, Chaleff, who gained prominence in criminal law as the defender of the Hillside Strangler, represented Erik. It is rumored that Abramson and Chaleff are each being paid $700,000. Psychological abuse is a constant theme in articles written about the brothers, and will probably be the basis of the defense strategy when the case comes to trial. There are even whispers—shocker of shockers—of sexual abuse in the Menendez family.

Jose Enrique Menendez was an American success story. A Cuban émigré, he was sent to the United States by his parents in 1960 at age fifteen to escape from Castro's Cuba. His father, a onetime soccer star, and his mother, a former champion swimmer, stayed behind until their last properties were seized by Castro. Young Jose, who excelled in swimming, basketball, and soccer, won a swimming scholarship to Southern Illinois University, but he gave it up when he married Mary Louise Andersen, known as Kitty, at the age of nineteen and moved to New York. He earned a degree in accounting at Queens College in Flushing, New York, while working part-time as a dishwasher at the swank "21" Club in Manhattan, where, later, successful and prosperous, he would often dine. Then began a career of astonishing ascendancy which took him through Hertz, where he was in charge of car and commercial leasing, to the record division of RCA, where he signed such high-earning acts as Menudo, the Eurythmics, and Duran Duran. By this time he and Kitty had had two sons and settled down to a graceful life on a million-dollar estate in Princeton, New Jersey. The boys attended the exclusive Princeton Day School and, urged on by their father, began developing into first-rate tennis and soccer players. Their mother attended every match and game they played. When Jose clashed with a senior executive at RCA in 1986, after having been passed over for the executive vice presidency of RCA Records, he uprooted his family, much to the distress of Kitty, who loved her life and house in Princeton, and moved to Los Angeles. There he leapfrogged to I.V.E., International Video Entertainment, a video distributor which eventually became Live Entertainment, a division of the hugely successful Carolco Pictures, the company that produced the Rambo films of Sylvester Stallone as well as some of Arnold Schwarzenegger's action films. Jose Menendez's success at Live Entertainment was dazzling. In 1986 the company lost $20 million; a year later, under Menendez, Live earned $8 million and in 1988 doubled that. "He was the perfect corporate executive," I was told by one of his lieutenants. "He had an incredible dedication to business. He was focused, specific about what he wanted from the business, very much in control. He believed that whatever had to be done should be done—with no heart, if necessary."

The family lived at first in Calabasas, an upper-middle-class suburb of Los Angeles, inland beyond Malibu, where they occupied one house while building a more spectacular one on thirteen acres with mountaintop views. Then, unexpectedly, almost overnight, the family abandoned Calabasas and moved to Beverly Hills, where Jose bought the house on Elm Drive, a six-bedroom Mediterranean-style house with a red tile roof, a courtyard, a swimming pool, a tennis court, and a guesthouse. Built in 1927, rebuilt in 1974, the house had good credentials. It had previously been rented to Elton John. And Prince. And Hal Prince. And a Saudi prince, for $35,000 a month. Erik Menendez, the younger son, transferred from Calabasas High to Beverly Hills High, probably the most snobbish public school in America. Lyle was a student at Princeton University, fulfilling one of the many American dreams of his immigrant father.

They were the ideal family; everyone said so. "They were extraordinarily close-knit," an executive of Live Entertainment told me. "It was one big happy family," said John E. Mason, a friend and Live Entertainment director. They did things together. They telephoned one another several times a day, about tennis matches and girlfriends and the results of exams. They almost always had dinner together, which, in a community where most parents go to parties or screenings every night and leave their children to their own devices, is a rare thing. They talked about world events, as well as about what was happening in Jose's business. On the day before the catastrophic event, a Saturday, they chartered a boat called *Motion Picture Marine* in Marina del Rey and spent the day together shark-fishing, just the four of them.

On the evening of the following day, August 20, 1989, the seemingly idyllic world that Jose Menendez had created was shattered.

With their kids at the movies in Century City, Jose and Kitty settled in for a comfortable evening of television and videos in the television room at the rear of their house. Jose was in shorts and a sweatshirt; Kitty was in a sweatshirt, jogging pants, and sneakers. They had dishes of strawberries and ice cream on the table in front of the sofa where they were sitting. Later, after everything happened, a neighbor would report hearing sounds like firecrackers coming from the house at about ten o'clock, but he took no notice. It wasn't until a hysterical 911 call came in to the Beverly Hills police station around midnight that there was any indication that the sounds had not been made by firecrackers. The sons of the house, Lyle and Erik, having returned from the movies, where they said they saw *Batman* again after they couldn't get into *License to Kill* because of the lines, drove in the gate at 722 North Elm Drive, parked their car in the courtyard, entered the house by the front door, and found their parents dead, sprawled on the floor and couch in the television room. In shock at the grisly sight, Lyle telephoned for help. "They shot and killed my parents!" he shrieked into the instrument. "I don't know . . . I didn't hear anything . . . I just came home. Erik! Shut up! Get away from them!"

Another neighbor said on television that she had seen one of the Menendez boys curled up in a ball on the lawn in front of their house and screaming in grief. "I have heard of very few murders that were more savage," said Beverly Hills police chief Marvin Iannone. Dan Stewart, a retired police detective hired by the family to investigate the murders, gave the most graphic description of the sight in the television room. "I've seen a lot of homicides, but nothing quite that brutal. Blood, flesh, skulls, It would be hard to describe, especially Jose, as resembling a human that you would recognize. That's how bad it was." According to the autopsy report, one blast caused "explosive decapitation with evisceration of the brain" and "deformity of the face" to Jose Menendez. The first round of shots apparently struck Kitty in her chest, right arm, left hip, and left leg. Her murderers then reloaded and fired into her face, causing "multiple lacerations of the brain." Her face was an unrecognizable pulp.

The prevalent theory in the days following the murders was that it had been a Mob hit. Erik Menendez went so far as to point the finger at Noel Bloom, a distributor of pornographic films and a former associate of the Bonanno organized-crime family, as a possible suspect. Erik told police and early reporters on the story that Bloom and his father had despised each other after a business deal turned sour. (When questioned, Bloom denied any involvement whatsoever.) Expressing fear that the Mob might be after them as well, the brothers moved from hotel to hotel in the aftermath of the murders. Marlene Mizzy, the front-desk supervisor at the Beverly Hills Hotel, said that Lyle arrived at the hotel without a reservation two days after the murders and asked for a two-bedroom suite. Not liking the suites that were available on such short notice, he went to another hotel.

Seven months later, after the boys were arrested, I visited the house on Elm Drive. It is deceptive in size, far larger than one would imagine from the outside. You enter a spacious hallway with a white marble floor and a skylight above. Ahead, to the right, is a stairway carpeted in pale green. Off the hallway on one side is an immense drawing room, forty feet in length. The lone piece of sheet music on the grand piano was "American Pie," by Don McLean. On the other side are a small paneled sitting room and a large dining room. At the far end of the hallway, in full view of the front door, is the television room, where Kitty and Jose spent their last evening together. On the back wall is a floor-to-ceiling bookcase, filled with books, many of them paperbacks, including all the American-history novels of Gore Vidal, Jose's favorite author. On the top shelf of the bookcase were sixty tennis trophies—all first place—that had been won over the years by Lyle and Erik.

Like a lot of houses of the movie nouveau riche still in their social and business rise, the grand exterior is not matched by a grand interior. When the Menendez family bought the house, it was handsomely furnished, and they could have bought the furniture from the former owner for an extra $350,000, but they declined. With the exception of some reproduction Chippendale chairs in the dining room, the house is appallingly furnished with second-rate pieces; either the purchase price left nothing for interior decoration or there was just a lack of interest. In any case, your attention, once you are in the house, is not on the furniture. You are drawn, like a magnet, to the television room.

Trying to imagine what happened that night, I found it unlikely that the boys—if indeed it was the boys, and there is a very vocal contingent who believe it was not—would have come down the stairs with the guns, turned right, and entered the television room, facing their parents. Since Jose was hit point-blank in the back of the head, it seems far more likely that the killers entered the television room through the terrace doors behind the sofa on which Kitty and Jose were sitting, their backs to the doors, facing the television set. The killers would probably have unlocked the doors in advance. In every account of the murders, Kitty was said to have run toward the kitchen. This would suggest, assuming she was running away from her assailants, that they had entered from behind.

Every person who saw the death scene has described the blood, the guts, and the carnage in sick-making detail. The furniture I saw in that room was replacement furniture, rented after the murders from Antiquarian Traders in West Hollywood. The original blood-drenched furniture and Oriental carpet had been hauled away, never to be sat on or walked on again. It is not farfetched to imagine that splatterings of blood and guts found their way onto the clothes and shoes of the killers, which would have necessitated a change of clothing and possibly a shower. There is no way the killers could have gone up the stairs, however; the blood on their shoes would have left tracks on the pale green stair carpet. The lavatory beneath the stairs and adjacent to the television room does not have a shower. What probably happened is that the killers retreated out the same terrace doors they had entered, and went back to the guesthouse to shower and change into clothes they had left there. The guesthouse is a separate, two-story unit beyond the swimming pool and adjacent to the tennis court, with a sitting room, a bedroom, a full bath, and a two-car garage opening onto an alley.

There is also the possibility that the killers, knowing the carnage twelve-gauge-shotgun blasts would cause, wore boots, gloves, and overalls. In that event, they would have only had to discard the clothes and boots into a large garbage bag and make a dash for it. One of the most interesting aspects of the case is that the fourteen shell casings were picked up and removed. I have been told that such fastidiousness is out of character in a Mafia hit, where a speedy getaway is essential. There is a sense of leisurely time here, of people not in a hurry, not expecting anyone, when they delay their departure from a massacre to pick the shell casings out of the bloody remains of their victims' bodies. They almost certainly wore rubber gloves to do it.

Then they had to get rid of the guns. The guns, as of this writing, have still not been found. We will come back to the guns. The car the killers left in was probably parked in the guesthouse garage; from there they could make their exit unobserved down the alley behind the house. Had they left out the front gate on Elm Drive, they would have risked being observed by neighbors or passersby. Between the time the killers left the house and the time the boys made the call to the police, the bloody clothes were probably disposed of.

On the day before the fishing trip on the *Motion Picture Marine*, Erik Menendez allegedly drove south to San Diego and purchased two Mossberg twelve-gauge shotguns in a Big 5 sporting-goods store, using for identification the stolen driver's license of a young man named Donovan Goodreau. Under federal law, to purchase a weapon, an individual must fill out a 4473 form, which requires the buyer to provide his name, address, and signature, as well as an identification card with picture. Donovan Goodreau had subsequently said on television that he can prove he was in New York at the time of the gun purchase in San Diego. Goodreau had once roomed with Jamie Pisarcik, who was, and still is, Lyle Menendez's girlfriend and stalwart supporter, visiting him daily in jail and attending his every court session. When Goodreau stopped rooming with Jamie, he moved into Lyle's room at Princeton, which was against the rules, since he was not a student at the university. But then, Lyle had once kept a puppy in his room at Princeton, and having animals in the rooms was against the rules, too.

What has emerged most significantly in the year since the murders is that all was not what it seemed in the seemingly perfect Menendez household. There are people who will tell you that Jose was well liked. There are more people by far who will tell you that he was greatly disliked. Even despised. He had made enemies all along the way in his rise to the high middle of the entertainment industry, but everyone agrees that had he lived he would have gone right to the top. He did not have many personal friends, and he and Kitty were not involved in the party circuit of Beverly Hills. His life was family and business. I was told that at the memorial service in Los Angeles, which preceded the funeral in Princeton, most of the two hundred people who attended had a business rather than a personal relationship with him. Stung by the allegations that Jose had Mob connections in his business dealings at Live Entertainment, allegations that surfaced immediately after the murders, the company hired Warren Cowan, the famed public-relations man, to arrange the memorial service. His idea was to present Menendez as Jose the family man. He suggested starting a Jose Menendez scholarship fund, a suggestion that never came to fruition. It was also his idea to hold the memorial service in an auditorium at the Directors Guild in Hollywood, in order to show that Jose was a member of the entertainment community, although it is doubtful that Jose had ever been there. Two people from Live Entertainment gave glowing eulogies. Brian Andersen, Kitty's brother, spoke lovingly about Kitty, and each son spoke reverently about his parents. One person leaving the service was heard to say, "The only word not used to describe Jose was 'prick.' "

Although Jose spoke with a very slight accent, a business cohort described him to me as "very non-Hispanic." He was once offended when he received a letter of congratulations for having achieved such a high place in the business world "for a Hispanic." "He hated anyone who knew anything about his heritage," the colleague said. On the other hand, there was a part of Jose Menendez that secretly wanted to run for the U.S. Senate from Florida in order to free Cuba from the tyranny of Fidel Castro and make it a U.S. territory.

Kitty Menendez was another matter. You never hear a bad word about Kitty. Back in Princeton, people remember her on the tennis courts with affection. Those who knew her in the later years of her life felt affection too, but they also felt sorry for her. She was a deeply unhappy woman, and was becoming a pathetic one. Her husband was flagrantly unfaithful to her, and she was devastated by his infidelity. There has been much talk since the killings of Jose's having had a mistress, but that mistress was by no means his first, although he was said to have had "fidelity in his infidelity" in that particular relationship. Kitty fought hard to hold her marriage together, but it is unlikely that Jose would ever have divorced her. An employee at Live Entertainment said, "Kitty called Jose at his office every thirty minutes, sometimes just to tell him what kind of pizza to bring home for supper. She was a dependent person. She wanted to go on his business trips with him. She had June Allyson looks. Very warm. She also had a history of drinking and pills." Another business associate of Jose's at Live said, "I knew Kitty at company dinners and cocktail parties. They used to say about Kitty that she was Jose with a wig. She was always very much at his side, part of his vision, dedicated to the cause, whatever the cause was."

A more intimate picture of Kitty comes from Karen Lamm, one of the most highly publicized secondary characters in the Menendez saga. A beautiful former actress and model who was once wed to the late Dennis Wilson of the Beach Boys, Lamm is now a television producer, and she and her partner, Zev Braun, are developing a mini-series based on the Menendez case. Lamm is often presented as Kitty's closest friend and confidante. However, friends of Erik and Lyle decry her claims of friendship with Kitty, asserting that the boys did not know her, and asking how she could have been such a great friend of Kitty's if she was totally unknown to the sons.

Most newspaper accounts say that Karen Lamm and Kitty Menendez met in an aerobics class, but Lamm, who says she dislikes exercise classes, gave a different account of the beginning of their friendship. About a year before the murders, she was living with a film executive named Stuart Benjamin, who was a business acquaintance of Jose Menendez. Benjamin was a partner of the film director Taylor Hackford in a production company called New Visions Pictures, which Menendez was interested in acquiring as a subsidiary for Live Entertainment. During the negotiation period, Benjamin, with Lamm as his date, attended a dinner party at the Menendez house on Elm Drive. Lamm, who is an effusive and witty conversationalist, and Kitty spent much of the evening talking together. It was the beginning of a friendship that would blossom. Lamm described Kitty to me as being deeply unhappy over her husband's philandering. She claims that Kitty had tried suicide on three occasions, the kind of at-home suicide attempts that are more cries for help than a longing for death. Kitty had once won a beauty contest and could still be pretty on occasion, but she had let her looks go, grown fat (her autopsy report described her as "fairly well-nourished" and gave her weight as 165), and dyed her hair an unbecoming blond color that did not suit her. Lamm suggested that she get back into shape, and took her to aerobics classes, as well as offering her advice on a darker hair color. During the year that followed, the two women became intimate friends, and Kitty confided in Lamm, not only about Jose's infidelity but also about the many problems they were having with their sons.

Lamm said she met the boys three times, but never talked to them in the house on Elm Drive. She told me. "Those kids watched their mother become a doormat for their father. Jose lived through Lyle. Jose made Lyle white bread. He sent him to Princeton. He gave him all the things that were not available to him as an immigrant." Lamm finally talked with Kitty's sons at the memorial service at the Directors Guild. She was introduced to Lyle, who, in turn, introduced her to Erik as "Mom's friend." She said that Lyle had become Jose overnight. He radiated confidence and showed no emotion, "unless it was a convenient moment." Erik, on the other hand, fell apart.

Over the previous two years, the handsome, athletic, and gifted Menendez sons had been getting into trouble. Although a great friend of the boys dismissed their scrapes as merely "rich kids' sick jokes," two events occurred in Calabasas, where the family lived before the move to Beverly Hills, that were to have momentous consequences for all the members of the family. The brothers got involved in two very serious criminal offenses, a burglary at the home of Michael Warren Ginsberg in Calabasas and grand theft at the home of John Richard List in Hidden Hills. In total, more than $100,000 in money and jewels was taken from the two houses—not an insignificant sum.

Jose dealt with his sons' transgressions the way he would deal with any prickly business problem, said a business associate, by "minimizing the damage and going forward, fixing something that was broken without actually dealing with the problem." He simply took over and solved it. The money and jewels were returned, and

$11,000 in damages was paid. Since Erik was underage, it was decided that he would take the fall for both brothers, thereby safeguarding Jose's dream of having Lyle study at Princeton. Jose hired the criminal lawyer Gerald Chaleff to represent Erik—the same Gerald Chaleff who is now representing Lyle on the charge of murdering the man who once hired him to represent Erik on the burglary charge. Everything was solved to perfection. Erik got probation, no more. And compulsory counseling. And for that, Kitty asked her psychologist, Les Summerfield, to recommend someone her son could go to for the required number of hours ordered by the judge. Les Summerfield recommend a Beverly Hills psychologist named Jerome Oziel, who, like Gerald Chaleff, continues his role to the Menendez saga right up to the present.

Prior to the thefts, Erik had made a friend at Calabasas High School who would also play a continuing part in the story. Craig Cignarelli, the son of a prominent executive in the television industry, is a Tom Cruise look-alike currently studying at the University of California in Santa Barbara. Craig was the captain of the Calabasas High School tennis team, and Erik, who had recently transferred from Princeton Day, was the No. 1 singles player on the team. One day, while playing a match together, they were taunted by two students from El Camino High School, a rival school in a less affluent neighborhood. Menendez and Cignarelli went out to the street to face their adversaries, and a fight started. Suddenly, a whole group of El Camino boys jumped out of cars and joined the fray. Erik and Craig were both badly beaten up. Erik's jaw was broken, and Craig received severe damage to his ribs. The incident sparked a close friendship between the two, which would culminate in the co-writing of a movie script called *Friends*, in which a young man named Hamilton Cromwell murders his extremely rich parents for his inheritance. One of the most quoted passages from this screenplay comes from the mouth of Hamilton Cromwell, speaking about his father: "Sometimes he would tell me that I was not worthy to be his son. When he did that, it would make me strive harder . . . just so I could hear the words 'I love you, son.' . . . And I never heard those words." To add to the awful irony, Kitty, the loving mother who could not do enough for her sons, typed the screenplay in which her own demise seems to have been predicted. In the embarrassing aftermath of the burglaries, the family moved to the house on Elm Drive in Beverly Hills. Jose told people at Live Entertainment that he was upset by the drug activity in Calabasas and that the tires of his car had been slashed, but it is quite possible that these stories were a diversionary tactic, or smoke screen, created to cover the disgrace of his son's criminal record.

A further setback for the family, also partly covered up, had occurred the previous winter, when Lyle was suspended from Princeton after one semester for cheating in Psychology 101. Taken before a disciplinary committee, he was told he could leave the university voluntarily or be expelled. He chose to leave. This was a grave blow to Jose, who loved to tell people that he had a son at Princeton. Again taking over, he tried to talk the authorities at Princeton into reinstating his son, but this time the pressure he applied did not work. The suspension lasted a year. In a typical reaction, Jose became more angry at the school than he was at his son. He urged Lyle to stay on in Princeton rather than return to Beverly Hills, so that he would not have to admit to anyone that Lyle had been kicked out.

But Lyle did return, and worked briefly at Live Entertainment, where he showed all the worst qualities of the spoiled rich boy holding down a grace-and-favor job in his father's company. He was consistently late for work. His attention span was brief. He worked short hours, leaving in the afternoon to play tennis. He was unpopular with the career-oriented staff. "The kids had a sense of being young royalty," said an employee of the company. "They could be nasty, arrogant, and self-centered." But, the same person said, Jose had a blind spot about his sons. And tennis held the family together. Once, Jose took the Concorde to Europe just to watch Lyle play in a tennis tournament, and then came right back. However, for all the seeming closeness of the family, the sons were proving to be disappointments, even failures, in the eyes of their perfection-demanding father. Jose had apparently come to the end of financing his recalcitrant sons' rebellion, and there are indications that he planned to revise his will.

After the Calabasas debacle, Erik transferred to Beverly Hills High School for his senior year. His classmates remember him chiefly as a loner, walking around in tennis shorts, always carrying his tennis racket.

"A girl I was going out with lusted after him," a student told me. "She said he had good legs."

"Was he spoiled?"

"Everyone at Beverly High is spoiled."

Like his father, Lyle is said to have been a great ladies' man, which pleased Jose, but several of Lyle's girlfriends, mostly older than he, were not considered to be suitable by his parents, and clashes occurred. When Jose forbade Lyle to go to Europe with an older girlfriend, Lyle went anyway. A person extremely close to the family told me that another of Lyle's girlfriends—not Jamie Pisarcik, who has been so loyal to him during his incarceration—was "manipulating him," which I took to mean manipulating him into marriage. This girl became pregnant. Jose, in his usual method of dealing with his sons' problems, moved in and paid off the girl to abort the child. The manner of Jose's interference in so personal a matter—not allowing Lyle to deal with his own problem—is said to have infuriated Lyle and caused a deep rift between father and son. Lyle moved out of the main house into the guesthouse at the back of the property. He was still living there at the time of the murders, although Erik continued to live in the main house.

Karen Lamm told me that in her final conversation with Kitty, three days before the killing and one day before the purchase of the guns in San Diego, Kitty told her that Lyle had been verbally abusive to her in a long, late-night call from the guesthouse to the main house.

From the beginning, the police were disinclined to buy the highly publicized Mafia-hit story, on the grounds that Mafia hits are rarely done in the home, that the victim is usually executed with a single shot to the back of the head, and that the wife is not usually killed also. The hit, if hit it was, looked more like a Colombian drug-lord hit, like the bloody massacre carried out by Al Pacino in the film *Scarface*, which, incidentally, was one of Lyle's favorite movies.

Months later, after the arrests, the Beverly Hills police claimed to have been suspicious of the Menendez brothers from the beginning, even from the first night. One detective at the scene asked the boys if they had the ticket stubs from the film they said they had just seen in Century City. "When both parents are hit, our feeling is usually that the kids did it," said a Beverly Hills police officer. Another officer declared, two days after the event, "These kids fried their parents. They cooked them." But there was no proof, nothing to go on, merely gut reactions.

Inadvertently, the boys brought suspicion upon themselves. In the aftermath of the terrible event, close observers noted the extraordinary calm the boys exhibited, almost as if the murders had happened to another family. They were seen renting furniture at Antiquarian Traders to replace the furniture that had been removed from the television room. And, as new heirs, they embarked on a spending spree that even the merriest widow, who had married for money, would have refrained from going on—for propriety's sake, if nothing else—in the first flush of her mourning period. They bought and bought and bought. Estimates of their spending have gone as high at $700,000. Lyle bought a $60,000 Porsche 911 Carrera to replace the Alfa Romeo his father had given him. Erik turned in his Ford Mustang 5.0 hardtop and bought a tan Jeep Wrangler, which his girlfriend, Noelle Terelsky, is now driving. Lyle bought $40,000 worth of clothes and a $15,000 Rolex watch. Erik hired a $50,000-a-year tennis coach. Lyle decided to go into the restaurant business, and paid a reported $550,000 for a cafeteria-style eatery in Princeton, which he renamed Mr. Buffalo's, flying back and forth coast to coast on MGM Grand Air. "It was one of my mother's delights that I pursue a small restaurant chain and serve healthy food with friendly service," he said in an interview with *The Daily Princetonian*, the campus newspaper. Erik, less successful as an entrepreneur than Lyle, put up $40,000 for a rock concert at the Palladium, but got ripped off by a conman partner and lost the entire amount. Erik decided not to attend U.C.L.A., which had been his father's plan for him, but to pursue a career in tennis instead. After moving from hotel to hotel to elude the Mafia, who they claimed were watching them, the brothers leased adjoining condos in the tony Marina City Club Towers. "They liked high-tech surrounds, and they wanted to get out of the house," one of their friends said to me. Then there was the ghoulish sense of humor another of their friends spoke about: Sitting with a gang of pals one night, deciding what videos to rent for the evening, Erik suggested *Dad* and *Parenthood.* Even as close a friend as Glenn Stevens, who was in the car with Lyle when he was arrested, later told the *Los Angeles Times* that two days after the murders, when he asked Lyle how he was holding up emotionally, his friend replied, "I've been waiting so long to be in this position that the transition came easy." The police were also aware that Lyle Menendez had hired a computer expert who eradicated from the hard disc of the family computer a revised will that Jose had been working on. Most remarkable of all was that, unlike the families of most homicide victims, the sons of Jose and Kitty Menendez did not have the obsessive interest in the police search for the killers of their parents that usually supersedes all else in the wake of such a tragedy.

As the C.E.O. of Live Entertainment, Jose Menendez earned a base pay of $500,000 a year, with a maximum bonus of $850,00 based on the company's yearly earnings. On top of that, there were life-insurance policies. An interesting sidebar to the story concerns two policies that were thought to have been taken out on Menendez by Live Entertainment. The bigger of the two was a $15 million keyman policy; $10 million of what was with Bankers Trust and $5 million with Credit Lyonnais. Taking out a keyman life-insurance policy on a top executive is common practice in business, with the company being named as beneficiary. Live Entertainment was also required to maintain a second policy on Menendez in the amount of $5 million, with the beneficiary to be named by him. Given the family's much-talked-about closeness, it is not unlikely that Kitty and the boys were aware of this policy. Presumably, the beneficiary of the insurance policy would have been the same as the beneficiary of Jose's will. In the will, it was stated that if Kitty died first everything would go to Jose, and if Jose died first everything would go to Kitty. In the event that both died, everything would go to the boys.

The murders happened on a Sunday night. On the afternoon of the following Tuesday, Lyle and Erik, accompanied by two uncles, Kitty's brother Brian Andersen and Jose's brother-in-law Carlos Baralt, who was the executor of Jose's will, met with officials of

Live Entertainment at the company's headquarters to go over Jose's financial situation. At that meeting, it became the difficult duty of Jose's successor to inform the heirs that the $5 million policy with beneficiaries named by Jose had not gone into effect, because Jose had failed to take the required physical examination, believing that the one he had taken for the $15 million policy applied to both policies. It did not. A person present at that meeting told me of the resounding silence that followed the reception of that information. To expect $5 million, payable upon death, and to find that it was not forthcoming, would be a crushing disappointment. Finally, Erik Menendez spoke. His voice was cold. "And the $15 million policy in favor of the company? Was that in order?" he asked. It was. Jose had apparently been told that he would have to take another physical for the second policy, but he had postponed it. As an officer of the company said to me, "That anything could ever happen to Jose never occurred to Jose."

The news that the policy was invalid caused bad blood between the family and the company, especially since the immediate payment of the $15 million keyman policy gave Carolco one of its biggest quarters since the inception of the company. One of Jose's former employees in New York, who was close enough to the family to warrant having a limousine sent to take him from a suburb of New York to the funeral in Princeton, said to me, "The grandmother? Did you talk to her? Did she tell you her theory? Did she tell you the company had Jose taken care of for the $15 million insurance policy?" The grandmother had not told me this, but it is a theory that the dwindling group of people who believe in the innocence of the Menendez boys cling to with passion. The same former employee continued, "Jose must have made a lot of money in California. I don't know where all that money came from that I've been hearing about and reading about."

Further bad feelings between the family and Live Entertainment have arisen over the house on Elm Drive, which, like the house in Calabasas, is heavily mortgaged: Approximately $2 million is still owed on the Elm Drive house, with estimated payments of $225,000 a year, plus $40,000 a year in taxes and approximately $40,000 in maintenance. In addition, the house in Calabasas has been on the market for some time and remains unsold; $1.5 million is still owed on it. So, in effect, the expenses on the two houses are approximately $500,000 a year, a staggering amount for the two sons to have dealt with before their arrest. During the meeting on the Tuesday after the murders, when the boys were told that the $5 million life-insurance policy had not gone into effect, it was suggested that Live Entertainment might buy the house on Elm Drive from the estate, thereby removing the financial burden from the boys while the house was waiting to be resold. Furthermore, Live Entertainment was prepared to take less for the house than Jose had paid for it, knowing that houses where murders have taken place are hard sells, even in as inflated a real-estate market as Beverly Hills.

Ads have run in the real-estate section of the *Los Angeles Times* for the Elm Drive House. The asking price is $5.95 million. Surprisingly, a buyer did come along. The unidentified person offered only $4.5 million, a bargain for a house on that street, and the offer was hastily accepted. Later, however, the deal fell through. The purchaser was said to have been intimidated by the event that occurred there, and worried about the reaction neighborhood children would have to his own children for living in the house.

The arrangement for Live Entertainment to purchase the property from the estate failed to go into effect, once the police investigation pointed more and more toward the boys, and so the estate has had to assume the immense cost of maintaining the properties. Recently, the Elm Drive house has been leased to a member of the Saudi royal family—not the same prince who rented it before—for $50,000 a month to allay expenses.

Carolco, wishing to stifle rumors that Live Entertainment had Mob connections because of its acquisition of companies like Strawberries, an audio-video retailing chain, from Morris Levy, who allegedly has Genovese crime-family connections, and its bitter battle with Noel Bloom, hired the prestigious New York firm of Kaye, Scholer, Fierman, Hays & Handler to investigate the company for underworld ties. The 220-page report, which cynics in the industry mock as a whitewash, exonerated the company of any such involvement. The report was read at a board meeting on March 8, and the conclusion made clear that the Beverly Hills police, in their investigation of the Menendez murders, were increasingly focusing on their sons, not the Mob. An ironic bit of drama came at precisely that moment, when a vice president of the company burst in on the meeting with the news that Lyle Menendez had just been arrested.

Concurrently, in another, less fashionable area of the city known as Carthay Circle, an attractive thirty-seven-year-old woman named Judalon Rose Smyth, pronounced Smith, was living out her own drama in a complicated love affair. Judalon Smyth's lover was a Beverly Hills psychologist named Jerome Oziel, whom she called Jerry. Dr. Oziel was the same Dr. Oziel whom Kitty Menendez's psychologist, Les Summerfield, had recommended to her a year earlier as the doctor for her troubled son, after the judge in the burglary case in Calabasas had ruled that Erik must have counseling while he was on probation. During that brief period of court-ordered therapy, Jerome Oziel had met the entire Menendez family. Judalon Smyth, however, was as unknown to Lyle and Erik as they were to her, and yet, seven months from the time of the double murder, she would be responsible for their arrest on the charge of killing their parents.

On March 8, Lyle Menendez was flagged down by more than a dozen heavily armed Beverly Hills policemen as he was leaving the house on Elm Drive in his brother's Jeep Wrangler, accompanied by his former Princeton classmate Glenn Stevens. Lyle was made to lie on the street, in full view of his neighbors, while the police, with drawn guns, manacled his hands behind his back before taking him to the police station to book him for suspicion of murder. The arrest came as a complete surprise to Lyle, who had been playing chess, a game at which he excelled, until two the night before at the home of a friend in Beverly Hills.

Three days earlier, Judalon Smyth had contacted the police in Beverly Hills and told them of the existence of audiotapes in the Bedford Drive office of Dr. Oziel on which the Menendez brothers had allegedly confessed to the murders of their parents. She also told police that the brothers had threatened to kill Oziel if he reported them. Lastly, she told them that the two twelve-gauge shotguns had been purchased at a sporting-goods store in San Diego. All of this information was unknown to the Beverly Hills police, after seven months of investigation. They obtained a subpoena to search all of Oziel's locations. The tapes were found in a safe-deposit box in a bank on Ventura Boulevard.

Lyle's arrest was reported almost immediately on the local Los Angeles newscasts. Among those who heard the news was Noel Nedli, a tennis-team friend from Beverly Hills High who was Erik Menendez's roommate in a condominium that Erik was leasing for six months at the Marina City Club Towers, next to the condominium that his brother had leased with his girlfriend, Jamie Pisarcik. Erik was playing in a tennis tournament in Israel, where he had been for two weeks, accompanied by Mark Heffernan, his $50,000-a-year tennis coach. By a curious coincidence, Erik happened to telephone Nedli at almost the same moment Nedli was listening to the report of Lyle's arrest on the radio. It was merely a routine checking-up-on-everything call, and Nedli realized at once that Erik did not know about Lyle's arrest. He is reported to have said to Erik, "I hope you're sitting down." Then he said, "Lyle was just arrested."

"Erik became hysterical. He was crying, the whole nine yards," said a friend of Nedli's who had heard the story from him. This friend went on to say that the immediate problem for Erik was to get out of Israel before he was arrested there. Accompanied by Heffernan, who was not aware of the seriousness of the situation, the two got on a plane without incident, bound for London. There they split up. Heffernan returned to Los Angeles. Erik flew to Miami, where several members on the Menendez side of the family reside. An aunt advised him to return to Los Angeles and turn himself in. Erik notified police of his travel plans and gave himself up at Los Angeles International Airport, where he was taken into custody by four detectives. He was later booked at the Los Angeles County Men's Central Jail on suspicion of murder and held without bond.

According to Judalon Smyth, and the California Court of Appeals decision, she had stood outside the door of Dr. Oziel's office and, unbeknownst to the Menendez brothers, listened to their confession and threats. Dr. Oziel has denied this.

Approximately a year before any of the above happened, Judalon Smyth told me, she telephoned Jerome Oziel's clinic, the Phobia Institute of Beverly Hills, after having heard a series of tapes called

Through the Briar Patch, which had impressed her. She was then thirty-six, had been married twice, and was desirous of having a relationship and a family, but she tended to choose the wrong kind of men, men who were controlling. The *Briar Patch* tapes told her she could break the pattern of picking the wrong kind of men in five minutes.

She says Oziel began telephoning her, and she found him very nice on the phone. She felt he seemed genuinely interested in her. After Oziel's third call, she sent him a tape of love poems she had written and called *Love Tears*. She also told him she was in the tape-duplicating business. She found his calls were like therapy, and she began to tell him intimate things about herself, like the fact that she had been going to a professional matchmaker she had seen on television. "I was falling in love over the phone," she said. "You don't think someone's married when he calls you from home at night."

Eventually, he came to her house with two enormous bouquets. "The minute I opened the door I was relieved," she said. "I wasn't attracted to him. He was shorter than me, blond, balding, with a round face." She told me she was attracted to men who looked like the actor Ken Wahl or Tom Cruise. Oziel was forty-two at the time. "He kept trying to get physical right away. I said, 'Look, you're not my type. I'm not attracted to you.'" He said he just wanted a hug. "I said, 'Just because you know all this intimate stuff about me doesn't mean . . .'"

"Finally I gave in. It was the worst sex I ever had in my life. To have good sex you either have to be in love or in lust. I wasn't either. It was also awful the second time. The third time was better. I broke off with him four or five times between September and October. Then Erik Menendez came."

Although Dr. Oziel had not seen any members of the Menendez family since Erik's counseling had ended, when news of the murders was announced in August 1989, according to Smyth, he became consumed with excitement at his proximity to the tragedy. "Right away, he called the boys and offered his help." At the time, the boys were hiding out in hotels, saying they thought the Mafia was after them. "Jerry would go to where the boys were. He was advising them about attorneys for the will, etc. He had an I'll-be-your-father attitude."

At the end of October, Smyth told me, Oziel got a call from Erik, who said he needed to talk with him. Erik came at four on the afternoon of Halloween, October 31, to the office at 435 North Bedford Drive. There is a small waiting room outside the office, with a table for magazines and several places to sit, but there is no receptionist. An arriving patient pushes a button with the name of the doctor he is there to see, and a light goes on in the inner office to let the doctor know that his next patient has arrived. Off the waiting room is a doorway that opens into a small inner hallway off which are three small offices. Oziel shares the space with several other doctors, one of them his wife, Dr. Laurel Oziel, the mother of his two daughters.

Once there, Erik did not want to talk in the office, so he and Oziel went for a walk. On the walk, according to Smyth, Erik confessed that he and his brother had killed their parents. Lyle, who was at the Elm Drive house at the time, did not know that Erik was seeing Oziel for that purpose. Lyle did not know either that Erik had apparently also confessed to his good friend Craig Cignarelli, with whom he had written the screenplay called *Friends*.

When Smyth arrived at the office, Erik and Oziel had returned from their walk and were in the inner office. According to Smyth, Oziel wanted Erik to tell Lyle that he had confessed to him. Erik did not want to do that. He said that he and Lyle were soon going to the Caribbean to get rid of the guns and that he would tell him then. The plan, according to Erik, Judalon Smyth told me, was to break down the guns, put them into suitcases, and dump the bags in the Caribbean. On the night of the murders, the boys had hidden the two shotguns in the trunk of one of their parents' cars in the garage. The police had searched only the cars in the courtyard in front of the house, not the cars in the garage. Subsequently, the boys had buried the guns on Mulholland Drive. Smyth says Dr. Oziel convinced Erik that the boys would certainly be caught if they were carrying guns in their luggage. He also persuaded him to call Lyle and ask him to come to the office immediately.

It took ten minutes for Lyle to get to the office from the house on Elm Drive. Smyth says he did not know before he got there that Erik had confessed. When he walked into the waiting room, he picked up a magazine and chatted briefly with Smyth, assuming that she was another patient. "Been waiting long?" he asked her. He also pushed the button to indicate to Oziel that he had arrived. Oziel came out and asked Lyle to come in.

According to the California Court of Appeals decision, Smyth says she listened through the door to the doctor's meeting with the boys and heard Lyle become furious with Erik for having confessed. She told me he made threats to Oziel that they were going to kill him. "I never thought I believed in evil, but when I heard those boys speak, I did," she said.

The particulars of the murders she is not allowed to discuss, because of an agreement with the Beverly Hills police, but occasionally, in our conversation, things would creep in. "They did go to the theater to buy the tickets," she said one time. Or, "The mother kept moving, which is why she was hit more." Or, "If they just killed the father, the mother would have inherited the money. So they had to kill her too." Or, "Lyle said he thought he committed the perfect murder, that his father would have had to congratulate him—for once, he couldn't put him down."

Judalon went on to say, and it is in the opinion of the California Court of Appeals, that she was frightened that she might be caught listening if the boys came out of the office. She went back to the waiting room. Almost immediately, the door opened. "Erik came running out, crying. Then Lyle and Jerry came out. At the elevator, I heard Jerry ask if Lyle was threatening him. Erik had already gone down. Lyle and Jerry followed." From a window in the office, Smyth could see Lyle and Oziel talking to Erik, who was in his Jeep on Bedford Drive.

According to Smyth, Erik knew, from his period of therapy with Oziel after the burglaries, where the doctor lived in Sherman Oaks, a suburb of Los Angeles in the San Fernando Valley. Fearing the boys might come after him, Oziel called his wife and told her to get the children and move out of the house. "Laurel and the kids went to stay with friends," said Smyth. Oziel then moved into Smyth's apartment, the ground floor of a two-family house in the Carthay Circle area of Los Angeles.

In the days that followed, Smyth told several people what she had heard. She has her own business, an audio-video duplicating service called Judalon Sound and Light, in the Fairfax section of Los Angeles. Behind her shop, in which she also sells crystals, quartz, and greeting cards, there is a small office which she rents to two friends, Bruce and Grant, who also have a video-duplicating service. As self-protection, she told them that the Menendez boys had killed their parents. She also told her mother and father and her best friend, Donna.

Then Oziel set up another meeting with the boys. He told them on the second visit that everything they had told him was taped. According to Smyth, the original confession, on October 31, was not taped. What was taped was Oziel's documentation of everything that happened in that session and subsequent sessions with the boys, giving times and dates, telling about the confession and the threat on his life, "a log of what was happening during the time his life was in danger." Smyth further contends that, as time went on, the relationship between the doctor and the boys grew more stable, and the doctor no longer felt threatened.

She said that Oziel convinced the boys "he was their only ally— that if they were arrested he would be their only ally. He was the only one who knew they were abused children, who knew how horrible their home life was, who knew that Jose was a monster father, who knew that Kitty was an abused wife. He convinced them that if they had any hope of ever getting off, they needed him."

Meanwhile, the personal relationship between Smyth and Oziel deteriorated. In a lawsuit filed in the Superior Court of the State of California by Judalon Rose Smyth against L. Jerome Oziel, Ph.D., on May 31, three months after the arrest of the Menendez brothers, it is charged that while Smyth was receiving psychiatric and psychological counseling from defendant Oziel he "improperly maintained Smyth on large doses of drugs and, during said time periods, manipulated and took advantage of Smyth, controlled Smyth, and limited Smyth's ability to care for herself . . . creating a belief in Smyth that she could not handle her affairs without the guidance of Oziel, and convincing Smyth that no other therapist could provide the insight and benefit to her life that Oziel could."

In the second cause of action in the suit, Smyth charges that on or about February 16, 1990, defendant Oziel "placed his hands around her throat attempting to choke her, and pulled her hair with great force. Subsequently, on the same day, Defendant Oziel forced Smyth to engage in an act of forcible and unconsented sexual intercourse." According to the California Court of Appeals decision, approximately three weeks after the alleged attack, Smyth contacted the police in Beverly Hills to inform them about the confession she said the Menendez brothers had made to Oziel.

Oziel's lawyer, Bradley Brunon, called Smyth's allegations "completely untrue," and characterized her behavior as "an unfortunate real-life enactment of the scenario in *Fatal Attraction*. . . . She has twisted reality to the point where it is unrecognizable."

"The boys are *adorable*. They're like two foundlings. You want to take them home with you," said the defense attorney Leslie Abramson, who has saved a dozen people from death row. She was talking about the Menendez brothers. Leslie Abramson is Erik's lawyer. Gerald Chaleff is Lyle's.

"Leslie will fight to the grave for her clients," I heard from reporters in Los Angeles who have followed her career. "When there is a murder rap, Leslie is the best in town."

Abramson and Chaleff have worked together before. "We're fifty-fifty, but she's in charge," Chaleff said in an interview. They like each other, and are friends in private life. Abramson met her present husband, Tim Rutten, an editorial writer for the *Los Angeles Times*, at a dinner party at Chaleff's home.

During the arraignment in the Beverly Hills courthouse, I was struck by the glamour of the young Menendez brothers, whom I was seeing face-to-face for the first time. They entered the courtroom, heads held high, like leading actors in a television series. They walked like colts. Their clothes, if not by Armani himself, were by a designer heavily influenced by Armani, probably purchased in the brief period of their independent affluence, between the murders and their arrest. Their demeanor seemed remarkably lighthearted for people in the kind of trouble they were in, as they smiled dimpled smiles and laughed at the steady stream of Abramson's jocular banter. Their two girlfriends, Jamie Pisarcik and

Noelle Terelsky, were in the front row next to Erik's tennis coach, Mark Heffernan. Everyone waved. Maria Menendez, the loyal grandmother, was also in the front row, and aunts and uncles and a probate lawyer were in the same section of the courtroom. Several times the boys turned around and flashed smiles at their pretty girlfriends.

They were told to rise. The judge, Judith Stein, spoke in a lugubrious, knell-like voice. The brothers smiled, almost smirked, as she read the charges. "You have been charged with multiple murder for financial gain, while lying in wait, with a loaded firearm, for which, if convicted, you could receive the death penalty. How do you plead?"

"Not guilty, Your Honor," said Erik.

"Not guilty," said Lyle.

Later I asked a friend of theirs who believes in their innocence why they were smiling.

"At the judge's voice," she replied.

Leslie Abramson's curly blond hair bounces, Orphan Annie style, when she walks and talks. She is funny. She is fearless. And she is tough. Oh, is she tough. She walked down the entire corridor of the Beverly Hills courthouse giving the middle finger to an NBC cameraman. "This what you want? You want that?" she said with an angry sneer into the camera, thrusting the finger at the lens, a shot that appeared on the NBC special *Exposé*, narrated by Tom Brokaw. Her passion for the welfare of the accused murderers she defends is legendary. She is considered one of the most merciless cross-examiners in the legal business, with a remarkable ability to degrade and confuse prosecution witnesses. "She loves to intimidate people," I was told. "She thrives on it. She knows when she has you. She can twist and turn a witness's memory like no one else can." John Gregory Dunne, in his 1987 novel *The Red White and Blue*, based the character Leah Kaye, a left-leaning criminal-defense attorney, on Leslie Abramson.

"Why did you give the finger to the cameraman?" I asked her.

"I'll tell you why," she answered, bristling at the memory. "Because I was talking privately to a member of the Menendez family, and NBC turned the camera on, one inch from my face. I said, 'Take that fucker out of my face.' These people think they own the courthouse. They will go to any sleazoid end these days. So I said, 'Is this what you want?' That's when I gave them the finger. Imagine, Tom Brokaw on a show like that.

"I do not understand the publicity of the case," she continued, although of course she understood perfectly. "I mean, the president of the United States wasn't shot."

Before I could reply with such words as "patricide," "matricide," "wealth," "Beverly Hills," she had thought over what she had said. "Well, I rate murder cases different from the public." Most of her cases are from less swell circumstances. In the Bob's Big Boy case, the only death-penalty case she has ever lost, her clients herded nine employees and two customers into the restaurant's walk-in freezer and fired shotguns into their bodies at close range. Three died and four were maimed. One of those who lived had part of her brain removed. Another lost an eye.

"What's the mood of the boys?" I asked.

"I can't comment on my clients," she said. "All I can say is, they're among the very best clients I've ever had, as far as relating. Both of them. It's nonsense, all this talk that there's a good brother and a bad brother. Lyle is wonderful. They're both adorable."

In the avalanche of media blitz that followed the arrest of the Menendez brothers, no one close to Lyle and Erik was the object of more intense fascination and scrutiny than Craig Cignarelli, Erik's tennis partner, with whom he had written the screenplay *Friends*. A family spokesperson told me that in one day alone Craig Cignarelli received thirty-two calls from the media, including "one from Dan Rather, 'A Current Affair,' 'Hard Copy,' etc., etc. I can't remember them all. We had to hire an attorney to field calls." The spokesperson said that "from the beginning it was presumed that Craig knew something."

Craig, clearly enjoying his moments of stardom following the arrests of his best friend and best friend's brother, talked freely to the press and was, by all accounts of other friends of the brothers, too talkative by far. In articles by Ron Soble and John Johnson in the *Los Angeles Times*, Craig said he was attracted to Erik by a shared sense that they were special. He recalled how they would drive out to Malibu late at night, park on a hilltop overlooking the ocean, and talk about their hopes for the future, about how much smarter they were than everyone else, and about how to commit the perfect crime. They had nicknames for each other: Craig was "King," and Erik was "Shepherd." "People really looked up to us. We have an aura of superiority," he said.

As the months passed, it was whispered that Erik had confessed the murders to Craig. This was borne out to me by Judalon Smyth. But he confessed them in an elliptical manner, according to Smyth, in a suppose-it-happened-like-this way, as if planning another screenplay. It was further said that Craig told the police about the confession, but there were not the hard facts on which to make an arrest, such as came later from Judalon Smyth.

Craig's loquaciousness gave rise to many rumors about the two boys, as well as about the possibility that a second screenplay by them exists, one that parallels the murders even more closely. Craig has since been requested by the police not to speak to the press.

At one point, Cignarelli was presumed to be in danger because of what he knew, and was sent away by his family to a place known only to them. An ongoing story is that a relation of the Menendez brothers threatened Craig after hearing that he had gone to the police. The spokesperson for Craig wanted me to make it clear that, contrary to rumors, Craig "never approached the police. The police approached Craig. At a point Craig decided to tell them what he knew." When I asked this same spokesperson about the possibility of a second screenplay written by Craig and Erik, he said he had never seen one. He also said that the district attorney, Elliott Alhadeff, was satisfied that all the information on the confession tapes was known to Craig, so in the event that the tapes were ruled inadmissible by the court he would be able to supply the information on the stand.

Sometime last January, two months before the arrests, the friendship between the two boys cooled. That may have been because Erik suspected that Craig had talked to the police.

Earlier that month, during a New Year's skiing vacation at Lake Tahoe, Erik had met and fallen in love with Noelle Terelsky, a pretty blond student at the University of California in Santa Barbara from Cincinnati. The romance was instantaneous. "Erik's not a hard guy to fall for," said a friend of Noelle. "He's very sweet, very sexy, has a great body, and is an all-around great guy." Noelle, together with Jamie Pisarcik, Lyle's girlfriend, visits the brothers in jail every day, and has been present at every court appearance of the brothers since their arrest. Until recently, when the house on Elm Drive was rented to the member of the Saudi royal family, the two girls lived in the guesthouse, as the guests of Maria Menendez, the proud and passionate grandmother of Lyle and Erik, who believes completely in the innocence of her grandsons. Maria Menendez, Noelle, and Jamie are now living in the Menendezes' Calabasas house, which has still not been sold.

Five months had passed since the arrest. Five months of hearings and deliberations to see whether the audiotapes of Dr. Jerome Oziel were admissible in the murder trial of Lyle and Erik Menendez. Police seizure of therapy tapes is rare, because ordinarily conversations between patients and therapists are secret. But there are occasional exceptions to the secrecy rule, one being that the therapist believes the patient is a serious threat to himself or others. Only the defense attorneys, who did not want the tapes to be heard, had been allowed to participate in the hearings. The prosecution, which did want them to be heard, was barred. Oziel had been on the stand in private hearings from which the family, the media, and the public were barred. Judalon Smyth had also been on the stand for two days in private sessions, being grilled by Leslie Abramson. The day of the decision had arrived.

There was great tension in the courtroom. Noelle and Jamie, the girlfriends, were there. And Maria, the grandmother. And an aunt from Miami. And a cousin. And the probate lawyer. And others.

Then the Menendez brothers walked in. The swagger, the smirks, the smiles were all gone. And the glamour. So were the Armani-type suits. Their ever-loyal grandmother had arrived with their clothes in suit bags, but the bags were returned to her by the bailiff. They appeared in V-necked, short-sleeved jailhouse blues with T-shirts underneath. Their tennis tans had long since faded. It was impossible not to notice the deterioration in the appearance of the boys, especially Erik. His eyes looked tormented, tortured, haunted. At his neck was a tiny gold cross. He nodded to Noelle

Terelsky. He nodded to his grandmother. There were no smiles that day.

Leslie Abramson and Gerald Chaleff went to Judge James Albracht's chambers to hear his ruling on the admissibility of the tapes before it was read to the court. The brothers sat alone at the defense table, stripped of their support system. "Everybody's staring at us," said Erik to the bailiff in a pleading voice, as if the bailiff could do something about it, but there was nothing the bailiff could do. Everybody did stare at them. Lyle leaned forward and whispered something to his brother.

The fierce demeanor of Leslie Abramson when she returned to the courtroom left no doubt that the judge's ruling had not gone in favor of the defense. As the judge read his ruling to the crowded courtroom, Abramson, with her back to the judge, kept up a nonstop commentary in Erik Menendez's ear.

"I have ruled that none of the communications are privileged," said the judge. There was an audible sound of dismay from the Menendez family members. The tapes would be admissible. The judge found that psychologist Jerome Oziel had reasonable cause to believe that Lyle and Erik Menendez "constituted a threat, and it was necessary to disclose the communications to prevent a danger." There was no doubt that this was a serious setback to the defense.

Abramson and Chaleff immediately announced at a news conference that they would appeal the judge's ruling. Abramson called Oziel a gossip, a liar, and "less than credible." Neither Judalon Smyth's name nor her role in the proceedings was ever mentioned.

A mere eight days later, in a stunning reversal of Judge Albracht's ruling, the 2nd District Court of Appeals blocked the release of the tapes, to the undisguised delight of Abramson and Chaleff. Prosecutors were then given a date by which to file opposing arguments. Another complication occurred when Erik Menendez, from jail, refused to provide the prosecution with a handwriting sample to compare with the handwriting found on forms for the purchase of two shotguns in San Diego, despite a warning by the court that his refusal to do so could be used as evidence against him. In a further surprise, Deputy District Attorney Elliott Alhadeff, who won the original court ruling that the tapes would be admissible, was abruptly replaced on the notorious case by Deputy District Attorney Pamela Ferrero.

Since their arrest in March, Lyle and Erik Menendez have dwelt in the Los Angeles County Men's Central Jail, in the section reserved for prisoners awaiting trial in heavily publicized cases. The brothers' cells are not side by side. They order reading material from Book Soup, the trendy Sunset Strip bookshop. Eric has been sent *The Dead Zone*, by Stephen King, and a book on chess. They have frequent visits from family members, and talk with one friend almost daily by telephone. That friend told me that they have to pay for protection in jail. "Other prisoners, who are tough, hate them—who they are, what they've been accused of. They've been threatened." He also told me they feel they have lost every one of their friends. Late in August, when three razor blades were reportedly found in Erik's possession, he was put in solitary confinement, deprived of visitors, books except for the Bible, telephone calls, and exercise. That same week, Lyle suddenly shaved his head.

Los Angeles District Attorney Ira Reiner stated on television that one motive for the murders was greed. Certainly it is possible for a child to kill his parents for money, to wish to continue the easy life on easy street without the encumbrance of parental restrictions. But is it really possible for a child to kill, for merely financial gain, in the manner Kitty and Jose Menendez were killed? To blast holes into one's parents? To deface them? To obliterate them? In the fatal, *coup de grâce* shot, the barrel of one shotgun touched the cheek of Kitty Menendez. You wonder if her eyes met the eyes of her killer in the last second of her life. In this case, we have two children who allegedly participated in the killing of each parent, not in the heat of rage but in a carefully orchestrated scenario after a long gestation period. There is more than money involved here. There is a deep, deep hatred, a hatred that goes beyond hate.

The closest friend of the Menendez brothers, with whom I talked at length on the condition of anonymity, kept saying to me over and over, "It's only the tip of the iceberg." No amount of persuasion on my part could make him explain what the iceberg was. Months earlier, however, a person close to the situation mouthed but did not speak the word "incest" to me. Subsequently, a rich woman in Los Angeles told me that her bodyguard, a former cop, had heard from a friend of his on the Beverly Hills police force that Kitty Menendez had been shot in the vagina. At a Malibu barbecue, a film star said to me, "I heard the mother was shot up the wazoo." There is, however, no indication of such a penetration in the autopsy report, which carefully delineates each of the ten wounds from the nine shots fired into Kitty Menendez's body. But the subject continues to surface. Could it be possible that these boys were puppets of their father's dark side? "They had sexual hatred for their parents," one of the friends told me. This same person went on to say, "The tapes will show that Jose molested Lyle at a very young age."

Is this true? Only the boys know. If it is, it could be the defense argument that will return them to their tennis court, swimming pool, and chess set, as inheritors of a $14 million estate that they could not have inherited if they had been found guilty. Karen Lamm, however, does not believe such a story, although it is unlikely that Kitty would have revealed to her a secret of that dimension. Judalon Smyth was also skeptical of this information when I brought up the subject of sexual abuse. She said she had heard nothing of the kind on Halloween afternoon when, according to the California Court of Appeals decision, she listened outside Dr. Oziel's office door as Lyle and Erik talked about the murders. She said that last December, almost two months after the October 31 confession to Oziel, which was not taped, the boys, feeling that the police were beginning to suspect them, voluntarily made a tape in which they confessed to the crime. In it, they spoke of their remorse. In it, apparently, they told of psychological abuse. But sexual abuse? Judalon Smyth did not hear this tape, and by that time Dr. Oziel was no longer confiding in her.

October 1990

QUEENS
OF
THE ROAD

JUST WHEN you thought you knew all there was to know about the highly publicized Collins sisters, Joan and Jackie, or Jackie and Joan, comes the news that big sister Joan, the soap-opera superstar, whose divorces and romantic exploits have been making tabloid headlines for thirty years, has turned literary in her fifty-fifth year and is moving in on the printed-page turf of her little sister Jackie, the superstar novelist, whose eleven-volume *oeuvre* has sold 65 million copies in thirty languages throughout the world over the last two decades. Yes, friends, Joan Collins, between takes as the beloved bitch Alexis Carrington Colby on "Dynasty," has written her *own* novel, called *Prime Time*, about a top-rated soap opera on American television, with eight or ten characters, all of them actors and actresses, and a leading lady who has overcome obstacles, both personal and financial, to regain her stardom.

And as if that weren't enough, Joan's literary agent, the legendary Irving "Swifty" Lazar, a superstar in his own right, has sold Joan's book for a million bucks to, you guessed it, Jackie's publisher, Simon and Schuster, where her editor is another superstar, Michael Korda, a novelist in his own right, who—hang on to your hat—also happens to be Jackie's editor. (Lazar sold it abroad for an additional $2 million—$1 million in England alone—without showing one written word.)

"I get along very well with both of them," said Korda. "I'm very fond of them."

There are those who will tell you that Jackie isn't happy with the proximity, and neither is her superstar agent, Morton Janklow, who long ago moved in on Swifty Lazar's turf as the agent who got the most bucks for his writer clients. As a reaffirmation of Simon and Schuster's warm feeling for its massive money-maker, Michael Korda signed Jackie up for two additional books after the completion of her current contract.

"I don't like to talk figures," said Jackie Collins in her Beverly

Hills home about her new deal, "but I will say it's a record-breaking contract."

Michael Korda, from his New York office, added, "If this isn't the largest amount of money in American book publishing, it sure ought to be. It's about the same size as the Brazilian national debt." Then he added, almost as an afterthought, "But I also bought two more books from Joan."

"Is there a feud going on between them?" I asked.

"Probably so, at some level," he answered. "Jackie can't help but feel that Joan is crowding her territory."

Said Irving Lazar, "Certainly, there is sibling rivalry at times."

Said Joni Evans, formerly of Simon and Schuster, now publisher of Random House, "Of course, there has to be."

Said Morton Janklow, "Yes, Jackie and Joan have flare-ups, but since Simon and Schuster has both books, Irving and I can see to it that they don't come out head to head. So both sisters will have a couple great months."

The Collins sisters themselves are quick to tell you that there is no trouble between them at all, although their publicist, Jeffrey Lane, who is actually Joan's publicist, best pal, and traveling companion, but who doubled as Jackie's publicist for this article, laid down some ground rules for me to abide by, namely that if Jackie's name was used first in one sentence, then Joan's must be used first in the next, and that there was to be equal copy on each sister. Like that.

The fact is, I know both of these ladies. The first time I ever saw Joan was in 1957. She walked up off the beach in Santa Monica, California, where I was renting a beach house, wearing a bikini before anyone I knew was wearing a bikini, and asked if she could use the bathroom. She was then in the first of her two stardoms, the one that didn't last. Of course she could use the bathroom. In my scrapbooks I have pictures of her from the sixties, at parties my wife and I had in Beverly Hills: with Mia Farrow, before she married Frank Sinatra; with Ryan O'Neal, after he split from Joanna Moore; with Michael Caine, long before he married Shakira; and with Natalie Wood, after her first marriage to Robert Wagner. Joan was then in the second of her four marriages, to the English star Anthony Newley. In every picture she is having a good time.

Jackie I met much later. We sat next to each other at one of

Irving Lazar's Academy Awards parties at Spago. It struck me then how alike the sisters are, and also how different. Last year at the Writers' Conference in Santa Barbara, Jackie and I were both speakers, along with Thomas McGuane, Irving Stone, William F. Buckley, Jr., and others. Jackie arrived only minutes before she was scheduled to speak, in a stretch limousine with a great deal of video equipment to record her speech. Only, she didn't make a speech the way the rest of us did. The conference provided her with an interviewer, and the interviewer asked her questions. There wasn't an empty seat in the hall. "Can you give the writers here some advice?" the interviewer asked. "Write only about what you know," she told them. Later, when the floor was thrown open to questions from the audience, the audience was told in advance by the interviewer, "Miss Collins will answer no questions about her sister." Her sister was, at the time, involved in the highly publicized extrication from her fourth marriage.

"It's nonsense," said Jackie when I asked her about the rumors of a rift. "We're very amicable together."

"I don't have a rivalry with my sister," said Joan when I asked her. "People are always saying I have rivalries—particularly with Elizabeth Taylor and Linda Evans. I've never said a bad word about another actress, at least in print. And now they're saying I have this rivalry with Jackie. It's not true."

"Let me put it this way," said Jackie. "We're not in each other's pockets, but we're good friends. We're not the kind of sisters who call each other every day, but she knows I'm there for her."

"Jackie lives a totally different life from me," said Joan. "If I get five days off from work, I take off. I like Los Angeles, but I'm more European than she is in my outlook. I like staying up late. I like sleeping late. I like two-hour lunches, with wine. I do not like tennis, golf, lying by the pool. What I like doing here is to work very hard and then leave."

"We have a lot of the same friends," said Jackie. "Roger and Luisa Moore, Dudley Moore, Michael and Shakira Caine. Then Joan has *her* whole group of friends, and I have *my* whole group."

"I like getting on planes and going on trips," said Joan.

"*Hollywood Wives* gave me a high profile," said Jackie. "Before that, in England, I was always Joan's little sister. I was lucky to have made it in America before Joan hit in 'Dynasty.' What I love about Joan is that she's one of the great survivors. She did things ahead of her time that have since become accepted. She always lived her life like a man. She was a free spirit. If she saw a guy she wanted to go to bed with, she went after him, and that was unacceptable behavior at the time."

"Oh, God, Jackie, that's great," said Joan, touching the emerald of a borrowed necklace her sister was wearing for the shoot. "Is it yours?"

Jackie laughed. "No, darling."

"You should buy it for yourself," said Joan. "You can afford it."

Joan Collins is the embodiment of the kind of characters that Jackie Collins writes about. She is beautiful, famous, rich, was once a movie star, has been what is known in Hollywood as on her ass, meaning washed up and nearly broke, and then resurrected herself as a greater television star than she ever was a movie star. Jackie flatly denies that her character Silver Anderson in *Hollywood Husbands* was based on her sister, although Silver Anderson is a washed-up, middle-aged star who makes it back, bigger than ever, in a soap opera, who "wasn't twenty-two and didn't give a damn," and who "had a compact, sinewy body, with firm breasts and hard nipples."

Joan has been married and divorced four times. "I've always left my husbands," she said, about Maxwell Reed, Anthony Newley, the late Ron Kass, and the recent and unlamented Peter Holm, who asked for, but didn't receive, a divorce settlement of $80,000 a month. Her host of romances over the years, which she delineated in detail in her autobiography, *Past Imperfect*, have included Laurence Harvey, Warren Beatty, Sydney Chaplin, Ryan O'Neal, and Rafael Trujillo, the son of the dictator of the Dominican Republic, an affairette masterminded in the fifties by Zsa Zsa Gabor. She currently lives in a house that Joan Crawford might have lived in at the height of her fame. Built by Laurence Harvey but redone totally by Joan, it has a marble entrance hall and white carpets and white sofas and a peach bedroom with an Art Deco headboard and a spectacular view of the city of Los Angeles. She has posed for more than five hundred magazine covers, and many of them are framed on the walls of her office. She has diamonds for all occasions, and Bob Mackie and Nolan Miller design the glittering evening gowns she favors for her public appearances. Swifty Lazar says, "Joan is addicted to the precept that life is for fun and having a great time. She throws caution to the wind. It has brought her troubles at times. She has been broke when she didn't have to be. She is much less cautious than Jackie. She worries much less about what's going to happen in ten years. She lives totally in the present."

Known as a great hostess, she loves having parties as much as she loves going to them. She gives Sunday lunches, seated dinners for eighteen, and buffet suppers for forty, and recently she tented over her swimming pool and had several hundred of her nearest and dearest friends, mostly famous, in for a black-tie dinner dance, with, according to Swifty Lazar, "great music, great wines, and place cards," the kind of party that people in Hollywood always say they used to give out here but don't give anymore. She loves nightlife, and one of her complaints about Hollywood, where she has lived on and off since the 1950s, is that everyone goes to bed too early. As often as possible, every three weeks or so, she is on a plane to London for four or five days, because her three children are there. Tara and Sacha, twenty-five and twenty-three, by her marriage to Anthony Newley, are living on their own. Her other daughter, Katyana, called Katy, by Ron Kass, who died in 1986, is the child she literally willed back to life after she was struck by a car and hovered between life and death for weeks in an intensive-care unit when she was eight. Katy, now fifteen, attends school in London and lives in a rented flat with Joan's longtime English secretary and a nanny. Although Joan is said to party nonstop during her London weekends, it is to see her children that she travels there so often, and not to see her latest love, Bill Wiggins, known as Bungalow by the English tabloids because he has "nothing upstairs and everything down below." As of this writing he is no longer her latest love but just "a dear friend." "She loves it there," said Douglas Cramer, an executive producer on "Dynasty." "Next to the Queen, she's the queen."

"How do the producers feel about your traveling so much to England while the show is in production?" I asked Joan.

"They're quite accommodating, actually, because they want me back next season," said Joan.

"Are you coming back next season?"

"I would only do it on my terms. I would not want to be in every episode."

While Joan is known as a great hostess, Jackie is known as a great housekeeper. She cooks. She markets. She dusts. She has no live-in servants, only a cleaning woman three times a week, and her children have their household chores. At Christmastime, she presided over a family dinner for seventeen, including Joan, which she cooked and served herself, urging seconds and thirds on everyone, and then organized charades. She is a very concerned family person.

Like her sister, she has a tremendous drive to be on top. "Being number one in America means being number one in the world," she said. She has been married for over twenty years to Oscar Lerman, who co-owns discotheques in London and Los Angeles. Ad Lib, his famous London club of the sixties, was a favorite hang-out of the Beatles and the Stones. It was there Jackie conceived the idea for her about-to-be-released novel, *Rock Star*. Tramp, the Los Angeles branch of his London disco, is a hangout for young stars like Sean Penn and Timothy Hutton. Jackie goes there one night a week to watch the action and store away information. She married for the first time at the age of nineteen, but the marriage ended tragically when her husband overdosed on drugs. Her oldest daughter, Tracy, is from that marriage, and she has two more daughters by Oscar, Tiffany, twenty, and Rory, eighteen, who are not, absolutely not, she will tell you, "Hollywood kids," which will be the subject of the book after *Lady Boss*, which will be the book after *Rock Star*. All three girls live at home, in a deceptively large white house in the flats of Beverly Hills which Carroll Baker once bought with her *Baby Doll* earnings. It is definitely not the kind of house where Joan Crawford would have lived, but rather a house that screams family and family life. There are so many cars in the driveway it looks like a parking lot: Jackie's '66 Mustang and her two Cadillacs, Oscar's Mercury, her daughters' cars, and sometimes their boyfriends' cars. Every room has bookcases brimming over with books, most of them best-sellers of the Harold Robbins and Sidney Sheldon school, and so many paintings that they are stacked against the walls. Pictures of movie stars at movie-star parties, all taken by the famous author herself, who never goes to a party without her camera, line the walls of her powder room.

On my first visit to Jackie's home, two large yellow Labradors were flaked out on the white sofas in the living room, and she did not tell them to move. "Poor old thing, he's fifteen," she said about one of the dogs, and we moved to another room rather than disturb them.

When the doorbell rang later, the dogs charged for the door. Joan Collins, in a fox coat, had stopped by to have tea with her sister.

"Am I going to be jumped on by these wild animals?" she screamed from the front hall. All Joan's entrances are entrances. The day before, she had walked down a stairway wearing a—for her—demure dress. "This is my *jeune fille* look," she said in greeting. "Still trying after all these years."

"Joan's not crazy about dogs," Jackie explained to me, rising to take the dogs elsewhere. It occurred to me that Silver Anderson in *Hollywood Husbands* is not crazy about dogs either.

The sisters greeted each other with a kiss on each cheek. One had tea. One had coffee. They talked about movies they had seen the night before. They always see movies in friends' projection rooms or at studio screenings. Jackie had seen *The Last Emperor* at Roger Moore's house. Joan had seen *Baby Boom* at someone else's house. "It's my favorite movie. Diane is so good," she said about Diane Keaton. "She had one of the best scenes I ever saw." She then re-enacted it while Jackie watched. Whatever you hear about these two sisters having a feud, just remember this. They like each other. They laugh at each other's stories. They listen to each other, and they're proud of each other's success.

"We are the triumph of the immigrant," said Joan. "That's what America's all about. People dream that the streets are paved with gold, and my sister and I showed that they are. If only Mummy had lived to see the two of us now, she would have been so proud."

Their father, now in his eighties, they remember as aloof, strict, and austere when they were children. "English men are rather cool and into themselves," Joan said. He was a theatrical agent with Lew Grade, later Sir Lew Grade, now Lord Grade. But it was their mother, who died in 1962, whom both sisters spoke of in the most loving terms, as being affectionate and feminine and protective of them. There are pictures of her in both sisters' houses.

"We wish our mother was alive to see what's happened to us. She would have enjoyed this more than anyone," said Jackie.

Joan said it was not true, as I had heard, that she was so broke in 1981 that Aaron Spelling had to pay her grocery bills before she could return to California to do "Dynasty." "Where do these stories start?" she asked.

In a large album of color photographs on the tea table, there is a picture of Joan, taken by Jackie, at the party Joan gave to celebrate her recent divorce from Peter Holm, the toy-boy husband who almost made Joan look foolish, but didn't, because she laughed at herself first. In the photograph, she is wearing a T-shirt that says, "HOMEless," a gift from her friend David Niven, Jr. She is laughing, but behind her mascara'd eyes there is the unmistakable look, at once gallant and sad, of the Hollywood survivor.

When I asked her about Peter Holm, who is rumored to be writing a book called *Joan and Me*, she began to sing. It is a topic she is thoroughly sick of. "I wonder what's happened to him," she said finally.

"Do you care?" I asked.

She shrugged her shoulders.

"One of these days I just know I'm going to meet somebody with whom I would like to share my life," she said.

Later, as I was leaving, she called after me a variation on that line in *Tea and Sympathy*, "When you write about this, and you will, be kind!"

Jackie Collins is a high-school dropout and was a self-confessed juvenile delinquent at age fifteen. "I'm glad I got all of that out of my system at an early age," she said. She arrived in Hollywood at sixteen to visit her sister, then a contract player at Twentieth Century-Fox. Joan was just leaving to go on location for a film, and she tossed her sister the keys to her apartment. "Learn how to drive" was her only L.A. advice. Jackie said she started out her Hollywood

life with Joan's famous friends and the friends she made herself—
kids who pumped gas and waited on tables. She still draws on the
latter group for inspiration. In all her books, there are characters
who embody the underlying hostility of the have-nots for the
haves. Chauffeurs and gardeners urinate in movie stars' swimming
pools; hired waiters steal cases of liquor at A Group parties where
they serve; butlers sell their employers' secrets to the trash press.

Jackie's style is different from Joan's, but it's style. Watch her
walk into Le Dome for lunch, a superstar in action. Le Dome, on
the Sunset Strip, is the hot hot hot spot for the in movie crowd to
lunch these days. Outside the front door, fans with cameras wait
for the stars. "Look this way, Miss Collins," they yell when we
arrive, and she obliges, adjusting her head to the perfect angle,
smiling the friendly but not too friendly smile that celebrities use
for their fans. Inside, Michael Yhuelo, one of the owners, greets
her with open arms and gives her an air kiss near each cheek.
Waiters turn to look at her as if she were a film star rather than a
novelist. She walks through the terrace room and makes a turn
into the dining room to the table she has asked for in the far corner.
"Hi, Michelle," she calls to Michelle Phillips on the way. "Hi,
Jack," she calls to the columnist Jack Martin.

"I really love L.A.," she said. "In England, I grew up reading
Harold Robbins, Mickey Spillane, and Raymond Chandler." L.A.
to Jackie means strictly Hollywood, which she affectionately calls
the kiss-ass capital of the world. She loves the picture business, the
television business, the record business, and the people in them,
the stars, celebrities, directors, and producers. She is also a great
partygoer, but more in the role of observer than participant, someone doing research. Like all seasoned Hollywood people, she refers
to Hollywood as "this town." "One of the reasons I've gotten along
here is that I've never needed this town, or anything from anyone
here." As she said at the writers' conference last summer, "Write
about what you know." And what this lady knows about is Hollywood. Sue Mengers, the famed Hollywood actors' agent, now in
semiretirement, called *Hollywood Husbands* the definitive book
about Hollywood in the eighties. "Jackie got the feeling of this town
better than anyone ever caught it. She understands it."

"I love what I do," said Jackie. "I fall in love with my characters.

They become me, and I become them. They're part of me forever, even when I'm finished with them."

Her writing schedule is rigid. She works seven days a week, writing in longhand in spiral notebooks in a room she calls her study. On a good day she can write twenty pages. On a bad day she knocks off ten. When she gets to about seven hundred pages, she starts to bring the novel to an ending. She does not type; a secretary transfers her longhand to a word processor. Jackie is aware that her grammar is not always perfect, but that is the way she wants it. Once she asked her secretary to change anything she thought was wrong, and she then realized that her work lost in the translation to correct grammar.

"I never show *anything* to my publishers until after I finish writing the entire book," said Jackie. At the time I talked with her in December, she had not yet submitted *Rock Star* to Simon and Schuster, although it was coming out in April. Most books are not published until eight or ten months after submission. Confirming this, Michael Korda diplomatically said, "I would rather not have it this way." Only someone who has shown the same consistent success year after year could command that kind of leverage with a publisher.

Finally we get around to the subject of Joan Collins the novelist.

"Everybody wants to write a book once in their life," said Jackie about Joan's book, which she has not read. "If Joan can do it, good luck to her. She does everything well." She looked at her menu and continued: "I don't see Joan as becoming a novelist. I see it as a diversion for her. I've been a published novelist for twenty years. All eleven of my books have never been out of print." She thought over what she had said. "Of course, the fact that I've been offered the lead in a soap opera has nothing to do with her book!"

Joan Collins is the kind of woman you expect women to hate, but they don't. When her friends talk about her, they use the adjectives "indomitable" and "indefatigable." Her former agent, Sue Mengers, who handled the crème de la crème of Hollywood stars when she was still in the picture business, confirmed for me a story that Joan had told me. During Joan's down years, when the movie offers had stopped coming, Sue took Joan, whom she truly liked, out to lunch and told her she had to face up to the fact that after forty it was tough for actresses. "You have to realize that nothing more may happen in your career. Go home and concentrate on real life." Mengers went on to say that Joan cried a little that day, but she refused to give up. "Never," she said. "I'm so happy she proved me wrong," said Mengers. "Even Aaron Spelling, when he cast Joan in the part of Alexis, could not have imagined how strongly the public would have taken to her—especially women. The femme fatale number she plays is in good fun. In her own life, she has more women friends than any woman I know."

Joan Collins can carry on a conversation with you on the set of "Dynasty" at the same time she is being pinned up by one person, powdered by another, and having her hair sprayed by a third. She continues her conversation while she looks in a mirror that someone holds for her, checks her left side, checks her right, and makes a minute readjustment of a curl. She has been on movie sets since she was seventeen, and she retains the figure of a teenager and a bosom so superb that she recently had to threaten to sue the London *Sun* and *News of the World* after they reported that she had had a breast implant. She hadn't had a breast implant at all, and she got a retraction.

"Actually, I started writing novels when I was seven or eight," said Joan, about her new career as a novelist. " 'The Little Ballerinas,' 'The Gypsy and the Prince.' That kind of thing."

She is called to the set to shoot a scene with Linda Evans, a variation of half a hundred other confrontation scenes between Alexis and Krystle that have been shot in the six years that she has been on "Dynasty." Joan, as Alexis, paced back and forth in her office, reading a stock report, and Linda Evans, as Krystle Carrington, entered.

ALEXIS: What do you want, Krystle?

KRYSTLE: To go over a few things with you.

ALEXIS: Such as?

KRYSTLE: Your life.

ALEXIS: Is this some sort of joke?

KRYSTLE: I'm getting closer and closer to the truth of who and what you really are.

ALEXIS: I'm going to call security.

The director yelled, "Cut!" Joan returned to where we had been talking, and picked up the conversation as if a scene had not just been filmed. "I write in bed, on planes, under the hair dryer, on the set. Sometimes I write twelve to fifteen hours a day for a week, and then I don't touch it for a while. It's erratic, because it's a second career for me."

"Most of her manuscript comes in on the most extraordinary pieces of paper," says Michael Korda, who is working closely with her on her novel, as he did on her autobiography. "But every word is from her. Every revision. There is no ghostwriter, no helper, no hidden person. Her concentration is remarkable, given all the things going on in her life." Korda, the nephew of Sir Alexander Korda, the film producer, is an old acquaintance of Joan's from their teenage years in London. He remembers that when he was nineteen he took her to a party for Sonny Tufts at the house of Sir Carol Reed, but he adds that Joan did not remember this early date when he reminded her of it.

He thinks that when the two books come out the media will manufacture a rivalry between Joan and Jackie. "But if the time should ever come when the two of them are neck and neck on the *New York Times* best-seller list," he says, "I'm going to have a hot time of it."

March 1988

T

EARDOWN is the new word on everyone's lips in what has become known as the Platinum Triangle, the prestigious residential area of Los Angeles that encompasses Beverly Hills, Holmby Hills, and Bel-Air, and teardowns are rampant on almost every one of its fashionable streets. Sounds of hammering and drilling fill the air, and the once-quiet drives are jammed with cement mixers, cherry pickers, trucks, and lunch wagons as one of the greatest and most expensive building booms in real-estate history takes place. If *teardown* is a new word to you, it means buying a house, very often a beautiful house, for a great deal of money, and tearing it down in order to build a bigger house, for a great deal more money, on the same piece of land, a process that results, very often, in the construction of houses that are vastly overscaled for the size of the property on which they sit. The value of the land alone is so high that people are paying $3 million and up for an acre.

"We're in a renaissance out here. There's nothing like it in the world," said the enormously successful realtor Bruce Nelson as he drove me around the various high-priced areas in his pale yellow Rolls Corniche, in which the telephone never stopped ringing. "Excuse me," he said at one point, stopping in the middle of a sentence to answer the phone and discuss a deal with a possible buyer for the house of a Saudi Arabian prince, which the prince had bought a few years earlier from the shipping and real-estate magnate D. K. Ludwig, reportedly the richest man in America until recent business reversals in the Amazon region of Brazil toppled him from that lofty perch to a current net worth of a mere $550 million.

"All the great homes here were built in the thirties," Nelson continued after he hung up. "At that time, two-acre lots went for $15,000 or $20,000. Now the same properly goes for between $7 million and $10 million, but without the house." Nelson was not exaggerating. In fact, a few days later the *Los Angeles Times* reported in its real-estate column that a two-acre vacant lot in Beverly Hills had been sold by the film and record producer David Geffen for $7.45 million. Geffen had bought the land only a year and a half earlier for $3.85 million, and after having plans for a house drawn up had decided against building it. Even more amazing was the story of a young couple who had purchased eight acres in the Pacific Palisades for $6.5 million. Only two of the eight acres were flat; the rest was downhill. Yet even before the couple started to build, they had an offer of $24 million in cash for the land. And they refused it!

Real-estate agent Thelma Orloff, who was a show girl in the great days of the MGM musicals, holds court in the coffee shop of the Beverly Hills Hotel at 8:30 every morning, before leaving for her office. Still statuesque, she arrives each day to a chorus of "Hello, Thelma" from the regular breakfasters at the counter. Thelma Orloff has been around a long time, first as a show girl, then as an actress, wife, and mother, and now—stardom at last—as a real-estate agent *extraordinaire*. She recently celebrated fifty years of friendship with her best pal, Lucille Ball. She used to swim in Fanny Brice's pool in Holmby Hills, and can tell you every person who's lived in that house since Fanny died and what he paid. It is said that Thelma Orloff made the former television gossip celebrity Rona Barrett rich by turning over Beverly Hills real estate for her. As she drove me through the streets in her sleek black Cadillac, her comments on the houses of the famous were like an oral history of the area. "That's Eva Gabor's house, which is now up for sale; she bought it from Henry Berger after Anita Louise died. That's Betsy Bloomingdale's house, and up there next to it there used to be a one-story house that burned down; this developer bought it and has built a $7.8 million spec house, using every square inch of the land. Over there's Bonita Granville Wrather's house, which is about to come on the market. I went to Ann Warner with an offer of $30 million for her house, but she said, 'Forget it.'" Ann Warner is the widow of Jack Warner, of Warner Brothers, and her magnificent house, set on nine prime Beverly Hills acres, is considered one of the great estates of the area. Mrs. Warner, who lives in virtual seclusion in a few upstairs rooms in the house, has turned down offer after offer for her mansion. One real-estate agent told me she would probably accept $25 million for it on the condition that she have the right to live there for the rest of her life, with everything as it is.

In my early days in Hollywood, the grandest house of all to get into, once you had arrived socially, was the white Georgian mansion belonging to the late William and Edith Mayer Goetz. A famed Hollywood wit as well as a distinguished film producer, Bill Goetz was one of the earliest major art collectors in the film colony. His wife, Edie, the daughter of Louis B. Mayer, the legendary head of MGM in its heyday, and the sister of Irene Mayer Selznick, who was once married to David O. Selznick, before he married Jennifer Jones, was a Hollywood princess in every sense of the word, and, as Mrs. Goetz, became the undisputed social queen of Hollywood for decades. Her chef knew no peer in the community, and her guest lists were carefully honed as fine ivory. No outsiders in Edie Goetz's drawing room, ever. After dinner, there was always the latest movie, and as Mrs. Goetz's guests settled back into the sofas and chairs of her drawing room, designed by William Haines, a screen was lowered at one end of the room, obliterating for two hours Picasso's *Mother and Child*. It was heady stuff. Now the Goetzes are dead, their pictures have been sold in a recent auction that netted $85 million for their two daughters, and their lovely, graceful house is up for sale. Imagine my surprise, while having breakfast in the coffee shop of the Beverly Hills Hotel, to hear it casually referred to as a teardown—a $12 million teardown, but a teardown nonetheless. According to Bruce Nelson, the Goetz mansion, though swank in the extreme in its day, now needs "everything done. The Leonard Goldbergs offered $8 million cash, and were turned down." Another of the big realtors told me, "Streisand looked at it, but decided against it. Too much work." In all probability, the purchaser, whoever he or she may be, will raze the house to build a bigger and grander one. It's the trend. It's in the air. The talk is so pervasive and persuasive that you find yourself agreeing with the logic of buying a $10 million mansion in order to tear it down and build a $20 million one.

Some people will tell you that Columbia Savings in Beverly Hills started the teardown trend; a few residents will go so far as to say that Columbia Savings has just about ruined Beverly Hills. But the people who will always be most associated with the trend are the vastly rich television mogul Aaron Spelling and his wife, Candy. Over five years ago, the Spellings bought the old Bing Crosby house on one of the best streets in Holmby Hills for $10 million. It turned out that the cost of bringing the house up to date and redesigning it to the eighties needs of the Spelling family was prohibitive—it would be cheaper to tear it down and start over. The neighbors in the swank neighborhood were appalled, but the Spellings persevered. If all goes according to plan, they will finally be able to move into their French-style palace a year from now.

The Spelling house is the most discussed house in the city, and all other houses are compared with it. As of this moment, it is the largest by far of the many large houses being built. There was a time when houses were talked of in terms of how many rooms they had, but now all such discussions are in terms of square feet. The Spelling house is, give or take a thousand square feet or two, 56,000 square feet, approximately the size of a football field. An acre is 43,560 square feet, so the Spelling place is roughly an acre and a quarter of house. Probably not since Ludwig of Bavaria brought his country to the verge of bankruptcy with the extravagance of his palace-building has a residence been as publicly criticized as the Spelling house. Television newscasters have hovered over it in helicopters, pointing out to their viewers that it is being built for a family of only four. Comedians tell jokes about it. The fact remains that if the Spelling house had not been so prominently placed, so visible to the public eye, it would have been far less criticized. Budd Holden, a former set designer on "The Dinah Shore Show" who is now designing many of the most expensive L.A. homes, though not the Spelling mansion, has said of it, "It's mind-boggling, the space. Just beautiful." Four different real-estate agents told me that "some Japanese" had secretly gone through the Spelling house and offered $52 million for it.

"Do you mean the Spelling house is for sale?" I asked.

"No, no, of course it isn't for sale. But everything out here is for sale."

The mode of upscale spending is bewildering to longtime residents of Beverly Hills, who shake their heads in sadness at the evaporation of their once-charming community with its side-by-side pot-pourri of architectural styles. There is no remembrance of things past. "Beverly Hills has been destroyed. It's gone," one resident told me. New people moving in can't tear down fast enough. "New money wants new houses," said Stan Herman, a Beverly Hills realtor with eighteen agents working under him in an elegant office that sports a bar. Herman, who has a press agent and a press kit that lists the names of 131 famous people "who have lived in Stan Herman's homes," used to be married to Linda Evans of "Dynasty," and he moves in the fast lanes of Beverly Hills and Malibu life. Over the years he has bought many houses, redone them, and then resold them at enormous profit. He bought, for instance, the house Frank Sinatra lived in during his brief marriage to Mia Farrow in the 1960s, redid it entirely, even adding one of his trademarks, a wall urinal in the marble master bathroom, and then resold it to the theatrical producer James Nederlander and his wife for over $4 million. Herman says that if he had just held on to it until the teardown period started, he wouldn't have had to bother to do it over; he could have sold it for the same price without doing one thing. "There's megabucks here today. The Australians, the Japanese, people from Hong Kong. The Taiwanese money isn't here yet, but it's coming, and, of course, the French and the Italians. These people build enormous kitchens, the size of commercial kitchens, but they never cook, because they go out every night, and only the maids cook their own dinners in them." The big question everyone wants answered is, Who *are* these people who are knocking down all the houses and building new ones, putting as many square feet of house on the property as they can? Stan Herman said, "You'd think you would know, or should know, who someone is who has $10 million to spend on a house, but these days you don't."

KEEP OUT signs are posted everywhere to prevent the curious multitudes from staring in. Any sign of unauthorized entry brings a foreman yelling "Uh-uh" in no uncertain terms, meaning "*Out!*" and the grander places under construction have uniformed security guards. However, by arriving on the sites in Bruce Nelson's yellow Corniche and using "attitude," as Nelson calls it, I was able to gain entry to a surprising number.

Four of the most extraordinary new houses that I visited are being built by men in their early forties, most of them self-made men who acquired their fortunes during the Reagan years and who have probably been influenced by the flamboyance of Donald Trump's highly publicized life-style. In one instance, two houses on adjoining lots were torn down to build one 24,000-square-foot home for the couple and their three children, three nannies, and four maids. In another, two houses on adjoining lots were gutted, rebuilt, and joined together as one, encircled by a miniature railroad for the owners' two young sons. "You're only this age once. You may as well do it," one architect quoted his client as saying.

"We're talking all cash in these houses. There are no loans on any of them," said Bruce Nelson. "Vast fortunes have been coming into the Los Angeles area for years now, but very quietly."

Standing in the curve of a sweeping staircase, looking out over the marble-columned hallway, I said, "My God, these people could give a dance in this hall."

The contractor who had let me in answered, "They don't have to. There's a discotheque downstairs."

"Who is the owner?" I asked.

"He is not anyone you ever heard of," said the contractor.

Whoever these people are, they have not only a grand style in mind for their houses but also a grand style for the lives they intend to live in their houses once they are complete. In one *petit palais* under construction that I entered, the architect told me that the owner, described only as being "in airplane parts," had been so impatient to show off his vast new structure that he had increased the already large work staff of masons and bricklayers and agreed to pay them double and triple time to face the front of the mansion with red brick before Christmas so that he could give an outdoor party in the courtyard and let his friends see his work in progress.

"This is the only place in the world where real-estate agents become stars. I'm writing a novel about it," said real-estate agent Elaine Young. "What I'd really like to have is a three- or four-minute segment on the news dealing with real estate. When I first went into the business thirty years ago, there were only men in real estate, and older women. Real-estate people have been getting better- and better-looking. We just hired three new people in our office, two gorgeous girls and one handsome man. A man buying a $5 million house would rather buy from a beautiful woman than a homely one. It's such a personal business—we're in people's houses, in their bedrooms and their bathrooms. I love what I do. I could have gone into show business, but I ended up making a lot more money than some of the producers I've dated. We're sort of the periphery of show business."

A glamorous figure, Elaine Young lunches daily at the same table in the Polo Lounge of the Beverly Hills Hotel. An hour before I talked with her, she had been interviewed by another writer for another magazine. She was once married to the late film star Gig Young, who, years later, in the third week of a subsequent marriage, shot and killed his bride and himself in an unexplained mystery. Her hair is very very blond, her dress is very very pink, and her glasses have white frames. People turn to look at Elaine Young. "It's awesome," she said about the boom. "Every year I've said it can't go up any more, and then it does. Nothing hurts California real estate. Nothing. The rest of the country can get into a recession and California doesn't know. Even the earthquakes don't stop it. Did you feel the earthquake last night? I slept right through it."

Four or five times during the hour we spent together, the captain in the Polo Lounge brought her a remote-control telephone. "I told them not to put calls through," she said each time, and then took the call and transacted some business. "The Burt Reynolds house is up for sale for $6 million, and I've got some people interested," she said. "Burt's moving to Florida lock, stock, and barrel. It's the Japanese who are driving up the prices. They don't want anything over five years old. Even an older house redone they're not interested in. That's why there's so many teardowns. The Koreans are pretty much the same. I don't believe the prices! I have rentals for $40,000 a month. And there's no end in sight. Oh, God, here's another call. I told them not to put calls through."

In Europe, in the fifteenth century, laws called sumptuary laws were created to limit the excesses of the rich: the tower of a castle could be only so high, the length of a jeweled train only so long. "These people don't know when to stop," said Bruce Nelson about the new builders. "There are only two or three really great architects working in all this boom. What you're getting mostly is schlock. Look at this house. French balustrades and Corinthian columns. Everything is overbuilt. They don't know that the essence of elegance is simplicity. It's hard for them to stop. Now water is the new status symbol. I don't just mean Jacuzzis and very, very large swimming pools. Waterfalls are becoming very popular, and lakes."

At this point we drove into the courtyard of a $30 million spec house. I had been reminded by one real-estate agent to explain that a spec house did not mean a spectacular house, although it might very well be spectacular. A spec house is a house built on speculation, for sale to anyone with the necessary bucks. This $30 million spec house was being built right next door to an almost matching house. They were being built by two former business partners who reportedly no longer speak. Each house has a tennis court that is cantilevered out over Coldwater Canyon. The houses can be seen for miles around, and have caused outrage in the neighborhood. One Beverly Hills society figure, who lives directly below them, said, "I know it's terrible to talk about money, but my husband had to have $50,000 worth of shrubbery put in our lawn to block out those two monstrosities." The one I was allowed to enter has more gigantic marble columns than Hadrian's Villa. The master suite has his-and-her bathrooms of unparalleled luxury, with Jacuzzis, sunken tubs, and etched-glass doors. The floor of the dining room has clear glass panels that reveal an indoor swimming pool below. Leaving through the front door, which is eighteen feet high, the real-estate agent pointed to the house next door and said to me, "Imagine spending $30 million on this house and having that ugger right on top of you."

"Do you think this will sell?" I asked.

"Hell, yes," he said. "We're at the beginning of this boom. We're not at the end of it. No matter what happens to the economy, these people won't be affected."

The real big shots are taken by helicopter to look at property. That includes the very rich Japanese, members of the Saudi royal family, and agents representing the Sultan of Brunei's family. "I sold one house to a man from Hong Kong," said Bruce Nelson. "It always surprised me that he never wanted to see it when he was in town. Then I was told it was a subterfuge for the brother of the Sultan of Brunei. He paid $15 million for the house, but he's never moved in."

Brooks Barton, the patrician real-estate broker who is the first vice president of Coldwell Banker, spent hours in the air showing places to Sir James Goldsmith, the international financier, before Goldsmith abandoned the idea of living in Los Angeles and settled on Mexico instead. "The economy of Southern California is incredible, and growing all the time," Barton told me as he pointed out the Jerry Perenchio estate below. Although any spread with two acres is referred to as an estate by most brokers, there are only four major estates left that have not been broken up into smaller lots. One of them is the aforementioned Ann Warner estate. Another is the former Conrad Hilton estate in Bel-Air, which, like the Warner place, has nine acres. Now owned by the tremendously rich widower David Murdock, who is listed by *Forbes* magazine as being worth "well over $900 million," the property was described by one broker as "the perfect estate. You can't see it from the road. The driveway goes into a proper courtyard. The house opens onto the gardens." Another is the Knoll, considered by many to be the most beautiful house in Beverly Hills. The Knoll was built in the 1950s and lived in for many years by a Doheny heiress, Lucy Doheny Battson, whose family at one time owned four hundred acres in Beverly Hills. In 1975 Mrs. Battson sold the house for what was considered at the time the astronomical price of $2 million to the Italian film producer Dino De Laurentiis, who sold it six years later to the country-western star Kenny Rogers for $13 million. Rogers in turn sold it three years later to the Denver oil billionaire Marvin Davis for $20-plus million. Davis, who owned Twentieth Century-Fox Studios briefly and then sold it, and owned the Beverly Hills Hotel briefly and then sold it, and his popular wife, Barbara, are cutting a wide social swath in both the film community and the group that hovers around former president Reagan and Mrs. Reagan. The Davises' annual Christmas party in their new house is said to outdo for sheer splendor and movie star attendance any other party in the community in years and years. The last of the four great estates is the Bel-Air showplace known as the former

"It is," said Fernandez. Looking over the beautiful acreage, he said, "It's a dream of a job."

Despite all the hoopla connected with the Griffin estate, several highly placed people among the real-estate cognoscenti believe the house will never be built. "He's got ten in it now," they say, meaning $10 million. "You can buy Merv's land and Waldo Fernandez's blueprints for the house for $25 million."

But not to worry. There's always Robert Manoukian, an international figure of Armenian descent, who is a trusted friend of the Sultan of Brunei, and who also acts as his emissary. He negotiated to buy the Beverly Hills Hotel from Marvin Davis for the Sultan. Manoukian's new house, which is in the planning stages, is being designed by Budd Holden. It is to be built on 3.75 acres, on three descending lots, one of which was the old James Coburn estate, and, depending on whose version you believe, is going to be 58,000 square feet, 60,000 square feet, or 70,000 square feet. Fit for a king.

"Which is the Reagans' house?" I asked Brooks Barton in the helicopter.

"There," he answered, pointing down.

"Where?"

"There, that one."

"*That* little thing?"

"Yes."

Spoiled now by mansions of all sizes, styles, and shapes, I peered down critically at the modest ranch-style structure that is the new home of the former president of the United States and Mrs. Reagan—modest, at least in comparison with the houses in the neighborhood. It is a one-story, three-bedroom house of about 7,300 square feet (roughly the size of Candy Spelling's dressing room and closets), with pool, which friends of the Reagans bought for them for $2.5 million. Local rumor has it that Nancy Reagan does not enjoy having the house described as ranch-style. A block away on one side is the elaborate spec house designed by Budd Holden on 1.9 acres which recently sold for $15 million to the man from Hong Kong. On the other side is Jerry Perenchio's French château.

April 1989

HIGH ROLLER
The Phyllis McGuire Story

ONE DAY several years ago I was lunching at Le Cirque, arguably New York's most fashionable noontime restaurant, when my attention was drawn from my companions to three vaguely familiar-looking ladies of a certain age whom I at first mistook for triplets, since they were dressed identically in beige Chanel suits with matching bags, bracelets, pins, and honey-colored hairdos and were all speaking at the same time in an animated fashion. Seated at one of the very best tables, they were not unaware of the stir they were creating as they received the kind of deferential treatment from the sometimes haughty Le Cirque staff that Mrs. Astor or Mrs. Rockefeller might receive. The limitless curiosity of the socially inquisitive traveled from table to table: "Who are they?" And the answer came back, "The McGuire Sisters." A snap of the fingers—of course! The McGuire Sisters, the beautiful trio from Middletown, Ohio, who had had thirty hit records and given command performances for five presidents and the Queen Mother of England. One of the most popular singing groups of the fifties, discovered and made famous by Arthur Godfrey, they had by then been long out of circulation.

"Which one is Phyllis?" I asked the captain.

"In the middle," he answered.

"Wasn't she the—?"

Before I could finish my sentence, he nodded, *Yes, she was.* If I *had* finished my sentence that day at Le Cirque, it would have been, "Wasn't she the girlfriend of Sam Giancana?" Giancana, for decades one of the Mafia's most notorious and highly publicized figures, was also renowned for his role in the CIA plot to assassinate Fidel Castro, for his friendship with Frank Sinatra, and for his carrying on a love affair with Judith Campbell Exner at the same time she was having an affair with John F. Kennedy, the president of the United States.

Phyllis McGuire met Sam Giancana, according to legend, in Las Vegas in 1960, when the McGuire Sisters were performing there four times a year and pulling down $30,000 a week. Sam was a widower of fifty-two, and Phyllis, barely thirty, had already divorced Neal Van Ells, a radio/television announcer from Dayton, Ohio. Like many another Vegas performer, Phyllis had taken a liking to the gaming tables and had run up a hefty marker. As the story goes, Sam, spotting her, and liking her, went to Moe Dalitz, who ran the Desert Inn, and asked him how much the McGuire girl owed. Moe told him $100,000, a large marker at any time but enormous then. Sam is alleged to have said to Moe, "Eat it," meaning, in gangland parlance, erase the debt, which is different, of course, from paying the debt, but nonetheless it was a gesture not without charm and romantic appeal, especially since Sam followed it up with a suiteful of flowers. They fell in love.

For a time, the romance remained a well-kept secret, but wherever the trio traveled, Sam was there. In 1962, when the sisters were appearing at a nightclub in London, they were photographed there with their hairdresser, Frederic Jones, and Sam Giancana was also in the picture, with his arm wrapped around Phyllis. The photograph was flashed around the world, with enormous repercussions. The press and the public expressed a sense of outrage that the popular singer would associate with a person like Sam Giancana. In a tearful interview with the late gossip columnist Dorothy Kilgallen, Phyllis McGuire denied the rumors that she and Sam had been secretly married in Sweden, and also swore that she was never going to see Sam again. In 1968, the McGuires performed for the last time as a trio on "The Ed Sullivan Show," broadcast from Caesars Palace in Las Vegas. Since then, Phyllis has occasionally appeared as a solo act, as well as in musicals around the country, most recently in *Applause!* in Atlantic City.

Sam Giancana's life was ended in 1975, while he was cooking Italian sausage in the basement kitchen of his Oak Park, Illinois, home, by a shot from a High-Standard Duromatic .22 target pistol, with a silencer attached, fired into the back of his head. That shot was followed by a second, fired into his mouth after he fell to the floor, and then by a third, fourth, fifth, sixth, and seventh, which were fired upward into his chin, shattering his lower jaw, ripping through his tongue, and lodging in the back of his skull. The FBI believes to this day that the deliverer of the blasts was a friend of many years, who still lives in the Chicago area, and that Sam was murdered because he had refused to cut the Chicago Mob in on the gambling empire he had set up outside the United States, in Iran, Haiti, and Central and South America, as well as on five gambling ships he ran in the Caribbean. Furthermore, Sam had become old, he was in poor health, and it was time for a change.

Long before then, Phyllis and Sam had ceased being lovers, but they had remained friends and she had visited him on numerous occasions during his eight-year exile in Mexico. Both the Mob nobility and the show-business greats with whom Sam had hob-nobbed snubbed his Chicago funeral. Only Phyllis McGuire and Keely Smith, who had once sung with Louis Prima, arrived to pay their respects to Giancana's three daughters and to say farewell to Sam in his $8,000 silver casket.

For several years the McGuire Sisters have been planning a nightclub comeback. In February they performed at Rainbow & Stars in New York, and shortly after that, I made arrangements to interview Phyllis McGuire. "Don't mention Sam Giancana to her," people warned me, but not mentioning Sam Giancana when writing about Phyllis McGuire would be like not mentioning Richard Burton when writing about Elizabeth Taylor, or, in a more parallel situation, like not mentioning Nicky Arnstein when writing about Fanny Brice. As it turned out, I didn't have to bring up Sam's name, because Phyllis McGuire brought it up first. Their story has all the stuff of which myths are made.

I arrived in Las Vegas with elaborate directions for how to get from the airport to Rancho Circle, the exclusive enclave behind a guarded gate where she has lived for years. "Past the Lit'l Scholar Schoolhouse," I read from my instruction sheet, but the driver said he didn't need any instructions. "Everybody in Vegas knows where Phyllis McGuire lives."

From outside, the place looked like a suburban ranch-style house built in the fifties, but all resemblance to ranch-style life ended at the front door, which was opened by a man wearing a gun in a holster under his open suit jacket. Paul Romines has been her bodyguard for fourteen years. I stood for a moment in the hallway. To the right was a dining room with a mirrored floor. Through a door was a men's lavatory with two wall urinals side by side. Ahead was a replica of the Arc de Triomphe, which separated the hall from the living room. The living room was one of the largest I have ever been in, so large that a forty-four-foot-high replica of the Eiffel Tower did not seem to cramp the space. Beyond that was a vast area which included the formal dining room and, to the right of it, a bar with twelve bar chairs. To the left was an area identified by the bodyguard as the Chinese area, and to the right an area he designated as the French area. The windows, he informed me, were all bulletproof and could take a magnum shot, and at the touch of a button steel doors would drop from the eaves over all the windows, securing the house completely, fortress-style.

The floor of the living room was black and white marble. The rugs in the French area were Aubusson and Tabriz, and the walls were covered in rose damask. The chandeliers and sconces were Bavarian, with amber light bulbs. The mirrors on the walls were Venetian, and the chairs and sofas were all French, in multiple groupings, so many chairs that I lost count at sixty. That was when Phyllis McGuire came in.

She was dressed in a nautical style, with white flannel trousers and a white cashmere sweater with naval insignia on it. Her ear-rings were anchors. She was not at all what I was expecting, and from the moment she spoke I liked her. She was friendly, funny, gracious, utterly enthusiastic, constantly up, with boundless energy. And pretty, very pretty.

"Did anyone offer you a cup of coffee?" she asked. "Or any-thing?" She flung up her hands in mock exasperation and called into the kitchen, "Enice, take care of Mr. Dunne. And I'll have some coffee too. And some Perriers." She asked me, "Did you meet Enice? Enice Jobe? She's been with me for thirty-three years."

We sat on French chairs in the French area. "Is the music too loud?" she asked. "I can turn it down. Turn it down, Enice, will you, and put the coffee right here on this table."

I asked about the sisters, Dorothy and Christine, and she said, "We've been singing together since I was four years old. We sang in the car, using the windshield wiper for a metronome. My sisters are the most incredible harmony singers. I can start in any key, and they pick it up." The sisters got their start singing in the First Church of God in Middletown, Ohio, where their mother, an ordained minister, was an associate pastor.

"We were middle class," she said. "My father worked for forty-six years for Armco Steel. He made steel before there were jet furnaces, working at an open hearth, shoveling in the pig iron. He wore safety shoes and long thick underwear, safety shirts and gloves, and a hard hat. At night after work, his clothes were coated with salt from his sweat. When my sisters and I started making money, we asked our parents what they owed, and we paid off everything. We made my father retire, and ordered a custom-made Cadillac with a gold plaque on it that said, FOR ASA AND LILLIE MCGUIRE, FROM DOROTHY, CHRISTINE, AND PHYLLIS. We sent them all over the world."

Looking around the French area, she said, "Some of this furniture is very valuable, and some is just personal to me. That Aubusson should be hanging on the wall rather than be on the floor. A lot of the furniture and the paneling came from the house of Helen Bonfils in Denver, Colorado. Her father was the editor and publisher of the *Denver Post*. She was one of the finest women I ever knew. That desk belonged to Helen's father."

One thing I'll say about Phyllis McGuire, she's not hard to converse with. Raise any topic—with few exceptions—and she will talk away. She told me that one of the newspapers had called her a motor-mouth.

"Do you want to see everything?" she asked.

"Sure."

She took me through the house and grounds. There are eight acres and two guesthouses. "That's where my sisters stay when they come here to rehearse. The rest of the time they live in Arizona. They came to Vegas during the week and went home on weekends while we were getting ready for the comeback. We worked six to eight hours a day. We worked out and did stretching exercises in the mornings and did three hours each afternoon with Jim Hendricks, our pianist. One night I had Altovese and Sammy Davis over to hear the act. Chris and Dorothy each have their own bedroom and television set, and they share the living room and kitchen.

Sister Dorothy is no stranger to romantic headlines herself, having engaged in 1958 in a steamy love affair with fellow Arthur Godfrey singing star Julius La Rosa, which resulted in a public scolding on-air by Godfrey. Although the choirgirl image was tarnished, that affair caused no lessening of the group's popularity.

Behind the main house, we came to a moatlike area where Phyllis's twenty-three swans swim. "Those are the black Australian swans there," she said. "That one is about ready to hatch." Pointing to her tennis court, she said, "That's where Johnny Carson learned how to play tennis. It needs to be swept," she added, shaking her head.

"Someone told me all the flowers in your garden are fake," I said. She laughed and said, "Honey, I keep five gardeners."

In the pool house, noticing a crack in one of the windows, she picked up the telephone and called the main house. "Enice, tell maintenance there's a crack in the window of the pool house. Have him replace it, will you?" A bit farther on, she said, "Over there's my putting green. My waterfalls aren't on today—sorry."

Back in the house, she took me downstairs. "This is my nightclub. It even has a neon sign. The carpet rolls up and it's a dance floor underneath. The dance floor is in the shape of a piano. There have been lots of parties in this room. Over here is a blackjack table. Moe Dalitz gave me this table as a gift. I've taught more people how to play blackjack here at this table."

There is a beauty salon in the house, with several chairs and dryers so that the sisters, or houseguests, can have their hair done at the same time. In the health club, next to the beauty salon, are three changerooms and three massage tables next to one another, where three masseurs can work on three guests at the same time. "The steam room is always ready," she said, peering into a window of the steam room.

Her huge bathtub is part of her bedroom, and her closets are enormous. "This is all Chanel," she said, pointing to one area. "Over there, it's all Galanos, and there in that room is all Pauline Trigère." It was a tour she was used to giving. "This is for my furs.

The lynx, ermine, and sable are here. The older furs are over there. I keep a record of everything I wear so that I don't ever repeat with the same people. All my clothes are on a computer. So are all the books in my library, and all the furniture. They're all on video as well."

She picked up a model airplane. "This was my G-II," she said. "It had a sign saying, WELCOME ABOARD THE PHYLLIS SPECIAL. I've decorated the interiors of three planes. Do you feel like lunch?"

"Sure."

The mail had arrived. "Enice, I don't want to see the tabloids. The Searles across the street said there was something in them about us. Don't show me." We sat in the small dining room, and Enice, having given the mail to a secretary, brought in the lunch. "I have the greatest kitchens in the world," Phyllis said. "I don't cook, but I always have great chefs. And some of my maids have been with me for fourteen or seventeen years."

"How many people work for you in this house?" I asked, having noticed several in the background.

She began to count, looking up, looking over at Enice for verification, placing the forefinger of her left hand against the pinkie finger of her right hand, then against the ring finger, then the center finger, then against the other forefinger, and then repeating the process, at the same time reeling off a seemingly endless list of names—maids, cooks, guards, gardeners, drivers, secretaries.

"Twenty-eight," she said finally.

She thinks a great deal about security. "My limo driver carries a gun," she said. "But if they want to get you, they're going to get you. For me, it's the most secure feeling in the world when those steel doors are down."

Phyllis McGuire has a more elaborate life-style than most television and nightclub performers of the fifties whose stars have dimmed with time and the fickle musical tastes of the public, and nowhere is her wealth more visible than in her wondrous jewelry. No one who knows about jewels has not heard about her fantastic collection, which ranks among the best in the world, right up there with the famous collections of Elizabeth Taylor, Imelda Marcos, Candy Spelling, Mrs. Marvin Davis, and the fifth Baroness Thyssen.

Harry Winston, the great jeweler, once said to her, "If ever there was a lady meant to wear jewels, it's you." She told me, "There was a time when I was purchasing millions of dollars' worth of jewelry. I was one of Harry Winston's best customers." She paused for a moment and then added, "Maybe some Saudis were ahead of me. Jewels really turned me on then, and they still do. I wear the jewels, they don't wear me."

On the day I was in her house, most her jewels had been put in the vault because she was leaving imminently for a singing engagement with her sisters at the Moulin Rouge in Chicago. But a few were still at hand. "Enice," she called out, "bring in the canaries." The canaries consisted of a forty-two-carat yellow diamond set in a ring, surrounded by smaller diamonds, and some loose yellow diamonds which she was planning to have made into earrings. She examined her stones like a jeweler. "I'm not sure I like the way they put the diamonds around the canary," she said, "but I'm trying it this way." From the same package she pulled a twenty-eight-carat marquise-shaped diamond ring, which she called "one of the babies" because of its small size—small, at least, in comparison with some of her other rings. The canaries brought to mind a fairly recent drama in her life.

In 1979, she said, she took a D-flawless-diamond ring to Harry Winston's to have it cleaned and to have the prongs checked. When the ring was returned to her, it didn't seem to have the same sparkle it had had previously. Even now, a decade later, recounting the story, she held her hand up and examined her ring finger as if she were looking at the ring in question. She said that she had said at the time, "This can't be my ring. It doesn't sparkle the same." She said she had begun to question her own sanity. "I said to Enice, 'Is this my ring, Enice?' and she said, 'I think it is, Miss Phyllis.' But there is a process called cubic zirconia, where a fake diamond can be cut exactly to match a real diamond. I knew that my ring had been switched. I turned in one to be cleaned, and they gave me back another. I sued Winston for $60 million. They countersued me for $100 million." At the time, a spokesman for Winston denied the allegations "absolutely."

"I was only trying to recover my jewels," she continued. "I was deposed for three days at Foley Square in New York. I discovered the diamond wasn't mine at Christmas of '79, and the case was settled in '82." She seemed to be finished with her story.

"But what happened?" I asked.

"I'm not allowed to discuss the outcome of the suit. That's part of the agreement," she said, giving a helpless shrug, but neither her smile nor her attitude indicated any discontent with the outcome.

A spokesman for Winston told me the company had no comment to make.

Her conversation is peppered with the names of the very rich and very famous, with whom she has spent most of her time over the last twenty-five years. "I met Imelda Marcos at a party at Adnan Khashoggi's," she told me, and she and her sisters were scheduled to sing at the ninety-fifty birthday party of Armand Hammer, the billionaire philanthropist. Ann-Margret's name came up, and she said, "Let's call her." Ann-Margret was playing at Caesars Palace. She dialed the number. "This is Phyllis McGuire," she said to the telephone operator. "I'd like to speak to Ann-Margret. She's still sleeping? At two o'clock in the afternoon? My God, she only had one show last night. OK, tell her I called."

"New York is like roots for me," she said. "It was the first big city we saw after Ohio." For years she kept a Park Avenue apartment. Then she bought a town house on one of the most exclusive streets on the Upper East Side of Manhattan. "Do you know where Givenchy is? Two houses behind that." She bought the house, she said, "lock, stock, and barrel, including antiques, china, crystal, and silverware, from a son of King Fahd of Saudi Arabia," who was afraid of being assassinated, following the assassination of Anwar Sadat in Egypt, and took up residence instead in the Waldorf Towers, where many heads of state, and families of heads of state, stay for purposes of security. Phyllis loved the house dearly but spent only twenty-one days in it in 1987, so when her great friend Meshulam Riklis, the vastly rich ($440 million) financier husband of Pia Zadora, asked if he could buy it, she sold it to him. In order not to be without a nest in New York, she borrowed the Pierre-hotel apartment of another great friend, the vastly rich ($950 million) financier Kirk Kerkorian, and liked it so much that she talked Kerkorian into selling it to her, completely furnished.

"I'm a good businesswoman," she said, a fact that is borne out by most of her acquaintances. "If I weren't performing, I would have to constantly be working at something. I love business."

I didn't have to mention Sam Giancana. She brought him up. "I've had four serious involvements in my life, and one was a marriage. That was only for about ten minutes. Two of the men are still my friends, Simon Srybnik and Dr. Stanley Behrman, the head of oral surgery at New York Hospital. Even after Simon married Judy, and Stanley married Nancy, we stayed friends." She paused before continuing. "And then there was Sam." When she said Sam, she whispered his name. There is no doubt she loved him.

Even William Roemer, the former FBI agent who dogged Sam's life for a decade, says, "Phyllis really loved Sam, and Sam loved her." Phyllis's great friend the Broadway producer Dasha Epstein says, "She disappeared out of our lives when she was going with Sam. She said, 'I know it's difficult for my friends, and I understand.' That was so like Phyllis."

"My life is so much more than that—with Sam," Phyllis said. "That was only a chapter. I'm not ashamed of my past. I was doing what I honestly felt." She sat back in her rose damask Bergère chair and continued. "Sam was the greatest teacher I ever could have had. He was so wise about so many things. Sam is always depicted as unattractive. He wasn't. He was a very nice-looking man. He wasn't flashy. He didn't drive a pink Cadillac, like they used to say. He was a beautiful dresser. Dorothy Kilgallen thought he was my attorney when she met him. The two great losses of my life were my father and Sam."

She is now working on her autobiography to set the record straight. "I've got to get this out. I've got to get on with my life. It's holding me up. I have things to say that haven't been said," she told me. "Like about the late Mayor Daley of Chicago, even if his son is the new mayor." "It's a heavy-duty story," she was quoted in Marilyn Beck's column as saying. "I've been in thirty-four books in the last twelve to fifteen years, and it's time my story was finally told correctly. I don't need a Kitty Kelley doing to me what she did to Sinatra and [what she's doing to] Nancy Reagan."

She denies, for example, the story about the $100,000 marker that Giancana told Moe Dalitz to eat. "I never lost more than

$16,000 gambling at any one time," she said. She also discounts many of the stories about her in the book *Mafia Princess*, written by Sam Giancana's daughter Antoinette. "I tried to stop that book," she said. "It wasn't accurate. Toni got all her information through the Freedom of Information Act. She didn't know any firsthand. She and her father hadn't been close. She used to come and stay here, in the guesthouse."

In 1961, at the height of Phyllis's fame, her affair with Giancana was still not known to the public. The FBI, which tracked Giancana's every move, had chosen not to expose the relationship, understanding that such publicity would be detrimental to McGuire's career. But in the spring of that year, agents bugged their motel room in Phoenix and learned they would be traveling on American Airlines to New York with a stopover at O'Hare Airport in Chicago. The FBI decided to subpoena Phyllis with the proviso that if she cooperated with them by answering their questions in a room within the terminal, they would withdraw the subpoena and she would not have to appear the next day. She knew that if she were to appear, it would become publicly known that she was the mistress of the Mob chief. What the FBI agents asked her to do was cooperate with them in the future by letting them know where Sam was at all times. Phyllis agreed to do what they asked, and they took the subpoena back, but, according to several reliable sources, she didn't keep her promise.

William Roemer's job that day was to keep Giancana occupied while Phyllis was being questioned, and he and Giancana got into a screaming match at the airport, climaxing when Sam said he was going to have his friend Butch Blasi machine-gun him down. Roemer, probably the greatest authority on Sam Giancana, remembers him very differently from the way Phyllis does. His book, *Roemer: Man Against the Mob*, will be published in October by Donald I. Fine. He told me on the phone from his home in Tucson, "Sam was ugly, balding—wore a wig at the end of his life. Little, slight, dumpy, a deese-dem-dose guy, scum of the earth, killer, the dregs of society, the worst kind of person. We hated each other. I hated him, and he hated me."

Roemer said that the Mob was extremely upset with Giancana when he was going with Phyllis. They thought he wasn't minding the store. "He fell in love with her and traveled all over the world with her," Roemer said. He agrees that Phyllis, in the tradition of wives, daughters, and lovers of Mob members, knew little of Sam's life away from her. He told me that when Phyllis first thought about writing her book, she called him—Sam's nemesis—to say that she had met a lot of people during her years with Sam but that she didn't actually know who they were or what they had done. Some of them, she said, she knew only by their nicknames, like "Chuckie" (English), "Butch" (Blasi), and "Skinny" (D'Amato)— all figures in the racketeering life of Sam Giancana.

"Did Sam leave any money to Phyllis?"

"Nobody could ever prove that he left her money," answered Roemer. Although Giancana left an estate valued at only $132,583.16 when he died, that meant nothing. The kind of money that people like Sam Giancana have is not banked or left in the ordinary ways of money management. Roemer said it is possible that Giancana had a hundred million dollars.

"It very definitely hurt our careers for about a year," Phyllis McGuire said about her affair with Giancana. "We were blacklisted on TV, but that ended."

"In your interview with Dorothy Kilgallen, you said you were going to give him up," I said.

"Yes, I know. I said in that interview that I'd never see him again. Well, I did." She shrugged, and then threw out one of the amazing bits of information that flow freely from her tongue. "Kilgallen was murdered," she said. "She didn't commit suicide." Dorothy Kilgallen, who supposedly died of a sleeping-pill overdose in 1964, had in that same year interviewed Jack Ruby, the assassin of Lee Harvey Oswald, the man who assassinated President Kennedy. "I saw her three days before, dancing at El Morocco with Johnnie Ray. She was murdered. I didn't believe the suicide story then. I don't believe it now. Dorothy was the most beautiful corpse I ever saw."

Although Phyllis McGuire did not mention him in her list of suitors, there has been another romantic involvement since Sam, a bigger-than-life character named Mike Davis, and they are still close friends. The owner of Tiger Oil, Davis is based in Houston, but he is always on the move. Phrases like "my jet" pop up in his conversation, as do such names as Bunker Hunt, of the Texas Hunts, and Adnan Khashoggi, the international arms dealer, currently in hot water, with whom Davis has been a sometime partner. "Tiger Mike," as some people call him, is of Lebanese extraction. He was once the chauffeur of Phyllis's great friend Helen Bonfils, and married Bonfils upon the death of her husband in 1956. Helen Bonfils was reportedly in her late sixties at the time, and Davis was in his late twenties. Bonfils, who took over the running of the *Denver Post* when her father died, was also involved in producing Broadway shows. She helped finance Davis's start-up in Tiger Oil. Davis's interest in Phyllis began while she was still involved with Giancana. McGuire told me she once pulled him behind a slot machine and warned him, "You better stay away from me. Do you want to end up on the bottom of Lake Mead?"

On several occasions, Frank Sinatra's name came up in our conversation, and I sensed a certain amount of animosity. "We are cautiously friends," she said slowly. "He is the most talented but most contradictory person. He has surrounded himself with an entourage who yes him to death. How can you expand yourself surrounded by yes-men? I've stayed in his house, and he has bored me to death. He tells the *sa-a-ame* stories he's been telling for years, and all I ever heard were his records, which he played *over and over* again." She covered her ears as she told this. "I thought to myself, I'll never do that in my house with my records. You *never* hear my own music played on my system."

She recounted to me a story that I had read in Kitty Kelley's unauthorized biography of Sinatra, *His Way*. Sinatra, who was making $100,000 a week in Las Vegas, agreed, along with Sammy Davis, Jr., Dean Martin, and Eddie Fisher, to appear for nothing in a club called Villa Venice, which was a front for Giancana. Afterward, Giancana wanted to send a gift to each of them, and Phyllis picked out Sinatra's gift. She suggested sending Steuben crystal, having seen stemware in Sinatra's house that he told her was Steuben. "I say Steuben. Frank said Steu*banne*. He thought what he had was Steuben, but it wasn't. Steuben always says Steuben on the bottom, but his didn't. I called Gloria, who was Frank's secretary, to see if they should be monogrammed, but she said no to the monogram, because people tended to walk off with anything

SOCIAL DEATH
IN
VENICE

AT FIRST it seemed like a re-enactment of the sort of turn-of-the-century match Henry James or Edith Wharton might have written about, the marriage of a New World heiress and an Old World prince, a swap of money and title beneficial to both sides. Indeed, as we approach the turn of another century, the allure of grand titles for socially ambitious mothers with marriageable daughters seems not to have diminished, judging by the remarkable events in Venice during Easter weekend this year. No story by Henry James or Edith Wharton, however, would have ended with headlines such as this: HEIRESS JILTED AS BRIDEGROOM RUNS OFF WITH BEST MAN.

In this version of the tale, the heiress is an Australian named Primrose Dunlop, and the nobleman is the awesomely titled Prince Lorenzo Giustiniani Montesini, count of the Phanaar, Knight of Saint Sophia, Baron Alexandroff. A poor prince who claims to be "a small link in a chain that goes back to Constantine," Prince Giustiniani, known to his friends as Laurie, is employed as a steward on Qantas Airlines. Lorenzo Montesini, as he was then called, appeared on the social scene of Sydney in 1983, at a charity party at Fairwater, the mansion of Lady Fairfax, the widow of the Australian press lord. Affable, charming, socially adept, Lorenzo soon was in demand as an extra man. "He charmed his way into everyone's house here," one Sydney social figure told me. "He was asked to all the parties, between flights."

When the Egyptian-born Montesini, who is forty-four, chubby, bouncy, elfin, and very short, arrived in Sydney from Melbourne, he came with his longtime companion, Robert Straub, with whom he had served in Vietnam. In Woolloomooloo, a middle-class suburb of Sydney, the men converted two rose pink cottages into their home, which they filled with gilded mirrors, Persian carpets, rococo furnishings, and tables covered with framed photographs of well-known people. Montesini described the princely possessions as "family things."

Primrose Dunlop, the woman in question, was not a blushing debutante in her first bloom. Nor was she really an heiress, but merely the stepdaughter of a rich man who has two daughters of his own, who do not care much for their stepsister. Primrose is thirty-six, had been married before, briefly and unhappily, and is called Pitty Pat to distinguish her from her mother, Lady Potter, who is also named Primrose. Pitty Pat has had a variety of jobs over the years: she sold pots and pans in a department store, wrote social columns for two Sydney tabloids, did public-relations work for the British mogul Lord McAlpine, and, most recently, clerked as an eight-dollar-an-hour assistant to a haberdasher named John Lane, a great friend of her mother's, who sometimes escorted Lady Potter on the endless round of parties and boutique openings that her much older husband did not wish to attend.

Lady Potter, who once raised French poodles and is most often described by her friends as vivacious, became the fourth wife of Sir Ian Potter in 1975. Sleek, stylish, and very well dressed, she speaks in the grand vocal tones of a society lady. Her previous marriage, to Dr. Roger Dunlop, a surgeon, who is the father of Primrose, ended in divorce. Lady Potter, a tireless fund-raiser for charity, with a hardy appetite for publicity and social recognition, had set her sights far beyond Sydney and Melbourne. Described by an English acquaintance who has sat next to her at dinner on several occasions as "an expert dropper of key names meant to establish her credentials," Lady Potter is referred to in the Australian social columns as "the Empress" and is said to revel in her nickname. She is considered by many to be the queen bee of the Sydney-Melbourne social axis, and her public-relations consultant, Barry Everingham, has gone so far as to describe Sir Ian and Lady Potter as the closest thing that Australia has to royalty.

Sir Ian, eighty-eight, is one of the Australia's most respected businessmen, but age has caught up with the old man. A number of people I spoke with described him as slightly "gaga." Others said he was amazingly sharp for a man of his age. He played an integral, albeit passive, part in the Venetian nuptials, however, because his money was paying for everything. His fortune, which has been

was a nonromantic liaison reeking of ulterior motives on both sides. When Montesini and Robert Straub, whose relationship was causing titters in Lady Potter's circle, showed up at a party to celebrate the opening of a Chanel boutique in Sydney, John Lane, acting for Lady Potter, said to Lorenzo, "Don't be seen in public with that man again." The bride's family was less than enthusiastic when Lorenzo announced that Straub would be his best man. Dissension arose. There were rumors, all unconfirmed, that lurid photographs existed.

Stories persisted in Sydney society that the prince was in it for the money. He himself reported to Pitty Pat that John Laws, one of the highest-paid radio announcers in the world, had told him, while he was pouring champagne for him in the first-class cabin on a Qantas flight, that his title should be worth at least $2 million to the Potters. Lorenzo was shocked. "People suggest that there is money in this for me. That's utter rubbish," he protested.

Before their departure for Venice, the prince and his princess-to-be posed for pictures and gave an interview for a long article in *Good Weekend* magazine in the *Sydney Morning Herald*, and it was that article, with the royal-looking photographs, that began the unraveling of their plans. Previously unknown relations of the prince came out of the woodwork and mocked his pretentions, disputing both the title and his right to use it. One cousin, Nelson Trapani, a forty-nine-year-old retired Queensland builder, told the press, "Really, all this speculation about a title is a load of bulldust. I'd sooner sit down with a pie and watch the telly."

Nonetheless, the group, which included Father Kiss, who was to perform the ceremony, took off amid whispers that all was not as it was supposed to be, with either the title or the romance, or anything else. Dr. Roger Dunlop, Pitty Pat's real father, was so opposed to his daughter's choice of husband that he boycotted the wedding ceremony.

If Lorenzo was having second thoughts, he nonetheless went along with the plans, flying to Venice with Robert Straub and John Lane, Lady Potter's great friend, who had been assigned the paternal function of giving the bride away, owing to the refusal of her real father and the inability of her stepfather because of his age. The groom-to-be was the only member of the wedding party without a confirmed seat on the plane. He traveled standby economy-class at his own expense. A curious twist of alliances occurred during the trip. Lane, who had previously been unfriendly to Montesini and Straub and had warned them at the Chanel opening not to appear together in public, discovered, Lorenzo later said, that "we were really quite nice guys after all and not as bad as we had been painted."

On Good Friday, as Leo Schofield, an Australian journalist, and other guests were boarding their plane in Sydney for the long flight to Venice, they heard that the wedding had been called off.

What had up to then been merely a Sydney-Melbourne gossip-column story quickly turned into international headlines, and Pitty Pat and Lorenzo became, however briefly, household names, more famous in their disaster than they would ever have been in their marriage. "If it was publicity they all wanted," said one friend, "they have succeeded beyond their wildest dreams."

Although it was widely touted in the Australian press that the guest list had been made up of a glittering gaggle of international social-ites, there wasn't a recognizable name in the group. "Not a single man, woman, or dog in Venice ever heard of any of these people," said one longtime resident of the city.

There was a problem with accommodations from the beginning. Lord and Lady Potter and Pitty Pat were housed on an upper floor of the Palazzetto Pisani, and the prince, his best man, and John Lane were housed in a small flat on the ground floor, or water floor, consisting of two tiny rooms. The space was crowded and uncomfortable, and the bathroom facilities were not to the trio's liking. At a cocktail party held at the Palazzetto, which is owned by the Countess Maria Pia Ferri, another Venetian countess is said to have exclaimed to the bridegroom when he was introduced to her as Prince Giustiniani, "Oh, you must be related to my friend Cecy Giustiniani." Cecy Giustiniani is the venerable Dowager Countess Giustiniani, and soon telephones were jingling up and down the Grand Canal. People ran to their *Libro d'Oro*, the Italian book of nobility, but no one could find a Prince Giustiniani. Every Venetian with whom I spoke drew attention, often huffily, to the fact that "Prince" is not a Venetian title. "Count" is the title that counts in Venice, as any countess will tell you.

nance on his two-floor, 7,200-square-foot condominium with indoor swimming pool at the Olympic Tower on Fifth Avenue in New York; of unpaid helicopter lessons for his daughter, Nabila, even while the extravagant parties proclaiming denial of the truth continued. In fact, the more persistent the rumors of Khashoggi's financial collapse grew, the more extravagant his parties became. Nico Minardos, a former associate of Khashoggi's who was arrested during Iranscam for his involvement in a $2.5 billion deal with Iran for forty-six Skyhawk aircraft and later cleared, said, "Adnan is a lovely man. I like him. He is the greatest P.R. man in the world. When he gave his fiftieth-birthday party, our company was overdrawn at the bank in Madrid by $6 million. And that's about what his party cost. Last year he sold an apartment to pay for his birthday party."

Probably the most telling story in Khashoggi's downfall was repeated to me in London by a witness to the scene, who wished not to be identified. The King of Morocco was staying in the royal suite of Claridge's. The King of Jordan, also visiting London at the time, came to call on the King of Morocco. There is a marble stairway in the main hall of Claridge's which leads up to the royal suite. Shortly after the doors of the suite closed, Adnan Khashoggi, having heard of the meeting, arrived breathlessly at the hotel by taxi. Used to keeping company with kings, he sent a message up to the royal suite that he was downstairs. He was told that he would not be received.

Shortly after I was asked to write about Adnan Khashoggi, following his arrest, his executive assistant, Robert Shaheen, contacted this magazine, aware of my assignment. He said that I should call him, and I did.

"I understand," I said, "that you are the number-two man to Mr. Khashoggi."

"I am Mr. Khashoggi's number-one man," he corrected me. Then he said, "What is it you want? What will your angle be in your story?" I told him that at that point I didn't know. Shaheen's reverence for his boss was evident in every sentence, and his descriptions of him were sometimes florid. "He dared to dream dreams that no one else dared to dream," he said with a bit of a catch to his voice. He proceeded to list some of the accomplishments of his boss, whom he always referred to as the Chief. "The Chief was responsible for opening the West to Saudi Arabia. The Chief saved the Cairo telephone system. The Chief saved Lockheed from going bankrupt." He then told me, "You must talk with Max Helzel. He is a representative of Lockheed. Get him before he dies. He is getting old. Mention my name to him."

An American of Syrian descent, Shaheen went to Saudi Arabia to teach English in the late fifties, and there he met Khashoggi. He has described his job with Khashoggi in their long association as being similar to that of the chief of staff at the White House. Anyone wishing to meet with Khashoggi for a business proposition had to go through him first. He carried the Chief's money. He scheduled the air fleet's flights. He traveled with him. He became his apologist when things started to go wrong. After the debacle in Salt Lake City, he said, "People in Salt Lake City can't hold Adnan responsible. He delegated all responsibility to American executives, and it was up to them to make a success. Adnan still believes in Salt Lake City." And he became, like his boss, a very rich man himself through the contacts he made. At the close of our conversation, Shaheen told me that it was very unlikely that I would get into the prison in Bern, although he would do what he could to help me.

The night before I left New York, I was at a dinner party in a beautiful Fifth Avenue apartment overlooking Central Park. There were sixteen people, among them the high-flying Donald and Ivana Trump, one of New York's richest and most discussed couples, and a major topic of conversation was Khashoggi's imprisonment. "I read every word about Adnan Khashoggi," Donald Trump said to me.

A story that Trump frequently tells is about his purchase of Khashoggi's yacht, the 282-foot, $70 million *Nabila*, thought to be the most opulent private vessel afloat. In addition to the inevitable discotheque, with laser beams that projected Khashoggi's face, the floating palace also had an operating room and a morgue, with coffins. Forced to sell it for a mere $30 million, Khashoggi did not want Trump to keep the name *Nabila*, because it was his daughter's name. Trump had no intention, ever, of keeping the name.

He had already decided to rename it the *Trump Princess*. But for some reason Khashoggi thought Trump meant to retain the name, and he knocked a million dollars off the asking price to ensure the name change. Trump accepted the deduction.

"Khashoggi was a great broker and a lousy businessman," Trump said to me that night. "He understood the art of bringing people together and putting together a better deal than almost anyone—all the bullshitting part, of talk and entertainment—but he never knew how to invest his money. If he had put his commissions into a bank in Switzerland, he'd be a rich man today, but he invested it, and he made lousy choices."

In London, on my way to Bern, I contacted Viviane Ventura, an English public-relations woman who is a great friend of Khashoggi's. She attended Richard Nixon's second inauguration in January 1973 with him. Ventura told me more or less the same thing Shaheen had told me. "The lawyers won't let anyone near him. They don't want any statements. There's a lot more to it than we know. This is a terrible thing that your government is doing. Adnan is one of the most generous, most caring men."

The five-foot-four-inch, two-hundred-pound, financially troubled megastar was born in Saudi Arabia in 1935, the oldest of six children. His father, who was an enormous influence in his life, was a highly respected doctor, remembered for bringing the first X-ray machine to Saudi Arabia. He became the personal physician to King Ibn Saud, a position that brought him and his family into close proximity with court circles. Adnan was sent to Victoria College in Alexandria, Egypt, an exclusive boys' academy where King Hussein was a classmate and where the students were caned if they did not speak English. Later he went to California State University in Chico, and was overwhelmed by the freedom of the life-style of American girls. There he began to entertain as a way of establishing himself, and to broker his first few deals. Early on he won favor with many of the Saudi royal princes, particularly Prince Sultan, the eighteenth son, and Prince Talal, the twenty-third son, who became his champions. In the 1970s, when the price of Arab oil soared to new heights, he began operating in high gear. Although Northrup was his best-known client, he also represented Lockheed,

Teledyne National, Chrysler, and Raytheon in the Middle East. By the mid-1970s, his commissions from Lockheed alone totaled more than $100 million. In addition, his firm, Triad, had holdings that included thirteen banks and a chain of steak houses on the West Coast of the United States, cattle ranches in North and South America, resort developments in Fiji and Egypt, a chain of hotels in Australia, and various real-estate, insurance, and shipping concerns. The first Arab to develop land in the United States, he organized and invested many millions in Triad America Corporation in Salt Lake City. He became an intimate of kings and heads of state, a great gift giver, a provider of women, a perfect host, and the creator of a life-style that would become world-renowned for its extravagance. Even now, in the overlapping murkiness of deposed dictators, the baby Doc Duvaliers, those other Third World escapees with their nation's pillage, are living in the South of France in a house found for them by Adnan Khashoggi, belonging to his son.

Perhaps not surprisingly, having presented myself as a journalist from the United States, I was not allowed to visit Khashoggi in the prison at 22 Genfergasse in Bern. It is a modern jail, six stories high, located in the center of the city. The windows are vertically barred, and the prisoners take their exercise on the roof. At night the exterior walls are floodlit. For a city prison there is an amazing silence about the place. No prisoners were screaming out the windows at passersby. There were no guards in sight on the elevated catwalk. Much has been made of the fact that Khashoggi got his meals from the dining room of the nearby Schweizerhof Hotel, but that and a rented television set and access to a fax machine were in fact his only privileges. In the beginning, waiters in uniform from the hotel would carry the trays over, but they were photographed too much and asked too many questions by reporters. The waiters and the maître d' that I spoke with in the restaurant of the Schweizerhof were reluctant to talk about the meals being sent to the jail, as if they were under orders not to speak. The evening I waited to see Khashoggi's meal arrive, a young girl brought it on a tray. She was not in uniform. She got to the jail at precisely six, and the gourmet meal was wrapped in silver foil to keep it hot.

wide coverage, which caused great embarrassment to all members of the family, as well as an increased disenchantment with Khashoggi on the part of the Saudi royal family. Ultimately, Soraya received a measly $2 million divorce settlement, but, more important, she was also reinstated in the family. Right up to the bust and confinement in Bern, she attended all the major Khashoggi parties and even posed with Adnan and Lamia and their combined children for a 1988 Christmas family photograph.

Khashoggi's private life has always been a public mess. "I haven't spoken to my ex-uncle since 1983, after the Cap d'Ail scandal, when one of his aides went to jail for prostitution and drugs," said Dodi Fayed, executive producer of the film *Chariots of Fire* and the son of the controversial international businessman Mohammed Al Fayed, the owner of the Ritz Hotel in Paris and Harrods department store in London, over which there was one of the bitterest takeover battles of the decade. Dodi Fayed's mother, Samira, who died two years ago, was Adnan Khashoggi's sister. Khashoggi and Mohammed Al Fayed were once business partners. Since the business partnership and the marriage of Samira and Fayed both broke up bitterly, the relationship between the two families has been poisonous. Dodi Fayed's use of the term "ex-uncle" indicates that he no longer even considers Khashoggi a relation.

The Cap d'Ail affair had to do with a French woman named Mireille Griffon, who became known on the Côte d'Azur as Madame Mimi, a serious though brief rival to the famous Madame Claude, the Parisian madam who serviced the upper classes and business elite of Europe for three decades with some of the most beautiful women in the world, many of whom have gone on to marry into the upper strata. Partnered with Madame Mimi was Khashoggi's employee Abdo Khawagi, a onetime masseur. Madame Mimi's operation boasted a roster of three hundred girls between the ages of eighteen and twenty-five. A perfectionist in her trade, Madam Mimi groomed and dressed her girls so that they would be presentable escorts for the important men they were servicing. The girls, who were sent to Khashoggi in groups of twos and threes, called him *papa gâteau*, or sugar daddy, because he was extremely generous with them. In addition to their fee, 40 percent of which went to Madame Mimi, the girls received furs and jewels and tips that sometimes equaled or surpassed the fee. One of the greatest whoremongers in the world, Khashoggi was generous to a fault and provided the same girls to members of the Saudi royal family as well as to business associates and party friends. His role as a provider of women for business purposes was not unlike the role his uncle Yussuf Yassin had performed for King Ibn Saud. After the French police on the Riviera were alerted, a watch was put on the operations and the madam's telephone lines were tapped. In time an arrest was made, and the case went to trial in Nice in February 1984, amid nasty publicity. Madame Mimi, who is believed to have personally grossed $1.2 million in ten months, got a year and a half in jail. Khawagi, the procurer, got a year in prison. And Khashoggi sailed away on the *Nabila*.

Of more recent vintage is the story of the beautiful Indian prostitute Pamella Bordes, who was discovered working as a researcher in the House of Commons after having bedded some of the most distinguished men in England. In a three-part interview in the London *Daily Mail*, she made her sexual revelations about Khashoggi shortly after he was imprisoned in Bern, a bit of bad timing for the beleaguered arms dealer. Pamella was introduced into the great world by Shri Chandra Swamiji Maharaj, a Hindu teacher with worldly aspirations known simply as the Swami or Swamiji, although sometimes he is addressed by his worshipers with the papal-sounding title of Your Holiness. The Swami, who is said to possess miraculous powers, has served as a spiritual and financial adviser to, among others, Ferdinand Marcos, who credited him with once saving his life, Adnan Khashoggi, Mohammed Al Fayed, and both the Sultan of Brunei and the second of his two wives, Princess Mariam, a half-Japanese former airline stewardess. (Princess Mariam is less popular with the royal family of Brunei than the sultan's first wife, Queen Saleha, his cousin, who bore him six children, but Princess Mariam is clearly the sultan's favorite.) The Swami played a key role in the Mohammed Al Fayed–Tiny Rowland battle for the ownership of Harrods in London when he secretly taped a conversation with Fayed which vaguely indicated that the money Fayed had used to purchase Harrods was really the Sultan of Brunei's. The Swami sold the tape to Rowland for $2

man and Rosita Winston, the international socialites, who for years had leased the Clos, a house on the grounds of La Fiorentina. "She was out of the country before any mention of Donald's death was ever made," said Bert Whitley of New York, who leased another house on the grounds. The servant, who had been through previous scrapes with his employer, was left money in Bloomingdale's will, as were Rory Cameron and Jean-Louis Toriel, the Egyptian, who later also died of a heroin overdose. The newspapers reported that Bloomingdale's death had been caused by an overdose of barbiturates. No connection between the countess and the death of Donald Bloomingdale was ever made publicly. "But everybody knew," I was told over and over. "Everybody knew."

Probably nobody knew better what happened that night than Walter Beardshall, who was Lady Kenmare's butler and valet at the time and who remains her fervent supporter to this day. Now crippled by post-polio syndrome, Mr. Beardshall lives in Brooklyn, New York, where he is mostly confined to a motorized wheelchair. "I traveled around the world with Her Ladyship," he told me. "Elsa Maxwell spread the rumor that I was her gigolo, and everyone gossiped about us, but I wasn't. I was twenty-four at the time, and Lady Kenmare was sixty-two." According to Beardshall, the incident happened at the Sherry-Netherland. "Mr. Bloomingdale had a permanent suite at the Sherry-Netherland, and we were his guests there. He filled Lady Kenmare's room with flowers and everything. The next morning the telephone rang very early, and Her Ladyship asked me to come to her room as quickly as possible. 'How fast can you pack?' she asked. 'We're leaving for London.' We had only just arrived in New York. She said, 'I had dinner last night with Mr. Bloomingdale. He told me I could borrow his typewriter so that I could write Rory a letter. When I called him this morning, his servant told me that he was dead. I was the last person to see him alive. We have to leave. You know how the American police are.' "

After the Bloomingdale incident, Somerset Maugham dubbed his great friend Lady Kenmare Lady Killmore, although some people attribute the name to Noel Coward. At any rate the name stuck.

"Did Enid ever talk about Donald Bloomingdale?" I asked Anthony Pawson.

"It was always a tricky subject," he said. "She didn't talk too much about it, because of all the rumors going round."

"Did Rory talk about it?" I asked a lady friend of his in London.

"Those stories about Enid were never discussed. I mean, you can't ask if someone's mother murdered someone. Rory told me, though, that once, when she arrived on the *Queen Mary*, the tabloids said, 'Society Murderess Arrives,' " she replied.

"When Donald died in New York that time, we all expected to know more about it, but nothing came out," said Elvira de la Fuente. "She ran from New York after that."

Daisy Fellowes, another of the stunning women of the period and a famed society wit, maintained a sort of chilly friendship with Enid. The daughter of a French duke and an heiress to the Singer sewing-machine fortune, she didn't think Enid was sufficiently wellborn, describing her as "an Australian with a vague pedigree." Once, in conversation, Enid began a sentence with the phrase "people of our class." Mrs. Fellowes raised her hand and stopped the conversation. "Just a moment, Enid," she said. "Your class or mine?" After the Bloomingdale affair, Daisy Fellowes announced she was going to give a dinner party for twelve people. "I'm going to have all murderers," she said. "Very convenient. There are six men and six women. And Enid Kenmare will have the place of honor, because she killed the most people of anyone coming."

Lady Kenmare was aware of the stories told about her, and she was sometimes hurt by them. Roderick Coupe, an American who lives in Paris, told me of an occasion when the social figure Jimmy Donahue, a Woolworth heir, cousin of Enid's friend Barbara Hutton, and often rumored to have been the lover of the Duchess of Windsor, asked Enid to his house on Long Island. After a pleasant dinner, he began to ask her why she was known as Lady Killmore. She explained to him that it was a name that caused her a great deal of heartache. Donahue, who had a cruel streak, persisted. "But why do people say it?" he asked several more times. Enid Kenmare finally announced she was leaving. Donahue told her he had sent her car back to New York. Undeterred, she made her way to the highway and hitchhiked to the city.

"She was one of the most accomplished women. She rode. She shot. She fished. She painted very well. She sculpted. She did beautiful needlework. She cooked marvelously. There was nothing she couldn't do," said Tony Pawson. Looking through album after album of photographs of life at La Fiorentina, with its unending parties, one doesn't see an angry or worried face among the people pictured. Any age, any generation, eighteen to eighty, in and out of the house, and dogs everywhere. Although Lady Kenmare was thought of as a famous hostess, a word she greatly disliked, her lunch parties at La Fiorentina were often haphazard affairs, with unmatched guests. Celebrities such as Greta Garbo, Barbara Hutton, Claudette Colbert, Elsa Maxwell, and the Duke of Vedura came, but so did people no one had ever heard of. Guests would be thrown together—friends of Rory's, friends of hers, the well known and the unknown, the young and the old, the inexperienced and the accomplished—with no care as to a balance of the sexes at her table. Enid was diligently unpunctual, arriving, vaguely, long after her guests had been seated, once prompting Daisy Fellowes to remark on her hostess's absence, "Busy with her needle, no doubt." Another guest remembered, "She had no sense of time whatsoever. She'd arrive when the meals were over, or be dressed for the casino, in evening dress and jewels, in the afternoon." Tom Parr said, "She was an ethereal character, nice to us who were Rory's friends, adorable even, but then she'd float off." On one occasion, she was struck by the handsomeness of a young man sunning himself by her swimming pool. "Do please stay on for dinner," she said. "But, Lady Kenmare, I've been staying with you for a week," the young man replied.

"Enid was completely original. Very elegant. Very distinguished. She always made an entrance, like an actress, carrying a flower," said Jacqueline Delubac, a retired French actress who was once married to Sacha Guitry. She was always surrounded by dogs, "a mangy pack," according to John Galliher of New York. Walter Beardshall remembers her entrances more vividly. "All her guests would already be seated. First you would hear the dogs barking. And then you would hear her voice saying, 'Be quiet. Be quiet.' Then you would hear her high heels clicking on the marble floor. And then the dogs would enter, sometimes twenty of them, miniature poodles, gray and black. And then she would come in, with a parrot on one shoulder and her hyrax on the other." She fed her hyrax from her own fork; although at the cinema she would sometimes pull lettuce leaves from her bosom to feed it. Many people mistook the hyrax for a rat. It is a small ungulate mammal characterized by a thickset body with short legs and ears and rudimentary tail, feet with soft pads and broad nails, and teeth of which the molars resemble those of a rhinoceros and the incisors those of rodents. She taught the hyrax to pee in the toilet, standing straight up on the seat, and sometimes she let her guests peek at it through the bathroom window, keeping out of sight, since the hyrax was very shy. She trained her parrot to speak exactly like her. When the telephone rang, the parrot would call out, "Pat, the telephone," so that Enid's daughter, Pat, would answer it.

The fashion arbiter Eleanor Lambert often stayed with Rosita and Norman Winston in the Clos on Enid's property. She said that Lady Kenmare never seemed to sleep. She remembered looking out of her window during the night and seeing her walking through her garden dressed in flowing white garments, with the hyrax on her shoulder. "She looked like the woman in white from Wilkie Collins's book," Eleanor Lambert said.

"Enid was never social, really," said Elvira de la Fuente. "You could ask her to sit next to a prince or a waiter, and it never mattered to her." Indeed, the girl from Australia never went grand in the grand life she espoused and kept marrying into. She remained fiercely loyal to her Australian family back home, at one time investing money in the failing wine business even though her lawyers advised her not to. "They are my family," she said to them, according to Beardshall, who traveled to Australia with her. Along the way in her rise, she lost her Australian accent. Tony Pawson said she had "an accent you couldn't quite define, Americanized but not really American." James Douglas, who used to escort Barbara Hutton to La Fiorentina, said, "There was no trace of Australian at all, but sometimes her sister came from Australia to visit her, and then you could hear the way she once had talked." However, she did acquire irregularities of speech that were unique for a woman in her position at that time. According to Walter Beardshall, she used certain four-letter words before people started printing those words in books. He remembered a time when the Countess of Drogheda asked her, "What was Kenmare's first name, Enid?" Enid replied, "Fucked if I know. I was only married to him nine months before he died."

Some people say that Enid thought she would marry Somerset Maugham after Lord Kenmare's death, but more people scoff at this. "Nonsense!" said David Herbert. Tony Pawson agreed. "I don't believe she ever wanted to marry Willie Maugham. Unless it was for the money. Willie wasn't interested in ladies, you know." Jimmy Douglas said, "It's too ridiculous. What about Alan Searle [Maugham's longtime companion], for God's sake?" And Elvira de la Fuente said, "Enid has no friends, really, except Willie Maugham. She adored him. She and Maugham were a funny couple. They were intimate because of bridge. They played all the time. He was already old and grumpy at the time. It was companionship and affection, but there was no thought of romance."

At one time, friends say, Enid, who kept a residence in Monte Carlo and was a citizen of Monaco, harbored a desire for her daughter to marry Prince Rainier and become Her Serene Highness, the Princess of Monaco, but the prince showed no romantic inclinations toward Pat, nor did Pat toward the prince. Pat preferred dogs and horses, and was not cut out for princess life, or even society life on the Riviera, and soon decamped to Kenya and Cape Town to breed horses. Bearing no grudge toward the prince, Enid happily attended his wedding to Grace Kelly. As the tall, statuesque Lady Kenmare emerged from the cathedral at the end of the service, she was cheered by the crowds, who mistook her for a visiting monarch.

"Before anything else, Enid was a mother," said Yves Vidal of Paris and Tangier, who was a frequent visitor at the villa. "Most of the things she did, marrying all those men, were for the children more than herself." "She never *never* did what family people do—criticize and mumble about her children," said Elvira de la Fuente. Walter Beardshall said she tried to keep her drug taking from her children. "Once, Pat found one of her syringes. 'What's this, Mummy?' she asked. 'Oh, it's Walter's,' Lady Kenmare replied. 'He leaves his stuff all over the place. Get it out of here, Walter. Take it to your own room.' "

But it was with Rory, her older son, that she was the closest. "I always thought Rory was in love with Enid," said a London lady. "At Emerald Cunard's parties, they used to come in together, covered in rings and not speaking." Certainly they had an extremely close mother-son relationship. "It was really Rory's life that Enid came to lead, after all the marriages," said Elvira de la Fuente. "He used to say to her as a joke, 'Now you'll never find a fifth husband after you've killed four of them.' They lived as a couple, but it wasn't incestuous. Rory told Enid he was a homosexual when he was forty. She had never suspected. It was a terrible shock to her, but a shock she overcame in a day or two." Yves Vidal said, "She didn't really like social life. She was actually miscast in the grand life of a chatelaine and hostess of the Riviera." Another guest said, "She was in a way a passenger at La Fiorentina. As she got older, people began to think of it as Rory's house. This famous lady was always in the background. Sometimes she'd go for days without coming out of her bedroom."

The magnificent house, located on the finest property on the Riviera, commands the entrance to Beaulieu Bay. It was considered a strategic position during the war, and the Germans, who occupied the house, built extensive fortifications on their property against an Allied invasion. Near the end of the war they blew up the fortifications, destroying half of the house and most of the gardens. When the house was returned to the family, Rory redesigned it in the Palladian style, and the interiors were decorated by him. As Enid Kenmare grew older, she developed curvature of the spine, and her once-perfect posture gave way to a bent-over condition. She began leasing the house. Elizabeth Taylor and Mike Todd occupied it for a time, and for years the American philanthropist Mary Lasker rented it during the peak months. The house is now owned by Harding and Mary Wells Lawrence, the former chairman of Braniff Airways and the founder of the advertising agency Wells, Rich, Greene. Mary Lawrence said, "When we bought La Fiorentina, there were no lights in the bathrooms. Lady Kenmare couldn't bear to look at herself in the mirror anymore.

She moved to Cape Town, South Africa, where she bought a stud farm and raised racehorses. Her daughter, Pat, had preceded her there. For a while Enid employed Beryl Markham, the author of *West with the Night*, to train her horses, but the two women, who had known each other since Enid's marriage to Lord Furness, were such strong personalities that their partnership did not work out. Pat had two lions she had brought up from the time they were cubs that had the run of the house. A New York friend of Pat's who used to visit La Fiorentina every summer also visited the two women in Cape Town. She remembers seeing one of the lions drag an unperturbed Enid through the living room and out the French doors. "She was not remotely frightened, and later Pat told me, 'It happens all the time.' "

"Enid was mysterious," said Yves Vidal. "I remember once watching her run down the steps of La Fiorentina followed by her dogs. She was so beautiful, and she knew she was very beautiful. Until the end, she kept a wonderful allure. What made her life and ruined her life at the same time was her beauty.

March 1991

THE PASSION
OF
BARON THYSSEN

IT WAS a late-fall twilight on Lake Lugano. We were standing in the open window of an art-filled sitting room in the Villa Favorita, one of the loveliest houses in the world, looking out over the lake, listening to waves lap against the private dock below. Across the water the lights of Lugano, a city of 30,000 people and fifty banks in the Italian-speaking corner of Switzerland, were coming on. My companion in reverie, the Baron Hans Heinrich Thyssen-Bornemisza, has been looking out at the same view for over fifty years, since his father, Baron Heinrich Thyssen-Bornemisza, bought the seventeenth-century villa from Prince Friedrich Leopold of Prussia in 1932. For those who need an introduction, Baron Hans Heinrich Thyssen-Bornemisza is generally conceded to be one of the richest men in the world ("in the billions," say some people, "in the high hundred millions," according to others), as well as the possessor of one of the world's largest private art collections, which is rivaled in size and magnificence only by that of the Queen of England. It was the art collection I was there to discuss, for the baron, now in his sixty-seventh year, has begun to have thoughts about mortality, and for the last five years the disposition of his collection has been uppermost in his mind.

He is called Heini by those close to him, and that evening he was dressed in a dinner jacket and black tie, awaiting the arrival of guests for dinner. The Thyssen fortune, he was telling me, had been made originally in iron and steel in Germany. "My mother irons and my father steals," he said, in the manner of a man who has told the same joke over and over. Early in life, his father had left Germany and moved to Hungary, where he had married into the nobility; thus the title baron and the addition of the hyphen and the name Bornemisza. The current baron's older brother and two sisters were born in Hungary, but the Thyssen-Bornemisza family fled to Holland when the Communist leader of Hungary,

Béla Kun, sentenced the children's father to death for being a landowner. Heini Thyssen was born in Holland and spent the first nineteen years of his life there.

The baron's attention was distracted from his story by the arrival at the dock below of a flag-bedecked lake boat bringing his guests, thirty-one formally attired members of the Board of Trustees and the Trustees' Council of the National Gallery of Art in Washington, D.C., who were on a two-week tour of Swiss and Italian churches, museums, and private collections, headed by the gallery's director, J. Carter Brown. Among the members of this art-loving group were the Perry Basses of Forth Worth, the Alexander Mellon Laughlins and the Thomas Mellon Evanses of New York, and the Robert Erburus of Los Angeles.

"But it's too early," said the baron, looking down. "They've come too early. The baroness is not ready to receive them." And then he added, to no one in particular, "Send them away." He had his gun-toting American bodyguard tell the driver of the boat to spin the distinguished guests around the lake for half an hour and then come back. As we watched the drama from upstairs, we could hear Carter Brown call out, "Ladies and gentlemen," and then explain to his group that they were not to get off the boat yet but would instead take another short ride. This announcement apparently created some discord, because people began to get off anyway. The baron shrugged, sighed, smiled, and went down to greet them. Drinks were served on an outdoor loggia overlooking the lake. A night chill had set in, and the ladies hugged fur jackets and cashmere shawls over their short black dinner dresses and pearls. For some time the Baroness Thyssen-Bornemisza did not appear.

Tita Thyssen, a former Miss Barcelona and later Miss Spain, picked by a jury that included the American-born Countess of Romanoes and the great bullfighter Luis Domínguin, is the baron's fifth and presumably last baroness and, if all goes according to plan, his first and last duchess, for the *on-dit* in swell circles is that the King of Spain is prepared to confer on her the title of duchess when the Thyssen collection, or at least 700 of the A and B pictures in the 1,400-picture collection, goes to Spain permanently. That "permanently" is the catch.

"Where is she?" one wife asked, meaning their hostess.

"We heard she's not coming at all," said the lady to whom she spoke.

"I heard that too," said the first lady, and they exchanged "Miss Barcelona" looks.

But then the baroness did appear, the last arrival at her own party, although she was only coming from upstairs. She was stunning, blond, tanned from the sun, dressed in a long black strapless evening gown. "Balmain," I heard her say to someone. She has the persona of a film star and understands perfectly the technique of making an entrance. In an instant she was the center of attention, and earlier opinions of her were soon favorably revised. Like all the baron's wives, his fifth baroness is the possessor of some very serious jewelry. On her engagement-ring finger was a large marquise diamond that had once belonged to the baron's second wife, the ill-fated Nina Dyer, who married the baron at the age of seventeen and divorced him at the age of twenty-five to marry Prince Sadruddin Aga Khan, the half-brother of the late Aly Khan and the uncle of the current Aga Khan. Indifferent to gender when it came to love partners, Nina also dallied with a succession of ladies, who called her Oliver and vied with her husbands when it came to showering her with jewels. One of her most ardent admirers, an international film actress, gave her a panther bracelet designed by Cartier with an inscription in French which read, "To my panther, untamed by man." Before she was forty, Nina committed suicide. "She'd just had it," was the explanation someone who knew her gave me. Her jewelry, according to the baron, was stolen by her friends at the time of her death. Years later, he saw a picture of the marquise-diamond ring in an auction catalogue. Although it had no listed provenance, he recognized it as the diamond he had given Nina years before, and bought it back for his fifth wife for $1.5 million.

The baroness was wearing diamond-and-ruby earrings, and around her neck, hanging on a diamond necklace designed to accommodate it, was the Star of Peace, which she had told me earlier in the day was the "biggest flawless diamond in the world." I explained to one of the guests who gasped at its size that it was 167 carats. The baroness heard me say it. "One hundred and sixty-*nine*," she corrected me, and then, hearing herself, she roared with laughter.

Tita Thyssen speaks in a husky, international voice, often changing languages from sentence to sentence. She is fun, funny, and flirtatious, with a nature that is best described as vivacious. She is refreshingly outspoken, and makes no bones, for example, about her dislike of her immediate predecessor, the former Denise Shorto of Brazil, whose divorce from the baron was extremely acrimonious, resulting in a settlement rumored to be in the neighborhood of $50 million, in addition to jewels worth $80 million. At one point in the proceedings Denise Thyssen was briefly jailed in Liechtenstein for leaving Switzerland with unpaid bills in excess of $1.5 million, and the baron accused her of failing to return certain jewelry and other items belonging to his family. Ultimately, Denise was allowed to keep all the jewels, on the ground that they were gifts made to her during her marriage, not Thyssen heirlooms. "A gift is a gift," she was quoted as saying. We are talking here about very, very, very rich people. Now in her late forties, Denise Thyssen lives in Rome with Prince Mariano Hugo zu Windisch-Graetz, who is in his mid-thirties, and their liaison is not smiled upon by the prince's family. She refused to be interviewed for this article with the pointed comment that "Heini's present wife is very publicity-minded. This article belongs to her. I don't see my place in it."

"I believe in destiny," Tita Thyssen said, discussing the Star of Peace. "This stone proves to me that destiny is always there. I first saw it in the rough, before it was cut, in the Geneva office of Harry Winston, before I met Heini. They left me alone with it and let me play with it. They told me they were thinking of doing an adventure with somebody and cutting it. The person involved turned out to be Heini, but I did not know him yet. I talked with the store from time to time, and three times it was almost sold. Then Heini gave it to me."

Among the guests that evening was her friend and jeweler, Fred Horowitz, who used to be with Harry Winston and is now an independent jeweler with offices in Geneva and Monte Carlo. It was through Horowitz that the baroness met Heini Thyssen. She was staying with him and his then wife, Donatella, who is now married to the Mercedes-Benz heir Mick Flick, on their boat in Sardinia. "It was time for me to go back to my house on the Costa Brava, but my friends begged me to stay one more day, and I did," said the baroness. The next day Horowitz took her to a party on Heini Thyssen's yacht. "The look he gave me when we met, now that I know him better, is the look he gets when he sees a painting that he knows he is going to buy. He knew he was going to get it." Then she added, "Only I'm more expensive than a painting, and you don't have to change the frame with me." Her husband listened to her story, amused.

According to one guest on the Thyssen yacht that day, Tita and Heini remained aloof from the party and played backgammon for hours. Also on board was Thyssen's fourth wife, Denise, though their marriage was already in its last stages. Seeing her husband and Tita together for so long, she made a slighting remark of the "upstart" variety about Tita, and with that the two women's mutual dislike began.

"We have never been apart more than a day since we met," Tita said, taking her husband's hand. "We have been married three and a half years now, but we have been together seven. We discuss everything."

Spotting Fred Horowitz, she turned her attention from the National Gallery group to him. "It doesn't hang right," she said about the enormous stone she was wearing. Horowitz had made her the two-row necklace of matched diamonds from which the Star of Peace hung as a pendant. The diamond was too heavy for the necklace and tipped upward. For several minutes she and Horowitz and his new wife, Jasmine, also jewel-laden, discussed in French what was wrong with the diamond necklace. Then realizing that she was neglecting her guests, she turned back to them and said, in a playful, self-deprecating manner, "These are very nice problems to have."

At dinner we sat at five place-carded tables of eight, and she held her table in thrall, all the while chain-smoking cigarettes. The fifth baroness is steeped in the lore of her husband's family and, like him, is an expert storyteller. She told one story about Heini's stepmother, the beautiful Baroness Maud von Thyssen, who during her marriage to Baron Heinrich Thyssen, fell madly in love with twenty-six-year-old Prince Alexis Mdivani, "one of the marrying Mdivani brothers," as they were called. Alexis had just negotiated a lucrative divorce from the American heiress Barbara Hutton. The lovers rendezvoused in a remote village in Spain. After the tryst, Maud had to return to Paris, and the prince drove her to her train at breakneck speed in the Rolls-Royce that Hutton had given him. "There was a terrible crash," the baroness said. "Mdivani was killed. Maud's beautiful face was half-destroyed. Heini's father divorced her." At that point a waiter accidentally dropped a dozen dinner plates on the stone floor, with a crash that brought the room to silence. The baroness looked over, shrugged, and returned to her conversation with the same aplomb that her husband demonstrated at his table across the room. Why let a few broken plates ruin a good party?

A stranger to art before her marriage, the baroness has become deeply involved in her husband's collection, and if she is not as conversant as he on the subject of old masters, she has made herself more conversant than you or I—knowledgeable enough to be the main force behind her husband's selection of Spain, over England, West Germany, the United States, Japan, and France, as the resting place for his treasure. Many people consider the choice odd, since the baron himself has no real connection with Spain and no long-standing friendships there. It is the baroness's dream, however, according to one Spanish Tita watcher, to live in Spain and to be accepted by people who once neglected and even snubbed her.

There are pictures everywhere in the villa. Up a secondary stairway, outside the men's lavatory, hangs an Edvard Munch, and in every corridor is a profusion of pictures, around any one of which the average millionaire might build an entire room. The bar in the family sitting room is a seven-part coromandel screen, broken up to conceal a refrigerator, an icemaker, glasses, and liquor bottles. Walking through a drawing room that the baron and baroness almost never go into, we passed a Bonnard portrait of Misia Sert, and in a formal dining room so infrequently entered that the light switch didn't work—a room too large for intimate groups but not large enough for big groups from museums—hung a pair of Canalettos.

"Would you like to see our bedroom?" the baroness asked her guests.

Is the pope Catholic? Of course we wanted to see the bedroom, which contains three Pissarros, a Renoir, a Toulouse-Lautrec, a Winslow Homer, a Manet, and more that I don't remember. The pictures in the villa are quite different from the pictures that hang in the galleries of the museum next door—the Titians, the Tintorettos, the Carpaccio, the Goyas, and the El Grecos, which the baron would show the group the next day.

"Do you move these pictures with you to your other houses?" someone asked her.

"No, we have others."

Their bedroom, in contrast to most of the Mongiardino-decorated rooms, is soft and feminine, done in pale colors. It opens into Heini's enormous bathroom, which has a tub the size of a small pool, and into Tita's sitting room, which has an early Gauguin over the daybed and a Corot. Although it was October, the perpetual calendar on a side table still indicated June. The Thyssen-Bornemisza family crest is embossed on the message pad next to every telephone in the villa; the motto reads, *"Vertu surpasse richesse"*— Virtue surpasses riches.

The baroness opened the doors of closet after closet full of clothes. "Most of my clothes are still in Marbella," she said. She is dressed mostly by the Paris couturiers Balmain and Scherrer. When her schedule makes it impossible for her to attend the couture showings in Paris, the designers send her videotapes of their collections and she chooses from them.

"What's it like to live this way?" she was asked.

"It took me some time to get used to all this beauty," said the baroness quite modestly. "At first I was in shock."

"How long did it take before you got used to this kind of life?" I asked her.

"About two days," she answered, and burst out laughing at her joke.

Her native language is Spanish, which the baron does not speak well. His native languages are Dutch, Hungarian, and German, which the baroness does not speak well. When they are alone together, they speak sometimes in French and sometimes in English, heavily accented English, his Teutonic-sounding, hers with a very

ing a strand of perfect pearls, the size of large grapes, later changed to her sapphires, both blue and yellow, the baron's latest gift to her, and then to her rubies, and with each set came a different dress from Balmain or Scherrer. "Change of colors, I see," said the baron as he leaned over to examine one necklace.

Suddenly, surprisingly, from out of nowhere, as coffee was being served, the baroness turned to me and said, "Have you ever heard of Franco Rappetti?"

"Yes, I replied. I had heard of Franco Rappetti, but having come to Lugano to discuss the transfer of a great art collection from Switzerland to Spain, I had hardly expected to get into the darkest shadow in the life of the baron, yet here it was, offered up with the demitasse by the baron's fifth wife. Anyone who has ever dipped into the Thyssen saga has heard of Franco Rappetti, a tall, blond, handsome Roman who was at one time the baron's European art dealer. He was also—and this is no secret, at least in the social and art worlds in which the Thyssens moved—the lover of Denise, the fourth baroness, during her marriage to the baron. A onetime playboy, compulsive gambler, and drug user, Rappetti has been described to me by a woman who knew him well as a man who shared women with many powerful men. On June 8, 1978, while on a visit to New York, Rappetti, thirty-eight, went out a window at the Meurice, a building on West Fifty-eighth Street favored by artistic Europeans who keep apartments in New York. His mysterious death has fascinated society and the art world ever since.

"Did you hear how he died?" she asked.

"I heard he either jumped or was thrown out the window," I answered.

"Thrown," said the baroness, and then named the person who she believed had had it done. Only days before, a friend of mine had attended a lunch party in London following a memorial service for the Marquess of Dufferin and Ava; there the conversation had also turned to Franco Rappetti, for some reason, and one of the guests had named a well-known figure in the New York art world as the one who threw him out the window. The person the baroness named as having had Rappetti thrown and the person named at the London lunch party as having actually thrown him were not the same.

"He was thrown out the window," the baroness repeated. The baron was sitting with us but read a letter during the exchange. "He was going to have his face changed so he could not be recognized. He wanted to get away from someone."

"His faced changed?"

"Surgery." She named the person Franco Rappetti had wanted to get away from. "He was going to move somewhere and start a new life." She said that Rappetti had been acting in a hyper manner before the defenestration, and had been injected with a tranquilizer to calm him down. It was in that state that he was thrown.

Residents of the building who knew Rappetti disagree violently with the theory that he was pushed or thrown. "He was not murdered," said one emphatically. "He jumped. It's as simple as that. He was depressed. He had money problems."

Franco Rossellini, the Italian film producer and nephew of the great director Roberto Rossellini, lives in apartment 10-J of the building. He said that police came rushing into his apartment before he knew what had happened and asked him if he knew who had jumped out the window and saw the body, clad only in undershorts and an elaborate gold chain with charms and medals, lying ten floors below on the roof of a Volkswagen bus. "My God, for a moment I thought it was my butler," he told me. The body had come from the apartment above his, 11-J, where Rappetti had just arrived as a guest. One article written about the case stated that he had arrived "with a small suitcase and some very pure cocaine."

When the police left, Rossellini contacted Diane Von Furstenberg, the dress designer and perfume manufacturer, who was an acquaintance of Denise Thyssen's and who had, coincidentally, spoken with her on the telephone only a short time before. Although Denise Thyssen and Rappetti were in the city at the same time, supposedly neither knew the other was there. Von Furstenberg called the baroness at the Waldorf, realized she had not yet heard about Rappetti's death, put her mother on the telephone in order to keep Denise's line busy, and raced to the Waldorf Towers to break the news before she heard it from the police or news media. "Denise was hysterical," remembered Rossellini. Von Furstenberg then called Heini Thyssen in Europe to tell him what had happened, and contacted Rappetti's sister, who absolutely refused to believe that her brother had jumped. Later, Von Furstenberg accompanied Denise to the city morgue. Since Denise could not bear to go in and see her dead lover, Von Furstenberg identified the body. Only then was she able to relinquish the grieving baroness into the care of closer friends—Princess Yasmin Aga Khan, the daughter of Rita Hayworth; Nona Gordon Summers, then the wife of a London art dealer; and Cleo Goldsmith, the niece of international financier James Goldsmith.

"Nobody pushed him out," Rossellini asserted. "That is a fact. He was running away all the time. He was paranoid. He thought someone was after him. He was not eating anything anymore. He was afraid someone was trying to poison him."

Just as authoritatively, a woman who knew Rappetti well insists that he was not a suicide. "Oh, no, I don't believe Franco jumped. He was so vain about his looks, he would never have gone out the window in undershorts."

"It would be almost impossible to throw a six-foot-three-inch, well-developed man out the window," said Mariarosa Sclauzero, the person most likely to know the exact circumstances of the death. Sclauzero, a writer, still lives in Apartment 11-J, along with her husband, Enrico Tucci. They were both close to Rappetti, and Mariarosa was in the apartment at the time of the death, though in a different room. According to Sclauzero and Tucci, Rappetti had arrived in New York two days before and had registered at the Summit Hotel, after stopping to see Tucci at his office, where he told him, "There is no way out. I have nobody in the world I can trust anymore, not even my butler." Alerted by Tucci that Rappetti was in a highly excitable state, Sclauzero went to the Summit and brought him back to the apartment. He was indeed carrying a suitcase, but, Sclauzero maintains, it contained no cocaine, just clothes and a picture of his small son.

Rappetti kept saying over and over, "They're after me. They want me dead. If anyone asks for me, say I am not here." In the next hour, he tried several times to telephone someone in Switzerland, but he could not get through. There were also several calls for him, supposedly from Paris, but Sclauzero sensed that they were local calls and said that he was not there. Rappetti had left his watch in Paris, and asked to borrow one of Tucci's watches and a

T-shirt. He used the bathroom and went into one of the two bed-rooms of the apartment to rest. Mariarosa remained in the living room, reading. When the police knocked on her door, after leaving Rossellini's apartment, and asked if she had a guest, she followed Rappetti's instructions and said no. Realizing, however, that some-thing was wrong, she went into the bedroom and found the window wide open. Franco Rappetti was not there. On a table by the win-dow were the watch he had borrowed and the T-shirt, folded. She admits it was a mistake to lie to the police. Later she was grilled for six hours.

"Franco Rappetti was pushed, but not physically," Sclauzero told me as we sat in Apartment 11-J of the Meurice. "Other people brought him to this despair. What he never said was who or why." She said that Rappetti was convinced that he was being poisoned by a servant in Rome, who was being paid by "other people," and that he was being pursued. She denied reports that he had money problems, arguing that he was worth about $5 million in art at the time of his death. She also said that after his death all the paintings in his apartment in Rome disappeared overnight.

The death was declared a suicide. Several well-heeled friends who were approached to lend their private planes to fly Rappetti's body back to Italy refused, on the ground that it would be unlucky to fly the body of a suicide. The day following the death, Heini Thyssen arrived at the Waldorf Towers. An oft-repeated story in these circles is that, on his arrival, Heini asked, "Does Denise blame me?" It is generally acknowledged that he arranged for the broken corpse to be shipped back to Genoa, Rappetti's birthplace, in a chartered plane. The body was accompanied by the grief-stricken Denise Thyssen and her sister Penny, who is married to Jamie Granger, the son of film star Stewart Granger. There are those who say the body was shipped before an autopsy could be performed. There are others who believe that Rappetti was already dead when he was thrown from the window. The man who made the arrangements to ship the body for Thyssen was another art dealer he did business with. His name was Andrew Crispo.

Many people who once moved in the orbit of this charismatic art dealer now seek to distance themselves as widely as possible from him. To the baron's great distress, his name has frequently been associated in recent times with that of Crispo, who figured promi-

fellow. These pictures of my father's I have known for fifty years, and I've been collecting for thirty-five years so I know them all." Walking through the graceful galleries that his father built to house the early part of the collection and that he opened to the public after his father's death in 1947, Thyssen was drawing more interest from the browsing tourists and art lovers than the paintings themselves. He moved with the assurance of a celebrity, knowing he was being looked at and talked about. When people came up to ask him to autograph their Thyssen-Bornemisza catalogues, he was completely charming. As he signed the books, he would say a few words or make a joke. He was dressed, as he almost always is, in a blue blazer with double vents, which his London tailor makes for him a dozen at a time, gray flannels, and a striped tie. In his hand he carried a large, old-fashioned key ring, unlocking certain rooms as we entered them and then locking them again as we left.

"I bought this yesterday," the baron said, looking at a Brueghel painting of animals. "I bought it from my sister. It's not in the catalog. It belonged to my father, and my sister inherited it." He moved on. "Now, this picture I bought from my other sister." Although the baron inherited the major part of the collection when his father died, he has spent years buying back the pictures that his two sisters inherited. It is for this reason that he is determined that his collection be kept intact when he dies. Thyssen also had an older brother, whose story remains somewhat vague. "He lived in Cuba," said the baron. "Then he moved to New York and lived at the Plaza Hotel. He lived completely on vitamins. He ODed on vitamins."

"ODed?"

"Hmm, dead," he said. He walked into another room.

"This is my favorite picture," he said, peering as if for the first time at a Ghirlandaio portrait of Giovanna Tornabuoni, a Florentine noblewoman, painted in 1488. "She died very young, in childbirth. We have never known if the picture was painted before or after her death. It was in the Morgan Library in New York. They had to buy some books, so they sold it." He continued to make comments as he passed from one painting to the next: "A Titian, very late. He was almost ninety when he painted that . . . Who was that man who gave the big ball in Venice after the war? Beistegui, wasn't it? That pair of Tintorettos comes from him . . . Everything in this room was bought by me and not by my father. I call it the Rothschild room. All the pictures in this room I bought from different members of the Rothschild family . . . My father bought this Hans Holbein of Henry VIII from the grandfather of Princess Di, the Earl of Spencer. The Earl bought a Bugatti with the money. When the picture was shown in England, Princess Margaret said to me, 'Harry is one up on you.' She was talking about his six wives, and my five. I said, 'He didn't have to go through all these tedious legal proceedings I do.' "

Of course, only a fraction of the baron's pictures were on view. Several of his Degas were in New York at the Metropolitan Museum of Art. Some of his old masters had been lent to the U.S.S.R. and were at that moment in Siberia. Still others were on loan to exhibitions around the world. He shook his head at the complexity of owning such a large collection.

The baron unlocked a door, and we entered a part of his private museum called the Reserve. It is here that pictures for which there is no room in the galleries hang on both sides of movable floor-to-ceiling racks twenty to twenty-five feet high. In one room a restorer with a broken arm, on loan from the J. Paul Getty Museum in California, was cleaning a fifteenth-century Italian portrait. "We have no room for this Edward Hopper," the baron said of a picture of a naked woman sitting on a bed, "and there's no place for that Monet." He rolled the racks back. There was also no place for a Georgia O'Keeffe and an Andrew Wyeth and what seemed like several hundred others.

"That's a fake Mondrian there," he said, approaching it and squinting at it. "I bought it by mistake. An expert told me he saw Mondrian paint it, and I believed him."

"Why do you keep it?"

"I prefer to keep a small fake to a big fake," he said, smiling.

Behind a door, almost out of sight, hung a picture of the baron himself. He made no comment about the portrait until I mentioned it. "That's me by Lucian Freud," he said. The picture, which I had seen at the Lucian Freud exhibition at the National Gallery in Washington, is chilling; it suggests that there is a dark side to this billionaire. "I was getting a divorce at the time," he said, as if explaining Freud's unflattering rendition. People who know the baron well say that it is an extraordinarily accurate portrait. "That is Heini totally," said an American woman who had apparently known the baron extremely well for a short time between marriages and asked not to be identified. "He went into unbelievable mood swings."

Helmut Newton asked the baron to pose next to the Lucian Freud portrait. He did. "Your chin up a bit," said Newton. The baron raised his chin. "Maybe that's how I will look someday, but it's not how I look now." As we were leaving the room, he said, "There's another Greco."

Once the Spanish government agreed to put up the necessary capital to house the paintings, and figured out what compensation should be made to the heirs of Baron Thyssen for renouncing their claim to his pictures, the deal was more or less in order. The baron has five children, starting with Georg-Heinrich from his first marriage. He has two children by his third wife, the former Fiona Campbell-Walter: Francesca, known as Chessy, who is an actress, and Lorne, an aspiring actor. After their divorce, Fiona, a beautiful English model, fell madly in love with Alexander Onassis, Aristotle's son by his first wife, Tina Livanos. Although Fiona was acknowledged to be a positive influence on Alexander, who was younger than she, Aristotle Onassis despised her. In 1973, Alexander Onassis was killed in a plane crash. Thyssen also has a child, Alexander, by his fourth wife, Denise, as well as his adopted son, Borja, brought by Tita to the fifth marriage.

"All the paintings legally belong to a Bermuda foundation, a trust, made by Baron Thyssen," the Duke de Badajoz explained to me in his office in Madrid. "After all the proposals from all the countries were together, the Bermuda foundation met and decided the ideal solution would be to make a temporary arrangement and, if it worked out, to make the final solution."

The Spanish government will provide a palace known as the Villahermosa to house the Thyssen-Bornemisza collection. When the old Duchess of Villahermosa died almost sixteen years ago, the time of block-long palaces for private living was at an end, and her daughters, two duchesses and a *marquesa*, sought to sell it. The enormous pink brick palace was first offered to the Spanish government for a relatively modest amount of money. For whatever reasons, the government turned down the offer, and a bank purchased the palace. In order to make the building work as a commercial institution, the inside was stripped, so all architectural details of the once elegant structure have been obliterated, including what many people told me was one of the most beautiful staircases in Madrid. Then the bank went bankrupt, and the palace was bought by the Ministry of Culture, for more than five times what the government would originally have had to pay.

The palace is huge. There are two floors below ground level which will be made over for restaurants, an auditorium for lectures, and parking space. There will be three complete floors of galleries, and the top floor will be used for offices. Several hundred of the A and B pictures from the Thyssen collection will hang in the Villahermosa Palace. A convent in Barcelona is being refitted to hang seventy-five of the religious paintings in the collection. The rest will continue to hang in the private galleries of the Villa Favorita in Lugano.

The estimated time for the reconstruction of the palace is between eighteen months and two years. The ten-year loan period for the collection will not begin until the pictures are actually hung in the Villahermosa. In bottom-line terms, the loan of the pictures is in reality a rental for a ten-year period. "There is an annual fee of $5 million paid as a rent to the Bermuda foundation," said the Duke de Badajoz. Spain also has to provide insurance and security.

Critics of what has come to be known as the baron's Spanish decision say that he coyly received proposals from a host of suitors, playing one off against the other, when all the time he knew he was going to defer to his wife's wishes and send the collection to Spain, at least for a decade. Prince Charles flew to Lugano to lunch at the Villa Favorita in an effort to get the collection for England, and Helmut Kohl, the chancellor of West Germany, made a similar foray, offering a Baroque palace or a brand-new museum to house the collection. It is not out of the question that one or the other of these countries will be so favored when the baron's permanent decision is made. A London newspaper stated at the time of his last divorce that he had a tendency to ask for his gifts back, although the journalist was referring to jewels and not paintings. An interesting observation made to me by a prominent woman in Madrid was that, whatever decision is made, the Spanish pictures in the collection—the Velázquezes, the Goyas, the El Grecos—will never be allowed to leave the country. All the reports over the last year about the agreement have included the added attraction of Tita Thyssen getting the title of duchess. "It has never been part of the negotiation," said the Duke de Badajoz. "It is the king's privilege to grant such a thing." In fact, Baron Thyssen will be offered a dukedom, which would elevate the baroness to duchess. "Of course, you cannot make a duke for ten years," said the Duke de Badajoz, which means, in practical terms, that the baron and baroness would not be elevated to duke and duchess if at the end of the ten-year loan period they decided to remove the pictures to England, or France, or West Germany, or Japan, or the United States. In the meantime, the Spanish government has already decorated Baron Thyssen with the Grand Cross of Carlos III, one of Spain's highest honors, for outstanding service to the Spanish government, and has decorated the baroness with an Isabel la Católica medal, for outstanding civil merit.

For the present, Baron and Baroness Thyssen will be spending more and more time in Madrid to be near the Villahermosa during the reconstruction period and to take part in deciding how the collection will be hung. Their new house on the outskirts of Madrid, in an area that is reminiscent of the Bel-Air section of Los Angeles, is the kind of house that Californians talk about in terms of square feet. It is immense, with an indoor swimming pool next to the gymnasium, and an outdoor pool which may be one of the largest private swimming pools in the world. The décor is pure movie star: beige marble, beige terrazzo, beige travertine, indoor waterfalls, plate glass in all directions, and a security system that defies unwanted entry. "I want to get rid of all this," said the baroness after her first night there, waving her hands with a sweeping gesture at the custom-made beige leather sofa and chairs. "And all that in there," she continued, waving at the furniture in another of the many rooms, shaking her head at its lack of beauty. They bought the almost new house furnished. She said that she would give all this "modern furniture" to a benefit for the poor that the aristocratic ladies of Madrid were putting on and that she would furnish the new house with the antique furniture from Daylesford, which has been in storage since that estate was sold.

The Thyssens were scheduled to leave the following morning in their private plane for Barcelona, where the baroness and the Spanish opera singer José Carreras were to receive awards from the city of Barcelona. "It will be nice to settle down and decorate this new house. We are having the gardens all done over too. We've also bought the lot next door so there will be privacy. And there's the new house in Paris that I have to do over. All this traveling. It gets so tiring."

As we walked through her new gardens, she said, "When I die, I am going to leave all my jewelry to a museum. I hate auctions, when it says that the jewelry belonged to the late Mrs. So-and-so."

January 1989

JANE'S
TURN

REMEMBER, I've been in this business fifty-four years. I made eighty-six pictures and 350 television shows. I have not been idle." As she spoke, she leaned forward and her forefinger tapped the table to emphasize her accomplishment. The speaker was Jane Wyman, a no-nonsense star in her mid-seventies, who is one of the highest-paid ladies in show business. Her immensely successful television series for Lorimar, "Falcon Crest," is in its ninth year, and it is she, everyone agrees, in the centerpiece role of Angela Channing, that the public tunes in to see. She got an Academy Award in 1948 for *Johnny Belinda*, in which she played a deaf-mute who gets raped. She was nominated for Oscars on four other occasions, and she has also been nominated twice for Emmys. She has behind her what can well be called a distinguished career.

We met in a perfectly nice but certainly not fashionable restaurant called Bob Burns, at Second Street and Wilshire Boulevard in Santa Monica, California, not far from where she lives. Bob Burns is her favorite restaurant, where she has her regular table, a tufted-leather booth. It is one of those fifties-style California restaurants that are so dark inside that when you step in from the blazing sunlight you are momentarily blinded and pause in the entrance, not sure which way to go. When she arrived, I was already at the table. My eyes had become accustomed to the dark, and I was able to watch her getting her bearings in the doorway. It was twelve noon on the dot, and we were the first two customers in the restaurant. Even to an empty house, though, she played it like a star. She is taller than I had expected. Her posture is superb. Her back is ramrod-straight. She is rail-thin, too thin, giving credence to the speculation that she is not in good health. She walks slowly and carefully. Some people say she is seventy-two, some say seventy-five, others say older. What's the difference? She looks great. Her hairdo, bangs over her forehead, is the trademark style she has worn for years. "Is that you?" she asked, peering.

"Yes." I rose and walked toward her.

She held out her hand, strong and positive. The darkness of the restaurant was flattering to a handsome woman of a certain age, but that is not her reason for liking the place. "The three people who own it went to school with my kids," she said. The words "my kids" were said in the easy manner any parent uses when talking about his or her children. She happens not to be close to either of hers, but we didn't talk about that.

She is private in the extreme, almost mysterious in her privacy, a rich recluse who chooses to live alone, without servants even, in an apartment in Santa Monica overlooking the Pacific Ocean. She is a woman in control at all times. There is not a moment off guard. What you see is the persona she wants you to see, and she reveals nothing further. Any aspect of her career is available for discussion, but don't tread beyond. And for God's sake, I was told, don't mention you-know-who or she'll get up and walk out. Simply put, it pains her that a marriage that ended forty-one years ago seems to interest the press and public more than her career.

"The reason I enjoy TV more than pictures now is that I like the pace better. You've got so many hours to do so much, and you have to get it done. I was on *The Yearling* for eleven and a half months! Sometimes we only did two pages of dialogue in four days," she said. She shook her head in wonderment at the difference in the two media. She was ready to order lunch. "Are the sand dabs breaded?" she asked the waitress. "Why don't we have a Caesar salad first?" she suggested.

For several years before "Falcon Crest" went on the air, she was in a state of semiretirement, spending most of her time painting. Although I have not seen any of her pictures, I have heard from her friends that she is an extremely talented landscape artist. In 1979 her work was exhibited in a gallery in Carmel, California, and so many of the pictures were sold that she now has none of her own work in her apartment. During those years, she said, she was always being sent film and television scripts, "like *Baby Jane*, or playing a lesbian, and I didn't want to do that. But when I was sent the pilot script for 'Falcon Crest,' I could see so many facets to the character of Angela Channing. I said, 'I'll give it two years.' It's now nine."

"People say that you control 'Falcon Crest'," I said.

"I am a creative consultant only. They run things by me, or I run things by them. I just want to keep up the quality of the show," she replied. "I usually have my chair at an odd place on the set where no one can bother me. And I do help the young actors on the show. I hold a riding crop out, saying 'Don't do that!'"

"Is it true that actors on the show are told not to speak to you?"

"I hope not," she answered.

An actor who had appeared in a part that ran for three episodes told me that he had been informed by his agent, who in turn had heard it from the assistant director, that he was not to approach Miss Wyman on the set, as she did not like to be disturbed. He was also told never to go to her dressing room. He was also told that President Reagan was not to be discussed on the set, ever. The surprise to this particular actor was that Miss Wyman "could not have been more delightful, or friendly. She came right up and introduced herself. One time I did knock on the door of her dressing room. I told her that I didn't think that the scene that we were to do together worked, and she asked me in, and we went over it and made some changes.

Susan Sullivan, who played her daughter-in-law on the series for eight years, said, "Jane is the most professional person I have ever worked with. I have seen her battle through illnesses and fatigue and still keep working. She says, 'Let's get this done. We have a job to do,' and everyone gets behind her. She is always willing to help younger actors. She gave instructions nicely and with humor. She once told to me, 'You can tell anybody anything if you do it with humor.' She ruled the set with a kind and intelligent hand."

Rod Taylor, who plays her current husband in the series, agreed. "Sure, she rules the set, but everybody expects that. I adore her."

David Selby, who plays her son and has developed the closest friendship of any of the cast members with her, said, "Never once has she asked to be excused from standing in while the other actors in the scene are having their close-ups. She would be upset if you did your close-up without her. She has never once been late. If we go out to dinner, we go to her favorite little spot. I've never been to her apartment."

Another cast member said, "I've spent years working with her, and I still don't know her. She does not let herself be known."

An insider on the show had told me that an attempt would be made on Angela Channing's life in the new season of the series. "Is it true that you are going to be smothered with a pillow in the third episode and that the audience won't know whether you're dead or alive?"

Her eyes became very large. She was surprised that I knew that. She thought for a moment how to answer. "I *am* going into a coma for a while," she said. She has a way of letting you know when she is finished with a topic, without actually telling you that she is.

"Do you have a social life?" I asked.

"Not really. When you're on a series, it, the series, becomes your life. I don't go out." She gets up at 4:30 each morning the series is in production. "I can't drive in the dark, so I'm picked up by a studio driver. I leave my apartment at exactly 5:50. It's a long drive to the studio. I do my own makeup when I get there.

"I'm a great reader. And I have some close friends. We do a lot of telephoning. My friends understand me when I say, 'Everything is on hold until the series is finished.' " Among her closest friends are the two great film and television stars Loretta Young and Barbara Stanwyck, both of whom have had careers and led lives similar to Jane Wyman's. "Jane is a good girl. She's also a very determined woman," Barbara Stanwyck told me. "She has worked very hard for her successful career. I do mean hard, and she deserves all her success because she earned it." She then added, "I know this is a story about Jane, so be very good and very kind. She would be to you."

In an interview with Jane Wyman from the forties, published in a movie magazine of the period and discovered in the Warner Brothers archives at the University of Southern California, the writer noted, "Talking to her, one gets the impression she's wound up like a tight spring." Approximately forty years later, the same line could still be written about her, except for when she is talking about her career. Then she relaxes. She is a virtual oral historian of the decades she spent at Warner Brothers. She was under contract to Warner's for years, beginning in 1936 at $166 a week. She had been at Fox and Paramount before that. Somewhere along the line, her name was changed from Sarah Jane Fulks to Jane Wyman. "I stayed at Warner's until I went into television," she said. She started out as a wisecracking comedienne and singer, with no interest whatever in dramatic roles. "Jane Wyman has no yen for drama," read one of her early press releases. "Leave that to other people," she was quoted as saying. Her studio biography described her as "pert, vivacious, with plenty of pep. Jane Wyman is a human tornado." Not all of her films were distinguished, but her memory is as astonishingly sharp for details of the making of middling and less-than-middling films as it is for those of such classics as Billy Wilder's *The Lost Weekend*. "We were in a three shot," she said, remembering one B-picture incident. "I was in the middle. Jack Carson was on one side, and Dennis Morgan on the other."

The star names flew from her lips. She calls James Cagney Cagney and Bob Hope Hope. "Cagney was my dream man," she said. "Hope wanted me to do this picture with him. You know Hope." Ann Sheridan. Humphrey Bogart. Joan Blondell. Bette Davis. "Bette Davis's dressing room was right next to mine, but we were never friends." Olivia de Havilland. Errol Flynn. "Jack Warner would never put me into any of their costume epics. He said I had the wrong looks. I think Jack was probably right."

She had an early marriage to Myron Futterman, a New Orleans dress manufacturer, about whom almost nothing is known. In 1940 she married Ronald Reagan, a fellow contract player at Warner Brothers, with whom she made four films. Their wedding reception was held at the home of the most famous of all Hollywood gossip columnists, Louella Parsons, who was raised in Dixon, Illinois, where Reagan grew up. Every movie magazine of the period recorded the idyll of the young stars' marriage, in the approved, studio-orchestrated publicity jargon. When Jane became pregnant, the studio announced that she was expecting a bundle from heaven. The bundle from heaven was Maureen Reagan, now forty-eight, who was born in 1941. Four years later the young couple adopted a son, Michael. They were promoted by Warner's as the dream Hollywood couple, and every fan magazine monitored their lives. "Ronnie and I are perfect counterparts for each other. I blow up, and Ronnie just laughs at me. We've never had a quarrel, because he's just too good-natured," said Jane in one interview. Several years after that, the lovebirds became known in the press as "Those Fightin' Reagans," and rumors of a rift in the marriage were rampant. Louella Parsons, who thrived on such matters, told Jane in a column, "I want to write a story and settle all this talk once and for all." Jane was quoted by Louella as replying, "Believe me, I'm going to find out who has started all this talk. . . . Can't gossips let us keep our happiness?"

In 1947 the marriage did break up. "We're through," Jane said to a columnist during a trip to New York. "We're finished, and it's all my fault." Reagan found out about the termination of his marriage when he read it in the column. He gave long interviews to Louella and to her archrival, Hedda Hopper, both of whom took his side. "If this comes to a divorce, I'll name *Johnny Belinda* as co-respondent," Hedda Hopper quoted him as saying. Jane had become so immersed in her new career as a dramatic actress that she wore pellets wrapped in wax in her ears so that she would not be able to hear during the filming of the deaf-mute movie. Hedda Hopper had more to say on the subject: "I can't really believe it yet. I don't think Ronald Reagan does either. It caught him so flatfooted, so pathetically by surprise. I talked to Ronnie the day he read in the newspapers what Jane should have told her husband first."

They were divorced in 1948, the same year she won the Academy Award. Jane got custody of the two children, and Reagan got weekend visitation rights. Jane testified that her husband's overriding interest in filmland union and political activity had driven them apart. Friends speculated at the time that Jane's emergence as a bona fide star and Reagan's concurrent slide from box-office favor contributed to the breakup. Others felt that Jane was simply bored with him. Before the governorship and his truly remarkable rise as a recognized world leader, friends from that period remember, he did indeed engage in long, ponderous, yawn-producing discourses on a variety of subjects. An ongoing joke in Hollywood during his campaign for the governorship of California was a remark attributed to Jane Wyman about her former husband. When asked what he was like, she allegedly said, "If you asked Ronnie the time, he'd tell you how to make a watch."

In 1954 Reagan married the actress Nancy Davis, who had been a contract player at MGM. Not long afterward, Jane married the bandleader and musical arranger Freddie Karger, a popular and handsome man-about-town in Hollywood. She divorced him a year later. Karger is often mentioned in Marilyn Monroe biographies as one of her lovers. Years later Wyman married Karger again, and then divorced him again. She has not married since.

In 1954 Jane was converted to Catholicism through the intervention of her great friend Loretta Young. Her Catholicism is a mainstay in her life. In fact, when asked her age, according to friends, she very often replies, "I'm thirty-five." she is counting from the year of her conversion to Catholicism. "She goes to Mass all the time," said a member of the cast of "Falcon Crest." "Sometimes she even has Mass said in her room." One of the ongoing characters in the series is a Catholic priest. "We need a lot of advice, because some of the characters are Catholic in the show," said Jane. The priest character is played by a real priest, Father Bob Curtis, a Paulist.

After *Johnny Belinda*, her career totally dominated her life. "She told me she could never even cook a hamburger. She taught her kids early that she wasn't going to be there," said an actor friend of hers. She had made the long and difficult transition from contract player to leading lady to star, and she hung on to that position through the forties and into the mid-fifties, playing what she has called four-handkerchief roles in such classic films of the genre as *Magnificent Obsession* and *The Blue Veil*, which remains her favorite. "I was in the middle of the woman's cycle in picture making," she said. She talked about her contemporaries. "Greer, Irene, Olivia, Joan, Bette, Loretta, Barbara, and don't forget Ginger . . . I never really knew Ava." She was talking about Greer Garson, Irene Dunne, Olivia de Havilland, Joan Fontaine, Bette Davis, Loretta Young, Barbara Stanwyck, Ginger Rogers, and Ava Gardner. "The thing was, we were all different," she said. The *New York Times* film critic Bosley Crowther wrote about her in 1953, "Her acting of drudges has become a virtual standard on the screen." But then the cycle of women's films ended. She decided to retire in 1962.

Several seasons ago Lana Turner, who was one of the queens of MGM when Jane was one of the queens of Warner Brothers, came on "Falcon Crest" as a semiregular. From the beginning, there was a coolness between the two stars. Lana, according to one source, took five or six hours to get ready, and Jane, for whom promptness is a passion, could never tolerate that. Someone closely connected with the show told me that Jane watched Lana on a talk show one night and felt that she was taking credit for "Falcon Crest" 's coming in number two in the ratings. "Imagine her taking credit for the show's success," said Jane at the time. Lana did not appear on the show again.

In the old days of the studios and contract players, the young actors were taught how to conduct themselves in interviews. They never said anything negative about anyone, and that training is still evident today.

"Was there a difficulty between you and Lana Turner?" I asked.

"Enough said, right there," answered Jane Wyman. She looked at me in a way that said very clearly that Miss Turner was a topic she had finished discussing. Her praise for her fellow actors on the series is unqualified, however. "I love to work with David Selby." "Lorenzo Lamas can do almost anything. He's a wonderful dramatic actor." "I said, 'I want Rod Taylor in the show.' He was occupied doing something else. I said, 'We'll wait.' "

"I never asked anything about her children. I have never approached that relationship with her," said an actor on the series. "I think she was hurt by Michael's book, but she has never said one harsh word about them. The only time I ever heard her mention the name of the president, she said something kind."

Both of her children have written books in which they announced things to their parents that they had not told them before. Maureen wrote that she had been a severely battered wife in her first marriage, and Michael confessed that he had been sexually molested by a man when he was a child. Since Joan Crawford's daughter Christina wrote *Mommie Dearest*, it has become the vogue among the adult children of the famous to cash in on their privileged unhappiness by spilling the beans on their celebrity dad or mom. Maureen wrote that Jane had not come to her first wedding. Michael wrote that Jane had sent him away to boarding school when he was six. Even the siblings did not seem to get along. Michael, in his book, recounts an incident that happened when he was four years old. He told Maureen that he knew a secret. "What?" she asked. He told her that she was getting a new blue dress for Christmas. Infuriated that he had ruined her Christmas surprise, she snapped, "I know a secret too. You're adopted."

"Do you see your grandchildren?" I asked. Maureen has no children, but Michael has two, Cameron and Ashley.

"Once in a while," she replied slowly. The subject was approaching the danger area. "They're in school when I'm working. They're adorable kids, Cameron and Ashley. Cameron's always saying to me, 'Gramma, how old are you?' And I said, 'I'm as old as my little finger.' And he says, 'How old is that?' and I say, 'As old as I am.' "

"Have you always been so reluctant to be interviewed?" I asked.

"No," she said. "My life's an open book. Everyone knows everything about me. There are all those magazines with lies in them." She had ordered a Diet Coke, and she took a sip. "I used to be interviewed a lot. But the last time I was, I had what seemed to be a very nice interview with the reporter, and then the piece came out. The first line was something like 'This is the president's ex-wife.' That's when the guillotine fell. I don't have to be known as that. I've been in this business longer than he has. It's such bad taste. They wouldn't say it if I was Joe Blow's ex-wife. It wouldn't even be mentioned."

With that said—and it was the closest she got to the unmentionable subject, the former president of the United State—she shifted topics abruptly. "We're going to have fun this year on the series. We have such a good producer, and the writers are wonderful. I feel like I'm doing the first show. The enthusiasm is just wonderful. The 'Falcon Crest' that I want is going on this year."

However reluctant she may be to discuss it, how can her relationship with Ronald Reagan not be discussed? She is the only former wife of a United States president in the history of the country. It is certainly true that if she had been married to Joe Blow it would never be mentioned. Her marriages to Myron Futterman, who manufactured dresses, and to Freddie Karger, who led the dance band on the roof of the Beverly Hilton Hotel in Beverly Hills, are never mentioned. But between those two marriages was her longest marriage, to a movie star of the period, with whom she had two children and who later became the governor of the state of California and then the president of the United States. It is part of her history. It will be the lead in her obituary when she dies.

It is a curious coincidence of fate that the eight years of her emergence as the First Lady of television should almost exactly parallel the eight years of her former husband's second wife's emergence as the First Lady of the land. The relationship between the two women is, has always been, and ever will be poisonous, although Jane Wyman has never uttered a single word in public about or against Nancy Reagan. Apparently Mrs. Reagan has not returned the courtesy. There are publishing rumors that her forthcoming book, My Turn, contains several obliquely critical allusions to Jane Wyman in reference to the bringing up of the two children Jane had during her marriage to Ronald Reagan. "Jane was a star. Nancy never was," a Los Angeles socialite acquainted with both said to explain the bad blood between the two women. "For seventeen years, Jane has kept her mouth shut. Nancy hates Jane with such a passion because it's the only part of Ronnie that she doesn't control. If you had mentioned Ronnie to Jane, she would have gotten up and walked out." A person friendly with Nancy Reagan told me that in the scrapbooks she keeps of newspaper clippings about her romance and marriage to Ronald Reagan, all mentions of Jane Wyman have been blacked out. In turn, a person friendly with Jane Wyman told me in private Jane sometimes refers to Nancy Reagan as Nancyvita.

Until recently, Jane was a regular and favored patron of the famed Hollywood restaurant Chasen's, as well as a close personal friend of Maude Chasen, the widow of David Chasen, who founded the restaurant fifty-three years ago. Although her friendship with Maude continues, she is, by unstated mutual agreement, almost never seen there these days. Chasen's has become the more or less official restaurant of the recent president and his wife, and Jane Wyman's absence from the premises averts the possibility of a chance encounter.

A journalist friend told me about interviewing the former president in the private quarters of the White House. He had been warned in advance that the name Jane Wyman was never mentioned in the presence of the First Lady. But since Miss Wyman had been married to the president for eight years, the journalist ventured very cautiously, when they were deep into the conversation, to bring up her name. To his surprise, the president began to tell a friendly anecdote about his first wife. Midway through the story, Nancy Reagan walked into the room. Without a second's hesitation, the president shifted to another topic right in the middle of a sentence, and the subject of Miss Wyman did not come up again.

Every star of Jane Wyman's caliber pays a price for fame, and she has endured for over fifty years. Although she is husbandless and vaguely estranged from her children, her splendid isolation must not be confused with loneliness. Where she is is where she has always wanted to be from her early contract days.

Like all success-oriented people, she is not without her detractors. Robert Raison was Jane Wyman's agent for nearly thirty years, as well as her friend and sometime escort to social functions in the television industry. He was also the agent of Dennis Hopper, Michelle Phillips, and all of the Bottoms brothers. He had a reputation for developing close friendships with his clients. He negotiated the seven-year deal for Jane when she decided to play the role of Angela Channing on "Falcon Crest." At the end of the seventh year of the series, Raison heard from Jane's lawyer that he was through. "When she fired me, she never told me herself. I heard it from her lawyer," said Raison. When he asked why, the lawyer told him to call Jane and discuss it with her. "I did," said Raison. "I told her I wanted to hear it from her mouth. You know what she said?"

"No."

"She said, 'You and me, Bobby, we've run out of gas.' I was going to sue her, but the lawyers settled it for a given amount of money. I can't discuss that amount."

Raison is now writing a book about his years with Jane Wyman. It is tentatively titled *Jane Wyman, Less than a Legend: A Memoir in Close-Up*. Although angry and hurt, Raison still expresses residual tenderness for his former client. "Two days after the assassination attempt on the president, Jane sent him flowers to the hospital in Washington. Several days later, the president personally called to say thank you for the flowers," Raison recalled recently. He answered the telephone when the president called. "He said to me, 'Thank you for taking care of her, Bobby,' " said Raison.

The check came. In an interview situation like this one, the interviewer always picks up the check. As I reached for it, Jane Wyman tapped my hand and shook her head. "This is on Lorimar," she said.

We walked outside into the brilliant sunlight. Her red Jaguar was parked in the number-one space of the Bob Burns parking lot. We shook hands. "Where else can you meet such fascinating people and go to such places as people in our business do?" she said. "It's a fabulous life."

In an era of tell-all, Jane Wyman has made the decision to tell nothing. No confessions. No revelations. It's her life, and it's private. There are those who say it is her duty to inform historians of the eight years she shared with a man who later became the president of the United States, years that encompassed the peak of his minor movie stardom, his presidency of the Screen Actors Guild, and his role in the ignoble House Un-American Activities Committee hearings. But she sees it differently, and that's the way it is.

"She's one tough lady," said one of the cast members of "Falcon Crest." Yeah, but a lady.

November 1989

IT'S A
FAMILY AFFAIR

IT WAS a family affair. The father, the mother, the three sons, the two daughters, the estranged wife of one of the sons, a grandchild, boyfriends and girlfriends of all the children. And there were the father's half-sister and the mother's sisters and almost all their husbands, and a good many of their children. And cousins, lots of cousins, city cousins and country cousins, including, in the host's own words, "masses of Guinnesses." And friends, but only close friends, hardly a jet-setter in the whole bunch. This was, remember, a family affair.

But what a family and what an affair. Lord Glenconner, of England, Scotland, and the islands of Mustique and Saint Lucia in the British West Indies, who used to be called Colin Tennant before he inherited his father's title, was celebrating his sixtieth birthday in very grand style. For openers, he had chartered a brand-new 440-foot four-masted sailing vessel called the *Wind Star*, possibly the prettiest ship afloat, with a crew of eighty-seven, and had installed 130 of his nearest and dearest in its seventy-five staterooms, complete with VCRs and mini-bars, for a week-long cruise from Saint Lucia to Martinique to Bequia to Mustique, with parties all along the way, every noon and every night, culminating in a costume ball called the Peacock Ball at the Glenconner's place, which some people call a palace, on the beach in Mustique. And should there have been any question of the financial burden imposed by such an adventure, Lord Glenconner had taken care of that too, by paying the fares of all his guests from London to Saint Lucia, where he owns a second estate, called the Jalousie Plantation, which he plans, in time, to turn into a hotel and health spa. And should there have been any problem about rounding up a suitable costume for the lavish India-theme ball, Lord Glenconner had even anticipated that. In his travels to India over the past year, while he was preparing for his birthday celebration, he had purchased a variety of kurtas and Aligarh trousers and turbans and ghagra/cholis and harem dresses in a whole range of sizes and styles and had had them transported to the *Wind Star* so that his guests could pick out what they liked. There were even two seamstresses on board to make any necessary alterations. The only thing you had to provide was your own jewelry. He drew the line at that. But he did have a hairdresser for the ladies, who doubled as a barber for the men, and a masseuse and a masseur. And 360 movies to choose from for the VCRs, including 58 pornographic ones. And all taxi rides on the various islands were to be paid for by Lord Glenconner. And there was to be absolutely no tipping. Lord Glenconner had taken care of all that. It was, all the way around, a class act.

I arrived in Saint Lucia the day before the plane from London arrived, and was met at Hewanorra airport by Lord Glenconner and his estate manager, Lyton Lamontagne, at whose house I spent the first night. Lyton Lamontagne, a native of Saint Lucia in his late twenties, and his wife, Eroline, went to school together in the town of Soufrière. He is handsome and she is beautiful. A trusted confidant of Lord Glenconner's, Lamontagne traveled to India with him last year and was instrumental in carrying out the farsighted and sometimes seemingly impossible plans of the eccentric lord. Glenconner feels, as do others I saw in Saint Lucia, that in time Lyton Lamontagne could become the prime minister of the island. The Lamontagnes refer to Lord Glenconner as Papa, as do many of the natives on both Saint Lucia and Mustique, and there is a sense in their relationship of the nineteenth-century British Empire builder and his devoted overseer. In Soufrière, Glenconner lives in an old wooden house on the town square, so primitive that it has no electricity or running water, although it will have at some point in the future. He has to go to the nearby Texaco station to use the bathroom or wash, and this sort of inconvenience seems to appeal to him, although it is at variance with his elegance of manner, which is sometimes almost effete. He wears large straw hats, and for his birthday week he always dressed in white or black.

Lord Glenconner talked briefly about several last-minute dropouts from the party. Mick Jagger could not take the time out to attend, although Jerry Hall would be joining the group when the boat docked in Mustique. David Bowie could not come. Lord Dufferin and Ava was ill. Carolina Herrera had to finalize a perfume deal in New York. Glenconner rolled his eyes in disappointment. He rolls his eyes a great deal, in exasperation, or wonder, or over lapses of taste. His own lapses, however, take on a sort of aristocratic whimsy, at least in his mind. He once allowed himself to be photographed defecating by the side of the road in India and sent the pictures to *Vanity Fair*.

We sailed in a small open boat to the Jalousie Plantation, where one of the main events of the week-long celebration was going to take place several days hence. His plantation lies between two peaks called the Pitons. The original house, on what was once a sugar plantation built by the French in the seventeenth or eighteenth centuries, is long gone, but stone walls from the original waterwheel are still standing. The principal house now is a small wooden bungalow, onto which had just been added a covered porch for the picnic party. The bungalow, which has gingerbread trimmings, was painted pink with yellow shutters, green floors, and blue interior walls, and looked like a set from the musical *House of Flowers*. Gamboling happily around the scene of preparations was a frisky young elephant called Bupa, which Glenconner had bought from the Dublin zoo and had sent out to his plantation. A native painter was finishing a mural on one side of the house, and Lord Glenconner examined the lavender leaves and red and orange flowers closely. "No, no, no, I don't like that color red at all," he said to the painter. "There's far too much brown in that red. I want a red red." They found a red red.

Then we went for the first of two trips to the airport, to meet Lady Glenconner, known as Lady Anne, who was arriving from Mustique with the eldest of her three sons, Charles, as well as her daughter-in-law, Tessa Tennant, the wife of her second son, Henry, and Viscount Linley, the son of Princess Margaret by the Earl of Snowdon. The contingent from London, which included the Glenconners' twin teenage daughters, Amy and May, was arriving on a second plane several hours later. Another son, Christopher, was arriving from Mexico. On the way to the airport Glenconner had the driver stop the car several times so that he could cut wild lilies growing by the side of the road to present to his wife. Lady Anne is a lady-in-waiting to Princess Margaret. Such close friends are the Glenconners of the princess that they have been living at Kensington Palace as her houseguests for nearly a year while their new London house has been undergoing extensive renovations and decoration. "I sleep in what was Tony Snowdon's dressing room, just this far from Princess Margaret," Lord Glenconner told me. He said when they were moving out of their old house, Princess Margaret came to help them pack; she donned a working smock borrowed from a maid and wrapped china in newspapers.

"I thought surely you'd have had a steel band on the tarmac when the plane arrived," Lady Anne said to her husband, patting her hair beneath a straw hat and supervising the transfer of all the luggage to the van that would take us to the boat. She is blond and calm and attractive.

"I hadn't thought of it," replied Glenconner, and I felt that in his mind he was trying to figure out if he could do just that before the plane from London arrived a few hours later. Although they are married and live together, or at least live under the same roof when the separate schedules of their lives overlap, they speak to each other with the friendly distance of a divorced couple meeting at their child's wedding.

Their oldest son, Charles, called Charlie, thirty, looked pale and disheveled. His father told him to wash his face and get a haircut as soon as we got on the ship. Although Lord Glenconner has publicly disinherited his eldest son, who is a registered heroin addict, with an announcement in the London *Daily Mail*, there seems to be no lessening of affection for him, nor is there any sort of middle-class covering up of a family embarrassment. "My son Charlie is a heroin addict and has been ever since he was fifteen," said Glenconner openly, not only to me but to several other people encountering the situation for the first time. Charlie remains a part of the family, disinherited but not cast out, and loved by all. In time he will become Lord Glenconner, for titles must go to the eldest son, but the estates, fortune, and castle in Scotland will pass to his brother Henry, who is estranged from Tessa, by whom he has a son, Euan, three.

When we got to the pier where the *Wind Star* was docked, the fence was padlocked, and two armed guards stared at us as if we were usurpers, making no attempt to open the gates for the van to enter. "I am the lessee of the boat," called out Lord Glenconner from the backseat of the van. The guards did not react. "Just say Lord Glenconner," said Charles from the front seat to his father. "I am Lord Glenconner," called out Lord Glenconner. The gates were opened.

Standing on deck, we watched the London crowd arrive, hot and tired and bedraggled, and trudge up the gangplank. A Mrs. Wills had lost her keys, and there was a great to-do. "Where's Mark Palmer?" someone called out. "I can't find my suitcases," someone else wailed. John Stefanidis, the famed London interior decorator, who helped the Glenconners with the Great House in Mustique and who is currently doing up their new London house, remarked to his deck companions, Lord and Lady Neidpath, with whom he had flown over from Mustique, "Rather elite, having arrived early."

In typical English fashion, no one was introduced. Those who already knew one another stayed together and looked at the others. There were no passenger lists in the staterooms, so it was impossible to put names to faces. Even during lifeboat drill, when we were separated into small groups, they did not introduce themselves. After a few days, people began to come into focus as one-line descriptions were repeated over and over: "He's Princess Margaret's son." "She's Rachel Ward's mother." "He was recently fired by Mrs. Thatcher." "She's the Duke of Rutland's sister-in-law."

One passenger of interest was Barbara Barnes, on holiday from Kensington Palace, where she is nanny to the royal princes, William and Henry. Nanny Barnes, a popular figure on the ship, used to be nanny to the children of Colin and Anne Glenconner, and the Princess of Wales had given her time off to attend the celebration and visit her former charges.

For a week we heard no news of the outside world. We were hermetically sealed in the elegant confines of the *Wind Star* when we were not ashore being picnicked. There was swimming off the ship and in the pool, and gambling in the casino, and a gym to work out in, and bars to drink at, and a disco to dance in, and all those videos, including the fifty-eight pornographic ones, with titles like *For Your Thighs Only* and *Lust on the Orient Express*, and even a library. John Nutting read the recent biography of Lord Esher. His wife read a biography of Francis Bacon. The Honorable Mrs. Marten read the new biography of Anthony Eden. Prince Rupert Löwenstein read the biography of Frank Sinatra by Kitty Kelley. Conversation, which never lagged, from breakfast to bedtime, was all about themselves. They never tired of discussing one another. One Englishman described the degree of friendship with another man on board as being not quite on farting terms.

"Tell me, how is young Lord Ivar Mountbatten, over there with the pretty Channon girl, related to Dickie?"

"He's through the Milford Haven branch."

"Claire tells me Tony Lambton's writing a biography of Dickie Mountbatten that's going to tell everything."

"Oh dear."

"The Guinnesses all stick together, have you noticed?"

"Lord Neidpath is very proud of his feet."

It is said that on all private boat trips the most unifying factor for harmony is a mutual dislike of one particular person aboard, and this trip was no exception. By the third day, all had agreed that they loathed the same certain person, and from that moment on, tales of that person's every move and statement were circulated.

"Don't believe any rumors unless you start them yourself," cautioned Lord Glenconner, in regard to all the rumors that were circulating about the trip. From passing yachts we heard that Michael Jackson was on board the *Wind Star*, but the person the passengers in the passing yachts mistook for Michael Jackson was called Kelvin Omard, a London actor and great friend of Henry Tennant, Lord Glenconner's second son. "Did you see *Water* with Michael Caine?" asked Tessa Tennant, Henry's wife. "Kelvin played the waiter."

"How much do you suppose this is all costing?" I inquired tentatively one day at lunch on Martinique, fully expecting to be put in my place with imperious stares for daring to ask such a vulgar question. I meant the whole week of it: the plane fares, the *Wind Star*, the parties, parties, parties, and the ball that was to come.

"That's what we're all wondering" was the immediate and unexpected answer, from one of my lunch companions, not a Tennant, at a table of Tennants. "We figure about a half-million." I didn't know if she meant pounds or dollars, but since she was English, I assumed pounds. As the week progressed, revealing constant new considerations on the part of our host for his guests, the cost question was brought up again and again, not only by me, an almost lone American on a boatload of Brits, but by a number of Brits as well.

"Colin is not limitlessly rich," said another passenger a few days later at dinner on board the *Wind Star*, pursuant to the same question. When I wrote down the phrase "not limitlessly rich," his wife said, "My God, you're not going to quote my husband, are you?"

"All I know is he sold some items at Sotheby's in order to charter the *Wind Star*, and paid for the charter in installments," offered someone else.

"Where is Lord Glenconner's money from?" I asked over and over.

"Sugar in the West Indies, nineteenth century, I would think" was one reply.

"Imperial Chemical" was another.

Lord Glenconner's explanation seemed to answer the question. "My great-grandfather invented the Industrial Revolution."

Like a mysterious shadow, a second ship was known to be looming in the distance, the *Maxim's des Mers*, the floating sister of the famed Parisian restaurant, carrying "the American crowd." At some point we would be rendezvousing with them. In speculation preceding the ball week, it had been rumored that Mick Jagger, David Bowie, Michael Caine, and others too famous for words would be among its passengers, supplying the magic mix of show biz with swells that guarantees fascination on both sides. At the helm of the *Maxim's des Mers*, at least as organizer of the famous, was André Weinfeld, the husband of Raquel Welch, and an invitation every bit as grand as the one to the Peacock Ball sent by Lady Glenconner and the one to a beach picnic on the morning following the ball sent by H.R.H. the Princess Margaret, countess of Snowdon, had been dispatched by Miss Welch and Mr. Weinfeld bidding us, the passengers on the *Wind Star*, and other guests who would be joining our party in Mustique, to a dinner on board the *Maxim's des Mers* on the evening preceding the ball. Already, even before our rendezvous, rumors of defections from their guest list had circulated. We knew that such stalwarts of the international social scene as Carolina and Reinaldo Herrera and Ahmet and Mica Ertegün had dropped out, not to mention Mick and David, as they were referred to, meaning Jagger and Bowie, who had long since changed their plans.

The *Maxim's des Mers* came side by side with the *Wind Star* in the cove in front of Lord Glenconner's Jalousie Plantation on Saint Lucia. The other boat was squat and inelegant next to our trim, patrician four-master, the battle lines were instantly drawn. No amount of interior Art Nouveau tarting up of the *Maxim's des Mers* could belie its minesweeper origins. The A group–B group distinction between the two parties could not be denied by even the most generous-hearted. It carried right down to the crew of the *Wind Star*, who snubbed the crew of the *Maxim's des Mers*. "Rather like being on the wrong side of the room at '21,' " remarked a *Wind Star* passenger about the *Maxim's des Mers*, which others were already referring to as the *Mal de Mer*. The celebrity guests that Mr. Weinfeld was able to produce arrived onshore for the barbecue at the plantation. Vastly fat native women were dressed up in Aunt Jemima gear, a fourteen-piece steel band played nonstop, the elephant frolicked with the guests, and at one point Lyton and Eroline Lamontagne, got up as Scarlett O'Hara and Rhett Butler, drove down a mountain in a horse and buggy to be introduced by Lord Glenconner as his distinguished neighbors from the next plantation. Rum punch and more rum punch, and still more rum punch was consumed. And the sun beat down.

Heading Mr. Weinfeld's star list was the amply bosomed Dianne Brill, the New York underground cult figure often referred to in the gossip columns as the Queen of the Night. Although Miss Brill is a good sport, a good mixer, and a genuinely funny lady, even she could not bring about any real mixing between the passengers of the two ships. "Who do you suppose *they* are?" someone in our party asked about a trio of ladies. "In trade, I would think," said Prince Rupert Löwenstein playfully, "above a boutique and below a department store." André Weinfeld explained that because it was Thanksgiving, most of the people he had invited had backed out, and he had brought along a substitute crowd. Indeed, his wife,

Raquel Welch, had not yet joined the company, but he assured us she would be along in time for her party on board the *Maxim's des Mers*.

In Mustique the inner circle widened to admit some new arrivals. Adding more than a dash of American glamour to the British festivities were two tall and sleek American beauties, Jean Harvey Vanderbilt, of New York, and Minnie Cushing Coleman, of Newport and New Orleans. On Mustique the groups within the group of the *Wind Star* began to divide up into splinter groups. "We're going to Ingrid Channon's house for lunch," said Mrs. Vyner. "We've been asked for drinks at Princess Margaret's house," said Mrs. Nutting. "We're having a box lunch at Macaroni Beach," said the ones who weren't invited to any of the private houses.

"What happens if you don't call Princess Margaret ma'am?" asked one of the new American arrivals.

"You don't get asked back," came the reply.

On the morning of Raquel Welch's party aboard the *Maxim's des Mers*, a telex arrived for Lord Glenconner from the star, saying that a contract negotiation prevented her from attending her own party. Lord Glenconner rolled his eyes in disappointment, but any attentive observer could also detect an element of anger in the eye roll. His last star had fallen by the wayside. From that moment on, Raquel Welch, who had always been referred to as Raquel in anticipation of her arrival, was referred to by one and all as Miss Welch.

"I think this is the rudest thing I have ever heard," fumed one of Lord Glenconner's guests, and then proceeded to fume against all Americans for Miss Welch's rudeness, especially since a member of the royal family had consented to attend her party.

"But Miss Welch is not American, Julian. She's English," said his wife.

"Oh dear," said her husband, calmly accepting the correction, although he had been right to begin with.

"If she can't be bothered to attend her own party, I can't be bothered to attend it either," said another guest.

"Disgraceful!"

"Movie stars always back out at the last minute."

"They're insecure in social situations."

"You don't suppose they're getting a divorce, do you, Mr. Wein-feld and Miss Welch?"

On the night of the ball, after a whole week of partying, guests ran up and down the passageways of the *Wind Star* borrowing feathers, remarking on one another's costumes, pinning and sewing up each other—all with the excitement of boarding-school students preparing for the annual spring dance. John Stefanidis had gone to Paris to borrow jewelry to wear with his Indian costume from Loulou de la Falaise, who works for Yves Saint Laurent, and indeed his pounds of pearls, rhinestone necklaces, and long drop earrings were the most elaborate jewelry at the ball—after the host's, that is.

All during the evening, Lord Glenconner's eyes shone with the excitement of an accomplished creation—a symphony composed, an epic written, a masterpiece painted. Wearing a gold crown and ropes of pearls, he was dressed in white magnificence, his high collar and robes heavily encrusted with gold embroidery. The Glenconner house, called simply the Great House, is a Taj Mahal–like palace designed by the ultimate stage and ballet designer-fantacist, the late Oliver Messel, uncle of Lord Snowdon, former husband of Princess Margaret. Magical even in broad daylight, by night, for the ball, it was bathed in pink and turquoise fluorescent light, which gave the illusion of a Broadway-musical version of India. Handsome, almost nude black males from Saint Lucia and Mustique, their private parts encased in coconut shells painted gold, with strips of gold tinsel hanging from their shoulders to the ground, lined the pink-carpeted walkway to the house. Inside the double doors, more natives, in pink and blue Lurex fantasies of Indian dress inspired more by *The King and I* than by *The Jewel in the Crown*, stood cooling the air with giant peacock feather fans on poles.

Standing under a pink marquee, with the palm-tree-lined beach in the background and the *Wind Star*, fully lit, on the sea beyond, Lord and Lady Glenconner, with their son Charlie by their side, received their elaborately dressed guests while their son Henry called out the names as they arrived.

"Mrs. Michael Brand," called out Henry Tennant.

"I am the Honorable Mrs. Brand, not Mrs. Michael Brand," corrected Mrs. Brand.

The natives on the island of Mustique call Princess Margaret simply Princess, with neither an article preceding nor a name following. Well, Princess was late, and the procession that was to open the ball could not take place until Princess arrived, because Princess was the principal participant. The fact was, Princess had arrived at the Great House, but she was still sitting in Lady Anne's bedroom, which boasts a silver bed with silver peacocks on the head- and footboards. One story had it that Raquel Welch had also finally arrived on the island, and that Princess, not wishing to be outdone by her, as she had been the previous evening, when Miss Welch had not shown up at her own party, where Princess was an honored guest, was delaying the procession until after Miss Welch's arrival. If such was the case, Princess lost another round.

Finally, despairing of Miss Welch's ever arriving, the royal procession started. The sisters of Lady Anne, Lady Carey Basset, with one of her three sons, and Lady Sarah Walter, with her husband, Prince and Princess Rupert Löwenstein, and the Americans, Miss Jerry Hall and Mr. and Mrs. James Coleman, Jr., moved slowly from the house to the receiving tent. They were followed by Viscount Linley, in a white peacock headdress, which he never removed for the whole night, and his beautiful girlfriend, Susannah Constantine. Then came Princess Margaret, the great friend of the Glenconners. On her head, complementing her dress, which was a gift from Lord Glenconner, she wore a black velvet headband tiara-style, onto which her maid, that afternoon, had sewn massive diamond clips. Her resplendence had been worth the wait.

"Her Royal Highness, Princess Margaret, Countess of Snowdon," called out Henry Tennant. All the Indian-clad ladies dropped in curtsies as she passed, and all the men bowed their heads. Under the tent, Lady Anne kissed her on both cheeks before doing a deep curtsy. Then Lord Glenconner removed his crown, as did his son Charlie, and they bowed to Princess.

When Princess Margaret first saw the Indian sari that Lord Glenconner had had made for her in India, she exclaimed, "I've been dreaming of having a dress like this since I was six." During dinner a maid spilled a tray of potatoes on the dress, but Princess's dinner partners, Sir John Plumb, the eighteenth-century historian, and John Nutting, an English barrister of note, were able to right the wrong with a minimum of fuss and very little stain.

Miss Welch, the lone dissenter from Indian costume, finally arrived during dinner, dressed in a gray metallic shirred evening gown and shoulder-length metallic shirred evening gloves, which she kept on while she ate. She was seated between Prince Rupert Löwenstein, a noted wit and conversationalist, and Mr. Roddy Llewellyn, the extremely affable suitor, before his marriage, of Princess Margaret, at whose Mustique house he and his wife, Tania, were houseguests, but conversation with the film star was pretty much uphill.

"Have you read the Sinatra biography?" Prince Rupert asked her.

"No," she said, "but I made a picture with Frank. If Frank likes you, he's behind you all the way. He wrote me a letter when my father died." Then she massaged her neck with her hand and said, "My neck's out. I've been wearing a neck brace, but I couldn't wear a neck brace with this dress to Colin's party. It's stress. I've been under a lot of stress. Would you get my husband, please? I need my pills for my neck. André, would you get my pills for my neck. Two of the yellow ones."

"They're back on the boat," joked Prince Rupert. "In the Dufy suite."

"No, I'm not staying on the boat," she said. "I'm at the Cotton House."

At the far end of Lord Glenconner's enormous swimming pool stands a maharajah's pleasure palace, discovered in India, purchased in India, and then brought to Mustique, along with two Indian stonemasons to put it together again. Constructed entirely of white marble, it has lattice marble screens on all four sides, which gives the interior constant dappled light by day. By night, for the ball, its interior was illuminated by gold fluorescent light, and smoke from smoke pots drifted through the lattice screens. A plan to have Raquel Welch emerge from the pleasure palace as part of the entertainment portion of the evening had been scratched, and an alternative plan had been substituted: another princess.

Princess was not the only princess at Lord Glenconner's ball.

Princess Josephine Löwenstein was there, as well as her daughter, Princess Dora Löwenstein. And then there was Princess Tina— just Tina, no last name. Princess Tina provided the cabaret entertainment, appearing late in the evening in front of the pleasure palace, doing gymnastic gyrations while she balanced full glasses of something on her head and pelvic area. The crowd surged out to watch her—blacks and swells vying for the good positions from which to view the tantalizing spectacle. One heavily wined English lady sat in the reflecting pool in front of the pleasure palace and pulled up her skirts to the refreshing waters. "My God, look at her —she's showing her bush!" another lady cried out.

Thrice Miss Welch upstaged Princess Margaret. She didn't show up at her own party on the *Maxim's des Mers*, at which Princess Margaret was a guest. She arrived later than Princess Margaret at the Peacock Ball. And on the day following the ball, at Princess Margaret's party, a picnic luncheon on Macaroni Beach, under the same pink marquee from the ball of the night before, transported after dawn from the Great House, Miss Welch, accompanied by Mr. Weinfeld, made another late entrance, as the princess and her guests were finishing dessert. Miss Welch was all smiles as she greeted her hostess. Princess inhaled deeply on her cigarette through a long holder protruding from the corner of her mouth, exhaled, pointedly looked at her watch, wordlessly established the time, and then returned the greeting with a stiff smile. One-upmanship was back in the royal corner.

That night, Lord Glenconner's party drew to a close with a farewell dinner aboard the *Wind Star*. New friends were exchanging addresses. Bags were being packed. Princess arrived on board and was seated at the right of Lord Glenconner. People said over and over again that they would never forget the week-long celebration. John Wells, who writes the "Dear Bill" column in *Private Eye*, rose and in mock-Shakespearean rhetoric recited a long poem to our host which ended with these lines addressed to Princess Margaret:

> *Your Royal Highness, may I crave*
> *Leave not only to ask God to Save*
> *The Queen, your Sister, but to bless*

> *The Author of our Happiness—*
> *This Prospero, Magician King*
> *Who makes Enchanted Islands sing;*
> *King Colin, at whose mildest Bate*
> *King Kong himself might emigrate!*
> *So charge your Glasses, Friends, to honour*
> *Our reckless Host, dear Lord Glenconner.*

Amid cheers and tears, Lord Glenconner rose. Dressed all in black, his energies spent now, his production over, he thanked the people who had helped him in his yearlong preparations: Lyton Lamontagne, Nicholas Courtney, and others. He thanked his son Charlie "for getting a little better," he thanked his son Henry and Henry's friend Kelvin for working out the treasure hunt on the island of Bequia. He thanked his daughter-in-law Tessa for her constant assistance. He did not thank Lady Anne, who seemed not to notice not being thanked. "You all say you'll never forget," he said wistfully. "But you do, you know. You do forget. I can't even remember my own wedding day."

March 1987

GRANDIOSITY
The Fall of Roberto Polo

IN RETROSPECT it's always easy to say, "Oh, yes, I knew, I always knew," about this one or that one, when this one or that one comes to a bad end or winds up in disgrace. Any number of people who knew Roberto Polo have told me that when they first heard that disaster was about to befall him, they said to the person who informed them, "I'm not surprised, are you?" and the informant invariably replied that he or she was not surprised either.

Polo, a thirty-seven-year-old Cuban-born American citizen with residences in Paris, New York, Monte Carlo, and Santo Domingo, is currently in prison in Italy, where he was arrested in June. He is wanted for questioning in Switzerland, France, and the United States concerning the alleged misappropriation of $110 million of his investors' money. At the time of his arrest, he had been a fugitive from the law for five weeks, and had been rumored either to have sought and bought refuge in Latin America or to have been murdered by the very people he was said to have swindled, on the theory that, if caught, he might reveal their identities.

"Roberto had so many personas it was hard to know which was the *real* person," one of his former employees said to me in describing him. A middle-class Cuban with dreams of glory, Polo appeared to be many things to many people, from family man to philanderer, from elegant boulevardier to preposterous phony, from fantasizer to fuckup of the American Dream. A man with the capacity to endear himself to many with his likability and charm and to enrage others with his grandiosity and pomposity, he provided uniformity of opinion among those who knew him in one thing only: He had exquisite taste.

I first met Roberto and his extremely attractive wife, Rosa, a Dominican by birth, the daughter of a diplomat and the cousin of a former president of that country, in 1984, at a small dinner for eight or ten people in New York, at the home of John Loring, senior vice president of Tiffany & Co. They were the youngest couple in the group, known to all the guests but me.

It was not until we sat down to dinner that I noticed the extraordinary ring Rosa Polo was wearing, a diamond so huge it would have been impossible not to comment on it. As one who has held up the hands and stared at the ice-skating-rink-size diamonds of Elizabeth Taylor, Candy Spelling, and Imelda Marcos, I realized that the young woman across from me was wearing one bigger and perhaps better than all of them. I asked her about it, and before she could reply Roberto called down from his end of the table and gave me the whole history of the jewel. It was the Ashoka diamond, a 41.37-carat D-flawless stone named after Ashoka Maurya, the third-century B.C. Buddhist warrior-emperor. Polo had bought it for his wife from the Mexican movie star Maria Felix.

Clearly the Polos were a young couple of consequence, but it was hard to get a line on them. Rosa was quiet, almost shy, a Latin wife who lived in the shadow of her husband, and Roberto sent out mixed signals. He was said to be a financial wizard, and he had his own company called PAMG, for Private Asset Management Group. He handled the monetary affairs of a select group of very rich foreign investors with assets in the United States.

He reclined in languid positions that first evening, and his talk was decidedly nonfinancial, about jewelry and fashion and Jacob Frères, Ltd., an antiques shop that had recently opened on Madison Avenue at Seventy-eighth Street, which was run by Rosa's brother, Federico Suro. They sold ormolu-encrusted furniture fit for palaces, and massive porcelain urns, all at prices in the hundreds of thousands of dollars. Roberto was obviously a genuine aesthete, mad about beautiful things, and his interest in fashion, which would become obsessive in the years ahead, was already evident. As a graduate student at Columbia in the early seventies, he had worked at Rizzoli, the art book store, and had come up with the idea of doing a show called "Fashion As Fantasy," with fashion designers showing clothes as art objects.

They were a couple in a hurry, or rather Roberto was in a hurry, and Rosa was swept along in his vortex. He had reportedly created his wife, turning her from a sweet Latin girl into a sleek and glamorous international figure. He picked out her clothes, told her what jewels to wear, chose their dinner guests, did the seating, and ordered the flowers and menu. He went to the collections in Paris with her, and in one season spent half a million dollars on clothes for her. He had a passion for jewelry and a knowledge of gemology. His role model, according to the interior designer and socialite Suzie Frankfurt, was Cosimo de' Medici.

"I didn't want it said I was just a rich boy," he said in an early interview, before his woes, as if he were the heir to a great fortune instead of an alleged usurper of other people's money. Like a Cuban Gatsby, an outsider with his nose pressed to the window, Roberto Polo wanted it all and he wanted it quick, and he saw, in the money-mad New York of the eighties, the way to achieve his ambitions.

July 1988. The picture was improbable. A young blond girl of extraordinary loveliness, wearing a light summer dress, was leaning against the pay-telephone booth in the courtyard of the prison in Lucca, an Italian walled town between Pisa and Florence. She was reading an English novel and occasionally taking sips of Pelligrino water from a green bottle. On the roof above her, a guard with a submachine gun paced back and forth on a catwalk in the scorching Tuscan sun. There was about the girl a sense of a person waiting.

I was waiting too, reading a day-old English newspaper and leaning against the fender of a dented red Fiat. I had been waiting for a week for a permit that was never to come, from the Procura Generale in Florence, to visit the most famous detainee in the prison. Roberto Polo had been arrested by the Italian police the week before in the nearby seaside village of Viareggio, after an alleged attempt, by wrist slashing, to commit suicide. Bleeding, believing himself to be dying, Polo had made farewell telephone calls proclaiming his innocence to one of his investors in Mexico, to members of his family, and to a former associate, the man who had set the case against him in motion.

It occurred to me, watching the young girl, that we were there for the same reason. I offered her my *Daily Mail*, and she said that she hadn't seen an English paper for days. She knew a girl whose name was in Nigel Dempster's column. "She's always in the papers," she said. We exchanged names, and it turned out that I knew the mother of her stepsisters in New York.

"Why are you here?" I asked. We had stepped through rope curtains into the shade of the Caffè la Patria, a bar and tobacco shop adjacent to the prison.

"I'm with people who are seeing someone inside," she said cautiously.

"Roberto Polo?" I asked.

"Yes."

"That's why I'm here," I said.

"I supposed you were," she replied.

The previous week I had made my presence and purpose known to Gaetano Berni, the Florentine lawyer retained by Polo's family. Berni had explained to me that Polo was fighting extradition to Switzerland. "It is better for him to remain in Italy," he had said. "The Swiss will be harder on him. Besides, there is insufficient evidence to extradite him. He didn't kill. He didn't deal drugs. He's not Mafia. As the judge pointed out, he was not escaping when he was arrested.

My new friend, Chantal Carr by name, was the girlfriend of Roberto Polo's brother, Marco, a banker in Milan, where she also lived. Early that morning she had driven Marco and his father, Roberto Polo, Sr., to Lucca in her tiny Italian car. Even for the family of such an illustrious prisoner, visiting hours were restricted to one hour a week, on either Saturday or Sunday.

When Chantal Carr saw Marco Polo come out of the prison, she joined him, and I could see her telling him that I was in the bar, hoping to talk to him. Marco Polo is thirty-three, younger than his brother by four years, and handsome. His hair is black and curly, combed straight back. He has the look of the rich Italian and Latin American playboys who disco at Regine's. Standing in the hot sun, he was weeping almost uncontrollably while Chantal Carr patted him comfortingly on the back. Behind him stood his father, a smaller man with wounded eyes. Roberto Polo, Sr., seemed desolated by the disgrace that had befallen his family, as well as by the shock of having just seen his son in such awful circumstances.

"My brother is devastated. He is destroyed," said Marco when he came into the café. The prison was filthy, he told me, the food inedible. Prisoners with money could purchase food and sundries in the prison store, but they were not allowed to spend more than 450,000 lire, or $350, a month. Roberto Polo, one of the few prisoners to have that kind of money, had spent his whole month's allowance in the first few days of his imprisonment. During the time I was in Lucca, he could not even buy stamps.

"I am living in subhuman conditions . . . with murderers, thieves, drug traffickers, etc.," Polo wrote in a press release from his cell. For two hours each morning, they were allowed to pace back and forth in an enclosed patio for exercise. "He is totally incommunicado. He does not know that people have come to see him," said Marco. The only visitors he was allowed to have were his lawyers and members of his immediate family, but even they were not allowed to bring him a prescription he needed or a brand of toothpaste he requested—only food.

Marco expressed shock at the newspaper coverage of his brother's dilemma. "They have convicted him without a trial," he said.

The family was hoping to obtain Roberto's release on bail. That afternoon the lawyers were due, Gaetano Berni from Florence and Jacques Kam from Paris. It seemed in keeping with the glamorous aspects of Roberto Polo's recent life that Maître Kam, the principal lawyer he had picked to defend his interests at the time the warrant for his arrest was issued, was also the lawyer of Marlene Dietrich, the late Orson Welles, Dior, and Van Cleef & Arpels. "Speed is of the essence," said Marco. "Everything comes to a standstill in August. The judicial system closes down. Of course, even if bail is granted, all his money has been frozen."

All around us in the café, waiting for the afternoon visiting hours to start, were prisoners' relatives, many with small children. Looking at them, Marco said, "Roberto wants to see Marina, his daughter. But Rosa and he have decided that it is best she not come. She is five. She would remember."

I asked about Rosa, who was expected in Lucca the following day from Paris, and whom I had spoken with a few days earlier. "Rosa has not cried once," replied Marco, and there was an implied criticism in his voice. It is a known fact among all their friends that Rosa Polo and her husband's mother have never gotten along. Rosa, however, who had every reason to be outraged at the posi-

tion she found herself in, had been staunchly loyal to her beleaguered husband when I spoke with her. She is, after all, the
daughter of a diplomat. Shortly after her husband's disappearance
five weeks before his arrest, the French police confiscated $26 mil-
lion in paintings and furnishings from the couple's Paris apartment,
leaving Rosa and her daughter only mattresses on the floor to sleep
on. "This whole thing has been a double cross," she had told me.
"We know who has been feeding everything to the press. When the
press destroys you, it is hard for anyone to ever believe you." The
person who she believed had double-crossed her husband was Alfredo Ortiz-Murias, the former associate of Roberto Polo who had
received one of his farewell calls. "We are united," she had said to
me about Roberto and her.

Marco and his father were also scornful about Alfredo Ortiz-
Murias. "He was always jealous of my brother," Marco said. Ortiz-
Murias was the principal witness in the suit brought against Polo
by Rostuca Holdings, Ltd., an offshore company operating out of
the Cayman Islands, whose money was managed by Polo's company, PAMG. It came out in the conversation that the man behind
the company known as Rostuca was the governor of one of the
poorest states in Mexico. I remembered Gaetano Berni saying to
me a few days earlier, about this same man, "What kind of person
has $20 million in U.S. dollars *in cash* outside his own country?
Even Mr. Agnelli or Mr. Henry Ford, when he was alive, did not
have $20 million in cash." He had grimaced and shaken his head.
The implication was clear.

"Will you tell me the circumstances of Roberto's arrest?" I asked
Marco.

"I have heard three stories. I do not know which one is the
truth," he replied, dismissing the subject.

I had heard several stories too, the first from Alfredo Ortiz-
Murias in New York, about his farewell call from Roberto. According to Ortiz-Murias, who had blown the whistle on Polo, Roberto
had said to him, "Good-bye, Alfredo. It's 6:30 A.M. in Europe. I am
sorry you felt that way about me. Good-bye." When I asked Ortiz-
Murias what his reaction to the call was, he said, "He was trying to
make me feel guilty."

I had also heard from Pablo Aramburuzabala, one of Polo's

investors, a well-to-do Mexican businessman whose wife is the god-mother of the Polos' daughter, that Roberto had called his house four times to say that he was going to commit suicide. "The first three times I was out, but my wife spoke to him. He was calling from a public telephone. When I talked with him, he said he had never done anything wrong. He gave me the address in Viareggio and said that I could call Interpol if I wanted. He said he was full of blood and didn't have too much time. Then he must have called his mother. She called me to say that Roberto was dead. She said she didn't know where to go to claim his body. I gave her the address in Viareggio. Then the brother, Marco, called from Tokyo. Marco said that Roberto had been picked up by an ambulance and was in the hospital in Viareggio."

Roberto Polo gave his own version of his arrest in a press release: "I ate some fish which apparently made me very sick, because early in the morning, I called my brother (who lives in Milan), who speaks Italian, in order to ask him to call the police station to have them send a doctor because I felt like I was dying. My brother, who has a friend in Viareggio, asked his friend to call the police in order that they send a doctor to see me. By the time the doctor arrived, I had already vomited and had some tea: I felt much better. However, the doctor took my blood pressure, stated that it was a bit high, then left. A few hours later (I was already dressed to go to the beach on my bicycle), the police returned without the doctor and asked me to go with them to the station. . . . I was interro-gated. . . . After that I was taken, handcuffed, to the prison where I am in Lucca."

It seems odd that a person wanted by the police in three coun-tries would call his brother in Milan to call the police in Viareggio to get a doctor for an attack of food poisoning. According to Gae-tano Berni, the Florentine lawyer, Roberto himself called for an ambulance. It seems odd also that nowhere in Polo's account of the events in Viareggio does he mention Fabrizio Bagaglini. Only Gaetano Berni would speak about Bagaglini when I brought up the name. He said, "Fabrizio stayed until the arrest." We will come to Fabrizio Bagaglini.

"Were you separated by a screen when you saw your brother?" I asked Marco Polo.

"No, we were able to embrace him."

"Was he wearing the ribbon?" Chantal Carr asked Marco.

"Yes," he replied.

Three weeks before Polo vanished, the French government had made him a Commander of the Order of the Arts and Letters in gratitude for his having donated to the Louvre Museum Fragonard's painting *The Adoration of the Shepherds* and a crown of gold, emeralds, and diamonds that had belonged to the Empress Eugénie.

"Does he wear a prison uniform?" I asked.

"No, he wears his own clothes. His body is clean. His clothes are clean. The place is filthy and horrible, but my brother looks classy. My brother is the classiest person I know."

In 1982 the Polos moved from a one-bedroom apartment on Lexington Avenue to a large Park Avenue apartment, for which they spent $450,000. That move signaled the beginning of their rise. They had a Botero in the dining room and a picture by Mary Cassatt of a woman reading *Le Figaro*, which Roberto later sold at Christie's for $1 million. "He took to buying paintings and then selling them a year later," said Alfredo Ortiz-Murias. "He had no attachment to anything. Everything he bought was for sale." Their only child, Marina, was born in 1983, while they were living in the Park Avenue apartment. The child's godfather was the Count of Odiel, whose wife is a cousin of the King of Spain. Early in 1984, Roberto bought a five-story town house on East Sixty-fourth Street for $2.7 million. Four years later, Ramona Colón, Polo's administrative assistant and office manager at the time of this purchase, stated in an affidavit filed with a New York civil suit, "I first became suspicious that not all of the clients' money was being invested as required. At that time Roberto directly or indirectly purchased a town house . . . and directed [an assistant] to transfer money, in the approximate amount of the purchase price of the town house, from clients' time deposits maturing at that time to an account at European American Bank on 41st Street, New York, and then to an account in the name of ITKA, at Crédit Suisse in the Bahamas. I believe that the ITKA account was Roberto Polo's personal account."

The redecorating of the new house from top to bottom—a job that would have normally taken anywhere from a year to two years —was done in six weeks, and Roberto was his own decorator. His men worked seven days a week, at the same frantic pace that his near neighbor Imelda Marcos had set when she did over her new town house on East Sixty-sixth Street in time to give a party for the international arms dealer Adnan Khashoggi. He brought special upholsterers from England to install the green damask on the library walls. People who watched Polo during this period said that he worked like a man possessed in creating the perfect setting, as if he knew that his good fortune couldn't last. The dark-paneled dining room on the first floor was large enough to seat thirty-six comfortably, and the living room on the floor above was the size of a small ballroom, with a white damask banquette along one wall and ample space to hang the young couple's astonishing and ever-growing art collection. He sold his Impressionist art to make room for his new and even more impressive collection of eighteenth-century French paintings, Fragonards and Bouchers and Vigée-Lebruns, mostly purchased through the Wildenstein gallery in New York. In order to get insurance for the paintings, he had to have steel shutters installed on all the windows; at the push of a button, these dropped and plunged the interior of the house into total darkness.

He also moved his offices. He had started PAMG in the bedroom of his apartment. Then he had shared a small office with several other people. Next he had taken space at 101 Park Avenue. Now he rented grand offices on the forty-third floor of the General Motors Building on Fifth Avenue.

More and more, Roberto Polo began to be talked about. His antiques buying at auctions and in shops in New York and Paris was nonstop, and he always paid the top prices. A former associate of his described Roberto on a spree in Paris, going from shop to shop, buying $3 million worth of antiques to stock Jacob Frères. On one occasion Rosa wore $6 million in emeralds. On another, she pushed her baby's stroller through Central Park wearing a T-shirt and jeans, the Ashoka diamond,and a million-dollar strand of pearls. Roberto, no slouch in the jewelry department himself, wore a ring with a 10.5-carat Burmese ruby worth over $1 million. He was so meticulous that when he bought a picture for his office he would have a picture hanger come from Wildenstein to install it. He was a terror at home; one out-of-place ashtray or a table not dusted properly could drive him into a rage. On the other hand, when he had people to lunch at the town house, in the midst of all that grandeur he might serve his guests grilled-cheese sandwiches on paper plates, which a servant would pick up from a nearby luncheonette. He could not stand to be alone; he even took people on the Concorde with him so that he would not have to fly alone. He ran his multimillion-dollar business mainly from his house, on one rotary telephone without even call waiting, and held meetings there in darkened rooms.

My second encounter with the glamorous Polos was at a charity ball for Casita Maria, the oldest Hispanic settlement house in New York. Apart from the ball for the Spanish Institute, the Casita Maria Fiesta is considered to be *the* Latin party of the year in New York. A new and interesting way for rich social aspirants to get their name known in smart circles is to underwrite charity parties, and in 1985 Polo underwrote the Casita Maria ball. It was the custom of Casita Maria to present three prominent people with gold medals, and in previous years honored guests had included Placido Domingo and Dame Margot Fonteyn. That year the honorees were the Colombian painter Fernando Botero, former secretary of the treasury William Simon, and the film star Maria Felix, who was enormously popular in Mexico but, unlike her sister star Dolores Del Rio, little known in the United States. People say that Polo had an obsession with this septuagenarian actress, whom he had met through his mother, and from whom he had purchased the Ashoka diamond as well as a diamond snake necklace of extraordinary workmanship made by Cartier, both of which adorned Rosa Polo that night.

At the last minute, Maria Felix canceled, informing the committee that she had broken her ankle. So Polo and his brother-in-law, Federico Suro, put together an eleven-minute montage of Felix's film clips as a substitute for the no-show star. He had promised the glittering crowd a celebrity, and he delivered instead badly edited clips, far too long and in Spanish. Soon the audience in the Grand Ballroom of the Plaza Hotel grew bored, and began to talk and laugh as if the film were not going on. Polo became petulant, then furious, and at the end of the film he went up to the microphone and berated the audience for their bad manners. He said he was glad Maria Felix was not there.

At this outburst, looks were exchanged across the tables, the kind of looks that clearly said, Who the hell is this little upstart to lecture us on manners? To make matters worse, Roberto's mother, who he had told people had once been an opera singer at La Scala, rose and applauded her son's speech.

"That night Roberto was finished in New York," said a Venezuelan society woman who resides in the city. Actually, he wasn't finished in New York that night. People with vast sums of money are never finished in social life as long as they keep picking up the checks, and Roberto Polo continued to pick up the checks for large dinners at Le Cirque and other fashionable restaurants, where he would sometimes order wine that cost a thousand dollars a bottle and take only a sip or two of it.

Some people are mesmerized by money. It covers all defects. Even people who suspected that something was not quite right about Polo overlooked his flaws and listened to him with rapt attention. Like a peacock, as soon as he met someone he wanted to impress, he would spread his feathers and show off all his colors, telling of his paintings, his furniture, his wife's jewels, his financial acumen, his social achievements. Often he would close this self-congratulatory catalog with the words "and only thirty-six"—his age at the time.

These same people, however, were beginning to speculate about who Roberto Polo was and where all his money came from. "We manage money for wealthy individuals," he would say. But talk was rampant that some of the money he managed was dirty money, meaning that he was laundering money, or drug-trafficking, or running arms. One former associate, however, who subsequently broke with him, told me he firmly believes that the clients' money was clean. The company served as financial adviser to a group of Mexicans, Latin Americans, and Europeans who happened to have money—often a great deal of money—in the United States. In most cases, however, it was illegal for these clients to have money invested secretly outside of their own country. In Spain, for instance, the government can confiscate all the Spanish holdings of an individual who has undeclared investments in the United States. At Citibank, where Polo had worked before founding PAMG, he became an account executive, but several times he was passed over for assistant vice president even though he attracted business to the bank. In 1981 he left to found his own company, which would serve the same function as the bank but with more personalized attention given to clients than the bank gave. PAMG arranged financial transactions for investors, and most of the money was in time deposits.

Although some former clients—Pablo Aramburuzabala, for one —say that they did not authorize Polo, or PAMG, to invest their money in art, Polo did entice new business to PAMG with a glossy brochure picturing his specialty in investments: paintings, jewels, and real estate. "Otherwise, his clients could have gone to Morgan Guaranty," said his lawyer Jacques Kam.

One of the great titans of Wall Street, who later refused to comment on his statement, is reported to have said about Roberto Polo, after meeting him at a small dinner party and listening to him talk, "There's something wrong. If there's that much money, I would have heard about him." He was echoing the old saying, "If they have the right kind of money, they're known at the bank."

"All of us, we may not know each other, but we know who each other is," said a New York social figure from a prominent Latin-American family, "and no one, not a single soul, knew anything about Roberto Polo or his family. Ask any of the Cubans we know. Never *heard* of Roberto Polo."

A New York fashion designer who was thinking of bringing out a fragrance backed by Polo was warned, "Do not touch him with the end of a barge pole."

Shortly after completing the town house, Polo gave a dinner for Amalita Fortabat, who is said to be the richest woman in Argentina. Many New York social figures attended. "Where did you get that fabulous Fragonard, Roberto?" someone asked him. "My parents brought it with them out of Cuba," he replied. People knew that wasn't the truth, but no one called him on it. "He bought the Fragonard at Wildenstein's, but he liked the old-money, old-family sound of his version of the acquisition," said a person who was present. Often he would point out a piece of his furniture by saying, "The twin to that is in Versailles."

Upper-class Cubans in New York and Florida are amazed by the stories Roberto Polo would tell of his family's background. "There is no mention of the Polo family in the old Social Registers from the days before Castro," said a Cuban lady in New York. Another said, "We know our own. The Polos were not in the clubs, and the boys did not go to either of the two schools everyone we know went to." Still another said, "He learned everything so fast. Just seven years ago, he was wearing black shoes and white socks." She paused and added, "He was always polite, very well mannered. I think he is to be admired for the myth he has created about himself. He really does think his family built all the oil refineries in Cuba. His family was perfectly nice—an engineer, or something like that, his father was—but they were certainly not a family that went about in social circles.

Like Imelda Marcos, who has spent a lifetime upgrading the circumstances of her birth, Polo had a tendency to paint a more aristocratic picture of his family than the truth would bear out. Even in stir, facing a long incarceration and sharing a cell and a toilet that doesn't work with two other prisoners, he issued a press release emphasizing the grandeur of his background. He quotes from early magazine articles written about him in which he was described as "the darkly handsome, wealth Cuban refugee, son of Countess Celis de Maceda." He describes his father as having been, "like his father before him," a "very rich playboy" in Cuba, as if—even if it were true, which it appears not to be—it were an admirable thing to be the son and grandson of wealthy playboys. He also says, "On my father's side of the family the wealth came from the construction business; they built various oil refineries and industrial plants for Standard Oil Company, the Bacardi plants in Nassau and Puerto Rico, and parts of the United Fruit Company in Costa Rica. . . . My mother's family was wealthy, but less than my father's. However, whatever wealth they missed (compared to my father's family) they made up in a more aristocratic, artistic, and generally more socially prominent background. . . . My mother's nobiliary title came to her as the oldest child in her family through her grandmother; I inherited this title, which I have never used nor pretend to (even though there are those who want to make me a social climber, hardly necessary given my higher education, refinement, and family upbringing relative to my American counterparts, because I am the oldest child in my family."

Roberto Polo was born in Havana on August 20, 1951, the older of two sons of Roberto Polo, an engineer, and his wife, Maria Teresa. The family fled Cuba in the wake of Castro and moved to Peru, where they suffered serious financial losses when the government nationalized their business. They then moved to Miami, where Roberto and Marco went to school. Their mother, a trained opera singer, became a hospital nutritionist after they left Cuba. An aspiring artist, Roberto attended the Corcoran School in Washington on a scholarship from age fourteen to eighteen, and then graduated from the American University in Washington, where he met his future wife's brother, Federico Suro. He studied philosophy and art. He moved to Montreal in order to avoid the draft for the Vietnam War, but he was later classified 4-F due to curvature of the spine and flat feet. He then got a master's degree in painting and sculpture at Columbia University, and while he was there he took his first job, at Rizzoli. After Columbia, he joined Citibank.

In an article in *Women's Wear Daily* this year, he said of his wife's family, "My in-laws are very wealthy. My wife's uncle was the president of the Dominican Republic. His name was Antonio Guzman. His brother died of cancer and left a huge fortune. I left Citibank to oversee that money." In fact, the Suro family is intellectually prominent and highly respected, but it is not a rich family. Dario Suro, Rosa Polo's father, is considered to be one of the greatest Dominican painters. He became the cultural attaché at the embassy in Washington in 1963, under Ambassador Enriquillo Del Rosario, who is now an ambassador to the United Nations. Rosa Polo's mother, Maruxa Suro, was the first cousin of the late president Antonio Guzman, but since the pay at the embassy was low, Mrs. Suro, in order to provide her children with a good education, worked for a time in the dress department of Lord & Taylor in Washington. Rosa, after moving to New York, studied first at the Harkness School of Ballet and then at the Joffrey Ballet school until she married Roberto in 1972.

Soon after Polo started in business for himself, old friends began

charm his way into French society with gifts and flowers, and he took tables in restaurants for fifteen or twenty people. Rosa became best friends with the wife of the antiques dealer Jean-Marie Rossi, who is the granddaughter of the late General Franco of Spain.

Polo hired the fashion consultant Eleanor Lambert to advise him on the buyout of the Miguel Cruz company. Cruz was paid a salary of $120,000 a year and a royalty on gross sales, although Polo claimed in an interview with *Women's Wear Daily* that he paid Cruz a minimum annual salary of $500,000. His intention was to vault Cruz into the ranks of the elite international designers of expensive ready-to-wear and to rival the houses of Giorgio Armani and Gianni Versace.

To launch the venture, Polo made an agreement with a retailer named Scarpa to turn her shops in Venice and Milan into Miguel Cruz boutiques. Scarpa received merchandise on consignment. Polo made a similar deal with a boutique owner on the island of Capri, and he paid $300,000 for the renovation of the shop. By the time the business opened, Polo had three boutiques, an office in the General Motors Building in New York with a rent of approximately $12,000 a month, and a showroom and warehouse in Milan. In spite of this huge overhead, Polo decided to launch an enormous advertising campaign. In the first season he spent $700,000 for media (media means buying space) and $30,000 on production. For the spring 1986 collection, there was an $800,000 advertising budget. For the fall 1986 collection, Polo spent $900,000 on advertising.

Consider, now, PAMG's contract with its investors: PAMG received a fee of one-half of 1 percent for managing an account. So on a $1 million account the annual fee would be $5,000. On a $100 million account, the fee would be $500,000. Therefore, people who worked for PAMG naturally began to wonder where the money was coming from to run the Miguel Cruz dress business as well as to cover Polo's continued buying of art and jewelry.

From the beginning, Polo played an active part in advertising and promotion, hiring the models, flying them to New York to be photographed, even staging the fashion shows. Fashion experts say that the campaign didn't work commercially, even if the photography was sometimes great. Like so much about Roberto Polo, his advertising sent out mixed signals; there was confusion as to whether he was selling his wares or his models. He claimed that he would make the name of Miguel Cruz known through the shock value of the ads. "We're living in a society that wants to be shocked," he told one interviewer. A Robert Mapplethorpe photograph for the Miguel Cruz men's line showed the back of a seated naked man removing a sweater over his head. For the women's line, a two-page ad showed a dimly lit female model in a black jeweled evening dress with one fully lit naked man behind her and another sitting on the floor in front of her.

It enraged Polo that while no one questioned the propriety of Calvin Klein's massively nude advertising campaign, which was going on at the same time, his own campaign was labeled prurient and offensive. "They object to my ads but not to Calvin Klein's." The advertisement showing the bull's-eye picture with the male rump may have offended one segment of the public, but a more lurid segment bombarded the New York office for copies of it.

Polo always knew more about everything than the experts. Soon he started directing Mapplethorpe's photo sessions, and Mapplethorpe, a bit of a prima donna himself, resented the interference. Eventually there was a falling-out, and Mapplethorpe resigned the account. Not to be topped, Polo wrote the photographer a letter firing him, and sent copies to several prominent people in New York.

Despite all the fanfare and hype, the Miguel Cruz line was a disaster almost from the beginning. The clothes were often badly made, delivery dates were missed, and orders were canceled. "I don't care about your four pages in Vogue—the clothes are not in my store" became a common complaint. It got to the point where the company was doing $1 million in advertising and only $100,000 in sales. In the fall of 1987, when all the collections of all the designers in Paris, New York, and Milan were showing skirts above the knee, Miguel Cruz was showing skirts down to the ankle. At that point Polo stepped in to give Cruz artistic advice on how the clothes should look, and he began writing memos telling him what colors and fabrics to use.

Unlike Polo's art acquisitions, which could be sold at a profit, the Miguel Cruz fashion venture was a bottomless pit. It is estimated that Polo lost between $12 million and $15 million on it, but he remained adamant in his belief that the clothes were beautiful and that the company was going to be a big success. He didn't want anyone to tell him the truth. He had a blind spot about Miguel Cruz, and he could not accept criticism. He thought that if he spent an enormous amount of money on advertising he should be rewarded with good reviews. He wrote irate letters to Polly Mellen of *Vogue* and Carrie Donovan of the *New York Times* threatening to pull his ads when they criticized the collections, and he had to be restrained from mailing a mocking letter to Hebe Dorsey, the late beloved fashion editor, demanding a retraction because she had mistakenly said Miguel Cruz designed in Rome in the fifties when she meant the sixties. He had the idea that American editors could be bought. One of the most powerful women in fashion, who asked that she not be identified, told me that on the morning after one of the collections was shown in Milan she received in her hotel room a box containing a full-length black coat lined in sable. She tried it on, modeled it in front of a mirror, wrapped it up again, and returned it to Roberto Polo at the Miguel Cruz office. A former employee told me that Hebe Dorsey had returned many such gifts.

Peter Dubow, the owner of a company called European Collections Inc., was hired by Polo as a consultant to use his retailing contacts to penetrate the American stores. Dubow, who, like a lot of Roberto Polo's employees, is still owed a great deal of money in salary and expenses, says, "The easy speculation is that Roberto didn't care if the collections weren't good, that he was simply getting dirty money back into circulation. But he did care. He cared passionately."

One day in Paris, in the magnificent apartment on Quai Anatole-France, Dubow said to Polo, "We need someone to stage the fashion shows. We need an art director for the advertising."

"That's what I do," replied Roberto quietly.

Trying another tack, Dubow said about the latest collection, "It's not good enough. It's totally lacking in commerciality." He even went a step further. "It is ugly, Roberto."

Polo said, "How many Fragonards do you own?"

"None," replied Dubow.

With a gesture, Polo indicated his possessions in the drawing room where they were seated. "Do you own furniture like this?"

"No," said Dubow.

"Well, I think Miguel's collection is beautiful," said Polo, in his superiority, settling the matter. "I cannot imagine how ready-to-wear can be any more beautiful than this."

It is a curious quirk of Roberto's business sense that he gave priority to the evening dresses he presented as free gifts to society women in New York to wear to publicized social functions at a time when stores he depended on for business were not getting their shipments on time and orders were being canceled. To set things right, Roberto hired his brother, Marco, to be chief of production for the fashion house. There had always been a rivalry between the two brothers, particularly for the affection of their mother, and it was she who asked Roberto to take Marco into the company. Marco had wanted to go into the investment side of Roberto's business, not the fashion side, because he thought he knew more about banking than Roberto did. "When I was a kid, I used to beat the shit out of my brother, and now he's this big man ordering me around," Marco complained to an American employee of the business. At Miguel Cruz, Marco did a good job of putting the business in order, but the quality of the workmanship remained poor and orders were rarely delivered on time.

Late in 1987, at a party in Milan for the opening of a collection, Polo met Fabrizio Bagaglini. A sometime actor, sometime model, the twenty-five-year-old Bagaglini became a dominant figure in the life of Roberto Polo over the next seven months, right up until Polo's actual arrest in Viareggio. Shortly after meeting Fabrizio, Polo hired him to do his public-relations work, although Bagaglini was not known to have any experience or skill in that field.

In an interview conducted before the warrant went out for Polo's arrest, but published after, Nadine Frey of *WWD* wrote, "As a last gesture, [Polo] gave a mini-tour of his apartment, as Barry White blared out of a speaker somewhere and a handsome Roman aide de camp hustled out to make a lunch reservation." Roberto showed off Fabrizio as if he were a painting. He told people that he wanted to make Fabrizio the vice president of the perfume company he was planning to start, to be called Le Parfum de Miguel Cruz.

Bagaglini began wearing Roberto's wristwatch, an eighteen-karat-gold Breitling, and Polo gave him a Ferrari Testarossa, worth $134,000, at a time when the unpaid bills and salaries at the Miguel Cruz office in New York amounted to $600,000. On several occasions, Polo said to my friends, "I have had three passions in my life: my wife, Rosa, my daughter, Marina, and Fabrizio." However, he persistently claimed that the friendship with Fabrizio was no more than a friendship.

Glamorous pictures of the glamorous Polos began appearing in all the fashionable magazines in France, usually showing them elegantly posed amid their museum-quality possessions. Elsewhere in the world, meanwhile, Mexican, Latin American, and European investors in PAMG were demanding to know where all the Polo money was coming from. "Roberto took too high a profile. He was too much in the papers, lived on far too grand a scale. His investors didn't like it, especially as he was living on a far grander scale than they," said Alfredo Ortiz-Murias, Polo's associate. Ortiz-Murias had at one time been Roberto's superior at Citibank. He had left the bank to form his own money-management firm, but, according to Polo, it had not done well, and he later joined PAMG, bringing his own clients with him. Ortiz-Murias claims to have introduced Roberto Polo to everyone in New York, but Polo says otherwise. The former associates are now bitter enemies.

Polo's behavior became more and more extreme. According to an employee of Miguel Cruz's men's wear in Milan, "The stories he told about himself became more and more fantastic, brilliant strokes of genius—how he had bought things at one price and sold them a short time later at enormous profits, like a pearl he bought for half a million dollars and resold for a million. He said, 'I always have $10 million in cash on hand.'"

Once, he showed up in the lobby of the Hotel Palace in Milan and requested twenty-five rooms for important people he was flying in to see the Miguel Cruz collection. The hotel, part of the CIGA hotel group, owned by the Aga Khan, was totally booked for the fashion week of the Milan collections and therefore unable to provide these accommodations. Polo made a loud scene. "Get the Aga Khan on the telephone!" he screamed indignantly.

He met Grace Jones and signed her up as a runway model for

three shows. At a time when the company was in serious trouble, he offered her $50,000 for each appearance. Jones wisely insisted on being paid in advance before each show.

He became a confider of intimate secrets, assuring each confidant that he or she was the only person he could trust. "I find that I wake up in a different bed each morning," he told an associate, who later discovered he had shared the same intimacy with his publicist and a number of friends. In October 1987, during the collections, he called several people, some he didn't even know very well, sobbing, saying he was getting a divorce. Rosa was said to be jealous of the female models in the shows, and at one point she packed and left Milan for Paris. There she remembered she had left her jewelry behind in the hotel safe, so she returned, and everything was all right between them again.

One observer told me that Polo got "weirder and weirder." He dieted down to 145 pounds and began to dye the hair on his chest.

Last February, amid persistent widespread rumors of imminent financial troubles, he appeared at a sale in Monte Carlo with Fabrizio Bagaglini and a whippet dog and paid $500,000 for a pair of chairs by the French furniture-maker Sené, chairs so rare that they could not be taken out of France.

That same month, Pablo Aramburuzabala, who had been Roberto Polo's first major client and who had a sort of father-son relationship with him, flew from Mexico to Paris to confront him about all the rumors. "The investors were nervous and not happy hearing all the publicity he was getting, being described as a Cuban-American millionaire," he told me. "He didn't have time to make that kind of money unless he was doing something wrong. People start to do little things and get away with it, and then start to take more and more. I gave him his chance. My wife is the godmother of his daughter. I met Roberto at Citibank. Then he started being money manager with me. It was just a matter of calling several banks to see which bank gave the best interest. I would see him four times a year, and he would tell me how my portfolio was. In February I asked him, 'Do you have financial problems?' He said no. He said that Mr. Ortiz-Murias was making trouble. I said to him, 'I don't think you have that kind of money.' I never authorized him to deal with art. He said that he had a syndicate of people for buying art. He told me he was managing a billion dollars. When I commented on Rosa's jewels, I was told that some of her jewels were lent by jewelers as a way of advertising. I said to him, 'I need some money. You have to give me some money back.' After a while I received part of it, not even 30 percent of the amount. Later, another small part, even smaller than the previous payment. I realized that things were in terrible shape. He promised to come to Mexico to straighten things out, but he never came."

The New York office of Miguel Cruz was run on money that was sent each month from Geneva. It took approximately $200,000 a month to keep the New York end of the business going, and more often than not only half that amount was sent. Salaries and bills went unpaid. By the end of 1987 there were bills in excess of $1 million. "A lot of people have been hurt by the unpaid bills, including Miguel Cruz himself," said Peter Dubow. "Miguel always paid his bills, and the matter was highly embarrassing for him."

In the fall of 1987, Roberto Polo made his biggest play for social recognition, as well as a last-ditch bid to promote the flailing fashion line, by underwriting two famous balls, the Save Venice ball in Venice to help restore the Church of Santa Maria dei Miracoli, followed seventeen days later by the Chantilly Ball in France to benefit the Institute of France. They attracted the crème de la crème of international society. With rumors everywhere that he was financially strapped, Polo spent over $600,000—some say closer to a million—on the two events. In addition, it was reported in society columns that he flew guests from all over the world by private jet to attend the parties. The talk of the Save Venice ball was Rosa Polo's jewels, in all the colors. She swam each day in the swimming pool of the Hotel Cipriani in a different bathing suit with a necklace of precious stones to match. Meanwhile, the people in the warehouse in Milan had to pass the hat to pay for the gasoline to get the collection to the Chantilly Ball. After that they sent the collection to New York for the fashion week there, but the New York office didn't have the money to get it out of customs.

Polo's hope, apparently, was that his new perfume company would rescue his collapsing empire. At a cost of nearly $1 million, he built a new office for Le Parfum de Miguel Cruz on Avenue Marceau in Paris. He hired as the president of the company

Jacques Bergerac, the fifties movie star, who had been married to Ginger Rogers and Dorothy Malone, and who had more recently —before the takeover by Ronald Perelman—been a high-ranking executive at Revlon. He also hired the New York architectural and design firm of de Marsillac Plunkett to design the bottles and packaging. He himself played an important part in choosing the scents for the perfume. The perfume business, however, is considered a seven-to-one shot for success, and it usually takes two to three years before profits begin to show. To finance Le Parfum and perhaps to settle with his disgruntled investors, who were beginning to demand their money back, Polo is reported to have sold $22 million in jewels between February and May.

He drew more international press by announcing that he had donated to the Louvre the Empress Eugénie crown, valued at $2.5 million, and Fragonard's *The Adoration of the Shepherds*, valued at between $2.5 million and $5 million. At a well-publicized ceremony attended by sixty guests in evening clothes, the French government expressed its gratitude by making him a Commander of the Order of Arts and Letters.

Next Polo announced that he was putting his famous collection of eighteenth-century French paintings up for sale. In what is thought to have been an I'll-pat-your-back-if-you-pat-mine gesture, Pierre Rosenberg, the distinguished curator of paintings at the Louvre, wrote the preface to the catalog for the sale, even though it is frowned on in museum circles for museum people to become involved in such commercial enterprises. To counteract the speculation that he was selling his collection to meet the demands of his investors, or to save his failing dress business, or to finance his perfume business, Roberto Polo wrote the foreword to the beautiful catalog, in which he said, "Collectors can be divided into two groups: those who satisfy their appetite by the endless accumulation of things and those who are most excited by the 'hunt,' the search and research of things. The latter kind of collector satisfies his appetite and curiosity for the collectible once he has it and squeezes out of it, as from a ripe fruit, all the juice that it has to give, then moves on to a different collectible . . . I am one of those collectors." Polo said he expected the sale to bring in between $18 million and $20 million.

.   .   .

When Alfredo Ortiz-Murias returned home from the Venice and Chantilly balls, he observed to Ramona Colón that he had seen a change in Roberto's personality. Ramona Colón told him that she thought Roberto had been transferring clients' money to "third parties." Ortiz-Murias claims that that was his first knowledge of malfeasance on the part of Polo. Colón stated in her affidavit that Polo would direct her to transfer a client's time deposit to the PAMG-NY account and then to the ITKA account. "I noticed that some client time deposit cards were marked 'PAMG' in Roberto's handwriting. Although these time deposit cards were regularly updated and statements sent to the clients continued to report these time deposits, I believe that the entries and statements were fraudulent and that the time deposits no longer existed. . . . Sometime in mid-1984, I calculated the total shown on all cards marked 'PAMG' and the total was about $37 million." Colón also stated in her affidavit, "I saw Roberto take home shopping bags full of client transfer records and other client information. Since I worked with the files on a daily basis, I know he never brought the records or information back. On one occasion, when Alfredo Ortiz-Murias requested some information on one of his clients and the record could not be found, Roberto explained that he had probably burned it in his fireplace by mistake. Also, during that time, Roberto instructed me to erase all the time deposit computer records. He told me that if they could not be erased, he would throw the computers into the river. Following Roberto's instructions, I contacted a man at Commercial Software, Inc., and he instructed me on how to erase the computer records, which I did."

Alfredo Ortiz-Murias began to notify his own clients and others that there was trouble, and the clients began to place calls on their assets, meaning, in layman's terms, they wanted their money back, immediately. In one of his letters from prison, Polo has said, "Rostuca advised PAMG in December 1987 that it wished to terminate its relationship; the other clients did the same in April and May of 1988; this means that PAMG was in the obligation to repay its clients between December of 1988 and June of 1989, at the earliest. Now as before this scandal, PAMG is prepared to pre-pay, but

Alfredo is not interested, because as he said, 'I hate Roberto. I only want his blood.' "

When too many of Polo's investors demanded their money at the same time, it was like a run on the bank. He could not meet their demands. But that, his defenders say, did not make him a crook.

A Swiss arrest warrant was issued on April 30. The Swiss were expecting Polo to appear at the opening of the exhibition of twenty-six paintings that were to be auctioned on May 30, but he didn't show up. In the meantime the Swiss judge got in touch with the French police, and an international arrest warrant was issued. At that time Polo made a call from Paris to Milan from a street telephone. "Don't call me at home," he said. "The telephones are tapped."

On May 8, Roberto Polo and Fabrizio Bagaglini were in Haiti. Polo intended to start a new collection of pictures to replace his collection of French masterpieces. An American friend, Kurt Thometz, and his wife were in Paris at the time. They visited the Polo apartment and said there were already between thirty-five and forty Haitian paintings in one room. Roberto was also buying Dominican art, including some new works by his father-in-law.

On May 11, Polo was seen at a jewel auction in Geneva, selling.

On May 12, he was seen in the South of France with Rosa, Fabrizio, the child, the nanny, and Julio Cordero, Rosa's cousin, who was the manager of the Geneva office, and his wife.

On May 15, the group was in Monte Carlo, and Polo's life seemed out of control. With an international warrant out for his arrest, he arrived that afternoon at the Hôtel de Paris apartment of Baby Monteiro de Carvalho, the richest man in Brazil, to watch the Grand Prix, which raced by in the square below. He was accompanied by Rosa, Marina, and Fabrizio, and other guests commented that he seemed harassed.

On May 16, police entered the office of the Miguel Cruz perfume company in Paris and told the staff that Roberto Polo was under arrest. The feeling, according to Ortiz-Murias, is that perhaps the employees alerted Polo. He and his family returned from the South of France that night. Rosa and the child went to the apartment, but Roberto did not. Instead he went to a hotel.

On May 17, Roberto disappeared.

On May 18, at nine o'clock in the morning, the police and detectives walked into the Polo apartment. Rosa was there. The police seized $26 million in furniture and paintings, leaving her with only two mattresses on the floor. Rosa asked the police if she could keep her engagement ring, and they let her.

The Ferrari Testarossa was seized in Monte Carlo.

In the days that followed, several people in New York had direct-dial overseas calls from Polo. Eleanor Lambert told me, "He didn't give his name. He simply said, 'You know who this is, don't you?' I said yes, and he went on to say that all the stories about him were lies spread by Alfredo Ortiz-Murias, and that in time his name would be cleared." People who knew him best said that he would not allow the police to catch him, that he would take sleeping pills.

"I wouldn't be surprised if he was dead," said an antiques dealer in New York.

"A suicide?" I asked.

"No, murdered."

"Murdered?"

"You must understand that there are a lot of people who don't want him to be found, because he could incriminate them."

In addition to the investors who did not want to be identified, several of the antiques dealers Polo did business with in Europe were said to have been paid partially in their own country and partially in Switzerland, a practice not only frowned upon but considered criminal in some countries.

The whereabouts of Roberto Polo and Fabrizio Bagaglini between May 16 and the end of June, when they turned up in Viareggio, remains a mystery, although the most persistent speculation at the time, later proved incorrect, was that they were in Peru, Chile, or Brazil. Alfredo Ortiz-Murias believes that Polo was hiding out in an apartment in Paris, because Rosa Polo, who was then under surveillance, left her apartment each afternoon and went to the Hôtel Ritz on the Place Vendôme to use the public telephone, presumably to call her husband. In on of the press releases Polo wrote from the prison in Lucca, he says about this period, "Prior to going to Viareggio, I had been in my apartment in Monte Carlo, at the Hôtel de Paris (also in Monte Carlo), at the Hôtel Hermitage (also in Monte Carlo), at Hôtel Le Richemond in Geneva (registered in my name), and before that in Port-au-Prince in Haiti with friends and Santo Domingo, Dominican Republic, with family." There is no doubt that he was in all those places, but earlier than May 16. There is further speculation that the French police did not want to make the arrest in France because a nephew of President Mitterand, Maxime Mitterand, was an employee in the Geneva office of PAMG, Ltd.

On May 30, the auction of Polo's French masterpieces went on in Paris as scheduled. Five days earlier, Ader Picard Tajan, the auctioneer, had called a press conference to explain that the sale would be a "forced one" and that he would be the "receiver" for the courts. Surprisingly, the highly publicized sale did not draw crowds. The $14 million realized from it was $3.4 million less than had been expected. There was talk in art circles that if the works donated to the Louvre by Polo had been purchased with money that was not his own the Louvre would have to return them.

After Polo's arrest in Viareggio, Fabrizio Bagaglini returned to Rome, where he remained for two weeks. From there he went to Paris and then on to London with a rich Argentinean girlfriend.

As of this writing, Roberto Polo has been denied bail by the Italians. Here in America, in addition to the ongoing investigations reportedly being conducted by the IRS and the SEC, the FBI is now allegedly involved in collecting evidence to see if there has been mail fraud, if, as Ramona Colón claimed in her affidavit, Polo sent false statements to his investors each month. On East Sixty-fourth Street in Manhattan, the gray stucco Italianate front of the Polo's town house is cracked and peeling. Inside, the lights stay on day and night. All the furniture is gone except for a set of six upholstered chairs, a chaise longue, and a sofa, all covered in chintz, that were left behind in the sitting room of the master bedroom, and an Aubusson rug, folded in one corner. On the front door is a notice that says, "Warning: "U.S. Government seizure. This property has been seized for non-payment of internal revenue taxes, due from Roberto Polo, by virtue of levy issued by the District Director of the Internal Revenue Service."

From prison Roberto Polo wrote me saying he was reading *One Hundred Years of Solitude* while awaiting the determination of his fate. He also issues communiqués and ultimatums, as if he were in the best bargaining position. In response to the criticism that his life-style surpassed that of the people whose money he handled, he wrote, "It is quite stupid to state that my lifestyle is better than that of my clients: I have a better education and sense of the quality of life, as well as make more money than any of them singly! Does the President or Chairman of the Board of Citibank, for example, live better than most of the bank's clients? Of course he does! PAMG, Ltd. has clients who are worth U.S. $20,000,000, but who don't know any better than to buy their clothes at Alexander's when they visit New York or who dine at coffee shops!"

From Mexico City, Pablo Aramburuzabala said, "Yesterday Polo said that if we didn't accept his offer to accept the money that had already been frozen he was going to tell everyone who we were. I said that my money is not dirty money. He can go ahead and tell."

In New York, Alfredo Ortiz-Murias says he has received irate calls from Roberto Polo's mother in Miami. She says she will not rest until she sees Alfredo in jail. Chantal Carr has become engaged to Marco Polo. Rosa Polo continues to live with Marina in the stripped-down apartment in Paris. The Miguel Cruz fashion house is defunct, and the perfume company is at a standstill. Everyone is waiting.

Jacques Kam, Polo's French lawyer, told me when he was in New York on the case, "There are many things in the stories that are quite wrong, 100 percent wrong." He added, "It is not the round that counts. It is the match. This whole case could boomerang."

Like the people who danced the nights away in the various discotheques of Imelda Marcos and then, after her fall from grace, pretended not to have known her, or claimed to have only met her, many of the recipients of Roberto Polo's largess act now as if the Polos had been no more than passing acquaintances, although they attended their parties and accepted free evening dresses from the ill-fated Miguel Cruz collections. Such is life in the fast lane. There are those, however, who remember Roberto Polo differently, for example the Chilean painter Benjamin Lira and his artist wife, Francisca Sutil. "The Roberto Polo we know doesn't match with this man we have been reading and hearing about," Lira said.

They remember their friend Roberto as a devout family man and a loving and generous friend, with whom they went to concerts and films and galleries, and with whom they spent long evenings in their loft or in the Polos' town house, discussing art.

"Roberto's understanding of art goes far beyond taste," said Francisca Sutil. Eleanor Lambert agreed: "He was not just showing off. He was someone with real destiny. He could have been one of the great authorities on art, another Bernard Berenson."

October 1988

DANSE MACABRE

The Rockefeller and the Ballet Boys

Thereis no one, not even his severest detractor, and let me tell you at the outset of this tale that he has a great many severe detractors, who will not concede that Raymundo de Larrain, who sometimes uses the questionable title of the Marquis de Larrain, is, or at least was, before he took the road to riches by marrying a Rockefeller heiress nearly forty years his senior, a man of considerable talent, who, if he had persevered in his artistic pursuits, might have made a name for himself on his own merit. Instead his name, long a fixture in the international social columns, is today at the center of the latest in a rash of contested-will controversies in which wildly rich American families go to court to slug it out publicly for millions of dollars left to upstart spouses the same age as or, in this case, younger than the disinherited adult children.

The most interesting person in this story is the late possessor of the now disputed millions, Margaret Strong de Cuevas de Larrain, who died in Madrid on December 2, 1985, at the age of eighty-eight, and the key name to keep in mind is the magical one of Rockefeller. Margaret de Larrain had two children, Elizabeth and John, from her first marriage, to the Marquis George de Cuevas. The children do not know the whereabouts of her remains, or even whether she was, as a member of the family put it, incinerated in Madrid. What they do know is that during the eight years of their octogenarian mother's marriage to Raymundo de Larrain, her enormous real-estate holdings, which included adjoining town houses in New York, an apartment in Paris, a country house in France, a villa in Tuscany, and a resort home in Palm Beach, were given away or sold, although she had been known throughout her life to hate parting with any of her belongings, even the most insubstantial things. At the time of her second marriage, in 1977, she had assets of approximately $30 million (some estimates go as high as $60 million), including 350,000 shares of Exxon stock in a custodian account at the Chase Manhattan Bank. The location of the Exxon shares is currently unknown, and documents presented by her widower show that his late wife's assets amount to only $400,000. Although these sums may seem modest in terms of today's billion-dollar fortunes, Margaret, at the time of her inheritance, was considered one of the richest women in the world. There are two wills in question: a 1968 will leaving the fortune to the children and a 1980 will leaving it to the widower. In the upcoming court case, the children, who are fifty-eight and fifty-six years old, are charging that the will submitted by de Larrain, who is fifty-two, represents "a massive fraud on an aging, physically ill, trusting lady."

Although Margaret Strong de Cuevas de Larrain was a reluctant news figure for five decades, the facts of her birth, her fortune, and the kind of men she married denied her the privacy she craved. However, her children, Elizabeth, known as Bessie, and John, have so successfully guarded their privacy, as well as that of their children, that they are practically anonymous in the social world in which they were raised. John de Cuevas, who has been described as almost a hermit, has never used the title of marquis. He is now divorced from his second wife, Sylvia Iolas de Cuevas, the niece of the art dealer Alexander Iolas, who was a friend of his father. His only child is a daughter from that marriage, now in her twenties. He maintains homes in St. James, Long Island, and Cambridge, Massachusetts, where he teaches scientific writing at Harvard. Bessie de Cuevas, a sculptor whose work resembles that of Archipenko, lives in New York City and East Hampton, Long Island. She is also divorced, and has one daughter, twenty-two, by her second husband, Joel Carmichael, the editor of *Midstream*, a Zionist magazine so reactionary that it recently published an article accusing the pope of being soft on Marxism. Friends of Bessie de Cuevas told me that she was never bothered by the short financial reins her mother kept her on, because she did not fall prey to fortune hunters the way her sister heiresses, like Sunny von Bülow, did.

Margaret Strong de Cuevas de Larrain, the twice-titled American heiress, grew up very much like a character in a Henry James novel. In fact, Henry James, as well as William James, visited her father's villa outside Florence when she was young. Margaret was the only child of Bessie Rockefeller, the eldest of John D. Rockefeller's five children, and Charles Augustus Strong, a philosopher and psychologist, whose father, Augustus Hopkins Strong, a Baptist clergyman and theologian, had been a great friend of old Rockefeller. A mark of the brilliance of Margaret's father was that, while at Harvard, he competed with fellow student George Santayana for a scholarship at a German university and won. He then shared the scholarship with Santayana, who remained his lifelong friend. Margaret was born in New York, but the family moved shortly thereafter to Paris. When Margaret was nine her mother died, and Strong, who never remarried, built his villa in Fiesole, outside Florence. There, in a dour and austere atmosphere, surrounded by intellectuals and philosophers, he raised his daughter and wrote scholarly books. His world provided very little amusement for a child, and no frivolity.

Each year Margaret returned to the United States to see her grandfather, with whom she maintained a good relationship, and to visit her Rockefeller cousins. Old John D. was amused by his serious and foreign granddaughter, who spoke several languages and went to school in England. Later, she was one of only three women attending Cambridge University, where she studied chemistry. Never, even as a young girl, could she have been considered attractive. She was big, bulky, and shy, and until the age of twenty-eight she always wore variations of the same modest sailor dress.

Her father was eager for her to marry, and toward that end Margaret went to Paris to live, although she had few prospects in sight. Following the Russian Revolution there was an influx of Russian émigrés into Paris, and Margaret Strong developed a fascination for them that remained with her all her life. She was most excited to meet the tall and elegant Prince Felix Yusupov, the assassin of Rasputin, who was said to have used his beautiful wife, Princess Irina, as a lure to attract the womanizing Rasputin to his palace on the night of the murder. In Paris, Prince Yusupov had taken to wearing pink rouge and green eyeshadow, and he supported himself by heading up a house of couture called Irfé, a combination of the first syllables of his and his wife's names. Into this hothouse of fashion, one day in 1927, walked the thirty-year-old, prim, studious, and unfashionable Rockefeller heiress. At that time Prince Yusupov had working for him an epicene and penniless young Chilean named George de Cuevas, who was, according to friends who remember him from that period, "extremely amusing and lively." He spoke with a strong Spanish accent and expressed himself in a wildly camp manner hitherto totally unknown to the sheltered lady. The story goes that at first Margaret mistook George de Cuevas for the prince. "What do you do at the couture?" she asked. "I'm the saleslady," he replied. The plain, timid heiress was enchanted with him, and promptly fell in love, thereby establishing what would be a lifelong predilection for flamboyant, effete men. The improbable pair were married in 1928.

From then on Margaret abandoned almost all intellectual activity. She stepped out of the pages of a Henry James novel into the pages of a Ronald Firbank novel. If her father had been the dominant figure of her maidenhood, George de Cuevas was the controlling force of her adult existence. Their life became more and more frivolous, capricious, and eccentric. Through her husband she discovered an exotic new world that centered on the arts, especially the ballet, for which George had a deep and abiding passion. Their beautiful apartment on the Quai Voltaire, filled with pets and bibelots and opulent furnishings, became a gathering place for the *haute bohème* of Paris, as did their country house in St.-Germain-en-Laye, where their daughter, Bessie, was born in 1929. Their son, John, was born two years later. Along the way the title of marquis was granted by, or purchased from, the King of Spain. The Chilean son of a Spanish father, George de Cuevas is listed in some dance manuals as the eighth Marquis de Piedrablanca de Guana de Cuevas, but the wife of a Spanish grandee, who wished not to be identified, told me that the title was laughed at in Spain. Nonetheless, the Marquis and Marquesa de Cuevas remained a highly visible couple on the international and artistic scenes for the next thirty years.

When World War II broke out, they moved to the United States. Margaret, already a collector of real estate, began to add to her holdings. She bought a town house on East Sixty-eighth Street in New York, a mansion in Palm Beach, and a weekend place in

Bernardsville, New Jersey. She also acquired a house in Riverdale, New York, which they never lived in but visited, and one in New Mexico to be used in the event the United States was invaded. In New York, Margaret always kept a rented limousine, and sometimes two, all day every day in front of her house in case she wanted to go out.

Although Margaret had inherited a vast fortune, she was to inherit a vaster one through the persistence of her husband. George de Cuevas's wooing of his wife's grandfather, old John D. Rockefeller, turned Margaret from a rich woman into a very rich woman. While John D. had bestowed liberal inheritances on his four daughters during their lifetimes, he believed in primogeniture, and in his late seventies he turned over the bulk of his $500 million fortune to his only son, John D. Rockefeller, Jr., the father of Abby, John D. III, Nelson, Laurence, Winthrop, and David. He retained the income for himself. Margaret at the that time was indifferent to her inheritance, but George, for whom the prospect of Rockefeller millions had surely been a lure in his choice of a life mate, was not one to sit back and watch what he felt should be his wife's share pass on to her already very rich Rockefeller cousins. He set about to charm his grandfather-in-law, and charm him he did. He even became his golfing companion. Rockefeller had never come across such a person as this eccentric bird of paradise that his granddaughter had married. Surprisingly, he not only was amused by him but genuinely liked him. The family legend goes that one day George took Bessie and John by the hand to the old man and said, "Do you want to see your great-grandchildren starve because their mother has not been taken care of the way the rest of the Rockefellers have been?" The tycoon calmly assured him that Margaret would be provided for. Old John D. then began investing his enormous income in the stock market and in the last years of his life made a second fortune, the bulk of which he left to Margaret on his death, when she was forty years old.

In 1940, in Toms River, New Jersey, George de Cuevas became an American citizen and renounced his Spanish title, claiming he would henceforth be known as merely George de Cuevas. However, he continued to be referred to by his title, and once his role as a ballet impresario grew to international prominence, he changed the name of the company associated with him throughout his career from the Ballet de Monte Carlo to the Grand Ballet du Marquis de Cuevas. From 1947 to 1960 the marquis toured the company all over the world, with the financial support of his wife, who donated 15 percent of her income to his troupe. He introduced American dancers to France and French dancers to America, and soon became a beloved figure in the dance world. The impresario Sol Hurok in his biography described him as "a colorful gentleman of taste and culture . . . perhaps the outstanding example we have today of the sincere and talented amateur in and patron of the arts."

Actually, de Cuevas is better remembered for one episode of histrionics and temperament than for any of his productions. In 1958 the dancer and choreographer Serge Lifar, then fifty-two years old, became angry when the marquis's company changed the choreography of his ballet *Black and White*. After a heated exchange of words the marquis, who was seventy-two at the time, slapped Lifar in the face with a handkerchief in public and then refused to apologize. Lifar challenged de Cuevas to a duel, and the marquis accepted. Although neither of the combatants was known as a swordsman, épées were chosen as the weapons. The location of the duel was to be kept secret because dueling was outlawed in France, but more than fifty tipped-off reporters and photographers showed up at the scene. The encounter was scheduled to last until blood was drawn. For the first four minutes of the duel Serge Lifar leapt about while the marquis remained stationary. In the third round the marquis forced Lifar back by simply advancing with his sword held straight out in front of him, and pinked his opponent. It was not clear, according to newspaper accounts of the duel, whether skill or accident brought the marquis's blade into contact with Lifar's arm. "Blood has flowed! Honor is saved!" cried Lifar. Both men burst into tears and rushed to embrace each other. Reporting the event on its front page, the *New York Times* said that the affair "might well have been the most delicate encounter in the history of French dueling."

As a couple, the Marquis and Marquesa de Cuevas became increasingly eccentric. "It was unconventional, their marriage, but, curiously, it worked," said Viscountess Jacqueline de Ribes, who was a frequent guest in their Paris apartment. "There were always people waiting in the hall to have an audience—it was like a court," said one family member. Another longtime observer of the inner workings of the de Cuevas household, Jean Pierre Laclouche, said, "Margaret was always in her room during the parties. She hated coming out, but usually she finally did. She gave in to all of George's pranks. She didn't care. He made life interesting around her." George de Cuevas often received visitors lying in bed wearing a black velvet robe with a sable collar and surrounded by his nine or ten Pekingese dogs, while Margaret grew more and more reclusive and slovenly in her dress. She always wore black and kept an in-residence dressmaker to make the same dress for her over and over again. When she traveled to Europe, she would book passage on as many as six ships and then be unable to make up her mind as to which she wanted to sail. If she wanted to go from Palm Beach to New York, she would book seats on every train for a week, and then not be able to make the commitment to move. Once, unable to secure a last-minute booking on a Paris-Biarritz train and determined to leave, no matter what, she piled her daughter, her maid, ten Pekingese dogs, and her luggage into a Paris taxicab and had the driver drive her the five hundred miles to Biarritz. The trip took three days.

George de Cuevas liked to entertain, and he filled their homes with society figures, titles, celebrated artists and dancers, and a constant flow of Russian émigrés. "At the Cuevas parties were such as the Queen Mother of Egypt, Maria Callas, and, of course, Salvador Dalí, who was a regular in the house," said Mafalda Davis, an Egyptian-born public-relations woman who was a great friend of George de Cuevas. George was a giver of gifts. He bought old furs and jewels from the poor Russians in Paris and gave them away as presents. He gave the Viscountess de Ribes a sable coat, and he gave Mrs. Gurney Munn of Palm Beach a watch on which he had had engraved "May the ticking of this watch remind you of the beauty of a faithful heart."

Somehow, in the midst of this affluent chaos on two continents, Bessie and John de Cuevas were raised. A relative of the family told me that Margaret had a good and strong relationship with her children. "Not a peasant-type relationship," he said, "not conventional," meaning, as I understood him, not many hugs and kisses, but strong in its way. Another relative said, "After a short period with her children—and later with her grandchildren—she was ready to send them out to play or to turn them over to their nanny. Margaret, who throughout her life was notorious for never being on time, arrived so late for her daughter's coming-out party at the Plaza Hotel in New York, which was attended by all of her Rockefeller relations, that she almost missed it. When Bessie was seventeen she met Hubert Faure, who became her first husband. "She was an extraordinary-looking person," said Faure about his former wife, with whom he has retained a close friendship. "English-American in intellect with a Spanish vitality behind that." Hubert Faure, now the chairman of United Technology, was not at the time considered a catch by the Marquis de Cuevas, who wanted his daughter to marry a Spanish grandee and possess a great title. But Bessie exhibited an early independence: she went ahead and married Faure in Paris in 1948, when she was nineteen, with no family and only another couple in attendance. John, her brother, was also married for the first time at an early age. The children, as Bessie and John are regularly referred to in the upcoming court case with Raymundo de Larrain, have at times shown a bemused attitude about their life. Once, when questioned about her nationality, Bessie described herself as a third-generation expatriate. John, during a brief Wall Street career, was asked by a colleague if he could possibly be related to a mad marquesa of the same name. "Yes," he is said to have replied, "she is a very distant mother."

The apex of the social career of George de Cuevas was reached in 1953 with a masked ball he gave in Biarritz; it vied with the Venetian masked ball given by Carlos de Beistegui in 1951 as the most elaborate fete of the decade. France at the time was paralyzed by a general strike. No planes or trains were running. Undaunted, the international nomads, with their couturier-designed eighteenth-century costumes tucked into their steamer trunks, made their way across Europe like migrating birds to participate in the *tableaux vivants* at the Marquis de Cuevas's ball, an event so extravagant that it was criticized by both the Vatican and the left wing. "People talked about it for months before," remembered Josephine Hartford Bryce, the A&P heiress, who recently donated her costume from the ball to the Metropolitan Museum of Art. "Everyone was dying to go to it. The costumes were fantastic, and people spent most of the evening just staring at each other." As they say in those circles, "everyone" came. Elsa Maxwell dressed as a man. The Duchess of Argyll, on the arm of the duke, who would later divorce her in the messiest divorce in the history of British society, came dressed as an angel. Ann Woodward, of the New York Woodwards, slapped a woman she thought was dancing too often with her husband, William, whom she was to shoot and kill two years later. King Peter of Yugoslavia waltzed with a diamond-tiaraed Merle Oberon. And at the center of it all was the Marquis George de Cuevas, in gold lamé with a headdress of grapes and towering ostrich plums, who presided as the King of Nature. He was surrounded by the Four Seasons, in the costumed persons of the Count Charles de Ganay; Princess Marella Caracciolo, who would soon become the wife of Fiat king Gianni Agnelli; Bessie, his daughter; and her then husband, Hubert Faure. As always, Margaret de Cuevas did the unexpected. For days beforehand, her costume, designed by the great couturier Pierre Balmain, who had paid her the honor of coming to her for fittings, hung, like a presence, on a dress dummy in the hallway of the de Cuevas residence in Biarritz. But Margaret did not appear at the ball, although, of course, she paid for it. She may have been an unlikely Rockefeller, but she was still a Rockefeller, and the opulence, extravagance, and sheer size (four thousand people were asked and two thousand accepted) of the event offended her. She simply disappeared that night, and the party went on without her. She did, however, watch the arrival of the guests from a hidden location, and a much repeated, but unconfirmed story is that she sent her maid to the ball dressed in her Balmain costume.

George de Cuevas increasingly made his life and many homes available to a series of young male worldlings who enjoyed the company of older men. In the early 1950s Margaret de Cuevas purchased the town house adjoining hers on East Sixty-eighth Street in New York. The confirmation-of-sale letter from the realty firm of Douglas L. Elliman & Co. contained a cautionary line: "The Marquessa detests publicity and would appreciate it if her name weren't divulged." An unkind novel by Theodora Keogh, called *The Double Door*, depicted the marriage of George and Margaret and their teenage daughter. The double door of the title referred to the point of access between the two adjoining houses, beyond which the wife of the main character, a flamboyant nobleman, was not permitted to go, although the houses were hers. The drama of the novel revolved around the teenage daughter's clandestine romance with one of the handsome young men beyond the double door. Inevitably, the marriage of George and Margaret de Cuevas began to founder, and for the most part they occupied their various residences at different times. They maintained close communication, however, and Margaret would often call George in Paris or Cannes from New York or Palm Beach to deal with a domestic problem. Once when the marquesa's temperamental chef in Palm Beach became enraged at one of her unreasonable demands and threw her breakfast tray at her, she called her husband in Paris and asked him to call the chef and beseech him not only to quit but also to bring her another breakfast, because she was hungry. George finally persuaded the chef to recook the breakfast, but the man refused to carry it to Margaret. A maid in the house had to do that.

At this point in the story, Raymundo de Larrain entered the picture. "Raymundo is not just a little Chilean," said a lady of fashion in Paris about him. "He is from one of the four greatest families in Chile. The Larrains are aristocratic people, a better family by far than the de Cuevas family." Whatever he was, Raymundo de Larrain wanted to be something more than just another bachelor from Chile seeking extra-man status in Paris society. He was talented, brilliant, and wildly extravagant, and soon began making a name for himself designing costumes and sets for George de Cuevas's ballet company. A protégé of the marquis's to start with, he soon became known as his nephew. An acquaintance who knew de Larrain at that time recalled that the card on the door of his sublet apartment first read M. Larrain. Later it became M. de Larrain. Later still it became the Marquis de Larrain.

In Bessie de Cuevas's affidavit in the upcoming probate proceedings, she emphatically states that although various newspapers have described de Larrain as the nephew of her father and suggested that he was raised by her parents, there was no blood relation between the two men. In a letter to an American friend in Paris, she wrote, "He is not my father's nephew. I think he planted the word long ago in Suzy's column. If there is any relationship at all, it is so remote as to be meaningless." Yet as recently as November, when I spoke with de Larrain in Palm Beach, he referred to George de Cuevas as "my uncle." That fact of the matter is that Raymundo de Larrain has been described as a de Cuevas nephew and has been using the title of marquis for years, and he was on a familiar basis with all members of the de Cuevas family. Longtime acquaintances in Paris remember Raymundo calling Margaret de Cuevas Tante Margaret or, sometimes, perhaps in levity, Tante Rockefeller. In her book *The Case of Salvador Dalí*, Fleur Cowles described the Dalí set in Paris as follows: "On May 9, 1957, the young nephew of the Marquis de Cuevas gave a ball in honor of the Dalís. According to Maggi Nolan, the social editor of the *Paris Herald-Tribune*, the Marquis Raymundo de Larrain's ball was 'unforgettable' in the apartment which had been converted . . . into a vast party confection," with "the most fabulous gala-attired members of international society." Fleur Cowles then went on to list the guests, including in their number the Marquis de Cuevas himself, without his wife, and M. and Mme. Hubert Faure, his daughter and son-in-law. Although Cowles did not say so, George de Cuevas almost certainly paid for Raymundo's ball.

Along the way de Larrain met the Viscountess Jacqueline de Ribes, one of the grandest ladies in Paris society and a ballet enthusiast to boot. "Before Jacqueline, no one had ever heard of Raymundo de Larrain except as a nephew of de Cuevas. Jacqueline was his stepping-stone into society," said another lady of international social fame who did not wish to be identified. The viscountess became an earlier admirer of his talent, and they entered into a close relationship that was to continue for years, sharing an interest in clothes and fashion as well as the ballet. Raymundo de Larrain is said to have made Jacqueline de Ribes over and given her the look that has remained her trademark for several decades. A famous photograph taken by Richard Avedon in 1961 shows the two of them in exotic matching profiles. At a charity party in New

York known as the Embassy Ball, chaired by the Viscountess de Ribes, Mrs. Winston Guest, and the American-born Princess d'Arenberg, Raymundo de Larrain's fantastical butterfly décor was so extravagant that there was no money left for the charity that was meant to benefit from the event. In time the viscountess became known as the godmother of the ballet, and she, more than any other person, pushed the career of Raymundo de Larrain.

After the publication of *The Double Door*, the de Cuevases were often the subject of gossip in the sophisticated society in which they moved, but somehow they had the ability to keep scandal within the family perimeter. The relationship of both husband and wife with the unsavory Jan de Vroom, however, almost caused their peculiar habits to be open to public scrutiny. A family member said to me that at this point in Margaret de Cuevas's life she fell into a nest of vipers. Born in Dutch Indonesia, Jan de Vroom was a tall, blond adventurer who dominated drawing rooms by sheer force of personality rather than good looks. A wit, storyteller, and linguist, he had en eye for the main chance, and like a great many young men before him looking for the easy ride, he attached himself to George de Cuevas. De Vroom was quick to realize on which side the bread was buttered in the de Cuevas household, and, to the distress of the marquis, who soon grew to distrust him, he shifted his attentions to Margaret, whom he followed to the United States. At first Margaret was not disposed to like him, but, undeterred by her initial snubs, he schooled himself in Mozart, whom he knew to be her favorite composer, and soon found favor with her as a fellow Mozart addict. He got a small apartment in a brownstone a few blocks from Margaret's houses on East Sixty-eighth Street and was always available when she needed a companion for dinner. She set him up in business, as an importer of Italian glass and lamps. From Europe, George de Cuevas tried to break up the deepening intimacy, but Margaret, egged on by her friend Florence Gould, ignored her husband's protests. As the friendship grew, so did de Vroom's store of acquisitions. He was a sportsman, and through Margaret de Cuevas's bounty he soon owned a sleek sailing boat, a fleet of Ferrari cars, a Rolls-Royce, and—briefly, until it crashed—an airplane. He also acquired an important collection of rare watches.

Raymundo de Larrain and Jan de Vroom detested each other, and Jan, in the years when he was in favor with Margaret, refused to have Raymundo around. De Vroom had no wish to join the ranks of men who made their fortune at the altar; he was content to play the rule of son to Margaret, a sort of naughty-boy son whose peccadilloes she easily forgave. A mixer in the darker worlds of New York and Florida, he entertained her with stories of his sub-terranean adventures. Often, in her own homes, she would be the only woman present at a dining table full of men who were disinterested in women.

In 1960 the Marquis de Cuevas, in failing health, offered Raymundo de Larrain, with whom he was now on the closest terms, the chance to create a whole new production of *The Sleeping Beauty*, to be performed at the Théatre des Champs Élysées. De Larrain's *Sleeping Beauty* is still remembered as one of the most beautiful ballet productions of all time, and it was the greatest box-office success the company had ever experienced. The marquis was permitted by his physicians to attend the premiere. "If I am going to die, I will die backstage," he said. After the performance he was pushed out onto the stage in a wheelchair and received a standing ovation. George de Cuevas attended every performance up until two weeks before his death. He died at his favorite of the many de Cuevas homes, Les Délices, in Cannes, on February 22, 1961. Margaret, who was in New York, did not visit her husband of thirty-three years in the months of his decline. In his will George left the house in Cannes to his Argentinean secretary, Horacio Guerrico, but Margaret was displeased with her husband's bequest and managed to get the house back from the secretary in exchange for money and several objects of value.

Although Margaret had never truly shared her husband's passion for the ballet, or for the ballet company bearing his name, which she had financed for so many years, she did not immediately dis-band it after his death. Instead she appointed Raymundo de Lar-rain the new head of the company. There was always a sense of dilettantism about George de Cuevas's role as a Maecenas of the dance—not dissimilar to the role Rebekah Harkness would later play with her ballet company. The taste and caprices of the mar-quis determined the policy of the company, which relied on the box-office appeal of big-star names. This same sense of dilettantism carried over into de Larrain's contribution. The de Cuevas company has been described to me by one balletomane as ballet for people who normally despise ballet, ballet for society audiences, as opposed to dance audiences.

De Larrain's stewardship of the company was brief but not undramatic. In June 1961 he played a significant role in the political defection of Rudolf Nureyev at the Paris airport when the Kirov Ballet of Leningrad was leaving France. The story has become romanticized over the years, and everyone's version of it differs. According to de Larrain, Nureyev had confessed to Clara Saint, a half-Chilean, half-Argentinean friend of de Larrain's, that he would rather commit suicide than go back to Russia. In one account, Clara Saint, feigning undying love for the departing star, screamed out to Nureyev that she must have one more kiss from him before he boarded the plane and returned to his homeland. Nureyev went back to kiss her, jumped over the barriers, and escaped in a waiting car as the plane carrying the company took off. De Larrain says that Clara Saint had alerted the French authorities that there was going to be a defection, and she advised Nureyev during a farewell drink at the airport bar that he must ask the French police at the departure gate for political asylum. He says that Nureyev spat in the face of the Russian security official. For a while Nureyev lived in de Larrain's Paris apartment, and the first time he danced after his defection was for the de Cuevas company, in de Larrain's production of *The Sleeping Beauty*. "He danced like a god, but he also had a spectacular story," de Larrain told me. At one of his first performances the balcony was filled with communists, who pelted the stage with tomatoes and almost caused a riot. People who were present that night remember that Nureyev continued to dance through the barrage, as if he were unaware of the commotion, until the performance was finally halted.

In Raymundo de Larrain's affidavit for the probate, he assesses his role in Nureyev's career in an I'm-not-the-nobody tone: "With the help of Margaret de Cuevas we made him into one of the biggest stars in the history of ballet." The professional association between de Larrain and Nureyev, which might have saved the de Cuevas ballet, did not last, just as most of de Larrain's professional associations did not last. "Raymundo and Rudolf did not have the same point of view on beauty and the theater, and they fought," explained the Viscountess de Ribes in Paris recently. "Raymundo had great talent and tremendous imagination. He had the talent to be a stage director, but neither the health nor the courage to fight. He was very unrealistic. He didn't know how to talk to people. He was too grand. What Raymundo is is a total aesthete, not an intellectual. He wanted to live around beautiful things. He was very generous and gave beautiful presents. Even the smallest gift he ever gave me was perfect, absolutely perfect," she said. Another friend of de Larrain's said, "Raymundo had more taste and knowledge of dancing than anyone. His problem was that he was unprofessional. He couldn't get along with people. He had no discipline over himself." When the Marquesa de Cuevas decided in 1962 not to underwrite the ballet company any longer, it was disbanded. Then, under the sponsorship of the Viscountess de Ribes, de Larrain formed his own ballet company. He began by producing and directing *Cinderella*, in which he featured Geraldine Chaplin in a modest but much publicized role. The viscountess, however, couldn't afford for long to underwrite a ballet company, and withdrew after two years. Raymundo de Larrain then took to photographing celebrities for *Vogue, Town & Country,* and *Life.* His friends say that he had one obsession: to "make it" in the eyes of his family back in Chile. He mailed every newspaper clipping about himself to his mother, for whom, de Ribes says, "he had a passion."

For years Margaret de Cuevas's physical appearance had been deteriorating. Never the slightest bit interested in fashion or style, she began to assume the look of what has been described to me by some as a millionairess bag lady and by others as the Madwoman of Chaillot. "Before Fellini she was Fellini," said Count Vega del Ren about her, but other assessments were less romantic. Her nails were uncared for. Her teeth were in a deplorable state. She had knee problems that gave her difficulty in walking. She covered her face with a white paste and white powder, and she blackened her eyes in an eccentric way that made people think she had put her thumb and fingers in a full ashtray and rubbed them around her eyes. Her hair was dyed black with reddish tinges, and around her head she always wore a black net scarf, which she tied beneath her chin. She wrapped handkerchiefs and ribbons around her wrists to hide her diamonds, and her black dresses were frequently stained with food and spilled white powder and held together with safety pins. For shoes she wore either sneakers or a pair of pink polyester bedroom slippers, which were often on the wrong feet. Her lateness had reached a point where dinner guests would sit for several hours waiting for her to make an appearance, while Marcel, her butler of forty-five years, would pass them five or six times, carrying a martini on a silver tray to the marquesa's room. "She drank much too much for an old lady," one of her frequent guests told me. Finally her arrival for dinner would be heralded by the barking of her Pekingese dogs, and she would enter the dining room preceded by her favorite of them, Happy, who had a twisted neck and a glass eye and walked with a limp as the result of a stroke.

Her behavior also was increasingly eccentric. In her bedroom she had ten radios sitting on tables and chests of drawers. Each radio was set to a different music station—country-and-western, rock 'n' roll, classical—and when she wanted to hear music she would ring for Marcel and point to the radio she wished him to turn on. For years she paid for rooms at the Westbury Hotel for a group of White Russians she had taken under her wing.

In the meantime Jan de Vroom had grown increasingly alcoholic and pill-dependent. "If someone's eyes are dilated, does that mean they're taking drugs?" Margaret asked a friend of de Vroom's. "I've been too kind to him. I've spoiled him." Young men—mostly hustlers and drug dealers—paraded in and out of his apartment at all hours of the day and night. In 1973 two hustlers, whom he knew, rang the bell of his New York apartment. On a previous visit they had asked him for a loan of $2,000, and he had refused. When de Vroom answered the bell, they sent up a thug to frighten him and demand money again. Jan de Vroom, in keeping with his character, aggravated the thug and incited him to rage. A French houseguest found de Vroom's body: his throat had been cut, and he had been stabbed over and over again. Although he was known to be the person closest to Margaret de Cuevas at that time in her life, her name was not brought into any of the lurid accounts of his murder in the tabloid papers. De Vroom's body, covered from the chin down to conceal his slit throat, lay in an open casket in the Westbury Room of the Frank E. Campbell Funeral Chapel at Madison Avenue and Eighty-first Street. Except for a few of the curious, there were no visitors. A little-known fact of the sordid situation was that, through the intercession of Margaret de Cuevas, the body was laid to rest in the Rockefeller cemetery in Pocantico Hills, the family estate, although subsequently it was shipped to Holland. The killers were caught and tried. There was no public outcry over the unsavory killing, and they received brief sentences. It is said that one of them still frequents the bars in New York.

Into this void in the life of the Marquesa Margaret de Cuevas moved Raymundo de Larrain. People meeting Margaret de Cuevas for the first time at this point were inclined to think that the cultivated lady was not intelligent, because she was unable to converse in the way people in society converse, and they suspected that she might be combining sedatives and drink. The same people are uniform in their praise of Raymundo de Larrain during this time. For parties at her house in New York, Raymundo would invite the guests and order the food and arrange the flowers, in much the same way that her late husband had during their marriage, and no one would argue the point that Raymundo surrounded her with a better crowd of people than Jan de Vroom ever had. He would choreograph a steady stream of handpicked guests to Margaret's side during the evening. " 'Go and sit with Tante Margaret and talk with her, and I will send someone over in ten minutes to relieve you,' " a frequent guest told me he used to say. "He was lovely to her." Another view of Raymundo at this time came from a New York lady who also visited the house: "He was so talented, Raymundo. Such a sense of fantasy. But he got sidetracked into money-grubbing." Whatever the interpretation, Margaret de Cuevas and Raymundo became the Harold and Maude of the Upper East Side and Palm Beach. Bessie de Cuevas, in her affidavit, acknowledges that "Raymundo was always attentive and extremely helpful to my mother, particularly in her social life, which consisted almost exclusively of gatherings and entertainments at her various residences."

On April 25, 1977, at the oceanfront estate of Mr. and Mrs.

Wilson C. Lucom in Palm Beach, the Marquesa Margaret de Cuevas, then eighty years old, married Raymundo de Larrain, then forty-two, in a hastily arranged surprise ceremony. The wedding was such a closely guarded secret that Margaret de Cuevas's children, Bessie and John, did not know of it until they read about it in Suzy's column in the New York *Daily News*. Bessie de Cuevas's friends say that she felt betrayed by Raymundo because he had not told her of his plans to marry her mother. Among the prominent guests present at the wedding were Rose Kennedy, Mrs. Winston Guest, and Mary Sanford, known as the queen of Palm Beach, who that night gave the newlyweds a wedding reception at her estate. In her affidavit Bessie de Cuevas states, "I had visited with my mother at some length at her home in New York just about two months before. She was clearly aging but we talked along quite well about personal and family things. She said she would be leaving soon to spend some time at her home in Florida. She did not in any way suggest that she was considering getting married. After I read the article, I called her at once in Florida. She could only speak briefly and seemed vague. I assured her that of course my brother John and I wanted anything that would make her comfortable and happy, but why, I asked, did she do it this way. Her reply was simply, 'It just happened.' "

Wilson C. Lucom, the host of the wedding, was also married to an older woman, the since-deceased Willys-Overland automobile heiress Virginia Willys. Lucom, who had trained as a lawyer, never practiced law but had served on the staff of the late secretary of state Edward Stettinius. Shortly after the wedding, in response to an inquiry from the Rockefeller family, he sent a Mailgram to John D. Rockefeller III, the first cousin of Margaret Strong de Cuevas de Larrain, stating his position as the representative of the marquesa and now of de Larrain. "Do not worry about her or be concerned about any rumors you may have heard," the Mailgram read. "She was married at our house with my wife and myself as witnesses. It was a solemn ceremony, and she was highly competent and knew precisely that she was being married and did so of her own free will being of sound mind." Bessie de Cuevas says in her affidavit, "I had never met or heard my mother speak of Mr. Lucom."

For the wedding, Raymundo told friends, he gave his bride a wheelchair and new teeth. He also supervised a transformation of her appearance. "You must understand this: Raymundo cleaned Margaret up. Why, her nails were manicured for the first time in years." He got rid of the white makeup and blackened eyes, and he supervised her hair, nails, cosmetics, and dress. "Margaret was never better cared for" is a remark made over and over about her after her marriage. De Larrain would invite people to lunch or for drinks and wheel her out to greet her guests; he basked in the compliments paid to his wife on her new appearance. However, lawyers for the Chase Manhattan Bank, which represents Bessie and John de Cuevas's interests, told me that the two health-care professionals who cared for the marquesa at different times in 1980 and 1982 recalled that de Larrain did not spend much time with his wife, and that she would often ask about him. But when attention was paid by him, it would be lavish; he would send roses in great quantity or do her makeup. Since he had arranged it so that no one would become close to his wife, "she was particularly vulnerable to such displays of charm and affection." During her second marriage, she became known as Margaret Rockefeller de Larrain. Although this was illustrious-sounding, it was incorrect, for it implied that she was born Margaret Rockefeller rather than Margaret Strong. "The snobbishness and enhancement were de Larrain's," sniffed a friend of her daughter's.

Shortly after the marriage, Sylvia de Cuevas, the then wife of John de Cuevas, took the marquesa's two granddaughters to visit her in Palm Beach. She says she was stopped at the front door by an armed guard, who would not let them enter until permission was granted by Raymundo. Soon other changes began to take place. Old servants who had been with the marquesa for years, including her favorite, Marcel, were fired by de Larrain. Bessie de Cuevas claims in her affidavit that he accused them of stealing and other misdeeds. Long-term relationships with lawyers and accountants were severed. Copies of correspondence to the marquesa from Richard Weldon, her lawyer for many years, and Albert Remmert, her secretary and financial adviser for many years, reflect that her directives to them were so unlike her usual method of communication that they questioned the authority of the letters.

Shortly thereafter both men were replaced. Another longtime secretary, Lillian Grappone, told Bessie de Cuevas that her mother
had complained of the fact that there were constantly new faces
around her. During this period the many houses of the marquesa
were sold or given to charity, among them her two houses on East
Sixty-eighth Street in New York, which had always been her favorite as well as her principal residence. Bessie de Cuevas claims in
her affidavit that her mother sometimes could not recall signing
anything to effect the transfer of these houses. At other times she
would talk as if she could get them back. On one occasion she
acknowledged having signed away the houses but said she had been
talked into it at a time when she was not feeling well. Her father's
villa in Fiesole, where she had grown up, was given to Georgetown
University. The house in Cannes was given to Bessie and John de
Cuevas. Her official residence was moved from New York to Florida, but she was moved out of her house of many years on El Bravo
Way in Palm Beach to a condominium on South Ocean Boulevard.
Several people who visited her at the condominium said that she
seemed confused as to why she should be living there instead of in
her own house. Other friends explain the move as a practical one:
The house on El Bravo Way was an old Spanish-style one on several floors and many levels, badly in need of repair, and for an
invalid in a wheelchair life was simpler in the one-floor apartment.
  During this period the financial affairs of the marquesa were
handled more and more by Wilson C. Lucom, the host at the
wedding. Bessie de Cuevas states in her affidavit, "I think my mother's belief that Lucom would safeguard her interests against de
Larrain only highlights her lack of appreciation for the reality of
her circumstances." Bessie de Cuevas tells of an occasion when she
visited her mother at the Palm Beach condominium and Lucom
"taunted" her by boasting that he and de Larrain were drinking
"Rockefeller champagne." "My mother's total dependence on de
Larrain is reflected in an explanation she gave for why she did not
accompany de Larrain to Paris on a trip he made concerning her
holdings there. De Larrain told her no American carrier flew to
Paris any longer, and since my mother did not care for Air France,
it was best for her not to go. Plainly, my mother had lost any
independent touch with the real world."

Access to her mother became more and more difficult for Bessie de Cuevas. When she called, she was told her mother could not come to the telephone. Some friends who visited the marquesa say that she would complain that she never heard from her daughter. Others say that messages left by Bessie were never given to her. In 1982 Raymundo de Larrain took his wife out of the country, and they began what lawyers representing the de Cuevases' interests call an "itinerant existence." She never returned. They went first to Switzerland, then to Chile, where he was from and where they had built a house, and finally to Madrid, where de Larrain was made the cultural attaché at the Chilean embassy. There Margaret died in a hotel room in 1985. Bessie de Cuevas saw her mother for the last time a few weeks before she died. Neither Bessie nor her brother has any idea where she is buried.

Certainly there was trouble between the Rockefeller family and the newlywed de Larrains from the time of the marriage. After the change of residence from New York to Florida, David Rockefeller urged his cousin to donate her two town houses at 52 and 54 East Sixty-eighth Street to an institution supported by the Rockefeller family called the Center for Inter-American Relations. The appraisal of the two houses was arranged by David Rockefeller, and the appraiser had been in the employ of the Rockefellers for years. He evaluated the two houses at $725,000. Subsequently Margaret de Larrain was distressed to hear that these properties, which she had donated to the Center for Inter-American Relations, were later sold to another favorite Rockefeller forum, the Council on Foreign Relations, for more than twice the amount of money they had been appraised at.

Raymundo de Larrain, in his affidavit for the probate proceedings, says that his wife's male Rockefeller cousins discriminated against the females of the family. "Not only did her cousin-trustee [John D. Rockefeller III] want to dominate her life and tell her how to spend her trust income, but wanted also to dictate and approve how she spent her non-trust personal principal and income. My wife strongly resented their intrusion in her personal life. . . . Her position was that her money was hers outright, not part of her trust, and that she and she alone was to decide how she spent it or what gifts she—not they—would make." Later in the affidavit, de Larrain says that his wife's trustees "wanted her to give virtually all her personal wealth away to her children long before she even thought of dying. Then they would control her through their control of her trust income."

De Larrain said that his wife had been generous with her two children, but that they were not satisfied with her gifts of millions to them. "They wanted more and more." After giving her children more than $7 million, she refused to transfer her personal wealth to them. Even after her gift of $7 million, he claimed, the trustees cut her trust income. "My wife was shocked and distressed at the unjust and cruel and illegal actions of the cousin-trustees in pressuring her to give millions to her children and then breaking their agreement not to cut her trust income. This further alienated her from her family. She felt cheated and a victim of a plan by the family and the Chase Manhattan Bank."

On February 21, 1978, a year after her marriage, Margaret de Larrain, at age eighty-one, revoked all prior wills and codicils executed by her. "I have personally destroyed the original wills in my possession, namely, two original wills dated February 14, 1941, and an original will dated April 26, 1950, and an original will dated May 14, 1956, and an original will dated May 17, 1968, and an original will dated June 11, 1968." Thereafter, Margaret de Larrain added two codicils to a new will of November 20, 1980. In the first, she stated that she had already transferred her fortune to her husband, and she made him the sole beneficiary and sole personal representative of her estate. In the second, she expressed her specific wish that her only two children and two grandchildren receive nothing. De Larrain ended his affidavit with this statement: "There is abundant testimony that my wife was entirely competent when she later added the two codicils which expressed that she wanted to give the property to me, her husband. She did this because her children neglected her and she had provided abundantly for them in her lifetime by giving them approximately $7 million in gifts."

It might be added that Margaret's will did not set a precedent in the stodgy Rockefeller family. Her mother's sister, Edith Rockefeller McCormick, who divorced her husband, Henry Fowler McCormick, heir to the International Harvester fortune, and then engaged in a series of flamboyant affairs with male secretaries, which caused her father great embarrassment, in 1932 bequeathed half of her fortune to a Swiss secretary.

Pending the upcoming court case, Raymundo de Larrain has dropped out of public view. When he is in Paris, he lives at the Meurice Hotel, but even his closest friends there, including the Viscountess de Ribes, do not hear from him, and he has dropped completely out of the smart social life that he once pursued so vigorously. On encountering Hubert Faure, the first husband of Bessie de Cuevas, in the bar of the Meurice recently, he turned his back on him. In Madrid he stays sometimes at the Palace Hotel and sometimes at less well known ones. He has been seen dining alone in restaurants there. Sometimes he nods to former acquaintances, but he makes no attempt to renew friendships. He has also been seen in Rabat and Lausanne. In the past year he has made two substantial gifts to charity. He gave a check for $1 million to the Spanish Institute in New York, and, as a member of the board of the Spanish Institute said at a New York party, "The check didn't bounce." He also recently gave a check for $500,000 to Georgetown University to supplement the gift of his late wife's father's villa in Fiesole to Georgetown. "You have to figure that if Raymundo gave a million dollars to the Spanish Institute *before* the trial, he must have already squirreled away at least $10 million," said a dubious Raymundo follower in Paris recently.

This is not a sad story. The deprived will not go hungry. If the courts are able to ascertain what happened to Margaret Strong de Cuevas de Larrain's fortune in the years of her marriage and to decide on an equitable distribution of her wealth, already rich people will get richer. As a woman friend of Raymundo de Larrain said to me recently, "Raymundo will be bad in court, nervous and insecure. If there's a jury, the jury won't like him." She thought a bit and then added, "It's only going to end up wrong. If you don't behave correctly, nothing turns out well. I mean, would you like to fight the Rockefellers, darling?"

February 1987

THE WINDSOR
EPILOGUE

O N APRIL 2, 1987, in Geneva, A. Alfred Taubman, the Michigan mall millionaire who has become the *grand seigneur* of the auction world, put on an auction which, for sheer showmanship, rivaled the finest hours of the late P. T. Barnum, the *grand seigneur* of the circus world, who immodestly called his circus the greatest show on earth. Mr. Taubman, no shrinking violet himself, pitched his tent, or rather his red-and-white striped marquee, on the banks of Lake Geneva and papered the house with some of the grandest names in the *Almanach de Gotha*—nonbidders, to be sure, but the swellest dress extras in auction history. Sprinkled among the princesses, the countesses, the baronesses, and an infanta were the buyers who meant business: dealers from New York and London, Japanese businessmen, a Hollywood divorce lawyer, representatives of the Sultan of Brunei and Prince Bernhard of the Netherlands, not to mention a battery of bidders who, because they did not wish to travel or like to be looked at, were connected by phone to Sotheby's in New York and Geneva. Under the red-and-white striped marquee, after six months of an unparalleled publicity blitz, the gavel was finally raised on the opening lot of the sale of the jewels and love tokens of the late Duchess of Windsor, the American woman from Baltimore for whom a king gave up his throne. What followed was a jewel auction against which all jewel auctions to come will be compared.

In the month preceding the sale, the jewels, which I heard an English woman in Geneva describe as "frighteningly chic," traveled from Paris, where they had been under the protectorship of Maître Suzanne Blum, the Duchess's lawyer and a key figure in the story, to Palm Beach and New York—all with great fanfare and hype generated by Sotheby's, the 243-year-old London-based auction house which took over New York's Parke-Bernet Galleries in 1964, in order to woo the rich Americans who were expected to be the chief buyers in Geneva. In both cities, Alfred Taubman, the owner and chairman of Sotheby's since 1983, hosted smart parties so that all the right people, like Mrs. Astor and Malcolm Forbes and the other heavy hitters, might have a leisurely view of the treasure trove that a besotted monarch has showered on his twice-divorced ladylove. Mr. Taubman, a hale and hearty sixty-two, whose assets are estimated in the *Forbes*-magazine list of the four hundred richest people in America at $800 million, and his beautiful younger wife, Judy, a former Miss Israel who once worked behind the counter at Christie's, the rival auction house, handing out catalogs, are high-profile figures on the New York and Palm Beach Social circuits. "Selling art is a lot like selling root beer," he once said.

Duchess fever swept New York. "The romance of the twentieth century," we heard over and over. In actual fact, it was not a romance that can bear very close scrutiny: the love story of a masculine woman of middle age, who was probably never once called beautiful in her life, and a Peter Pan king, who resisted responsibility and composed embarrassing love letters. "A boy loves a girl more and more and is holding her so tight these trying days of waiting," he wrote to her when he was forty-two. Be that as it may, royal romance was in the air. By day the hoi polloi, willing to wait in line for three or four hours just to pass by the jewel-filled vitrines, turned out in such record numbers that the *New York Times* reported the event on its front page. Public interest was so great that Sotheby's desisted from running advertisements in the newspapers and cut back plans to show the jewels on local television shows because the security force at the auction house could not handle any more people than were already jamming its halls.

Although the British press reported even more avidly than ours every detail of the presale hype, the traveling jewel show bypassed England. From a public-relations point of view, Sotheby's felt it best not to open old wounds or to stir up adverse criticism when such big bucks were at stake. Fifty years after Edward VIII gave up his throne for the woman he loved, his duchess, even in death, remains a controversial figure in that country, still disliked and still unforgiven by a generation that blames her for taking away from them a beloved king. A close friend of Princess Margaret, brimming with insider information straight from the palace, informed me, "The royal family hated her. Simply hated her."

Her American admirers felt very differently, of course. As one of them said to me in Geneva, "The English didn't get her. The English still don't get her. They should erect a statue to Wallis Windsor in every town in the realm for taking away their king."

The Duchess's sale lasted two days. The Hôtel Beau-Rivage, where Sotheby's is, was where the action was, but the Hôtel Richemond, directly next door, was unmistakably smarter. That was where the Taubmans stayed. The sale of the Duchess's jewelry was also the occasion of a Sotheby's board-of-directors meeting, and the Sotheby's board of directors, as assembled by Alfred Taubman, is the swellest board of directors in big business today, boasting such illustrious names as Her Royal Highness the Infanta Pilar de Borbón, Duchess of Badajoz, who happens to be the sister of the King of Spain, for starters, as well as the Right Honourable the Earl of Gowrie, the Earl of Westmorland, and Baron Hans Heinrich Thyssen-Bornemisza de Kaszon, who has the largest private art collection in the world after the Queen of England's, and such Americans as Henry Ford II, Mrs. Gordon Getty, and Mrs. Milton Petrie.

Society girls in the employ of Sotheby's, wearing black dresses and single strands of pearls, bristled with self-importance as they manned the telephones, dispensed press badges, sold catalogs, and gave terse replies to queries. The bars in both hotels were never not full, and the gossip was terrific, although not always reliable. "Absolutely not!" one indignant upper-class voice, overbrandied, rang out. "I don't care what you've heard! The Duchess of Windsor was not a man!"

Always, following the death of a prominent person, individuals come forward claiming to have had a closer acquaintance with the deceased than the facts would bear out. One favorite preoccupation among the insiders was minimizing the degree of familiarity certain people claimed to have had with the late Duke and Duchess. "So-and-so," they said, talking about a highly profiled man in New York, "was not nearly so close to the duchess as he says he was. The Duke would never have had him around." Or, "I visited the Duchess for years and I never once heard her mention So-and-so," naming an international lady.

A thousand smartly dressed people piled into the tent to find their ticketed seats, all carrying the glossiest and most gossipy auction catalog ever printed. At fifty dollars a copy, it promptly sold out, and is now a collector's item. Friends met. Men greeted men with kisses on both cheeks, and women did the same. On closed-circuit television sets around the tent a film was shown, but no one watched, because they were all looking at one another. "The world was fascinated by them," intoned a voice on the sound track, "and they were obsessed with each other. . . . The Prince of Wales's father, George V, had Mrs. Simpson's past investigated and decided she was not a suitable companion for his son. . . . Queen Mary called her an adventuress." Year after year of newsreels of their glittering and empty life flashed by: weekends at Fort Belvedere when the Duke was still king, their somber wedding at the Château de Candé, the two of them arriving here, arriving there, fashion plates both, stepping out of limousines, waving from the decks of ocean liners, sweeping into parties, relentlessly up to the moment, in all the very jewels that were about to be sold, the Duchess leading, the Duke following, she gleaming, he scowling, or smiling sadly. Behind it all, a voice sang, "The party's over. It's all over, my friend." But no one was listening either, because they were all talking to each other. The Princess of Naples, married to Victor Emmanuel, who would have been the king of Italy if history had gone another way, chatted up Prince Dimitri of Yugoslavia, who works for Sotheby's jewelry department, while his brother, Prince Serge of Yugoslavia, chatted up the Baroness Tita Thyssen-Bornemisza, ablaze in sapphires, who chatted up the Countess of Romanoes, who was wearing the diamond bracelet she had inherited from the Duchess of Windsor and who in turn chatted up the Infanta Beatriz of Spain, who chatted up Grace, Countess of Dudley, who chatted up Princess Firyal of Jordan, who chatted up Judy Taubman, while her husband, Alfred Taubman, the *grand seigneur,* radiating power and importance, carried a huge unlit cigar and smiled and waved and greeted.

Then the auction began.

From the first of the 306 lots, a gold-ruby-and-sapphire clip made by Cartier in Paris in 1946, the air in the tent was charged with excitement. A few moments later, lot 13, a diamond clip lorgnette by Van Cleef & Arpels, circa 1935, which was estimated to bring in $5,000, went to a private bidder for $117,000. The excitement began to build. Two lots later, when a pair of pavé diamond cuff links and three buttons and a stud, estimated to go for $10,000, went for $440,000 to a mysterious, deeply tanned man who was said to be bidding for the Egyptian who has taken over the Windsors' house outside Paris, the first applause broke out in the tent. People realized they were present at an event, engaged in the heady adventure of watching rich people acting rich, participating in a rite available only to them, the spending of big money, without a moment's hesitation or consideration. The sable-swathed Ann Getty, who wanted it known that she was there because of the board-of-directors meeting and not to bid, changed her seat from the fifth row to the first in order to be closer to the arena. By lot 91, a pair of yellow-diamond clips by Harry Winston, 1948, that went to the London jeweler Laurence Graff, one of the royal family's jewelers, for over $2 million, financial abandon filled the air with an almost erotic intensity, and it never lessened during the remaining hours of the sale. Powdered bosoms heaved in fiscal excitement at big bucks being spent. Each time the bidding got into the million-dollar range, for one of the ten or so world-class stones in the collection, the tension resembled the frenzy at a cockfight. Sotheby's employees manning the telephones waved their hands frantically to attract the auctioneer. People rose in their seats to get a better look at the mysterious Mr. Fabri, who bid and bid—money no object—on all the pieces directly linked to the love affair between Edward and Wallis. "The duke would have hated all this," said a friend of the duke's, shaking his head. "I'm surprised they're not auctioning off his fly buttons."

The auctioneer, like the judge at a trial, has the power to enthrall his audience. At the podium in Geneva was the tall and debonair Nicholas Rayner. It was he who first approached Maître Suzanne Blum, the keeper of the Windsor flame, about the disposition of the duchess's jewels. A notoriously difficult woman, the octogenarian Maître Blum is said to have been charmed by Rayner, and because of him she entrusted the jewels to Sotheby's. The charm that captivated Maître Blum captivated all the women in the tent as well. "Divine," said one woman about Rayner. "And separated," said another, as if that fact added to his glamour. Although he was criticized by a few purists for several times allowing the bidding to continue after he had dropped the gavel—he said that since the money was going to charity the ordinary rules did not apply—he won over far more people than he alienated. He had a sense of theater, realized that he was in a leading role, and understood exactly how to keep this audience in the palm of his hand. Graceful, witty, he was Cary Grant at forty, giving the kind of performance that turns a good actor into a major star. At the end of the second day, when the total sales had reached $50 million, the audience rose and gave Rayner a standing ovation which rivaled any that Lord Olivier ever received.

It was a sad disappointment to auction voyeurs that they could not turn around and stare at Miss Elizabeth Taylor raising her already jeweled hand to bid $623,000 for a diamond clip known as the Prince of Wales feathers brooch, which Richard Burton had once admired on the Duchess, for the simple reason that Miss Taylor had chosen to make her bid by telephone while sun-tanning next to her swimming pool in Bel-Air, California. They could not watch the multimillionaire dress designer Calvin Klein either, as he bid by telephone from New York $733,000 for a single-row pearl necklace by Cartier, or $198,000 for another single-row pearl necklace by Van Cleef & Arpels, or a mere $102,600 for a pearl-and-diamond eternity ring by Darde & Fils of Paris, or $300,600 for a pearl-and-diamond pendant by Cartier, for which he outbid the Duchess's friend and frequent New York hostess Estée Lauder, the cosmetics tycoon, and all for his beauteous new wife, Kelly. Expensive, yes, but Van Cleef & Arpels had told Calvin Klein it would take ten years to match pearls for the necklace he had in mind and cost several million dollars. He told the press that he was not going to wait for a special day to give them to Kelly. "The best presents just happen," he said.

Under the marquee, only Marvin Mitchelson, the Hollywood divorce lawyer, who built his fortune on the failed marriages of the famous, broke the rules of anonymity and had himself announced as the purchaser of the Duchess's amethyst-and-turquoise necklace for $605,000. He further wanted it announced that he dedicated the purchase to the memory of his mother, who had worked to put him through law school. Mitchelson also purchased a huge sapphire brooch for $374,000 for someone else, a client whom he would not name, although he tantalized the press by hinting that it was Joan Collins, whom he was representing in her latest divorce.

In seats every bit as good as the seats occupied by the Princess of Naples and Princess Firyal of Jordan sat two dark-haired beauties in Chanel suits—real Chanel suits, not knockoffs—who were there to bid, not gape. They scrutinized their catalogs, and they had mink coats folded over their knees. Their stockings had seams, a subtle signal to the cognoscenti of such things that they were wearing garter belts, not panty hose. Ms. X and Ms. Y, two international ladies of the evening, told me they were staying at the Richemond, where they felt as at home as they do at the Plaza Athénée or the Beverly Hills Hotel. Ms. X had her heart set on lot 26, a pavé diamond heart with a gold-and-ruby crown and the initials W. and E., for Wallis and Edward, intertwined in emeralds. It had been the twentieth-wedding-anniversary present of the Duke to the Duchess. Ms. Y had *her* heart set on lot 31, a single-row diamond bracelet with nine gem-set Latin crosses hanging from it. The Duchess had worn it on her wedding day in 1937 and had once remarked that the crosses represented the crosses she had to bear. Ms. X said about Ms. Y, jokingly, that she wanted the bracelet with the crosses to wear on her whipping hand. Used to the best, Ms. Y has a custom-made bag by Hermès to carry her whips in. She didn't get the bracelet with the crosses, which went for $381,000. Ms. X didn't get the pavé diamond heart either. It went for $300,000. "The prices just got out of hand. We were a couple of zeros too short," Ms. X told me during a break. "That heart probably belongs to Candy Spelling by now. Come and have tea tomorrow. We're free until ten."

Of course there was the inevitable Japanese, with millions at his disposal, who said he would have gone even higher than the $3.15 million he paid for the Duchess's solitary diamond. Hours later, no one could remember his name or his face.

There will be other jewel sales, even better jewel sales, but that night in Geneva, the jewel capital of the world, people wanted, at any price, no holds barred, something about which they could say, "This belonged to the Duchess of Windsor," because they knew that they were buying romance and history. Nowhere was this so evident as in lot 68, a pearl-and-diamond choker, which Nicholas Rayner carefully pointed out was imitation. The choker then sold for $51,000. The sale of the duchess's jewels, coming as it did only a few days after the $39.9 million sale of a Van Gogh sunflowers painting, whose chrome yellow paint had turned brown, made one realize the enormous amount of money there is in the world waiting to be spent, even for the imperfect, if the credentials are OK.

In the back of the tent, unknown to most of the people there, sat Georges Sanègre and his wife, Ofélia, the longtime butler and maid to the Duke and Duchess, quietly watching the personal possessions of their former employers make auction history. Not physically present, but prominently there in spirit, was the old and elusive Maître Blum, called Mrs. Blum by her detractors, who are legion. Maître Blum, who had met the Windsors in Portugal during World War II and then been their French lawyer for forty years, followed every moment of the auction by telephone from Paris and knew minute by minute everything that was going on.

Maître Blum's relationship with the former king and his duchess was strictly a business one. Social contact was limited to two dinners or lunches a year, and those in the context of business courtesy rather than friendship. The Duke was thought to have more regard for her than the Duchess, who, friends say, wanted to fire her after the Duke's death, but whose increasing mental confusion made this impossible.

"She lost her mind, you know," people told me about the Duchess, "during the last decade of her life." Or, "She was gaga." Or, "A veg." The *on-dit*, as these people say, meaning the gossip, or inside story, is that the Duchess insisted on having a final face-lift even though she was advised not to because of her age. Plastic surgeons in England and France declined to perform the operation, and warned her about the effects of anesthesia on people over seventy. Determined, she persevered. A plastic surgeon from another country performed the operation, in the course of which there was a technical difficulty with the anesthesia and the air to the Duchess's brain was briefly cut off. This is widely said to be the cause of the derangement that came on her after her husband's death. During her stay at Buckingham Palace at the time of the Duke's funeral, she often thought she was in Paris, and she mistook the Queen Victoria fountain, which she could see from the palace windows, for the Place de la Concorde. The Duke, before he died, aware that the Duchess's mind had begun to wander, entrusted her care to Maître Blum.

Shortly after the Duke's death, when the Duchess was in a confused and vulnerable state, all his private papers were confiscated, possibly under the direction of his cousin Lord Mountbatten, acting on behalf of the royal family. These papers now reside in the archives of Windsor Castle, unavailable to the public. Georges, the butler, is said to have hidden the love letters of the Duke and Duchess to prevent their being carried off in the same swoop. The letters he rescued were later published under the title *Wallis and Edward, Letters 1931–1937: The Intimate Correspondence of the Duke and Duchess of Windsor*.

It was the Duke's wish, so stated in his will, that the Duchess's jewels be removed from their settings after her death so that the pieces could never be worn by any other woman, but such was not the Duchess's wish. People who have had access to the Duchess's private papers tell me that several Americans tried to persuade the Duchess, because she was American, to leave her jewels, in whole or in part, to the Smithsonian Institution in Washington. Another suggestion was that she leave her jewels to the White House, as a permanent collection for the First Lady of the United States to wear. Although Maître Blum is most often blamed for nixing these American plans for the disposition of the collection, it was the Duchess herself who decided that France, the country that had given her refuge for fifty years, should be the beneficiary. There are unkind people who will tell you that if the Duchess had had her way, all her money would have been left to a dog hospital. The truth is, Maître Blum prevailed upon the Duchess to leave the money to the Pasteur Institute, the leading medical-research institution in France.

People familiar with the Windsors noticed, looking at the jewelry, that a great many pieces were missing. "What happened to all the Fulco di Verdura pieces?" they asked, referring to the designs of the Sicilian Duke di Verdura, whose scrapbooks show a great number of pieces he made for the Duchess which were not in the auction. Or, one heard in Geneva and later in New York, "All those marvelous things on her tables—her bibelots—what has become of those, we wonder?" The implication, each time the rhetorical question is asked, is that malfeasance was afoot. Michael Bloch, who edited the book of the couple's love letters, is adamant in his defense of Maître Blum. He affirms that she has not profited at all in the disposal of the estate, and his strong feelings are borne out by several other people close to the couple.

The Duchess had, in effect, an almost ten-year death, with nurses around the clock. The family fortune, in terms of hard cold cash, at the time of the Duke's death was around $1 million—not a great deal of money for people with their standard of living. The high cost of a royal death was prohibitive, and, curiously, the Duchess did not have medical insurance. From time to time during the years of the long illness, Maître Blum sold off pieces of jewelry, sets of china, or the odd Bergère chair or ormolu table to pay off the medical costs. Several years ago, for instance, Mrs. São Schlumberger of Paris bought a ruby necklace. A Sotheby's official assured me that the price she paid was at the top of the market at the time. Nate Cummings, the late American millionaire, collector, and friend of the Duke and Duchess, bought, among other things, a set of vermeil plates. Maître Blum also sold some bead necklaces in emeralds, rubies, and sapphires to the London firm of Hennell, who traveled to Beverly Hills with their wares before the auction. Candy Spelling, the wife of the television mogul Aaron Spelling and the possessor of one of the most spectacular jewel collections in the country, bought one of the necklaces. Another was sold to Mrs. Muriel Slatkin, the former owner, with her sister, Seema Boesky, the wife of the Wall Street swindler Ivan Boesky, of the Beverly Hills Hotel. A third was sold to Mrs. Marvin Davis, the wife of one of the country's richest men, who is, incidentally, the new owner of the Beverly Hills Hotel. Also, the Duchess gave away several pieces of her jewelry before she died. Princess Alexandra, a favorite niece of the Duke, received a piece. Princess Michael of Kent, whose own popularity in the royal family is on a par with the

Duchess's, won the heart of her husband's aunt by marriage by calling her in a letter "Dear Aunt Wallis," thereby likening her own marriage to that of the Windsors, and she too was rewarded.

The Duchess in her will mentioned certain people, like the American-born Countess of Romanoes, who received a diamond bracelet with an inscription from the Duke to the Duchess engraved on the back of it. When the item to be inherited was not specified, it was left to the discretion of Maître Blum, and in this role the mighty *maître* exerted her authority to the fullest. One lady of haughty bearing irritated Maître Blum exceedingly at the time of the Duchess's funeral by assuming too important a position and attitude among the mourners. Months later, her bijou of inheritance still undelivered, the haughty lady is said to have wailed to her friends, "Why does Maître Blum hate me so?" Her inheritance was the last to be distributed and the least important of the lot in both beauty and value.

No one lingers in Geneva. At fifteen minutes before eight the morning after the sale, Alfred Taubman, a huge unlit cigar balanced between his teeth, paced back and forth in front of the Hôtel Richemond, impatience in his every step. The auction was over, history made, he wanted to be gone. The jacket of his double-breasted gray flannel suit was unbuttoned. A cashmere scarf was wrapped Dickensian-style around his neck against the brisk lake breezes. By the curb three dark blue Mercedeses were being loaded with first-rate luggage, and he was directing the operation. Nervous minions offered assistance.

"How much . . . ?" someone started to ask him, meaning how much had the auction grossed.

"Forty-nine million plus," he answered, interrupting the question before it was finished. It was not the first time he had been asked the question since the night before, and he was proud of the figure.

"Call upstairs to Mrs. Taubman," he told the hall porter, walking back into the lobby of the hotel. "I left my yellow handkerchief behind. Tell her to find it." He walked back out to the street again. "C'mon. Let's get this show on the road." He did not like to be kept waiting. "Between Judy and Princess Firyal . . ." he said, shaking his head in exasperation at the delays women cause. Finally all was ready. "We're going to General Aviation, where my plane is," he said to the driver of the lead car.

The party was over, my friend.

In the six weeks that followed, two other notable jewel auctions took place. At Sotheby's in New York, the jewels of Flora Whitney Miller, the daughter of Gertrude Vanderbilt Whitney, were auctioned along with the jewels of a Romanian princess and the singer-actress Pia Zadora, among others. Back in Geneva, at Christie's, certain jewels of the Hon. Mrs. Reginald Fellowes, known as Daisy Fellowes, were sold in combination with jewelry from what the catalog listed merely as "various sources."

Unlike the Duchess of Windsor, both Mrs. Miller and Mrs. Fellowes, her contemporaries, were born to great wealth and great families. Mrs. Fellowes was the daughter of a French duke and a Singer-sewing-machine heiress. It was said that every time Mrs. Fellowes passed an advertisement for Singer sewing machines she crossed herself. Historically Daisy Fellowes is little more than a footnote in the memoirs and diary entries of social historians, although in fact she was just as relentlessly chic as the Duchess, far richer, and equally witty. She owned one of the largest yachts in the Mediterranean, the *Sister Anne*, one which the Windsors once sailed. Stories about her are endless. Once, a former footman with exceptional good looks, who had advanced himself from his position behind a dining-room chair to a seat at some of the best tables in the South of France, Palm Beach, and Beverly Hills, asked Daisy Fellowes if she missed her yacht, which she had recently sold. She looked at the fellow and answered, "Yes. Yes, I do. I miss it very much. Do you miss your tray?"

The auction of her jewels and the auction of the jewels of Flora Whitney Miller were dispirited occasions in comparison with the Windsor sale. "This won't be anything like that," a Christie's executive told me shortly before the Fellowes jewelry auction. "In all my years in the auction business," she said wistfully, in remembrance of things past, "I never saw anything like the Duchess's sale."

In the weeks following the sale, the Duchess's jewels began appearing on fashionable necks, wrists, and bosoms. Elizabeth Taylor arrived at Malcolm Forbes's party-of-the-year in Far Hills, New Jersey, wearing her Prince of Wales Plumes, and Mrs. Milton Petrie, who, when she was the Marquesa de Portago, was a great friend of the Duchess, walked into New York hostess Alice Mason's party for former president and Mrs. Jimmy Carter wearing the Duchess's articulated tourmaline-and-quartz necklace.

At another dinner party in New York, I heard Mr. Taubman describing, not immodestly, how he had restructured Sotheby's and made it a profitable company. "I computerized it. I got rid of the advertising department entirely. They were doing institutional advertising. I said to them, 'This isn't an institution. This is a business.' I didn't do wholesale firing, as everyone said. I kept the best people, but I brought in experts to go over every department. Now we have a working operation. When I took over the company, they were doing 350, 375 million a year. Last year we did 900 million. By the end of this year, I expect we'll do something like a billion two, a billion five, around there."

As far as the auction world is concerned, Mr. Taubman hit a peak with the sale of the Duchess's jewels. He made it the greatest show on earth. He took an estate appraised by his own experts at $7 million tops and, by means of hype and romance and showmanship, made it bring in over $50 million.

No matter how you slice it, though, Maître Blum emerges as the heroine of this tale. The Duchess of Windsor, unlike other ladies of the royal family she married into, was not a patroness of the arts or sciences. No orphanage or hospital ever knew her as a benefactress. Instead, she was the woman who defined the meaning of a life in society for her time. "Chic" and "stylish" were her adjectives of description. Her servants' livery was made by the same uniform maker who made the uniforms of General de Gaulle. Her days were spent preparing for the evening, telephoning friends, being massaged, being manicured, being coiffed, having fittings for her vast and ever-changing wardrobe, seating her dinners, choosing her china, ordering her flowers, having steamer trunks packed for their endless peregrinations in pursuit of pleasure. But fate stepped in to give a final importance to her life when Maître Blum suggested that the Pasteur Institute be the beneficiary of her will. At the time, no one could know that the Pasteur Institute would become the leading French medical institution involved in finding a cure for AIDS. Today, however, when the whole world is gripped with the fear of AIDS, the $45 million that the Pasteur Institute will receive from the sale of the Duchess's jewelry gives a sort of poetic finality to her life. Even, perhaps, the nobility that always eluded her.

August 1987

ROBERT MAPPLETHORPE'S
PROUD FINALE

N o one expected him to live for the opening, and there he was, on a high," said Tom Armstrong, the director of the Whitney Museum of American Art in New York. Whether the artist would or would not be present was the question that occupied the minds of all the people involved, in the days preceding the highly publicized and eagerly anticipated vernissage of the work of Robert Mapplethorpe, the photographer who took his art to the outer limits of his own experience, at the Whitney last July.

For nearly two years the rumors of Robert Mapplethorpe's illness had been whispered in the New York art and social circles in which he moved as a celebrated and somewhat notorious figure. The death in January 1987 of the New York aristocrat and collector Sam Wagstaff from AIDS had brought the matter of Mapplethorpe's illness with the same disease out into the open. Mapplethorpe, the principal inheritor of Sam Wagstaff's fortune, had once been Wagstaff's lover and later, for years, his great and good friend. The inheritance, believed to be in the neighborhood of $7 million —some say more, depending on the value of his art and silver collection—made the already much-talked-about Mapplethorpe, a famed figure of the night in the netherworld of New York, even more talked about, especially when the will was contested by the sister of Sam Wagstaff, Mrs. Thomas Jefferson IV of New York. Mapplethorpe has never avoided publicity; indeed, he has carefully nurtured his celebrity since his work first came to public notice in the mid-seventies.

That summer night at the Whitney Museum, there were sighs of relief when he did arrive for the opening, having been released from St. Vincent's Hospital only days before. He was in a wheelchair, surrounded by members of his entourage, carrying a cane with a death's-head top and wearing a stylish dinner jacket and black velvet slippers with his initials embroidered in gold on them

—a vastly different uniform from the black leather gear that had been his trademark. For those who had not seen the once-handsome figure in some time, the deterioration of his health and physical appearance was apparent and quite shocking. His hair looked wispy. His thin neck protruded from the wing collar of his dinner shirt like a tortoise's from his shell. But even ill, he was a man who commanded attention, and who expected it. A grouping of furniture had been placed in the center of the second of the four galleries where the exhibition was hung, and there he sat, with his inner circle in attendance, receiving the homage of his friends and admirers, a complex olio of swells and freaks, famous and unknown, that makes up the world of Robert Mapplethorpe. His eyes, darting about, missed nothing. He nodded his head and smiled, speaking in a voice barely above a whisper. "It's a wonderful night," person after person said to him, and he agreed. He was enjoying himself immensely. On the wall facing him hung *Jim and Tom, Sausalito*, his 1977–1978 triptych of two men in black leather, adorned with the accoutrements of sadomasochistic bondage and torture. In the photographs, Jim, the master, is urinating into the willing, even eager, mouth of Tom, the tied-up slave. "Marvelous," said one after another of the fashionable crowd as they surveyed the work. "Surreal" was the word that came to my mind.

However much you may have heard that this exhibition was not a shocker, believe me, it was a shocker. Robert Mapplethorpe was described by everyone I interviewed as the man who had taken the sexual experience to the limits in his work, a documentarian of the homoerotic life in the 1970s at its most excessive. Even his floral photographs are erotic; as critics have pointed out, he makes it quite clear that flowers are the sexual organs of plants. But the crowds that poured in that night, and kept pouring in for the following three months that the exhibition remained up, had not come just to see the still lifes of stark flowers, or the portraits of bejeweled and elegant ladies of society, like Carolina Herrera and Princess Gloria von Thurn und Taxis and Paloma Picasso, and of artist friends, like David Hockney and Louise Nevelson and Willem de Kooning, which are also very much a part of Mapplethorpe's oeuvre. They had come to see the sexually loaded pictures, freed of all inhibitions, that were hanging side by side with the above in the galleries of the Whitney, like the startling *Man in Polyester Suit*, in which an elephantine-size black penis simply hangs out of the unzipped fly of a man whose head is cropped, or the even more startling *Marty and Veronica*, in which Marty makes oral love to a stockinged and girdled Veronica, whose upper body is cropped off at her bare breasts. Mapplethorpe was a participant in the dark world he photographed, not a voyeur, a point he made clear by allowing a self-portrait showing his rectum—rarely considered to be one of the body's beauty spots—to be hung on the wall of the museum, with a bullwhip up it. The Mapplethorpe sexual influence is so great that in the otherwise scholarly introduction to the catalog of the show, Richard Marshall, an associate curator of the Whitney, made reference to this same photograph as the "*Self Portrait* with a whip inserted in his ass." That night, and on two subsequent visits to the exhibition, I watched the reactions of the viewers to the more graphically sexual pictures. They went from I-can't-believe-what-I'm-seeing-on-the-walls-of-the-Whitney-Museum looks to nudges and titters, to nervous, furtive glances to the left and right to see if it was safe to really move in and peer, and, finally, to a subdued sadness, a wondering, perhaps, of how many of the men whose genitalia they were looking at were still alive.

"On the opening night this amazing strength came to Robert," said Flora Biddle, the granddaughter of Gertrude Vanderbilt Whitney, who is the chairman of the board of trustees of the Whitney Museum, which her grandmother started. "At the end of the evening he got up and walked out, after he had come in a wheelchair."

Later, Mapplethorpe told me his feelings about the opening. "It was pretty good. I kept thinking what it would have been like if I'd been feeling better."

"You've become really famous, Robert," I said. "How does that feel?"

"Great," he said quietly, but shook his head at the same time. "I'm quite frustrated I'm not going to be around to enjoy it. The money's coming in, though. I'm making more money now than I've ever made before."

Today Mapplethorpe charges $10,000 for a sitting. His one-of-a-kind pictures sell for an average of $20,000 each. A Mapplethorpe

Shortly after we talked, Jim Nelson died. Nelson, a former hair-stylist for the television soap opera "All My Children," inherited 25 percent of Wagstaff's residuary estate, and Mapplethorpe inherited 75 percent. Nelson, aware that he was dying, wanted his money immediately, so Mapplethorpe, through their lawyers, bought out Nelson's share. As Nelson's life neared its end, he fulfilled a long-held dream and rented two suites on the *Queen Elizabeth 2*, one for himself and one for a companion, and sailed to England, where he stayed in a suite at the Ritz Hotel, and then took the Concorde back to New York. He spent the last day of his life making up a list of people he wanted to be notified of his death and another list of people he did not want to be notified, one of these being the person who told me this story.

Barbara Jakobson said, "It was great to observe Robert and Sam together. Sam got such a kick out of Robert, and Robert allowed Sam to be indulgent. Sam was a Yankee with cement in his pocket, but he was very generous with Robert. Sam always meant for Robert to have his money. I was very unhappy over the publicity about the will after Sam died."

Another close woman friend of both men, who did not want to be named, said, "Robert was looking for a patron, and along came Sam. Sam made Robert's career. He showed Robert this other way of life. Robert was into learning more than anyone I ever knew. When Robert met Sam, all the doors opened for him. Sam was his sugar daddy in a way."

Most of Wagstaff's money came from his stepfather, Donald Newhall, who left him and his sister shares of the Newhall Land and Farming Company in California, which later went public. Over the years, Wagstaff sold off some of his shares to buy his art, photography, and silver collections. In his will he left bequests of $100,000 each to the Museum of Modern Art, the Metropolitan Museum, and the New York Public Library, as well as $10,000 and the family silver to his sister, Mrs. Jefferson, and $10,000 to each of her three children.

"She's enormously rich," said Mapplethorpe about Mrs. Jefferson. "She didn't need the money."

"Then why did she contest the will?"

Mapplethorpe shrugged. "She needed entertainment," he said. In the long run, the litigation never went to trial; Wagstaff's sister decided against proceeding with the suit on the day of jury selection. Several subsequent lawsuits over Wagstaff's million-dollar silver collection, in which Mapplethorpe charged the New York Historical Society with "fraudulent conduct" in obtaining a five-year loan of Wagstaff's silver as he lay dying, were settled out of court.

Mapplethorpe's lawyer, Michael Stout, who handles many prominent people in the creative arts, said about him, "Robert is the most astute businessman of any of my clients. If there is a decision to be made, he understands the issues and votes the right way."

Although I had known Sam Wagstaff for years, my contact with Robert Mapplethorpe was minimal, no more than an acquaintanceship, so I was surprised when he asked me to write this article, and more surprised when he asked to photograph me. Two years ago, right after Sam Wagstaff died, when the rumors of litigation between his family and his heir over his will were rampant, I had thought of writing an article on the subject for this magazine. Mapplethorpe, however, let it be known through his great friend Suzie Frankfurt, the socialite interior decorator, that he did not wish me to write such a piece, and I immediately desisted. Later I saw him at the memorial service for Sam that was held at the Metropolitan Museum. Already ill himself, he made a point of thanking me for not writing the article.

I had met Mapplethorpe for the first time several years earlier, at a dinner given by the Earl of Warwick at his New York apartment. Although Mapplethorpe was then famous as a photographer, the celebrity that was so much a part of his persona was due equally to his reputation as a leading figure in the sadomasochistic subculture of New York. Indeed, he was the subject of endless stories involving dark bars and black men and bizarre behavior of the bondage and domination variety. He arrived late for the dinner, dressed for the post-dinner-party part of his night in black leather, and became in no time the focus of attention and unquestionably the star of Lord Warwick's party. He was at ease in his surroundings and, surprising to me, up on the latest gossip of the English smart set, telling stories in which Guinness and Tennant names abounded.

When coffee was served, he took some marijuana and a package of papers out of his pocket, rolled a joint, lit it, inhaled deeply, all the time continuing a story he was telling, and passed the joint to the person on his right. It was not a marijuana-smoking group, and the joint was declined and passed on by each person to the next, except for one guest who, gamely, took a few tokes and then passed out at the table, after saying, "Strong stuff." Unperturbed, Mapplethorpe continued talking until it was time for his exit. After he was gone, those who remained talked about him.

Like everything else about Robert Mapplethorpe, the studio where he now lives and works on a major crosstown street in the Chelsea section of New York, which was also purchased for him by Wagstaff, is enormously stylish and handsomely done. In 1988 it was photographed by *HG* magazine, and Martin Filler wrote in the accompanying text, "Mapplethorpe's rooms revel in the pleasures of art for art's sake and reconfirm his aesthetic genealogy in a direct line of descent from Oscar Wilde and Aubrey Beardsley through Christian Bérard and Jean Cocteau." There are things to look at in every direction, a mélange of objects and pictures, but everything has its place. Order and restraint prevail. "You create your own world," said Mapplethorpe. "The one that I want to live in is very precise, very controlled." It fits in with his personality that he pays his bills instantly on receiving them.

Each time we met, we sat in a different area. In the back sitting room of the floor-through loft space, the windows have elegant brown-black taffeta tieback curtains designed by Suzie Frankfurt, which seem both incongruous and not at all incongruous. Frankfurt, who maintains a complicated friendship with him, said, "Robert lives in the middle of a contradiction—part altar boy and part leather bar." That day he was wearing a black dressing gown from Gianni Versace, the Italian designer, and his black velvet slippers.

At one point he went into a paroxysm of coughing, and from the look he gave me I realized he didn't want me to see him like that. "Would you excuse me for a minute," he said. I got up and went to another part of the apartment until he called me back.

"Oh, I'm so sick," he said. "I've been throwing up all night. The nights are awful."

"When did you first know you had AIDS?" I asked.

"It was diagnosed as AIDS two years ago in October."

"Did you suspect beforehand that you had it?"

"Every faggot suspects beforehand."

He said that he had two nurses on twelve-hour shifts that cost him a thousand dollars a day. "But I'm lucky. I have insurance." He has been on AZT almost from the beginning. He worries constantly about friends who are less fortunate, specifically his black friends. In a conversation with Marlies Black, who assembled the Rivendell Collection of modern art and photography, which contains the largest selection of Mapplethorpe's work in the world, he once said, "At some point I started photographing black men. It was an area that hadn't been explored extensively. If you went through the history of nude male photography, there were very few black subjects. I found that I could take pictures of black men that were so subtle, and the form was so photographical." Now, musing on that, he said, "Most of the blacks don't have insurance and therefore can't afford AZT. They all die quickly, the blacks. If I go through my *Black Book*, half of them are dead."

When I sat for him to be photographed, I was nervous, even though he had asked me to sit. It was on a day that he was not feeling well. He had not slept the night before. He coughed a great deal. His skin was very pale. We sat on the sofa and talked while Brian English, his assistant, set up the camera and chair where I would sit for the picture. Although ill, Mapplethorpe kept working most days. He showed me pictures he had taken a day or two before of the three-year-old daughter of the actress Susan Sarandon, and he had arranged to photograph Carolina Herrera, the dress designer, as soon as he was finished with me. I was talking about anything I could think of, mostly about people we both knew, to postpone the inevitable. Finally, I told him I was nervous. "Why?" he asked. "I just am," I said. "Don't be," he said quietly. I was struck as always by his grace and manners, which seemed such a contradiction to the image most people have of Robert Mapplethorpe. Finally Brian placed me in the chair, and Robert got up and walked very slowly over to where the Hasselblad camera was set up. He looked in the viewfinder. He asked Brian to move a light. He made an adjustment on a lens opening. "Look to the left," he said. "Keep your head there. Look back toward me with your eyes." He was in charge.

Another time, I remarked that he was looking better. He told me that he was finally able to eat something called TPN, a totally nutritious substance which gave him 2,400 calories a day. "I don't actually eat. I'm fed mostly by tube. If I hadn't found this, I'd be dead by now. I couldn't keep any food down." And then he said a line I heard him say over and over. "This disease is hideous."

"My biggest problem now is walking. I have neuropathy, like when your foot's asleep. It's constant. It's in my hands too. If it weren't for that, I'd go out." His eyes moved toward the window. "I'd like to go to Central Park to see the new zoo. And I'd like to go back to the Whitney to see the show. I hear there are lines of people to see it."

He was born in a middle-class suburban neighborhood called Floral Park, which is on the edge of Queens, New York, the third of six children in a Catholic family of English, German, and Irish extraction. His mother is a housewife. His father does electrical work. He went to a public school in Floral Park, but he would have preferred to go to the Catholic school, which his younger brothers went to. Although he now says that Floral Park was a perfect place for his parents to raise a family, early yearnings in nonconformist directions brought his family life to a halt. "I wanted to have the freedom to do what I wanted to do. The only way to do that was to break away. I didn't want to have to worry about what my parents thought. When I was sixteen, I went to college at the Pratt Institute. That was when I began to live elsewhere."

Except for his brother Edward, the youngest of the six, who was at the studio each time I was there, he has not been close to his family for years, although he said that they are "closer since I told them I was sick, which was not too long ago."

"Did your parents come to see your show at the Whitney?" I asked him.

He shook his head no. "They intend to," he said. Then he added, "But they have come to see me here."

While still in school, he began living with Patti Smith, whom he

met in Brooklyn. Maxine de la Falaise McKendry remembered that
when Robert first met Smith he kicked a hole through from his
apartment to hers so that they could communicate better. "Patti
and I built on each other's confidence. We were never jealous of
each other's work. We inspired each other. She became recognized
first. Then she had a record contract. She pushed ahead. There
was a parallel happening to each career." Patti Smith, who is now
married with two children, lives in Detroit. "We talk to each other
all the time," he said.

"S&M is a certain percentage of Robert's work, and necessary to
show, to give a representation of his work," said Richard Marshall.
He told me that when they put the exhibition together there had
never been any idea of censorship, or any reservation about including offensive material, although, he added, "there are some
stronger pictures which do exist, some more explicitly graphic pictures, the uh, penetration of the arm." What Marshall was referring to was what Mapplethorpe calls his fist-fucking file. "Call
Suzanne," he said to me, speaking of his lovely young secretary,
Suzanne Donaldson, "and ask her, if you want to see the fist-
fucking file, or the video of me having my tit pierced." When certain of these photographs were shown at an art gallery in Madrid,
the gallery owner, who has since died of AIDS, was sent to jail.
    "There were some letters of protest about the show, but not in
great numbers at all," said Marshall. "We put up signs in three or
four locations, warning parents that the show might not be appli-
cable for children."
    Flora Biddle concurs. "I went on a tour of the show the night
before it opened with the Whitney Circle, which is the highest
category of membership. Richard Marshall talked about the pictures to the group, dealing with the pictures you could call the
most sexual, and spoke beautifully about them. The people in the
Circle were attentive and open to them. Afterward, people came
up and said they thought it was so wonderful the Whitney was
hanging this show."

Barbara Jakobson said, "Sometimes I'd drive downtown in my yellow Volkswagen to have dinner with Robert. Then, later, I'd drop

him off at the Mineshaft, or one of those places. God forbid he be seen having a woman drop him off, so I'd leave him a block away. I had no desire to see inside, but I once asked Robert to describe what it was like, in an architectural way. He said there were places of ritual. He told me how the rooms were divided, without telling me what actually went on. Once he showed me a sadomasochistic photograph. I said to him, 'I can't believe that a human being would allow this to be done.' He replied, 'The person who had it done wanted it to be done. Besides, he heals quickly.' Robert would find these people who enjoyed this. The interesting part is that they posed for him."

When I discussed this conversation with Mapplethorpe, he said, "I went to the Eagles Nest and the Spike to find models. Or I'd meet people from referrals. They'd hear you were good at such and such a thing, and call. I was more into the experience than the photography. The ones I thought were extraordinary enough, or the ones I related to, I'd eventually photograph."

"Were drugs involved?"

"Oh, yes. I've certainly had my share of drug experiences, but I don't need drugs to take pictures. They get in the way. However, drugs certainly played a big factor in sex at that time. MDA was a big drug in all this. It's somewhere between cocaine and acid.

"Most of the people in S&M were proud of what they were doing. It was giving pleasure to one another. It was not about hurting. It was sort of an art. Certainly there were people who were into brutality, but that wasn't my take. For me, it was about two people having a simultaneous orgasm. It was pleasure, even though it looked painful.

"Doing things to people who don't want it done to them is not sexy to me. The people in my pictures were doing it because they wanted to. No one was forced into it.

"For me, S&M means sex and magic, not sadomasochism. It was all about trust."

"If his S&M work were heterosexual, it wouldn't be acceptable," I was told by a world-famous photographer, who, because of Mapplethorpe's illness, did not wish to be quoted by name making critical remarks about him. "The smart society that has accepted his work has done so because it is so far removed from their own lives."

Even before the AIDS crisis, though, Mapplethorpe had begun to move away from the S&M scene as subject matter for his photography. One of his closest associates said to me, "Robert had gotten more and more away from being a downtown personality. He had been observing the uptown life for some time, and I think he wanted to become a society photographer. Once, leaving someone's town house on the Upper East Side, he said, 'I wouldn't mind living like that.' "

Carolina Herrera, the subject of one of Mapplethorpe's earliest and most celebrated society portraits, has known him for years, "long before he was famous." They met on the island of Mustique in the Caribbean in the early 1970s, when Herrera and her husband were guests of Princess Margaret, and Mapplethorpe, along with his English friend Catherine Tennant, was a guest of Tennant's brother Colin, who is now Lord Glenconner. Tennant remembers Mapplethorpe at the time wearing more ivory bracelets up his arms than the rebellious Nancy Cunard wore in the famous portrait Cecil Beaton book of her in 1927. When Mapplethorpe took Herrera's picture in a hotel room in New York, he had only a minimum of photographic equipment and no assistant. Herrera's husband, Reinaldo, had to hold the silver umbrella reflector for him. Mapplethorpe photographed Herrera wearing a hat and pearls, against a blank ground, and since then his style in social portraiture has remained as stark as in his nude figures, mirroring the sculptural influence of Man Ray more than the ethereal settings of Cecil Beaton.

On Friday evening, November 4, 1988, Robert Mapplethorpe gave a large cocktail party at his studio to celebrate his forty-second birthday. Incidentally, November 4 was also the birthday of Sam Wagstaff. Birthday celebrations have always been important to Mapplethorpe, according to Barbara Jakobson. She remembered other birthday parties in the past that Sam had given for Robert. " 'Sam is going to give me a party,' Robert would say way in advance."

At the peak of the birthday party, nearly two hundred people milled through the vast studio, among them the film stars Susan Sarandon, Sigourney Weaver, and Gregory Hines, all of whom had been photographed by Mapplethorpe. In the crowd were Prince and Princess Michael of Greece, the Earl of Warwick, Tom Armstrong of the Whitney Museum, gallery owner Mary Boone, Bruce Mailman, who was a managerial partner in the St. Marks Baths until it was closed down in the wake of the AIDS epidemic, and Dimitri Levas, the art director and principal stylist on Mapplethorpe's fashion shoots, who is said to be one of his heirs, as well as well-known figures from the magazine, gallery, auction, and museum worlds. And collectors. And people who were just friends. Inevitably, there were men in black leather, some wearing master caps, standing on the sidelines, watching. Everyone mixed.

Everybody brought gifts, wonderfully wrapped, and soon there was a mountain of them on a bench by the front door. Bouquets of flowers kept arriving throughout the party, including one of three dozen white roses in a perfect crystal vase. Waiters in black jackets moved through the crowd, carrying trays of fluted glasses of champagne. On several tables were large tins of beluga caviar, and Robert kept leaning over and helping himself.

Although there was certainly a sense that this was Robert Mapplethorpe's farewell party for his friends, there were no feelings of sadness in the studio that night. Robert, continually indomitable, provided his guests with an upbeat and optimistic celebration. He looked better than he had looked in weeks. He sat in his favorite chair, missing nothing, receiving guest after guest who came and knelt by his side to chat with him. Toward the end of the evening, he stood up and walked.

"This is Robert. This is his life. Everybody beautiful. Everybody successful," said one of the guests whom I did not know.

"Robert has style," said Prince Michael of Greece, surveying the event. "Personal style is not something you learn. It's something you have."

One of the most frequently asked questions these days is where Robert Mapplethorpe will leave his money when he dies. His lawyer, Michael Stout, refused to answer the question. But it is known that the photographer has recently set up the Robert Mapplethorpe Foundation, with a board of directors. Besides specific bequests to friends, the foundation will probably give money to the arts as well as to the American Foundation for AIDS Research (AmFAR), an organization with which Mapplethorpe had been associated since Sam Wagstaff's death. In a letter he sent out asking friends and acquaintances to pay $100 each to attend a private viewing of Sam Wagstaff's silver collection prior to its sale at Christie's in January, he wrote, "I have asked AmFAR to use the funds raised from this benefit to support community-based trials of promising AIDS drugs, a pilot program which will greatly increase patient access to treatments that may help extend their lives."

February 1989

THE LIGHT
OF HUSSEIN

PEOPLE CAME because she was beautiful, and were then awed by her brilliance. She had dispelled the fairy-tale image. This is no fairy tale. This is not a fairy tale at all," said Sarah Pillsbury, the Hollywood film producer, about her Concord Academy classmate Queen Noor al Hussein after the queen had spoken in the United States in October, defending the controversial role of her husband, King Hussein of Jordan, in the Middle East crisis. The Arab kingdom is precariously situated, bordered by Iraq, Israel, Syria, and Saudi Arabia. Should a war erupt, Jordan could become a battlefield. But in Amman, the capital, there was no overt sense of turbulence, or of a country close to war, during my visit two weeks later.

Foreign correspondents, on their way to and from Baghdad or Riyadh, talked in the bar of the Inter-Continental Hotel of atrocities and war, but taxi drivers and shopkeepers did not. Over dinner, the minister of information, speaking for the king, told a group of American journalists, "We don't want war. We are extremely nervous about military action in the area. We cannot afford to have a war. Jordan will be destroyed." But life seemed to go on as usual. In Petra, "the rose-red city half as old as time," I asked a Bedouin guide, "Don't you worry about the crisis?" "No," he replied, "we live our life in crisis. We have our faith. We're not afraid of death."

I had come hoping to see the American queen, whom I had heard speak several weeks earlier at the Brookings Institute in Washington, D.C., but my visit began inauspiciously. Checking into the Inter-Continental Hotel, I was confronted by a figure from the palace, Fouad Ayoub, who informed me that there were obstacles. The appointment for an interview with Her Majesty, he said, was unfixed, uncertain, and unpromised. There was a reluctance to let me meet with her until certain guidelines had been agreed upon, guidelines that were never going to be agreed upon. The best I was able to muster up was an evening visit with the only female member of the Jordanian senate, Laila Sharaf. An unpromising interview, of real interest to neither Mrs. Sharaf nor me.

The taxi driver who took me from the Inter-Continental to Mrs. Sharaf's house, high up on a hill on the outskirts of the city, spoke English but resisted all my attempts at conversation. There was, I was soon to discover, an underlying dislike of Americans in the country. In the taxi was a photograph of King Hussein next to one of Iraqi president Saddam Hussein, the man described by President Bush as worse than Hitler. King Hussein, who for many years positioned Jordan as a "moderate" Arab monarchy—who, indeed, has long been one of Washington's staunchest allies in the region —refused to join the anti-Saddam coalition. The surface reasons were apparent: Palestinians, who have sided with Iraq, account for more than half of Jordan's population, and the king could ill afford to ignore their interests. Even those Jordanians opposed to the brutal policies of Saddam Hussein are more opposed to the presence of American troops in the area. Although Jordan has abided by the U.N. sanctions against Iraq, the king's position severely strained his relations with the Bush administration and Saudi Arabia, which reacted by cutting off oil shipments to Jordan, leaving Iraq as its only supplier, and deepening the economic crisis.

At Mrs. Sharaf's large and handsome villa, the scent of night-blooming jasmine filled the air. The flower garden was in full bloom, and birds in great profusion sang on the roof. It was a setting of Middle Eastern luxe, marred only by the presence of an armed guard in a sentry box. I asked the taxi driver to wait for me in the courtyard. He was reluctant until I assured him that I would pay for his waiting time.

Laila Sharaf, the widow of a prime minister, is a distinguished woman in her own right, involved in cultural affairs. With the queen, she was active in starting the Jerash Festival of Culture and Arts, an annual program of dance, poetry, and music held in an ancient Roman amphitheater. The festival brought thousands of tourists to the country and was a boon to the economy, but with the beginning of the Gulf crisis, tourism became nonexistent overnight. Her butler brought a tray with glasses of lemonade, orange juice, cola, and water. We settled on comfortable sofas, and she began to describe to me the duties and accomplishments of the American queen.

A fiercely private woman until the recent events in the Middle East focused attention on her, Queen Noor has never captured the imagination of the American public in the way that Princess Grace of Monaco, her obvious counterpart, did. Comparisons to the late princess are said to disconcert, even annoy, her. In London recently, she attended the play *Love Letters* with her great friend Tessa Kennedy, the interior designer who decorated several residences of the Jordanian royal family. After the show, the queen went backstage to visit one of the stars, another old American friend, Stefanie Powers. A friend of mine who sat behind the queen said she was virtually unrecognized by the audience. She has never become a fashion darling of the international paparazzi in the manner of the Princess of Wales, the Duchess of York, and the two princesses of Monaco. However, since Iraq invaded Kuwait in August, the queen has had a much higher profile, becoming the most visible woman in the Middle East. She played a major role in helping to organize aid for the nearly three-quarters of a million refugees who fled from Kuwait and flooded into her adopted country. The presence of the refugees placed an enormous burden on Jordan's already stricken economy. Her main priority was to help get the refugees home, and to accomplish that she personally enlisted the aid of Richard Branson, the British music and entertainment entrepreneur, who owns Virgin Atlantic Airways. The queen had recently returned from the United States, where she had spoken publicly in New York and Washington and had been interviewed by Barbara Walters on "Nightline." On that program she evidenced her skill in evading ticklish questions. When Walters asked her to describe her impression of Saddam Hussein, she replied that she had met him only once, very briefly. When Walters continued, "When your husband comes home after he's had these meetings, how does he describe him?" the queen replied, "My husband and I discuss issues more than personalities."

She was criticized in Jordan by those who felt it was not the natural role of the wife of the king to give speeches about foreign policy. In addressing such criticism, Mrs. Sharaf said, "The queen not only understands the facts, but she has put herself on the same perspective as the Arabs. Her way of thinking is very Western, but she has absorbed the Arab side."

Outside the house, arrival sounds could be heard. The butler hurried into the room and spoke excitedly to Mrs. Sharaf in Arabic. "She is here," Mrs. Sharaf said, surprised.

"Who?" I asked.

She rose and rapidly made her way to the hall and opened the door. A BMW motorcycle was driving into the courtyard. On it was King Hussein, the longest-ruling leader in the Arab world. Sitting behind him on the seat, arms around his waist, was Queen Noor. A military vehicle filled with soldiers came up behind them.

Suddenly feeling like an intruder, I said, "Would you like me to leave?"

"No, no. Wait in that room," my hostess told me.

I retreated to the salon and listened as she greeted the king and queen. The royal couple said they had been out for an evening spin in the hills above Amman and had decided to call on Mrs. Sharaf. Then I heard the lowered voice of Mrs. Sharaf explaining my presence in the adjoining room.

Suddenly the door opened, and the queen walked into the salon where I was standing. She is thirty-nine years old, tall, slender, and exceptionally good-looking. She was wearing blue jeans and a loose-fitting light blue sweater, but her carriage was as regal as if she had been in coronation regalia. Her long honey-colored hair fell to her shoulders, kept in place by a headband. Despite the informality of her dress and the situation we found ourselves in, however, the formal distance of royalty prevailed. She had come to pay an impromptu call on a friend and had found an unexpected visitor. "Sir," she said in greeting. Later I discovered she addresses most men as "sir."

Her looks are American. Her handshake is American. Her eye contact is American. And yet, somehow, she is ceasing, or has even ceased, to be American. In Washington earlier in the month, when she spoke at the Brookings Institute, she had several times said, "Speaking as an Arab . . ." Lisa Halaby, Princeton '74, has truly become, during the twelve years of her marriage, the Queen of Jordan. Her voice is American, but her manner of speech is not. So deliberate is her prose style that at times I had the ridiculous feeling that she was translating in her mind from Arabic to English. She often interjects phrases such as "if you will" and "as it were." There is no chitchat. There are no short answers. Every sentence is carefully thought out and spoken in a modulated, complicated, sometimes convoluted manner.

Behind her, a moment later, the king appeared. He, too, was dressed for biking, in a black leather jacket and aviator glasses, but even though his attire was informal, his history enveloped him. The thirty-eighth-generation descendant of the Prophet, he has been on the throne of the Hashemite kingdom of Jordan for thirty-eight years. At the age of fifteen, he witnessed the assassination of his grandfather King Abdullah during a visit to the Al Aqsa Mosque in Jerusalem. The same assassin then fired at him, but the bullet was deflected by a medal on the tunic of his military-school uniform. Two years later, he succeeded his mentally unstable father, King Talal, to the throne. If he was distressed at finding a reporter present during a rare private moment in his overcast life, he gave no indication of it. We shook hands. In all the official photographs that hang in the shop windows and office buildings of Amman, the king stands considerably taller than the queen. In reality, the queen is taller than the king by almost a head. Mrs. Sharaf motioned us to sit, and the butler reappeared with his tray of juices and cola. In the awkward moments that followed, I said that although I had hoped to meet them I had never expected to encounter them on a motorcycle.

"We courted on a motorcycle," said the queen. I was struck by the old-fashioned word "courted." "It was the only way we could get off by ourselves." Then she added, with a slight nod of her head to the courtyard outside, where the king's guards were, "Of course, we were always followed."

They discussed the Nobel Peace Prize, which had been awarded that day to Mikhail Gorbachev. The king had sent him a telegram of congratulations. They discussed Vaclav Havel. The queen said she had never met Havel, but would like to. She added that their days of travel were limited, at least for the time being. Invariably, the conversation returned to the Gulf crisis. It is a constant in everyone's mind. It is the dark cloud over their country and monarchy. "The country has never been more united," she said.

Although she is a beautiful woman, her intelligence rather than her beauty is her dominant force. She has weathered gossip and criticism, but even those salon ladies, as they are called, meaning the upper-class ladies of Amman, who most disliked her in the beginning have a grudging respect for the manner in which she recently presented the views of her country in the United States. Her husband, who has been on the throne since his wife was one year old, is at the peak of his popularity in his country. Several times during the visit, he looked over at her and smiled. There is an open affection between them. When she returned from her recent trip abroad in the royal family's Gulfstream jet, the king was at the airport to meet her.

In the course of the conversation, the queen mentioned that she would visit the new site of the Jubilee School the next day. The Jubilee School is one of her pet projects, a three-year coeducational boarding school for the most gifted high-school students in the region, providing them with scholarships to develop their leadership potential.

After fifteen minutes I departed, leaving them to their visit. Outside, in the courtyard, the king's motorcycle had been parked by the front door. Eight soldiers carrying assault rifles hovered by the guardhouse waiting for their monarch. My taxi driver, who had been heretofore so disagreeable, was now wide-eyed with awe. He was convinced that the king had arrived by motorcycle at the hilltop villa specifically to meet with me in secret conference. I did nothing to dissuade him of his misperception. The following morning a call came from the palace, inviting me to go along with the queen on her visit to the Jubilee School. In the days that followed, every time I encountered the taxi driver at the taxi stand in front of the hotel, we shook hands and chatted amiably, but by that time I was being picked up by silver Mercedes sedans with soldier-chauffeurs provided by the palace, and had no more need of taxis.

Queen Noor al Hussein was born Lisa Najeeb Halaby on August 23, 1951, into a prominent Arab-American family. Her well-known father, Najeeb Halaby, known as Jeeb, was of Syrian descent. He headed the Federal Aviation Administration during the Kennedy-Johnson years and was at one time the president of Pan American World Airways. Lisa was fashionably educated at the National Cathedral School in Washington, D.C., and the Concord Academy in Massachusetts before entering Princeton University in its first coeducational freshman class. She wore a black armband to protest the Vietnam War and became one of the first women cheerleaders. "She wore white ducks. She was the most gorgeous thing you ever saw, with her long hair," recalled television producer Gillian Gordon, one of her classmates and still a close friend. After her sophomore year, she took a year off and moved to Aspen, Colorado, where she supported herself as a waitress. She also did work in the library of the Aspen Institute and indulged her passion for skiing. Returning to Princeton, she took her degree in architecture and urban planning. Her graduation yearbook picture shows a rather plain girl with long, stringy hair and a quizzical, faraway look in her eyes. Beside their pictures, most of her classmates have a paragraph about themselves, describing academic accomplishments and future dreams. But not Lisa Halaby. Beside her picture is a blank white space, startling in retrospect, as if her past had already been put behind her and her future as the queen of a Middle Eastern country was too unfathomable even to imagine.

After Princeton she traveled to Australia and Iran, where she was hired as an assistant by Marietta Tree, the director of the American branch of the British architectural and planning firm of Llewelyn-Davis, Weeks. The firm had been commissioned by the late Shah of Iran to replan the city of Teheran, and Lisa Halaby lived there for six months doing architectural drafting. From Teheran she went to Jordan, where her father was closely connected with the head of Alia, the Jordanian airline, to work on a plan for the creation of an Arab air university. She was introduced to King Hussein when he was attending a ceremony to mark the arrival of the first jumbo jet to join Alia, which later became Royal Jordanian airlines.

The king's first marriage, to Dina Abdul Hamid, whom he had met in London when still a schoolboy, took place in 1955, shortly after his nineteenth birthday. Dina, seven years his senior, was an intellectual with a university education and a keen understanding of the politics of the Arab world. The marriage was encouraged by his mother, Queen Zein, who admired Dina's intelligence and Hashemite credentials and was eager for her son to settle down. A daughter, Princess Alia, was born, but the marriage collapsed only eighteen months after the wedding. While Dina was on a holiday in Egypt, the king divorced her. For the next six years, Princess Dina was allowed to see her daughter only once. Many years later, Dina married a Palestinian commando who was also seven years younger than she.

In 1961, King Hussein married for the second time. His bride, Antoinette "Toni" Gardiner, was a nineteen-year-old English girl, the daughter of a lieutenant colonel serving in Jordan. They were introduced at a dance. Toni became a Muslim and adopted an Arab name, Muna al Hussein, meaning "Hussein's wish." Like Dina, Muna was made a princess, but not queen, and when Hussein announced the engagement on the radio, he described Muna as a Muslim, but not as an Arab. Her English background was left for a subsequent announcement. A year later a much-hoped-for son was born. Prince Abdullah was named after Hussein's slain grandfather. Another son followed, Prince Feisal, and twin daughters, Princess Zein and Princess Aisha. In addition, Alia, his daughter from his marriage to Princess Dina, was brought up by Princess Muna as one of her own family.

By the end of 1972, King Hussein had met and fallen in love with Alia Toukan, the daughter of a Jordanian diplomat. To the surprise of most people in Jordan, who were unaware of any problem in his marriage, the king divorced Princess Muna and married Alia, whom he made Queen of Jordan. In 1977, Queen Alia was killed in a helicopter crash while returning from visiting a hospital in the south of Jordan. The queen left behind two children, Princess Haya and Prince Ali, as well as an adopted daughter, Abir. Abir as an infant had survived an air crash in which her mother was killed. She was found alive, cradled in her dead mother's arms. Alia was moved by the baby's plight and adopted her from her father, a Jordanian truck driver. Abir was brought up in the palace on equal footing with her royal siblings. In the five years of her marriage, Alia had become a popular and beloved queen. The king was grief-stricken by her death, and the nation was plunged into mourning. For a while he withdrew into seclusion.

When the king met Lisa Halaby, the attraction between the two was immediate. Marietta Tree, who was visiting in Jordan at the time, remembers being told by Lisa that the king had asked her to lunch. Later that day, returning from a trip to Petra, Mrs. Tree asked, "How was the lunch?" Lisa told her, "It lasted five hours. He showed me the palace, and we played with the children." One of her close friends told me that she detested the word "dated" when speaking of her romance with the king. They "courted" for six weeks, escaping from the ever-watchful eye of Amman society, sometimes on the king's motorcycle for jaunts in the country and sometimes by helicopter for private dinners at Aqaba, the beach resort on the Red Sea, where the king maintains a summer residence.

Lisa Halaby converted to Islam and took the name Noor al Hussein, which means "light of Hussein." They were married on June 15, 1978, and the new queen became stepmother to the king's eight children, adopting Abir, who was then seven, and the two small children of Queen Alia. Sarah Pillsbury said of her old friend, "She was always very bright and very mature. We were always very impressed with her. She got in touch with me about a year after the wedding, and we have kept in touch since then. I was struck by her dignity and her determination to be the best wife and queen. The king never said to her, 'Do this. Do that.' She figured it out herself. Has she changed? None of us are the same people we were back then, and she's not, either." Another friend, and journalist Carinthia West, who attended the National Cathedral School with her, said, "Sure, it was hard for her in the beginning. She had no family. No buddies." It is a fact that there was a great deal of resentment toward the new queen at the beginning of her marriage, especially on the part of the fashionable ladies of Amman. There are indications also that jealousies occurred in the king's family over the new, fourth wife of the king. "It wasn't just because she's tall, blond, and American," a Jordanian woman told me. "It was because she became the queen." In the years that have followed, Queen Noor has had four children of her own. Prince Hamzah was born in 1980, Prince Hashim in 1981, Princess Iman in 1983, and Princess Raiyah in 1986.

When the queen goes about her daily duties, she travels in a motorcade, but there are no Daimlers, no Rollses, no Bentleys, no sirens, and no flags. This queen drives herself, in a jeep—a

Mercedes jeep, but a jeep nonetheless. She chooses who is going to ride with her, and her companions change during the day so that she can talk privately with her attendants or her guests. Her jeep is in the middle of the motorcade, preceded and followed by military vans with soldiers.

On several occasions I rode in the jeep with the queen. She drives the way she speaks, carefully. Unlike the English princesses, who are always being stopped for speeding, she does not drive fast. She is sometimes recognized by passengers in other cars, who lean out their windows to wave at her. She always smiled and waved back. At a busy five-way intersection in the middle of the city, one of the soldiers in the vehicle ahead of the jeep hopped out to halt traffic in all directions so that the queen and her party could go through. I don't like when they do that," she said. She stopped the jeep, shook her head, and waved the other cars through, sitting out the red light like any other driver. When the light turned green, she passed through the intersection. The traffic cop on duty smiled at her, and she waved back at him. "He knows me," she said.

After looking over the new facilities for the Jubilee School, she visited a school for girls, going from classroom to classroom, listening to children recite or perform, talking to as many of them as possible, giving her full attention to each conversation. About 50 percent of Jordan's population is under the age of fifteen. There is no bobbing and curtsying to her as there is to English royals making their official rounds in flowered hats. Rather, the queen extends her hand in the American manner and almost immediately engages in conversation. Her style of dress is extremely simple: Usually she wore a below-the-calf-length khaki skirt with a blue denim shirt and a blazer. She told me that when she was first married she was taken aside by an adviser and told that her duties would consist, for example, of cutting ribbons to open schools and buildings. She knew that her role would exceed such functions, but there was no precedent in the country for an activist queen. "I had always worked," she said. "My role has been a pioneering role."

When she is performing her official duties, she speaks only in Arabic. "It's my working language," she said. "I use no English when I am working with the people in the country, but I use both

English and Arabic with people in the scientific fields." She now speaks the language fluently but says, "I will never be a great poet in Arabic. It's such a challenging language." With the king, who was educated in England at Harrow and Sandhurst, she speaks both languages, but they converse primarily in English. "My children are completely bilingual, more than I could ever be. I spoke only Arabic with my first child. I hope and pray they won't have to study Arabic as a second language. I want them to think in Arabic. They all go to Arabic schools. Their courses are taught in Arabic, except for English courses. Arithmetic and science are taught in both languages."

"Do they have accents?"

"They don't sound like foreigners speaking English," she replied.

Once, talking about her children, she said, "I was so lucky I was raised the way I was, and that I traveled and worked before I was married. I want my children to do the same before they marry."

"Will you send your children to school abroad?"

"I once said to the headmaster of my husband's school, 'I will send my children to the best school for each one of them when the time comes.' They will study abroad. Each is entitled to have some time to compete equally with everyone else. Within Jordan, they will always be the sons of the king. There will be those who will surround them with too much attention, judge them too easily, even take advantage of them. To really learn how to stand on their own feet, they need to get away."

Despite growing anti-American sentiment, which in some circles extends to the queen, she is in daily touch with her subjects. "The people on the street like her. They get excited when they see her. They don't look *up* to her. They look *to* her for help. They see her as the female, the softer figure whom they can reach out to for help. She has been here twelve years now. She has grown in her job," said Dr. Sima Bahous, an assistant professor of journalism at Yarmouk University, north of Amman.

I went with Queen Noor to the village of Al Bassah, an hour's drive from the capital. It was the first visit ever paid to the village by a member of the royal family. Schoolchildren lined up on both sides of the road to greet her motorcade. Like a latter-day character out of Lesley Blanch's *The Wilder Shores of Love*, the queen walked through rows of clapping schoolboys and cadets to shake hands with the elders of the village. She entered a Bedouin tent and sat on a sofa that had been placed there for her. Opposite her on chairs sat the men of the village, who told her what they needed for the village. She replied in Arabic, promising them help, asking her aides to make notes, speaking in the same deliberate manner as when she speaks in English. Up the hill from the tent, women with covered heads watched from the porch of a house. When she finished with the men, she walked up the hill to the women. They crowded around her, several hundred of them, wanting to be near her. They held up babies. They kissed her hand. She addressed herself with special care to the problems of the women. "We are equal with the men and work together, plus raise our children," they told her. During the harvest, they said, they needed a kindergarten for their children while they worked in the fields. She promised to help them. She went into the olive groves and picked olives with the women, and then walked down into a green valley that looked biblical, where the villagers grew pomegranates and figs.

On the way back to the city, I drove in the jeep with the queen. High on a mountaintop in the distance was a beautiful sprawling estate looking down on the Dead Sea. It was the country house of Prince Muhammad, a brother of the king. "My husband and I were given land up there as a wedding present, but we never built," she said. "Maybe someday, something simple, a place to get away."

The king and queen maintain a large house in London as well as an estate in the English countryside, grand enough to have been lent to the Duke and Duchess of York to live in while their own country house was being built. But their main home is Al Nadwa, the cream-colored royal palace in Amman. As palaces go, Al Nadwa is more like a rich man's mansion than a monarch's royal residence. If all twelve of the king's children were home at the same time—an unlikely event—it would probably be a tight squeeze. A large estate set in the middle of the city, it is in a well-guarded compound with staff offices, guest residences, barracks, and several other palaces, one of which, the old palace of King Abdullah, the king's grandfather, is used by Queen Noor for her foundation and offices.

We sat in the English-looking garden under a white marquee, looking out over a lush green lawn. The marquee seemed to have permanent status in the garden, since the poles were covered with ivy. The lunch table was set for two. A butler wearing English butler clothes—dark jacket, striped trousers—carried the food on trays from the palace down a poplar-lined walkway to where we were sitting.

"This is my favorite room in the house," said the queen. "The garden is a recent thing. I put all this in. Gardening is something new for me. I wish I'd done it long before. It established an equilibrium with nature, putting my hands in the dirt, planting."

She looks as though she might have played field hockey in boarding school, but she complained about not getting enough exercise. "I do aerobics with a friend who comes here, and play tennis. We don't have a swimming pool." Plans were drawn up for one several years ago, but for security reasons it was never built. She likes to dispel the image of luxury living behind the palace walls. "I like being able to say, 'We don't have a pool.' "

"Have there been difficulties between you and other women in the royal family?" I had heard there was a chilly relationship with a sister-in-law and a former sister-in-law.

She shrugged. "I suppose it is the same in every family," she answered.

"Do you see Queen Zein?" The king's mother, Queen Zein, lives in a large, well-guarded house on Jubaiha, the road in Amman where most of the embassies are located. For years Queen Zein was the central figure in the royal family. After King Abdullah's assassination, she was a powerful influence on her son when he became king.

"If there is a family wedding, part of the celebration will always take place at her house," replied the queen carefully. "She came to see me in the hospital each time one of the children was born."

Ever since her marriage, the queen has been gossiped about. She has been accused of extravagance in clothes and jewels. She has also been accused of having had plastic surgery on her face, but her friends insist that clothes and jewels are not where her interests lie. "She is passionately interested in what's going on," says Marietta Tree. While I was in Jordan, a report was printed in an American newspaper that said she had recently purchased an estate in Palm Beach, Florida. When I asked her about it, she just smiled and shook her head in exasperation. "I am becoming inured to criticism. When you're in my position, people are always going to talk about you." She told me of a story that went around about her several years ago in which she was accused of purchasing a ring of extraordinary value. "Everyone knew someone who had seen the bill of sale, but it could never be found. It happened to Raisa Gorbachev too. I work with a wide variety of people from all segments of life. I'll never be approved of by everybody."

In all the time that I spent with her, there was never once when I felt I could have crossed the boundaries into the verbal intimacies of Americans meeting abroad. Her guard is never relaxed. Her conversation is without levity. It is not that she is humorless; it is simply that her sky is so darkened with the winds of war and its consequences that there is no time for laughter in her life. She is always addressed as Your Majesty. As an American, I found it difficult to call another American Your Majesty, but there is no other form of address. There are those in the court who address the king as Sidi, an affectionate term meaning "sir" or "My Lord," and address the queen as Sitti, meaning "My Lady," but I never did.

"How many assassination attempts have there been on the king?" I asked. I had been told there had been twenty-seven during his thirty-eight-year reign.

She waved her hands in front of her face as if to dispel my question. "I don't know. I don't want to know. My husband has learned from experience to be wise and prescient. He gives each moment of his life a maximum energy for good use. If we sealed ourselves off in a protective bubble, we wouldn't be able to reach out and touch and feel what people need. I feel they should be able to touch us. I'm willing to take the risk of being stampeded upon if it gives them hope. It runs against any security advice he has been given over the years. They feel he is not just a figurehead, or head of state in his office. He is there as a father to the people."

"Would you discuss the succession?" I asked her.

"At the moment, Prince Hassan, the king's brother, is the crown prince, so he is the king's successor. In this country, the succession has always been modified to accommodate. The monarchy should always be able to serve as a constructive and unifying force. The most important thing is that it serves the people of the country. For me, it's entirely in harmony with all I was raised to believe the role of the leader should be. It should not seek to protect its existence for its own sake."

When Prince Abdullah, the older son of Princess Muna, was born, in 1962, King Hussein named him as the crown prince, but since the country was in a constantly turbulent state, Hussein realized that a small child was not a reasonable successor. The king has two brothers. Prince Muhammad and Prince Hassan. Muhammad, who was next in line after the child Abdullah, was married to, and later divorced from, the international social figure Princess Firyal, who subsequently had a highly publicized liaison with the Greek shipping magnate Stavros Niarchos. After much consideration, the king bypassed Muhammad in favor of his younger brother, Prince Hassan, who is twelve years younger than the king. Oxford-educated and a brilliant public speaker, Hassan is considered the intellectual of the family. His wife, Princess Sarvath, is the daughter of a distinguished Pakistani leader and ambassador. Since the ratification of Hassan, the king has bypassed his two sons by the English Princess Muna and has named Prince Ali, his son by the Jordanian Queen Alia, as next in line after Prince Hassan. Prince Ali, now fifteen, attends Deerfield Academy in Massachusetts.

"I have heard it said that, because you are an American, you are becoming a liability to the king. Is that correct?"

She seemed surprised. "I haven't felt that. I have never felt it. I was born into an Arab-American family. My name, Halaby, is Arabic. I have returned to the Arab world. I am not aware that my Americanism is a liability."

Although most people in Amman dress in Western fashion, there is a growing group of Muslim fundamentalist women who have eschewed modern dress as a form of protest. "It has come out of the frustrations of the people," Sima Bahous had told me the day before. "Everybody wants an identity. It is more than a religious movement. If they unite behind a front, their voice will be heard."

"Do you feel threatened by the fundamentalists?" I asked the queen.

"I personally don't feel threatened, but I know that my work and what I have achieved could be threatened by them. Extremism will only feed off the economic inequalities. Traditionally, women in this area, even my mother-in-law, Queen Zein, wore their hair covered. It is part of the cultural tradition. As religious extremism started to develop, there came a form of dress that was devoid of color, that covered the body from head to toe. Over it is worn a headdress that is restrictive, an uglifying fashion psychologically, to defeminize, to desex, to make women totally unappealing, to negate their femininity. It is a symbol of submission. There is pressure brought to women to dress like that. I don't dress for the conservatives in society. At the same time, I don't dress the way Western women do, which would be immodest in this country."

"If war comes, do you fear losing your throne?"

"In the first place, I don't consider myself as having a throne. The only thing I would ever fear is if the peace and stability that the monarchy has offered to this country were destroyed, if all my husband struggled for, and what I have struggled for by his side, were lost. That is what I fear for. My happiness, satisfaction, and security do not come from the throne or the monarchy or having been privileged to carry the title of Queen of Jordan."

Her older son, Prince Hamzah, arrived from school and crossed the lawn to greet his mother. Dressed in a black T-shirt and light trousers, he looked like any American boy of ten arriving home from school, ready for playtime. In a garage on the opposite side of the palace, there were miniature Volkswagens and jeeps for the royal children, the kind that run on gasoline. Hamzah was joined by the princes' young American tutor. After greeting his mother and talking about the events of his school day, Hamzah pointed to the far end of the garden and asked, "Can we make some noise down there?"

The queen smiled and nodded to her son, and then resumed the conversation. "People are beginning to realize that we in Jordan don't conform to the worst stereotypes of the oil rich, or the worst stereotypes of the terrorists. Each Arab society is different from the others. For many in the Arab world, Saddam is a patriot. He represents someone who has stood up to the overwhelming forces of the West for what he believes in. He is against Western interference in Arab affairs. For many Arabs, whose history has been marked by Western interference over many decades, his tough stand is deemed to be courageous. Whatever happens, we shall follow King Hussein. For thirty-eight years, his humanity, experience, and wisdom have been what the people identify with."

In the background Prince Hamzah appeared from behind a tree, carrying a very realistic toy assault rifle. The tutor could be seen hiding behind another tree. The queen watched for a minute, shrugged, and said, "I guess he plays war with the boys."

It had turned dark. "Will you turn on the garden lights?" she called out to Prince Hamzah. Then her youngest child, Princess Raiyah, age four, arrived back at the palace from a children's music class. Dressed in pink jeans and a pink T-shirt, she raced to her mother. For several minutes they discussed the music class.

There was the beginning of a chill in the air. "The weather's going to change," she said. "This will be the last time I have lunch in the garden. It will soon be too cold to sit out like this. Sometimes there's even snow." She stood up. "Would you like to see the children's zoo?" she asked.

"If war comes, what will happen to Jordan?" I asked Sima Bahous.

"Some people think Jordan will suffer the most," she replied. "If it comes, the people in the streets will not be quiet. The youth of the country will not accept war without having a say in what will come about."

"Will the king survive?"

"War means change," she said. "Everything will be in danger. Not the king, who is popular, but the institution of monarchy."

On the night before I left Amman, the king and queen asked a small group of American journalists to dinner at the palace. On arriving there, each guest was given a seating plan showing where his or her place would be at the table. Thirty-five minutes after we had assembled and been served nonalcoholic drinks, the king and queen arrived in the reception room and, as a couple, moved around the room, greeting each guest. That night the queen wore tight black trousers and a loose-fitting black evening sweater. The king was wearing a dark business suit.

They did not sit at the head and foot of the long, narrow, elaborately set table. Instead, they sat opposite each other at the center of the table, so that during general conversation they were able to converse together. While we were served food passed by a staff of waiters, the king's plate was brought to him with food already on it. He ate almost nothing. Speaking in quiet tones, he held the attention of the entire table as he explained his role in trying to keep peace in the Middle East since August 2, when he had been awakened by King Fahd of Saudi Arabia at six o'clock in the morning to be told that the invasion of Kuwait had taken place. In the first forty-eight hours, he had gone off to mediate at the request of President Bush, President Mubarak, and King Fahd. He had been given assurances that there would be no condemnation of President Hussein, nothing to put him on the defensive. His efforts at peacekeeping, however, had been misunderstood, mistrusted, or rebuffed by former allies and friends. He seemed mired in personal melancholy, smoking cigarette after cigarette during the meal. Taking a cue from the king, a journalist seated to the left of the queen also lit up a cigarette. The queen mildly chastised the journalist for smoking, a chastisement clearly meant for the king.

Rising at the end of the dinner, the male reporters made a beeline for the queen, surrounding her to ask questions. From the sidelines, the king watched his wife at the center of the group of reporters and smiled proudly and affectionately. Lisa Halaby, Queen Noor al Hussein, had clearly come into her moment in time.

January 1991

OIL CITY LIBRARY
2 Central Avenue • Oil City, PA 16301

In Memory of

Paul Burtnett

Presented by

Northwest Savings Bank
Employees

THE GREATEST ADVENTURE

ASSOCIATION OF SPACE EXPLORERS

C. PIERSON
PUBLISHERS

G629.45
G798a

OIL CITY LIBRARY
2 CENTRAL AVENUE
OIL CITY, PA. 16301

ACKNOWLEDGEMENTS

A book of this magnitude and scope was made possible by the contribution of many talented people.

In particular the publisher thanks the astronauts and cosmonauts who participated in the project and the following people for their patience and input into what turned out to be a complicated project:

Victor Blagov, Dosmond Chew, Ted Everts, Edward Gibson, George Gibson, Dennis Hall, Christine Hoskins, Jim McMahon, Di Quick, Lim Gim Seng, Dick Underwood, Ingaret Ward and Peter Woodhead.

Photographs on previous pages:
Vladimir Kovalyonok emerging from Salyut-6 *to undertake an EVA.*
Sunset over the South American Atlantic coast, southern Brazil is on the horizon.

C. Pierson, Publishers
PO Box 87
Mosman NSW 2088
Sydney Australia

First published 1994
© Copyright 1994 Association of Space Explorers

This book is copyright. Apart from any fair dealings as permitted under the Copyright Act, no part may be reproduced by any means without permission. Enquiries should be addressed to the publisher.

The Greatest Adventure.
 ISBN 0 947068 19 8
 1. Manned space flight. 2 Astronauts. I. Association of Space Explorers.
 629.45

Consulting Editor: Dr Edward Gibson
Editor: Ingaret Ward
Designers: Di Quick and Dana Lundmark
Picture Research: Dick Underwood and Dennis Hall
All photography: courtesy of NASA and ASE Russia
Color Separations: Pica Overseas Pte Ltd
Printer: Stan Graphics Consultant, Singapore

CONTENTS

FOREWORD

James A. Michener

Space shuttle
Challenger
*lifts a crew of
eight into
Earth orbit, 30
October 1985.*

As I study the movements of humanity across the surface of Earth, I am awed by three adventures. Why did our early people, who must have been comfortable in their warm African settlements, ever decide to trek north into the fearfully inclement Arctic regions to live with snowscapes and reindeer? They must have been lured north by some powerful urge.

When they were more or less comfortably settled in the Arctic regions, whose characteristics they had now mastered, why did they feel compelled to cross the land bridge over the Bering Sea and wander south into Canada, the United States, Panama and Chile, all the way to Patagonia? They must have been driven south by the same kind of powerful urge.

And millennia later, when our American colonists were safely settled on the shores of the Atlantic Ocean, why did they feel compelled to move ever westward until they reached the Pacific, while at about the same time Russians, who were securely established in western Europe, felt driven to explore constantly eastward till they reached the shores of North America? I have been amused by philosophers who argue that Americans had some inborn drive to head toward the sunset, while Russians, almost the same kind of people, seem to have an inborn compulsion to move ever eastward toward the sunrise! From such speculations I decided that long before human beings took their first substantial steps into space, they had a desire not to move outward in any one direction or in search of any one goal, but a desire simply to explore. In our day, we are driven to explore outward to the limits of space, and this compulsion will never be satisfied by half-measures.

I felt such urges when I was five or six, wondering where the dirt road that led past our house would take me if I started down it, and this curiosity was converted into action when, at age twelve, I began wandering far from home and at fourteen set out with thirty-five cents in my pocket to explore the entire eastern seaboard of the United States, from Florida to Canada. Later I would venture out to all the continents, all the oceans, all the great mountain ranges, across the deserts and into the remote corners of my planet.

In the midst of these explorations, which have never ended, I became aware that a group of brilliant German scientists—in the pre-Hitler era—were applying the insatiable human thirst for exploration to a milieu of which I had been only slightly aware: outer space. From childhood I had studied the stars, memorized the constellations of the Zodiac and made myself familiar with Messier's list of the major nebulae, but I had failed to realize that we would relatively soon be able to leave Earth and soar out into space, thus directing our innate sense of exploration to a challenging new arena.

Once I learned what the Germans were attempting, I started looking into the accomplishments of our own space engineers and found to my surprise that they, too, were standing on the edge of space exploration. Some years later, because of my interest in space and my testimony before Congress to champion America's attempts to reach the moon, I was appointed to the board which advises our National Aeronautics and Space Administration, and from that vantage point, I help our nation explore space. Everything I saw firmed my belief that human beings have a psychological need to probe outward, and I stopped trying to explain to my friends why we were engaged in the great adventures of walking on the moon and sending our miracle machines out to the farthest planets. We were taking these steps because our ancestors, time and again, had done the same in their indefatigable exploration of all parts of Earth. We assumed the obligation because we had to.

But as I worked in the space program, I confronted one of the perplexing dichotomies of our time, one that none of my ancient exploring predecessors had had to confront. When Columbus, in 1491, stood on the shores of the Atlantic Ocean anticipating the world-changing voyage he was determined to make the next year in his frail caravels, he did not have the option of considering an enticing alternative to this perilous voyage: 'Why not just send the ships alone to explore the western seas? If they succeed and return safely, then we can follow with men.' The mechanisation of ships had not progressed to the point at which they could be dispatched unmanned. Men had to accompany them to ensure that they kept functioning and to bring them safely home with messages of what they had seen and accomplished.

But in the 1960s when the United States and the Soviet Union decided about the same time to explore the moon, they did face the tantalizing question of whether to do it by unmanned scientific probes that could photograph all

Later the subject of a United States postage stamp, the first Earthrise witnessed by human beings, Christmas 1968.

its aspects and send reports back to Earth, or whether they should employ people to do the job. Early in the debate I was caught in its tangles, and because I had been fairly good in mathematics and appreciated what properly designed engines could accomplish, I was an early proponent of relying on intelligent machines to explore space.

This decision then placed me in the Russian camp of space explorers. They, too, gambled on the sophisticated machine, and few Americans realize that capable unmanned Soviet space craft reached the moon and photographed it close up well before American ones did. It was the Soviet photographs that revealed the moon's hitherto unseen half.

It was obvious that our entire solar system could be explored by sophisticated machines whose cameras would send back to Earth binary signals—not actual photographs

as we know them, but rather the information on which photographs could be built or reconstructed—that would reveal the secrets of Venus, Jupiter, Saturn, Uranus and Neptune. Indeed, that has already been accomplished with staggering brilliance. Unmanned exploration works, and if we can somehow tease our great Hubble space telescope into working properly, its revelations are going to be mind wrenching.

As I was satisfying myself that we *could* accomplish miracles with relatively inexpensive unmanned flight, I became increasingly aware that the real question was: 'Should we?' The more I studied this problem, the more clearly I saw that the taxpayers of a democracy like ours would soon grow bored with merely mechanical explorations of space, regardless of the revolutionary photographs that resulted and the mind-changes such information produced. Our exploration of space would be

*Buzz Aldrin, second human to set foot on the
moon, 20–21 July 1969.*

endangered if it relied solely on machines. To retain the interest of the public, human beings had to be involved in the explorations. Space had to be inspected first hand by human beings whose reactions would enable the rest of us to understand and appreciate what was happening and how human thought was being modified.

Put in its bluntest terms, taxpayers will support a space program only if human beings are involved as passengers. If we rely solely on machines, interest will flag and support will vanish! On this sound principle, the American astronaut program, one of our outstanding successes in recent decades, was founded.

I have been told that it was President Eisenhower's initial decision that saved the program. When word went out that a new breed of men was to be projected into space with all the glory and danger that this implied, the managers of the program were probably suspicious that all the weirdos and romantic space buffs would flood the application process. Eisenhower said: 'Simple. We'll choose from among the military aviation pilots we already have', and thus the high professionalism of the early years was established. Quickly, however, we realized that nonmilitary types like scientists were needed in the program, and Ike himself might have been astonished when fairly soon women, too, were invited to become astronauts. (Russians preferred the name *cosmonaut*, and one of them, Valentina Tereshkova, became the first woman in space.)

The impeccable deportment of our astronauts and the Russian cosmonauts lent not only dignity to the projects, but also a keen understanding of what space exploration meant in human terms. In the previous volume to this book, *The Home Planet*, the astronauts, in brief passages from their notes, reported on what they saw and how it changed their attitudes toward their Earth and life upon it. None phrased their reactions more elegantly than Sultan bin Salman Al-Saud of Saudi Arabia, a passenger on *Discovery 5* in June 1985: 'The first day or so we all pointed to our countries. The third or fourth day we were pointing to our continents. By the fifth day, we were aware of only one Earth.'

In this volume the astronauts and cosmonauts take a major step forward. They write not single sentences or brief paragraphs, but substantial summaries of how their adventures into space affected them and, especially, how the discoveries they made have affected society in general.

These glowing words prove the validity of my earlier conclusion that to be meaningful, the exploration of space must involve human beings—wonderful as my cherished machines are, they cannot express themselves in words as resonant as these examples.

Where does all this leave me in my attitudes toward space and its ultimate meanings? I've spent a long apprenticeship trying to clarify my reactions, but they have never been better summarized than in a remarkable two-page color photograph I once saw. It shows in brilliant detail an area in the center of our galaxy where the nebulae Lagoon and Trifid are in the process of creating new stars and allowing old ones to die and return to primordial matter. The turbulence is majestic, with the chaotic brilliance of birth, but what impresses me even more is the blazing multitude of individual stars shown in this one small segment of the heavens. They remind me that our planetary system revolves about a smallish star in a galaxy that contains more than a billion stars, and that there are probably more than a billion similar galaxies, some much larger than our middle-sized one. This means that there can be a billion billion stars, many of which might carry with them planetary systems like ours. This means that a vast multitude of worlds like ours could exist in space.

We have what is almost a celestial imperative to solve the mysteries of space and to explore those fragments of it that are available to us. We must send humans to visit Mars to determine whether at one time it could have been a populated planet like ours, so that its history of radical change to an unpopulated desert might prefigure our own destiny. We should send unmanned probes to the outer reaches of our solar system, and we should continue to monitor space on the chance that some other civilization, millions of light years away, may have been sending signals into the vast void that separates the stars. When the first human left his safe abode in Central Africa to see what might be hiding in the next valley, he launched us on an inquisitive exploration that will never end.

In our generation, that outward thrust will be conducted by two agencies that have proved themselves: the skilled machine flying outward of itself, but bound electronically to commands from Earth, and the human astronaut-cosmonaut who takes shorter trips but who brings back interpretations that no machine could duplicate. This book focuses on the second half of our great adventure!

Lake Van in Eastern Turkey contrasts sharply with the snow-covered mountains and valleys.

PREFACE

Memories and thoughts, vivid when formed, have a way of evaporating with time. When they could be of value to those who follow, documentation, regardless of its form, becomes an obligation.

Thus, as we approached the 25th anniversary of our first lunar landing, the Association of Space Explorers offered its astronaut and cosmonaut members the opportunity to put in writing their recollections and reflections on their missions or their vision for the future. Though most space explorers are not writers by nature, many responded with significant effort to produce one or more essays.

From an editing standpoint, the reservoir of rich material that resulted presented a challenge. Space limitations precluded the inclusion of every submission, and most of the essays that are included had to be substantially shortened. Also, in the interest of editorial honesty (as well as of editor-preservation—this group is not noted for its timidity), extra care had to be taken to make only changes that increased the clarity of the message without altering its content.

The unflagging commitment and zeal of Charles Pierson, the publisher, and the hard work of Ingaret Ward, his extremely able in-house editor, energized the editing process. And in the end, the process turned out to be not only a challenge, but a pleasure, and even more, an enlightenment, as we anticipate the final result will be for you.

From a sampling of the trials and struggles encountered by the explorers flight after flight, the group's emotional roller coaster ride over a third of a century of triumphs and failures, and the resulting visions and convictions on what could lie ahead, one begins to grasp the legacy now at the doorstep of the current generation of policy makers. Clearly, space is a major frontier—finally open to humanity —an opportunity paid for by several significant national investments, the careers of hundreds of thousands of highly-skilled workers dedicated to a cause, and the lives of some of the colleagues of those who have written here.

A legacy, a trust ... where do we go from here?

Will we learn to use the zero gravity, the vacuum and the

vantage point of space for improving the quality of life down here on Earth, to use space as a focal point for human cooperation, and to respond to the incessant beckoning of new lands to be explored and settled? What stories will be available for telling in *The Greatest Adventure*, as published in 2027?

The answers lie, in large part, with you, the reader, the citizen. If the moments you spend with this book provide not only entertainment, but add to your understanding and enthusiasm for where we are now poised, then there is added hope that, together, we can stimulate the political wisdom and will to respond positively and decisively.

Edward Gibson
Editor

Unusual cloud formations seen from the MIR space station over the Atlantic Ocean.

INTRODUCTION

During an informal gathering at a rural French chateau in 1985, 25 astronauts and cosmonauts from 13 nations discussed with growing enthusiasm their common memories; viewing the sunlit expanse of a whole ocean, the jagged heights of an entire mountain range or the total length of a mighty river or deep canyon; or at night, the glimmering surfaces of moon-lit lakes and rivers, the sparkling lights of many of Earth's major cities or the glow of man-made conflagrations of crops or timber. But they had equally memorable impressions of what they did not see—borders separating the peoples of their nations.

As they talked, they realized that they had something else in common: a burning desire to adequately relate their incredible journeys to the people of the world who had sent them. They felt privileged to act as observers for all humankind, which had finally taken its first step outward from Earth and now paused to look back. And they felt compelled to publicize the true significance and potential of further steps toward the stars.

In this spirit, they founded the Association of Space Explorers (ASE). It was agreed that through annual meetings and more frequent communications, they would work together toward their common goals.

From the start, ASE members envisaged publishing a book of photographs and words to convey both the drama and beauty of their ventures. The result, *The Home Planet*, told a visceral tale of the universal human response to seeing our planet from afar. It presented the magnificence yet fragility of Earth in stunning photographs accompanied by brief personal recollections.

But these explorers soon realized that, collectively, they had another, and perhaps even more stirring tale to tell, one that required not only photographs and reflection, but essays that could even more convincingly put the reader in the mind, body and soul of the space explorer. Thus, *The Greatest Adventure*.

Together, the words and photographs presented here tell an exciting story, a sweeping story of the challenges faced before, during and after historic space flights, of intense and dangerous technical feats, of the nuts and bolts of working at the business end of this proud profession. They tell of the continuing flights of today and tomorrow, of the start of the greatest outward human migration imaginable. And in a more detailed way than accomplished before, they lay open the explorer's deeper thoughts and emotions for all to view.

In the end, however, the overriding theme of the stories told here, like the ASE itself, is that of a common humanity. Since the first meeting of the founding explorers, the ASE's membership has increased tenfold and the number of countries its members represent has doubled. This year of 1994, the year of the first edition of *The Greatest Adventure,* marks the 25th anniversary of humankind's first landing on the moon. Although this mission was an unprecedented human and technical achievement, it was driven by the Cold War between superpowers.

But, thankfully, the world is changing.

This year, the ASE will for the first time meet in Moscow for its tenth annual Congress. A Russian cosmonaut for the first time has flown aboard the American Space Shuttle. Plans are also in place for American astronauts to fly aboard Russia's *MIR* space station. And, most important to future generations, many European nations, Japan and Canada are joined together with America and Russia in an unprecedented international collaboration to design, build and operate a global space station for the benefit of all humankind.

The ASE salutes these efforts, a bold and critical next step in the exploration and use of space and in human cooperation—a continuation of *The Greatest Adventure.*

John Fabian
ASE Co-President, USA

Vladimir Kovalyonok
ASE Co-President, Russia

The classic view of a full Earth taken enroute to the moon at a range of about 26 000 miles, December 1972.

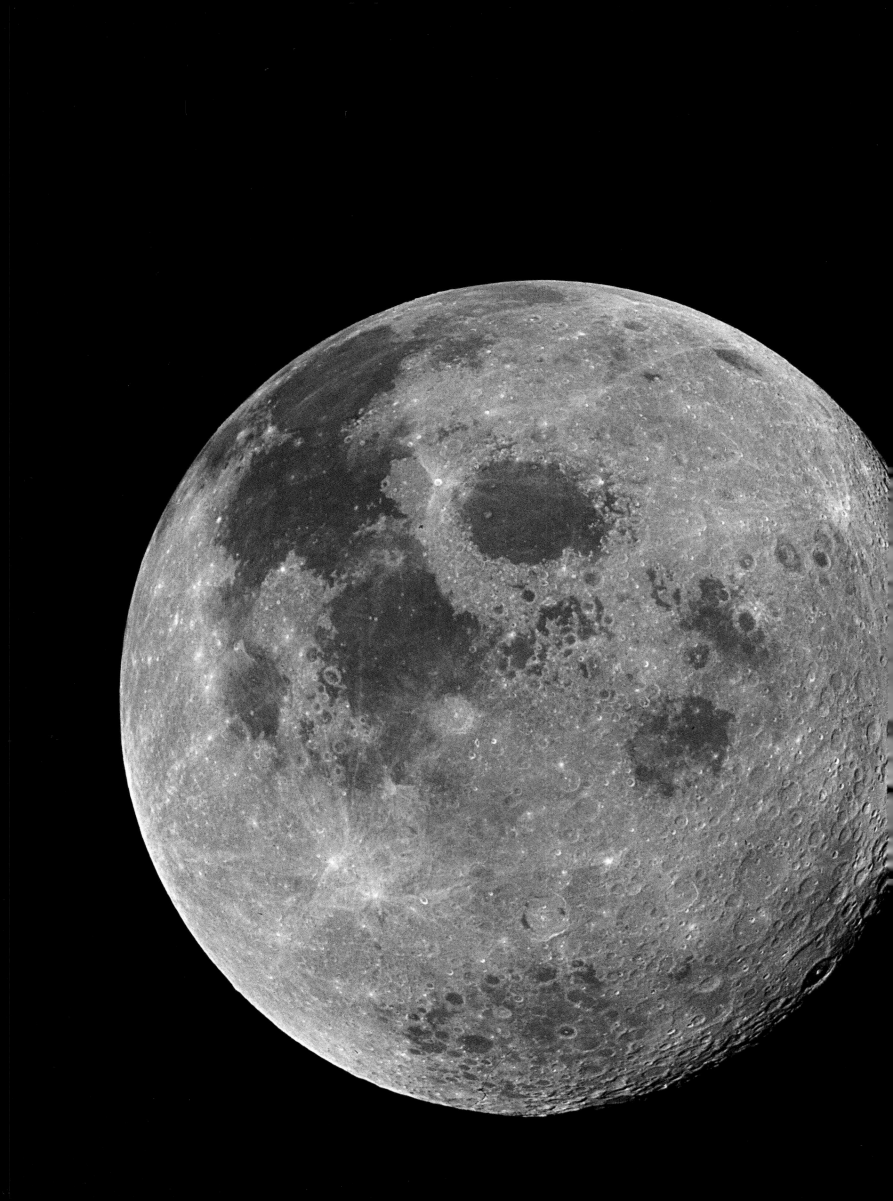

PART 1

THE URGE TO EXPLORE

A different view of a full moon as seen from Earth due to the alignment of Earth, moon and Apollo 17 spacecraft.

THE LAST FRONTIER

The sun lights up the horizon and silhouettes the cloud layers. The two orange 'suns' below the horizon are reflections on the double pane window of space shuttle Columbia.

We, as humans, have always gone where we have been able to go in order to satisfy our inquisitive nature, and if we now choose to turn our backs on further exploration, I think we all lose something substantial. Exploration produces a mood in us, a widening of interest, a stimulation of our thoughts, and I would hate to see it wither.

When we fail to push ourselves to the possible limits of our universe in a physical sense, it causes a mental slackening as well, and we are all the poorer for it. We should explore our universe by both microscope and telescope. And it is clearly wrong to argue that less emphasis on one will automatically cause a more powerful focus on the other.

Space is the only physical frontier we have left, and its continued exploration will produce real, if unpredictable, benefits to all of us who remain behind on this planet. That one cannot spell out in any detail what these benefits will be does not contradict or deny their potential existence. We all know examples of unexpected by-products of research, such as penicillin, and of our serendipity in new environments, but my favorite story goes back to 1783 when Ben Franklin witnessed the first public launching of a hydrogen balloon in Paris and was asked by a skeptic, 'Of what possible use is this new invention?'. Franklin replied, 'Of what use is a newborn babe?'.

Michael Collins, USA from *Carrying the Fire*

PROUD TO BE PART OF THE BEGINNING

Prerequisites: an active-duty test pilot with at least 1 500 hours of flight time and experience in jets; no more than 5 feet 11 inches in height or 39 years of age; and a Bachelor Degree or equivalent.

These were certainly new, maybe even slightly strange, job requirements—at least they seemed so back in 1958 when President Eisenhower instructed NASA to select candidates for Project Mercury.

After considerable poking and probing, Scott Carpenter, Gordon Cooper, Gus Grissom, Wally Schirra, Al Shepard, Deke Slayton and I survived the selection process.

Much preparation followed, including many hours in a simulator that closely duplicated what we would see in the *Mercury* capsule. Al Shepard got the first mission, a sub-orbital flight, followed by a second sub-orbital mission by Gus Grissom. On 20 February 1962 I made my flight aboard *Friendship 7*, a mission of three orbits—the first American orbital flight.

Commonplace to the astronaut or cosmonaut today, the sensations of space flight were new to us then, and sometimes very surprising. Significant pressure from G-forces thrust me into my seat during launch. At thrust cut-off, weightlessness registered on the capsule's instruments, yet it didn't register in my mind until a turn-around of the capsule brought me up in a sitting position. Pleasant, yes definitely a pleasant sensation, and contrary to the predictions of some scientists. Straps kept me in place, while my camera floated before my face, a natural place to stow it while I did other work. Also, there seemed to be little sensation of speed although I glided over Earth at about 5 miles per second, a speed many today still find difficult to comprehend.

It is hard to beat a day in which you see four spectacular sunsets and a brilliance of colors spread across the horizon. Thirty years ago, before pictures from space became commonplace, the view from *Friendship 7* was extraordinary. At first, most of Earth was covered by clouds until I passed over Australia and could see the lights of entire cities.

I was accompanied on my flight by what resembled huge masses of fireflies, tiny luminescent particles surrounding my spacecraft, which were later determined to be ice crystals formed by the steam released from the capsule's life support system.

The three orbits of *Friendship 7* demonstrated, as has been done many times since, that flight in space is rarely trouble free and the abilities of the human on board are usually underestimated. My flight plan called for me to switch from automatic to manual control over several hours in roll, pitch and yaw, one axis at a time, then two in various combinations, and then all three as a final proof of the human ability to control a spacecraft in flight. When the automatic system malfunctioned, I took over all the controls, all at once, for both the second and third orbits, as well as the re-entry, and had no problem doing so.

Certainly my flight in *Friendship 7* was rewarding, but perhaps the most gratifying aspect of my participation in the space program was the tremendous reception I received on my return, from Americans and around the world. My wife, Annie, and I will never forget the heartfelt warmth that the public extended to us. I am indeed proud to have had the privilege to take part in the beginning of our outward reach into space.

John Glenn, USA

The first American in space, Alan Shepard, lifts off atop a Redstone *booster 5 May 1961. His flight time was 15 minutes 22 seconds. John Glenn flew America's first orbital flight, 20 February 1962, flight time 4 hours 55 minutes 23 seconds.*

DEAR SON

7 May 1962
M. Scott Carpenter
PO Box 95 PALMER LAKE,
COLORADO

Dear Son,

Just a few words on the eve of your great adventure for which you have trained yourself and have anticipated for so long—to let you know that we shall share it with you, vicariously.

As I think I remarked to you at the outset of the space program, you are privileged to share in a pioneering project on a grand scale—in fact the grandest scale yet known to man. And I venture to predict that after all the huzzas have been uttered and the public acclaim is but a memory, you will derive the greatest satisfaction from the serene knowledge that you have discovered new truths. You can say to yourself: this I saw, this I experienced, this I know to be the truth. This experience is a precious thing; it is known to all researchers, in whatever field of endeavour, who have ventured into the unknown and have discovered new truths.

You are probably aware that I am not a particularly religious person, at least in the sense of embracing any of the numerous formal doctrines. Yet I cannot conceive of a man endowed with intellect, perceiving the ordered universe about him, the glory of a mountain top, the plumage of a tropical bird, the intricate complexity of a protein molecule, the utter and unchanging perfection of a salt crystal, who can deny the existence of some higher power. Whether he chooses to call it God or Mohammed or Buddha or Turquoise Woman or the Law of Probability matters little. I find myself in my writings frequently calling upon Mother Nature to explain things and citing Her as responsible for the order in the universe. She is a very satisfactory divinity for me. And so I shall call upon Her to watch over you and guard you and, if she so desires, share with you some of Her secrets which She is usually so ready to share with those who have high purpose.

With all my love,

Dad

Sunlight interplays between ocean and clouds over the Indian Ocean, about 1200 miles north of Wilkes Land, Antarctica.

25

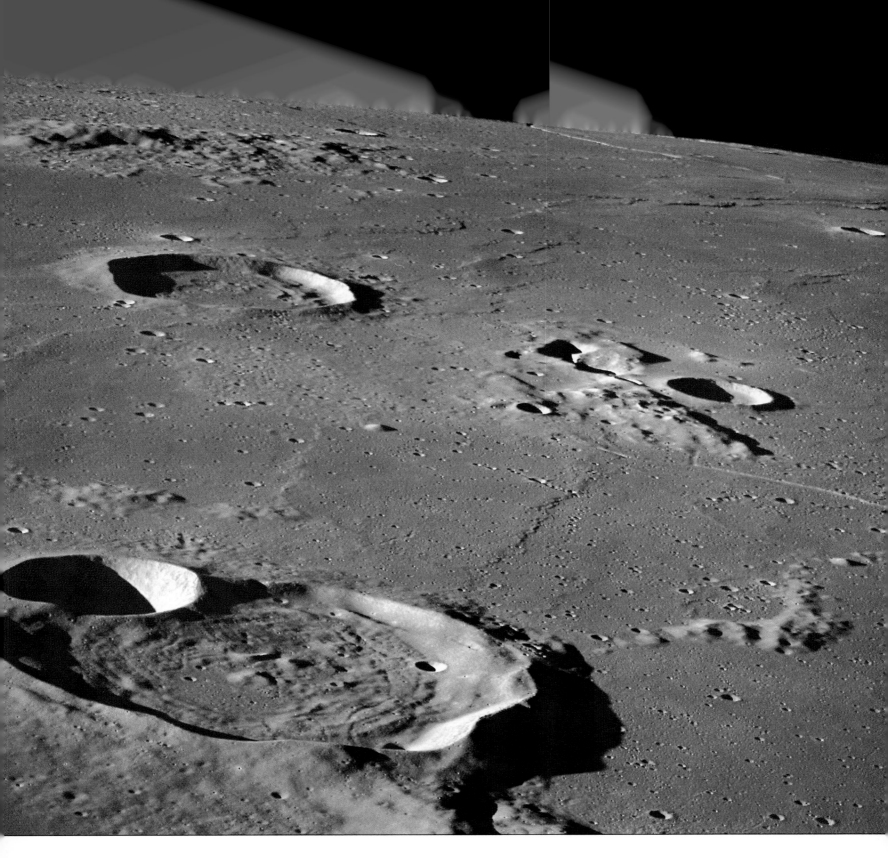

The craters Davy, Lassell and Lassell-C stand out in the Sea of Clouds.

WALLY'S LAST HURRAH

Apollo 7 was the first manned flight of the Apollo program. In one of those rare and envied opportunities, we would be the first to 'kick the tires and light the fire' on the newest and hottest flying machine. Such firsts are prized milestones in a test pilot's career—certainly more than I had dared hope for when I joined the space program.

At the time, Wally Schirra was 45 years old. The 'Old Pro' was saddled with two rookies (Don Eisele and me) on what is still the most ambitious first flight ever undertaken with any new vehicle—anywhere—anytime. *Apollo* 7 lasted for 11 days and had 3 people crowded into a cubicle the size of the back seat of a large American sedan.

In our profession, one man's opportunity frequently arises from another man's misfortune, and that was the case with the three of us. The first *Apollo* mission was originally scheduled to beflown by Gus Grissom and his crew two years earlier. When a spacecraft fire on the launch pad claimed the lives of our three friends, we inherited their key mission—the first giant step towards landing a man on the moon.

Since the exact cause of the fire was never determined, everything in the spacecraft considered to be a possible cause was changed. Finally, after five years of training, 21 months to recover from the fire, a half dozen crank letters and an untold number of last minute telephone calls from nervous engineers, we launched on a mission that would tell the world the American space program was back.

Everyone was aware that a second catastrophe following so closely after the *Apollo* fire could threaten the survival of the entire manned space effort. We shared the sense of urgency without feeling any anxiety about the mission.

Don Eisele and I achieved our objective of flying in space after five years of thorough and sometimes monotonous preparation. Crew training for *Apollo* 7 seemed aimed at reducing a magnificent and exciting experience to a routine, even 'boring' mission but it was also one of the primary reasons for our ultimate success.

On our second day in orbit, Wally Schirra woke up with the Grand Daddy of all head colds—hardly a fair reward for the three hours of sleep we had enjoyed following a launch day that was 23 hours long. Fair or not, our cozy little spacecraft was quickly turned into a used kleenex container. And our efficiency was lowered at the worst possible time—the beginning of the mission when the work load was the heaviest. It also raised the prospect of an early return with the risk of damage to Wally's eardrums from the pressure change during re-entry.

The cold left Wally feeling too wretched for several days to even get out of his sleep restraint. On the ground, he might have called in sick or gone to the doctor. We didn't have that luxury, and Wally's discomfort was magnified by the unrelenting demand of one complex test after another. Wally continued to perform, even from his 'sickbed', but the always critical schedule of activities made him more irascible by the day.

As spacecraft commander, Wally was in control of the spacecraft during those crucial times when our necks were on the line. It was Wally's hand on the abort handle during boost; he did most of the spacecraft maneuvering; and he flew the re-entry. A mistake by any of us could blow the mission or worse—the spacecraft—but Wally's responsibility carried with it the lion's share of the stress.

As interesting and challenging as space flight could be, over the years it could take its toll even on dedicated men. Wally Schirra once observed, 'This program devours people'.

In spite of close quarters, colds and flight plan changes, the mission wore on and the years of preparation paid off. *Apollo* 7 was routine but not boring, filled with accomplishment, a success by any measure—a great mission for Wally Schirra's last hurrah.

The *Apollo* 7 spacecraft was made of steel and other exotic materials, built to withstand lots of abuse. The more it was used the better a machine it became. But man is more fragile and wear and tear takes its toll—even when we may not be aware of it. We were proud of the work we accomplished, little realizing our faces were reflecting the strain of the three-year effort. The camera captured what we consciously ignored and only understand now, in retrospect.

Not as glamorous as the media image, *Apollo* 7 was certainly more challenging, interesting and rewarding. We did it right the first time!

Walter Cunningham, USA

Wally Schirra shows the physical strain of the mission commander.

Over page:
Distant mountains rise above the horizon of the moon. The lunar Rover tracks from the Apollo 17 *mission will be visible for millions of years.*

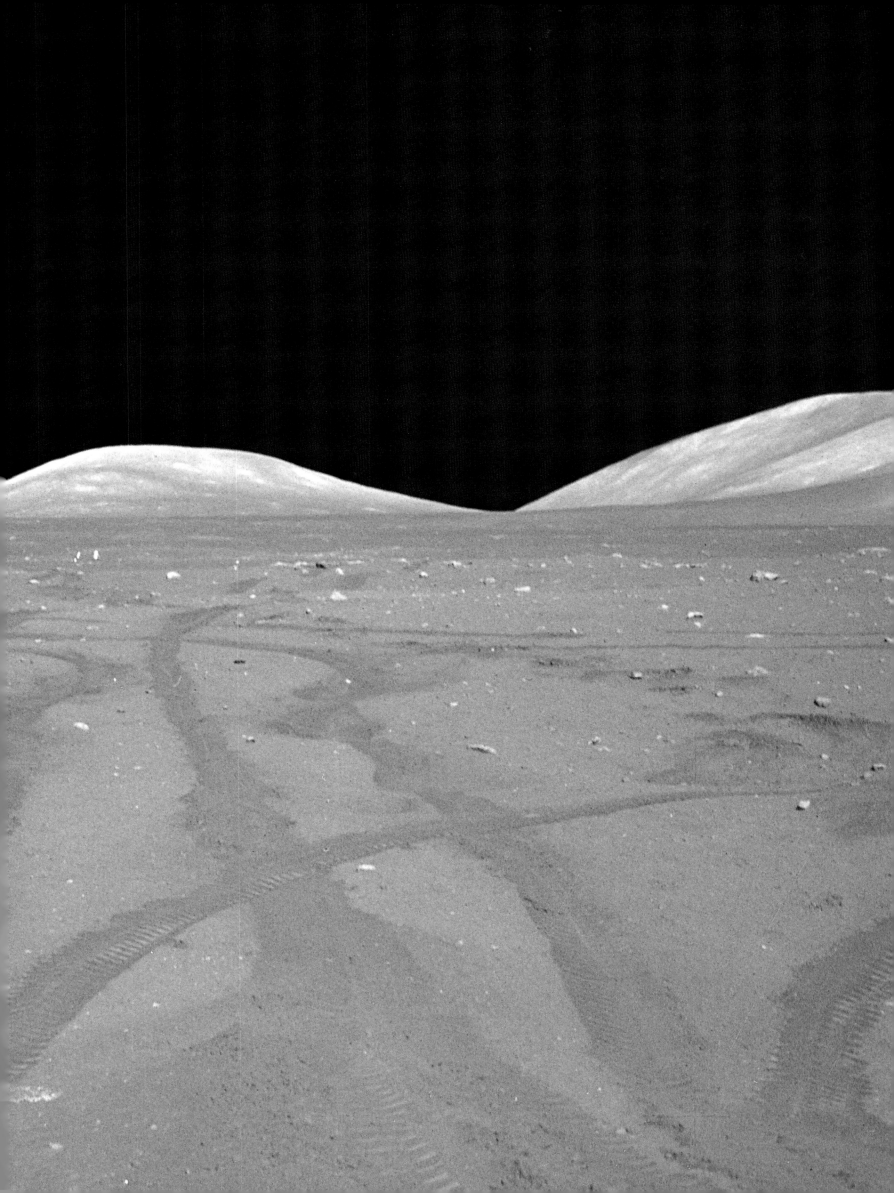

20 July 1969

Through the triangular windows of the lunar module, Neil and I watched an endless chaotic map of gray craters sweep underneath. Green digits on the small computer screen continued to blink as we flew westward over the lunar equator.

We had no sensation of falling as we glided backwards with our bodies parallel to the surface. We approached 'perilune', the lowest point on our coasting orbit and just 10 miles over the silent dust and craters below. Soon the computer would initiate the final 12 minutes of our landing attempt—powered descent.

'*Eagle,* Houston' the capcom, Charlie Duke, called from mission control, a quarter of a million miles away. 'If you read, you're go for powered descent.'

Charlie's voice was barely distinguishable in my headset. Since coming around the edge of the moon, from the side away from Earth, our voice and data link with Houston had been shaky. Mike Collins, orbiting 50 miles above us in the command module *Columbia,* heard Houston clearly.

Left: *Buzz Aldrin removing scientific experiments from the lunar module for deployment at the Tranquility Base 20-21 July 1969.*

Right: *A lunar 'farside' photo of an area never seen from Earth. The International Astronomical Union designates the large crater as #308. It has a width of about 50 miles.*

'*Eagle,* this is *Columbia*' Mike called, his voice calm. 'They just gave you a go for powered descent.'

The green digits flashed, announcing powered flight. Beneath our feet, propellants sprayed into the combustion chamber, ignited on contact, and spewed out a soundless plume of orange flame into the sunlit vacuum of space. The lunar module slowed as the computer throttled up the engine to full power. The pocked moonscape inched closer in my window. Four minutes into the burn, I began to feel weight in my arms caused by our first prolonged deceleration, a subtle imitation of gravity. My pressure boots flexed and my limbs settled inside my suit.

'*Eagle,* Houston. You are go' Charlie Duke announced, his voice clearer now through the hissing static. 'You are go to continue powered descent...'

The horizon moved across my window and settled at the bottom, as our lunar module completed a slow rotation about its vertical axis. A gradual pitch-over, or tilt about our horizontal axis, would soon bring the lander to its final descent attitude—feet toward the lunar surface. Again we saw Earth, only a partial disk of blue, white and brown, hanging far above the serrated horizon of the moon. As the engine fired and the pitch-over continued, Earth slipped out the top of my window.

Now my instrument panel came alive with winking data on our altitude. As we passed through 35 000 feet, we sensed the real speed of our descent for the first time. At that moment, an alarm we weren't prepared for flashed on our computer.

*Michael Collins'
startling photo-
graph showing
three satellites—
the Earth, moon
and Apollo 11.
Taken just prior to
docking with com-
mand and service
modules after the
historic first land-
ing on the moon
20 July 1969.*

Neil Armstrong, the first human to walk upon the moon, photographed inside the lunar module after completing the first moon walk.

Buzz Aldrin during lunar module checkout en route toward the moon.

'Twelve-oh-two' I called, unable to control the tension in my voice, 'twelve-oh-two.'

Neil and I exchanged quizzical but troubled looks. We were descending through 33 000 feet, and our primary computer had just signaled difficulty coping with the cascade of data coming in from the landing radar. The data screen went blank. All we could do was wait for the experts in mission control to decipher this alarm, but they were more than two light seconds away and any response therefore could not be immediate; it had an interminable four-second delay built into it.

To me, the alarm was ominous. Either the programing was incapable of managing the landing, or there was a hardware problem. In either case, the potential for catastrophe seemed obvious: our eventual ascent from the surface in 24 hours and our rendezvous with *Columbia* would place even greater demands on that computer. Still, we coasted toward the moon.

'Give us the reading on the twelve-oh-two program alarm' Neil called, voicing our tension.

We both eyed the large red ABORT STAGE button on the panel. Hitting it would instantly blast the lunar module's bulbous upper stage back toward *Columbia*—ending man's first attempt to reach the moon.

'Roger' Charlie called, the strain in his voice obvious. 'We've got...we're go on that alarm.' Charlie's transmission shredded with static again.

I felt an immense gulf separating that brightly lit control room in Houston from the dimly lit cabin of our lunar module. Neil nodded to me through his helmet, his eyes somber in the glow of the panel. Charlie's terse 'go' meant the guidance officers at mission control had judged the problem to be an acceptable risk. At this critical point, the time delay in our communications made a discussion of the situation impossible. We simply had to trust Houston.

Another alarm went off on the data screen! I fought the urge to shout a warning to Neil. Even after years as a fighter pilot and an astronaut, I felt that first hot edge of panic. I knew there had to be something seriously wrong with our guidance computer, and yet we were still descending. Again, mission control reassured us with a call of 'go'. They had dismissed the alarm as noncritical, but they couldn't take the time to explain why. We dropped through 20 000 feet, eating up altitude at 150 feet a second. As the lunar module continued tilting forward, our triangular windows filled with craters and humped ridges. During this phase we had to be sure we were heading toward a safe landing spot, but all we saw were gray craters and boulder fields. Again the alarms flashed, banishing data from our screen.

'Twelve alarm' Neil called. 'Twelve-oh-one.'

'Roger' Charlie acknowledged. 'Twelve-oh-one alarm.'

I licked my dry lips. This was a time for discipline. But the tension had me rigid inside my suit. We had to trust mission control.

'We're go' Charlie added. 'Hang tight, we're go. Two thousand feet...'

The pitch-over maneuver continued, giving us an excellent view of the hills and craters below us. Neil hunched over his hand controller, ready to take command if the automatic landing system led us into danger. I began a continuous series of readouts, giving both Neil and mission control a detailed description of our final descent.

At 500 feet, Neil was not satisfied with the landing zone. He took over control from the computer, slowed our descent from 20 feet per second to only 9, and then at 300 feet, reduced it to only 3 feet per second. The lunar module hovered above its cone of flame as Neil looked. He did not like what he saw. He stroked the hand controller, like a motorist fine-tuning his cruise control, and we scooted horizontally across a field of rubbly boulders. Slightly above 200 feet, our descent picked up speed. 'Eleven forward, coming down nicely' I called, my eyes scanning the instruments. 'Two hundred feet, four and a half down. Five and a half down. One sixty…Quantity light.'

The amber low-fuel light blinked on the master caution-and-warning panel near my face. The lumpy horizon of the moon hung at eye level. We were less than 200 feet from landing on the moon, but Neil again slowed the descent. Simultaneously, Charlie's voice warned, 'Sixty seconds.'

Although the ascent engine fuel tanks were full, they were completely separate from the big descent engine. Thus, we had a maximum of 60 seconds of fuel remaining in the descent stage before we had to land or abort. Yet Neil had slowed to a hover again as he searched the ground below.

'Down two and a half' I called. 'Forward. Forward. Good. Forty feet. Down two and a half. Picking up some dust. Thirty feet…'

Thirty feet below the lunar module's gangly legs, dust that had lain in place for over a billion years blasted radially outward in all directions with the plume of our engine.

'Thirty seconds' Charlie announced solemnly, but still Neil hovered.

The descent engine roared silently in my mind, devouring the last of its fuel supply. Again, I eyed the ABORT STAGE button.

'Drifting right' I called, watching the shadow of a foot-pad probe straining to touch the surface. 'Contact light.' We settled silently onto the moon with perhaps only 20 seconds of fuel remaining.

Immediately, I began preparing the module for a sudden abort ascent in the event the landing had damaged the *Eagle* or the lunar surface was not strong enough to support our weight.

'Ok, engine stop' I told Neil, reciting from the check list. 'ACA out of detent.'

'Got it' Neil answered quietly, disengaging his hand control system.

'Mode controls, both auto' I continued. 'Descent engine command override off. Engine arm off…'

'We copy you down, *Eagle*' Charlie Duke interrupted from Houston.

From the window before my face, I looked out over the alien rock and shadow of the moon and breathed inside my helmet, totally absorbed. A mile away the horizon curved into blackness.

'Houston' Neil called. 'Tranquility Base here. The *Eagle* has landed.'

Buzz Aldrin, USA

Neil Armstrong's footprint at Tranquility Base. Made on 20–21 July 1969, this footprint will probably be unchanged 20 million years hence.

36

Apollo 13: A Successful Failure

The coastline of Western Australia at Shark Bay is dramatized by the land-sea contrast. Freycinet Estuary is at the left edge, Hamelin Pool center and the Peron Peninsula between.

HARRUMPPHH!!!
No one suspected that the heater wiring was badly damaged but it was. When the tank was filled with liquid oxygen and the heater system turned on, a bomb waited to go off. At 55 hours, 53 minutes elapsed time, mission control called *Apollo 13.*

'13, we've one more item for you. When you get a chance, we'd like you to stir up your cryo tanks.'

* * *

I was the commander of *Apollo 13* on my fourth flight into space. Our mission was to land at a place called Fra Mauro in the hills of the moon. The geologists suspected that surface material found there was different in composition from the material brought back by *Apollo 11* and *12* crews. Our job was to prove their theory.

We departed from Cape Kennedy on Saturday, 11 April 1970 at 1313 hours CST. After approximately 30 hours, we changed our trajectory so that when we started our landing on the moon, the sun's shadows would highlight the rock formations. However, this new trajectory was not one of free return—it would not automatically take us home safely if something should happen to our spacecraft. In fact, it would take us back towards Earth, but our closest point of approach would be about 2 500 nautical miles—much too far out to make a successful landing.

We had no cause for concern. This maneuver had been done before and the spaceship was functioning perfectly. The friendly stars, and familiar sounds and smells of our surroundings had given us a sense of security. The three of us settled down for a routine flight to the moon.

On the way there, our two spacecraft were mated; that is, a tunnel connected our command and service module (*Odyssey*) with our lunar module (*Aquarius*). At approximately 54 hours after take-off, Jack Swigert took over watch duties in *Odyssey* while Fred Haise and I drifted through the tunnel to inspect *Aquarius.* We were on our way back to *Odyssey* when we heard the explosion.
HARRUMPPHH!!!

The short, muffled blast echoed through the spacecraft. The spacecraft rocked for a few brief seconds... then settled down and quiet again prevailed. I could tell by Fred's expression that he didn't know what had happened. A quick glance over to Jack told me the same. Jack's eyes were as wide as saucers, and he was probably asking himself 'Why am I here?'.

A red light flashed on our warning panel: low voltage on Main B electrical bus. Then two more lights blinked on: two of our three fuel cells had just died—our major source of electrical energy. One fuel cell would take us around the moon and back home, but without all three operating, our mission rules prevented a lunar landing. Endless months of training, my second flight to the moon, and now I can't land?!

I scanned gauges that monitored our oxygen tanks behind us in the service module: one read zero, and I could actually see the needle going down in the second one! I looked out the side window. The gaseous substance I saw escaping at a high speed from the rear of the spacecraft confirmed my suspicions. Soon we would be completely out of oxygen, and our third and last fuel cell would die, as would all our environmental control and electrical power. And, since we used electrical power to gimbal our rocket engine, our propulsion system was also about to become useless.

Inside *Odyssey* we did have a small battery and oxygen tank to use after we jettisoned our service module. But they were only designed to last five hours during the final plunge into Earth's atmosphere. At the time of the explosion, we were 90 hours away from home: 200 000 miles from Earth and heading away. Jack called mission control in Houston:

'Houston, we've had a problem. We've had a Main B bus undervolt. And we had a pretty large bang associated with the caution and warning here.'

We began our four-day struggle to return to Earth and to stay alive. Our situation in the command module became critical. Houston called:

'We figure you've got about 15 minutes worth of power left in the command module, so we want you to start getting over in the lunar module and getting some power on that.'

The control center didn't have to urge us to make the move. When that call came through, Fred and I were already threading our way through the tunnel into *Aquarius*. We knew our only chance for survival was to convert *Aquarius* into a lifeboat and use its systems to get home.

Our first task was time critical. We had to transfer the alignment from *Odyssey's* inertial guidance system to the guidance system in *Aquarius* before the power failed. The guidance system, coupled with the computers, gave us spacecraft attitude, position and velocity information, that was essential for performing the necessary course corrections. We completed the transfer just before *Odyssey's* power died. It was a close call. Without that information, the success of our future tasks would have been in jeopardy.

The course we were on would take us around the moon—but not back to Earth! We had to get back on a free return trajectory. All systems were turned on in *Aquarius*, and at 61 hours and 30 minutes since we left Cape Kennedy, we fired *Aquarius'* descent engine for about 30 seconds. We called Houston:

'Ok, burn's complete. Now we have to talk about powering down.'

Battery power in the lunar module was the problem. *Aquarius* was designed to last just 45 hours, half of what we needed. We would run out of electrical power long

before we could safely re-enter Earth's atmosphere. The obvious solution was to speed up our return. Our present course would put us in the Indian Ocean and required a total mission time of approximately 152 hours— too long.

Mission control had an idea. We would light *Aquarius'* descent engine a second time, about two hours after we passed the far side of the moon. It would have to be a long burn, but we might just increase our velocity enough to make a successful re-entry prior to running out of oxygen and other consumables. Besides, this maneuver would put our landing near our recovery force in the Pacific Ocean.

Left: *Ice had to be scraped off a command module window to obtain this photo of the damaged service module. It showed engineers what had gone wrong and how close the astronauts came to death in space.*

Above: *After the service module explosion, Apollo 13 had to pass beyond the moon before returning to Earth. The crew, not knowing if they would survive, continued to take a series of very valuable photos. This view shows the far side crater Tsiolkovski in contrast to the lighter lunar surface.*

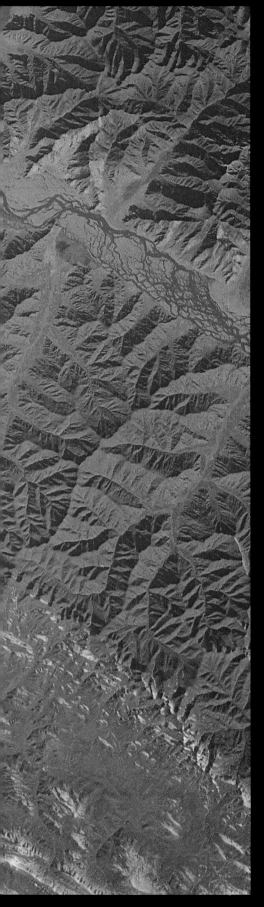

Lake Yamzho Yumco is located about 70 miles south-west of Lhasa.

Houston started to develop the procedures and our back-up crew was called in to test the plan in the simulator. We didn't have much time—the moon was less than 40 000 miles away, we were rapidly accerlerating towards it and, upon arrival, the lunar gravity would quickly sling us around to the far side and out of communication with Earth.

On Tuesday night at 1921 hours, *Apollo 13* swung behind the moon, lost contact with Earth and passed 164 nautical miles above the lunar surface. Mission control had passed up the necessary procedures for the long descent engine burn and we began preparations for the maneuver—only two hours away.

I noticed that both Fred and Jack were not paying too much attention to the upcoming critical maneuver. Instead, they had cameras in their hands.

'Gentlemen, what are your intentions?'

'We want to get some pictures of the far side of the moon.'

'If we don't get home, you won't get them developed!'

We finally got our act together and, at the correct time, began the four and half minute burn. Once back in contact with Houston, mission control closely monitored us. We shut down on time. It looked good. Houston confirmed it. We called:

'Now we want to power down as soon as possible.'

'We have a procedure ready' Houston replied.

Powering down meant everything! The only items left operating were the radio to talk to Earth and a fan to circulate the atmosphere in the spacecraft. All those exotic electronic devices like the guidance system, computer and digital autopilot were all turned off. We were flying by the seat of our pants. But again we ran into problems.

The attitude control rockets were never designed to control the attitude of the lunar module with a dead 60 000 pound command and service module attached to it, so, without the autopilot, I had to fly it manually. Pushing forward on the controller did not result in a pitch-down motion but some wild gyration in another direction. I had to learn to 'fly' all over again!

Controlling our attitude with all the electrical equipment turned off was important. We had lost our internal source of heat and were radiating more heat into space than we were getting from the sun. To try to heat up our spacecraft, we manually rotated it perpendicular to the

43

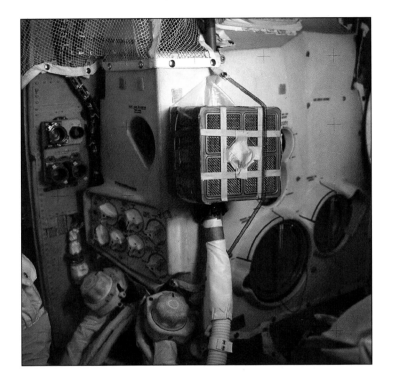

After the April 1970 mission to the moon's surface was aborted, astronauts Lovell, Haise and Swigert had to make adjustments to save their lives. One was to use the command module air purifiers in the lunar module. Here a lunar surface map connects the device to a hose and space suit, resulting in clean air to breathe.

sun, a maneuver we called the 'barbecue mode'. Yet all the metal fixtures felt cold and clammy, as moisture formed on everything. Even the windows began to frost over. The interior temperature kept dropping and finally reached about 35°F.

About this time, we faced another crisis. We were in danger of being poisoned by the carbon dioxide from our own exhalation! In the command module, the carbon dioxide was removed by square-shaped lithium hydroxide canisters in the environmental system. When the partial pressure of carbon dioxide got up to 7.5 mm Hg, we simply replaced the canister. But the command module was dead and its environmental control system useless to us. The lunar module also had an environmental control system, but it did not have enough lithium hydroxide canisters to support three men for four days. Also, we could not fit the square command module canisters into the lunar module round receptacle. A human engineering goof. The partial pressure of carbon dioxide approached 15 mm Hg when the engineers back at Houston thought of a solution. By using tape, plastic and cardboard they knew we had on board, they told us how to 'adapt' a command module canister to the lunar module system— we were saved by the ingenuity of the engineers!

One of the many emergency operations needed to make the Apollo 13 lunar module a livable lifeboat. Here, the late Jack Swigert and the cold hands of James Lovell are building a system to store urine in unused oxygen hoses.

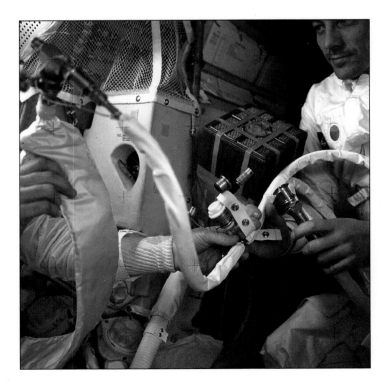

We returned our attention to our trajectory, which hopefully after our first maneuver, was now on a free return course home and within the narrow 2° pie-shaped entry corridor. We would enter the atmosphere at over 24 000 miles per hour and the entry angle could not be less than 5.5° or greater than 7.5° with respect to Earth's horizon. If we came in at too shallow an angle, we would skip off the atmosphere like a stone off water. If we came in too steeply, we would burn up in seconds like a meteor.

Houston used large, 110-foot radar antennas on Earth to constantly track us and plot our course home. They knew exactly where we were headed. At about 102 hours elapsed time into the mission, we received an ominous message from them. They could not understand what had happened. Perhaps we were still venting gas and it applied force on the spacecraft. Or maybe our guidance system alignment had been a little off. Whatever happened, we were no longer on the free return course. If we continued on the present trajectory, we would miss Earth's atmosphere by 99 miles and sail on in sun orbit—forever!

'Great!' I said. 'Just great! What are we going to do? We powered down our guidance system so we've lost any accurate attitude reference. Our computer is dead. The autopilot inoperative. Why, even the burst disk in the super critical helium tank, that pressurizes the descent engine fuel tanks, is about to blow. And when that happens, we will lose our descent engine!'

Mission control radioed that they thought they had a solution, but we would have to work fast. They reminded me of the emergency procedures we had tucked away in the back of *Apollo 8's* flight manual, last ditch procedures to be used if both the navigation and communications systems failed. Unfortunately, we had removed those procedures from the flight manual after *Apollo 8*. We never thought they would be used, and besides we never trained for double failures. Their reply was, 'You will have to use them now!'.

The procedures called for manually rotating the spacecraft, using our newly acquired 'flying skills', to put Earth in the lunar module window. In that window I had mounted a crosshair 'gunsight' that was used for rendezvous. If I could line up the terminator on Earth, the line between daylight and darkness, with the horizontal line of my gunsight, then the lunar module's descent engine would be properly positioned to correct our angle of entry into the

atmosphere. We had only one chance to make the maneuver: at the point in our flight home when we had just left the sphere of influence of the moon and had the least forward velocity.

Houston checked the procedures in the simulator. On board *Apollo 13* everyone was serious—no cameras were to be found. *Aquarius'* clock had failed, so I told Jack to time the burn with his Omega wrist watch. I knew that without an autopilot, it would be difficult to control the spacecraft's attitude to keep Earth in the window. But I had two three-axis attitude controllers in *Aquarius*, the primary and a backup. I told Fred to use the backup controller to maintain yaw control and I would control pitch and roll with the primary controller.

Two emergency electrical buttons were located on the left side of the console. One was labeled 'START' and the other 'STOP'. They were direct electrical links from the batteries to the descent engine. This was the one and only time they were ever used on an *Apollo* flight.

At the proper time, I pushed START. The engine came on full blast! Fred and I jockeyed Earth in the window. Fourteen seconds later, Jack yelled 'Stop!' and I pushed the button.

Mission control monitored the burn via telemetry: 'Ignition!…Thrust looks good…It shut down…Nice work.'

'Let's hope it was' we replied.

Space network radars soon confirmed that *Apollo 13* was comfortably back within the entry corridor!

During the rest of the flight, we just hung on. The temperature kept dropping. Fred and I pulled on our lunar boots. We tried to get some sleep, but the cold, damp environment made it almost impossible. The food was cold and tasteless. Finally, on Thursday evening, Jack began receiving procedures from mission control on how to power up the dormant *Odyssey* with the entry battery.

By Friday morning, the conclusion of the flight of *Apollo 13* was only hours away. Jack looked out the window and noted that 'Earth is whistling in like a freight train'—our velocity was approaching 24 000 miles per hour. By that time, all systems in the command module were on and operating. With a sigh of relief, he noted that the condensation did not short out any electrical equipment.

At approximately 138 hours elapsed time, we received permission to jettison our service module. This module

The Brahmaputra River in
*Tibet flows eastward in a
canyon south of Lhasa.*

contained our two large liquid oxygen tanks, the suspected location of the explosion. I was in *Aquarius*, straining to get a glimpse and photograph the service module as it drifted by:

'Ok, I've got her…there's one whole side of that spacecraft missing…right by the high gain antenna, the whole panel is blown out, almost to the base of the engine—it's really a mess.'

'Take pictures but don't make any unnecessary maneuvers' replied Houston.

'Man, that's unbelievable—looks like a lot of debris is just hanging out of the side near the S-band antenna.'

At about 141 hours elapsed time, Fred and I joined Jack back in *Odyssey*. The hatch between the two spacecraft was closed and we prepared to jettison *Aquarius*. She had been a good ship that supported three stranded astronauts for over 84 hours and provided the propulsion to get us home. We jettisoned *Aquarius* with less than four and a half hours of electrical power remaining. Houston gave her the final salute with 'Farewell *Aquarius*; and we thank you.'

Six hundred miles south-east of Samoa, the USS *Iwo Jima* patrolled the landing area. Search aircraft and rescue helicopters were already on station as *Odyssey* prepared for its flight through the atmosphere.

At 142 hours 40 minutes elapsed time, *Odyssey* slammed into the thin upper air at about 400 000 feet. A pink glow came through our windows, when the atmosphere started to decelerate the spacecraft, and the temperature on the heat shield rose to 5 000° F. The 'G' loading rose, peaked at 5 Gs, then leveled off at 3 Gs for over three minutes. The guidance system rotated *Odyssey* to control the direction of the lift vector, as it sought to guide the spacecraft to the designated landing spot. Thank God the guidance system and computer were not damaged during the long, cold, soak period.

Finally, when we reached 40 000 feet, the drogue chutes popped out followed by three beautiful main parachutes.

Odyssey splashed into the Pacific Ocean just a mile or so from the USS *Iwo Jima* at 1308 hours Friday, 17 April, after a flight lasting 142 hours, 54 minutes and 41 seconds.

But why did all this happen?

We learn in Aviation Safety School that most aircraft accidents are not caused by a chance malfunction but rather by a series of events that overcomes either the pilot or aircraft. Such was the case with *Apollo 13*.

Apollo 13's accident was set up five years before we lifted off. At that time, the prime contractor ordered the manufacturer of the liquid oxygen tanks to make the heater system in the tanks compatible with 65-volt DC power that was available at the Kennedy Space Center. In flight, the system used a 28-volt DC power supply. However, the higher voltage would allow certain tests and checkout functions to be accomplished more quickly. The contractor complied with the order, but he failed to replace the 28-volt thermostat in the heater system with one capable of handling a higher voltage.

This condition existed in all the *Apollo* spacecraft prior to *Apollo 13* and probably never would have been noticed if another incident had not happened to *Apollo 13's* oxygen tanks. One of the two tanks was dropped at the factory. It was originally scheduled for *Apollo 10*, but because of the incident it was recycled and assigned to *Apollo 13*. Approximately six weeks prior to launch, with the spacecraft already on the launch pad, the tank was filled with liquid oxygen and tested. No abnormalities were noted during the test, but the engineers could not drain the oxygen out after the tests were completed. It was decided to turn on the heater system and boil the oxygen from the tank.

The heater system remained on for eight hours—much longer than on any previous spacecraft oxygen system. As the heater temperature approached 80° F, the thermostat contacts started to open, to shut off the power and control the temperature. However, because the thermostat was designed for 28 volts, not 65, the contacts overheated and welded shut, and all protection was lost. Power to the heater was monitored by telemetry, but no one bothered to watch the readout to see that the power had actually turned off. It is now known through laboratory tests that the heater temperature approached 1 000° F.

This failure caused the explosion that ruptured our oxygen tank and doomed our mission to failure, yet the mission itself must be classified as a 'successful failure'. *Apollo 13* demonstrated the initiative and motivation of space engineers and technicians to salvage a crippled spacecraft under extremely demanding and trying circumstances. More personally, the excellent teamwork between the control center in Houston and the flight crew made it possible for me to tell this story.

James Lovell, USA

46

FLIGHT OF A LIFETIME

When I was a young lad looking at the moon, I had the feeling that I would be able to travel there someday. It was such a strong feeling that I told our neighbors and my parents. Their reaction was one of amazement. My mother said 'Son, that is ridiculous. Man will never be able to go to the moon. You should forget that right now.'

In July 1971, we were told that we were ready. Our spacecraft was also ready. We would go to the moon on *Apollo 15*.

Our slow drive to the launch pad was very quiet. Across from me sat Dave Scott, our commander, Al Worden, command module pilot, and Deke Slayton, commander of all the astronauts. Normally these men had a lot to say, but we all were thinking about the past—and the future.

The first lunar Rover carried to the moon and assembled there by astronauts Scott and Irwin is about to begin exploration near Hadley Rille.

I remembered back 10 years to a near-tragic, light airplane accident when the doctors said I would probably never fly again. Now, here I was driving out to the launch pad. My prayers really had been answered.

When we arrived at the pad, we entered the elevator and were taken slowly to the top. Everything was done slowly.

Once our helpers had the three of us tied down securely, they patted us on the shoulder, hopped out and closed the hatch. It went 'CLANG!' like a dungeon door and we knew it was too late to knock and say, 'Hey, open up. I've changed my mind.' But you know you would never change your mind anyway—we had waited and trained for nearly a lifetime and were eager to begin our journey. It was the most important thing we could do with our lives, and we were willing to give our lives for it, if necessary.

Silence settled in again. Occasionally there was a report from launch control as the countdown continued. Time went by so slowly, then it seemed to speed up during the last couple of minutes. Before I knew it, I heard the word 'Ignition'. Then I heard and felt all that tremendous power lifting us into space. It was about the happiest moment in my life. I noticed there were tears of joy trickling down my cheeks.

There was no sensation of speed even though we were going 25 000 miles per hour. We felt as if we were stationary in the blackness of space. We viewed Earth several times as it moved away from us: a basketball, then a baseball, then a golfball and finally the size of a marble, when we reached the moon.

The moon was completely dark as we approached. When we flew around the back side, we came into light and marveled at its surface. There were craters of every size, canyons and mountains. The color varied with the sun's angle. At the terminator, the line dividing light from darkness, the surface was dark gray, like molten metal. As we traveled toward the sun, the surface lightened to brown, then light tan and almost white directly below the sun.

We would be the first and really the only mission to explore the mountains of the moon. At the scheduled time we transferred into the lunar module, *Falcon,* for our descent to the surface of the moon.

We looked up into the blackness of space as the rocket fired to slow us. Then we dropped closer to the surface, skimmed over the ranges of the mountains and came into a

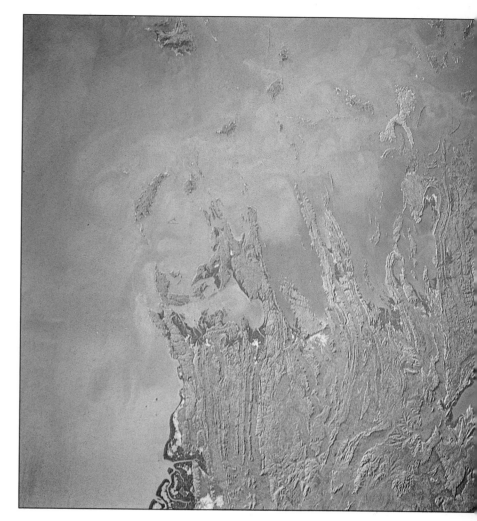

In Western Australia, the Wyndham Range reaches the sea. King Sound is lower right, Buccaneer Archipelago is on the left.

small valley. In the final approach, the lunar module pitched forward so that we could see the landing area and make final adjustments. We were startled to see the mountains looming high above us and to the left. We saw the desired landing spot, Hadley Base, and came straight down.

We hit very hard and held our breath as the telemetry data was sent to Earth, afraid our hard landing had damaged our spacecraft. In just a few minutes, we received word that everything looked fine. We could stay. We relaxed and congratulated each other with slaps on the back.

Hadley Base was our camping place for three days.

From here, we drove out to explore the canyon alley called Hadley Rille and the Appenience Mountains. The mountains around us were spectacular. They were 15 000 feet high. The surface reminded me of a desert on Earth but there was no life at all, not even a cactus. There was no sound. And then we looked out and up into black space. Earth was directly overhead but only a half-Earth. It was a beautiful jewel in the blackness, only the size of a marble. I looked for some sign of civilization but I could see none. Yet I knew it was my home. Here I was, standing on a completely dead world and looking at a world full of life, but I could not see the evidence of this life. I could easily cover Earth with my thumb.

I felt privileged to view Earth as God must view it. I realized that He made a very special home for me and you. I felt as though I were an advanced sensor sent out to experience another world. It was now my responsibility and opportunity to report back all that I saw and felt. I knew my life would never be the same. I had seen Earth from a heavenly perspective. We regretted that we had to leave the moon after our brief three-day stay, but we had already run out of water and had only a little oxygen left.

Anyone passing through our solar system would be attracted to the blue planet. They would know that the blue color indicated water on Earth. They would know that where there is water there is probably life. They might try to meet us. We, the blue planet, stand out as a beacon to all.

For the last 15 years, I have been sharing our adventure with people all around the world. As we view the pictures, we travel together to another planet.

Life has become fuller and richer as a result of space flight. I realize we are all crew on spacecraft Earth that is hurtling through space to an unknown destination. To reach it, we must take care of our spacecraft and each other. We all have new responsibilities since we have shared the space perspective.

Life has not been easy. We worked too hard on the moon. We lost essential electrolytes such as potassium, and our heart rhythms have become irregular. Since my return to Earth, I have developed a heart condition that might be related to my work in space. I have had two heart attacks, bypass surgery and just this past summer I had a heart arrest. I don't know how much longer I will be here, but I know that as long as I can share that space adventure, I will.

James Irwin, USA
Deceased 1991

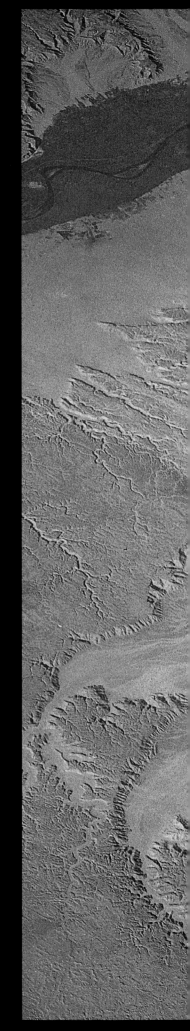

The great north flowing Nile River makes a bend in the vicinity of such ancient places as Quz, Luxor, Thebes and the Valley of the Kings.

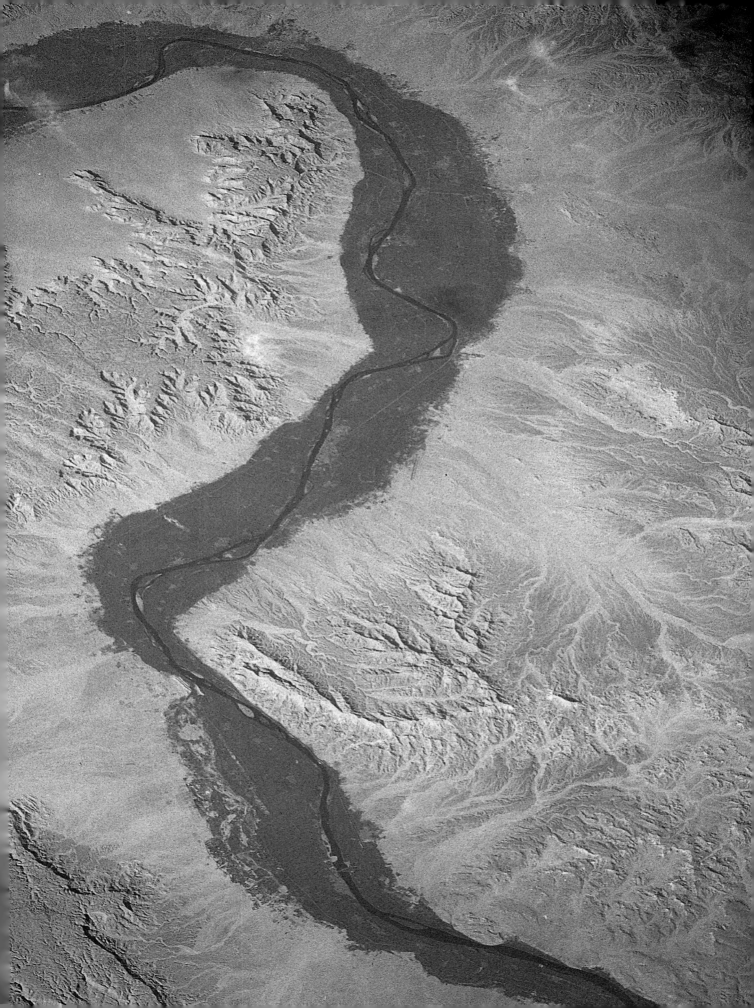

A Bitter-sweet Experience

Having had the good fortune to be selected for the first group of astronauts in the US space program, and the bad fortune not to fly until the last *Apollo*, I probably have a unique perspective on manned space exploration.

While my more fortunate associates in the USA and USSR were busy racking up one space first after another and having a ball, I was selecting, training, assigning, managing and de-briefing the US astronauts for almost 15 years. This job was especially frustrating, considering every astronaut thinks he is the best qualified to fly every mission, and I was no exception.

After escorting crews from the suit-up facilities towards the launch pad about 25 times, but having to drop off at the blockhouse every time, the opportunity to finally go all the way into orbit on *Apollo-Soyuz* gave me great pleasure. Like many things in life, it was also a bitter-sweet experience. Spending 16 years preparing to be the world's oldest rookie astronaut was not an enviable position. But on the flip side, there are millions who will never have the opportunity to fly in space, so it was certainly better late than never.

Apollo-Soyuz was not a major technological achievement. The *Apollo* command module had flown 14 previous flights, 9 of these to the moon. Although *Soyuz* had not been to the moon, it also had an extensive and successful flight record. The only new piece of hardware was the docking module, which provided the electrical and mechanical connections between *Soyuz* and *Apollo* and acted as an airlock to allow transfer between two spacecraft with different atmospheric compositions. Although simple in concept, the fact that the USSR side was built in Russia on the metric system, the US side in California on the British system and they mated successfully on the first try, might be viewed as a minor miracle.

I had the distinction of being designated the world's first, and, so far, only docking module pilot, placing me in command of the apparatus some have dubbed the world's highest and fastest flying sewer pipe.

I am happy to report it performed its functions almost flawlessly, up to and including its jettison with a full load of trash to perform a final orbital mechanics experiment. It was like seeing an old friend depart, since it served as my bedroom for 10 days and everybody's bathroom when we all gave in to that requirement after five days of stalling the inevitable. On my initial activation of and entry into the docking module, I almost passed out from some outgassing products present in the atmosphere and retreated into the command module until we cleaned them up. I'm sure the 'outgassing' from that final load we jettisoned would have been fatal to anyone forced to breathe it.

Technically, the *Apollo-Soyuz* flight was almost 100% successful. We hated to see the flight end and would have campaigned for an extension except we were reaching our red lines on expendables. The only unpleasant event before, during or after the flight occurred during re-entry when we accidentally ingested an almost-lethal dose of rocket propellant in the spacecraft. Fortunately, we survived to make the last parachute landing by a US crew.

Left: *No Cold War here—astronaut Thomas Stafford and cosmonaut Alexei Leonov meet in the hatchway connecting the Apollo and Soyuz modules during the Apollo-Soyuz Test Project, July 1975.*

Cloud patterns near the coast of Western Australia, at Fortescue River.

The real challenge and success of *Apollo-Soyuz* was in the field of international relations. The US and USSR had been active and vocal competitors for space firsts since my induction into the Mercury program. The challenge was clear and precise with national honor and international prestige at stake on both sides. The cosmonauts were beating our pants off: first man in space, first woman in space, first multiple man crew, first EVA, etc. We had confidence in our ability to ultimately make a comeback but weren't so sure it would happen before the first lunar landing.

My first encounter with 'the enemy' was in Athens, Greece, at an International Astronautical Federation conference. The initial formal meetings between US and Russian crews and government officials were slightly strained to say the least. However, we managed to arrange a private breakfast with just astronauts, cosmonauts and interpreters.

After a couple of bottles of Greek Metaxa brandy, we again concluded what I have known since World War II: pilots think alike and act alike world wide, independent of nationality and language. We have a common dislike for bureaucracy and the medical community in general. (I'd hasten to add this dislike does not include individual doctors, some of whom are my dearest friends and greatest supporters.) We also have a common enjoyment of flying and pretty girls.

After this meeting I believe we all felt the space race had more the character of a friendly, but spirited, athletic competition than a military battle for control of nations. Without exception, all the cosmonauts I have met since that encounter have been friends in the truest sense and I was particularly happy when one of them, Alexei Leonov, surfaced as commander of *Soyuz* for the joint mission.

Prior to our assignment to the crew, some astute soul made the decision that we should speak Russian and the cosmonauts should speak English during the mission. Theoretically, this action would reduce the chance of misunderstandings or mistakes in communicating. Undoubtedly it was sound logic, but more importantly, it also created the ability to communicate with the whole team and with the public of each other's country. It addressed the nut of what *Apollo-Soyuz* was all about. As we've already noted, the technological challenges were minimal. The whole purpose of the project was to use crews in space as a focal point to get the governments and people of the USA and USSR working together towards a common goal rather than continuing to compete in the Cold War. Learning each other's language was obviously a step in the right direction.

The language hurdle turned out to be the biggest training challenge for technocrats with few linguistic credentials. Worse than that, some of us were approaching senior citizen status. We spent more man hours on language training than any other single phase of flight preparation, and at times we thought we had reached a reasonable level of proficiency. This illusion was usually shattered at our next meeting with our Soviet counterparts, when it became apparent our fluent Houston Russian was drawing blank stares in Moscow. Ultimately, between our fractured Russian and the cosmonauts' fractured English, we communicated rather well. Some on both sides did very well, eventually, but I admit it never was easy for me.

The greatest challenge in the whole program was being last in line to give a toast. Having just downed a large number of vodkas in rapid succession, you had to mentally create a profound, unique toast then translate it to Russian. Friendship, motherhood, fatherhood, children, success and all the other easy subjects were already toasted and whatever you came up with that was unique, you didn't have the Russian vocabulary to express. Fortunately, the Russian people in general are gregarious, generous, friendly and have a good sense of humor. As in any interpersonal relationship, a smile goes a long way.

I think the real success of *Apollo-Soyuz* was accomplished on the ground during pre-flight and post-flight visits to each other's countries. Even though there were some rocky times at the diplomatic corps level after the mission, personal friendships have endured and will continue to do so. One of the most obvious and active legacies of *Apollo-Soyuz* was the creation and continuing growth of the Association of Space Explorers. This organization is carrying on the theme of international friendship through co-operation in space on a grand scale, and the founders are to be congratulated.

Deke Slayton, USA
Deceased 1993

Land degradation on the African continent creates enormous dust storms which can be over 7 miles thick.

Next page: *The Ar Rimal area of the Saudi Arabian Ar Rub Al Khali displays an almost uniform pattern of sand dunes. It is easy to understand why it is called the 'empty quarter'.*

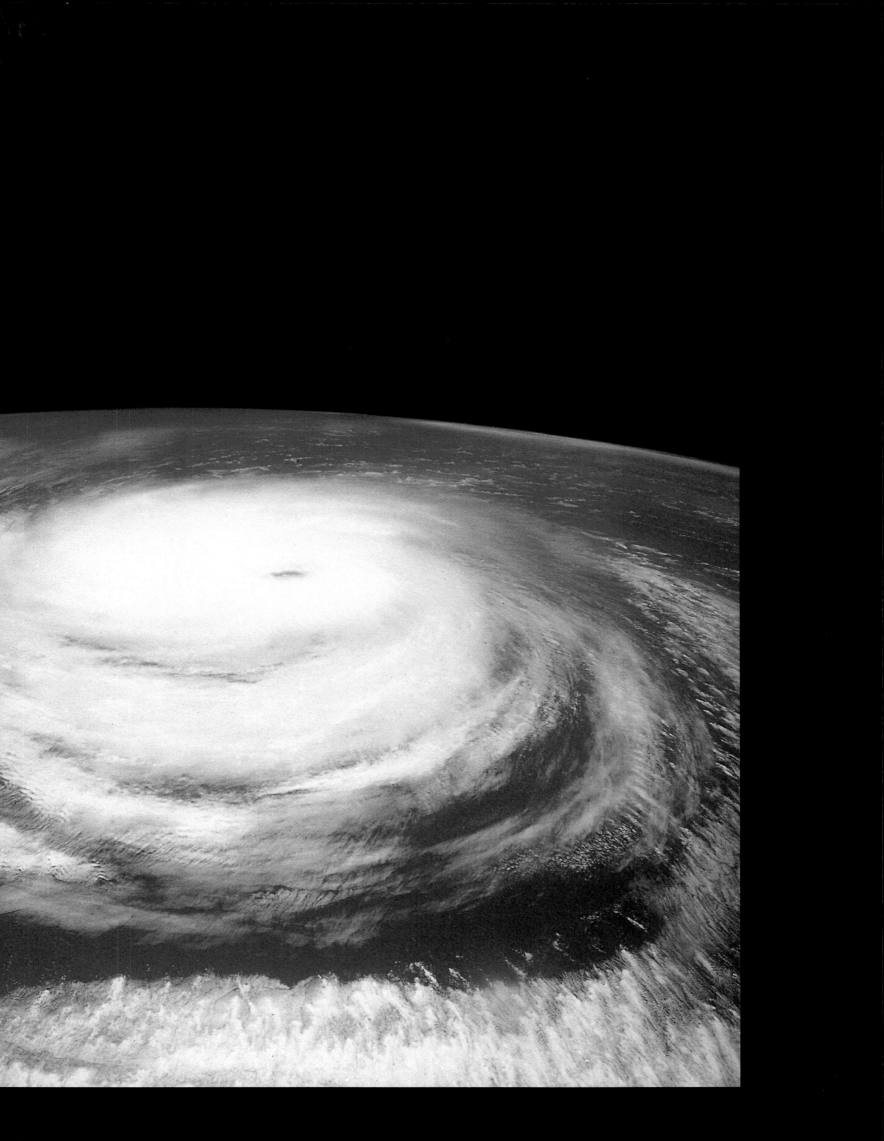

*The shuttle pallet satellite (SPAS-01)
took this photograph of space shuttle
Challenger in earth orbit using a
70 mm Hasselblad camera, June 1983.*

We jumped out and landed in chest-deep powdery snow. The emergency kit was retrieved, radios turned on, and tent erected. We had to act to keep from getting cold, for although warmly dressed and covered in material designed for landing at sea, we were drenched from the stress and strain of landing.

The silence was shattered by a screech. Our three 250-feet parachutes, filled like sails in the strong wind, pulled down a massive pine. Then the capsule began to move threateningly towards a 1 625-foot deep precipice, sliding along the layer of water that was being melted by its hot underside. Another problem: how to stabilize the capsule? Even though very little time had passed since our abortive launch 600 miles away, the emergency had been flashed to the rescue command, and while we were still returning from the sky, they were starting out to meet us.

We heard the roar of an aircraft engine. It circled, signaling to us that we had been found.

'Everything ok?' they asked.

'Sure' I replied. 'If you think *this* is ok.'

'How do you feel?'

'Like the weather' Oleg replied.

Now we were not so worried for ourselves, for we knew how things stood. We were more anxious for those back at Baikonur, who didn't.

The night became completely black. Crawling through the deep snow, we gathered dry sticks and piled them into a heap. Our emergency matches were proof against wind and rain, and we used the instruction booklet on emergency procedures for landing in unpopulated areas as kindling.

Melted snow and biscuits were all we wanted, then we sat quietly listening to the murmur of the pines, the sweep of the snow, and the whistling of the wind in the pine needles. Another plane appeared during the night, as if to remind us that we had not been forgotten.

Suddenly it seemed as if the weather realised it was hindering us: the wind lessened, the snow stopped, and the clouds disappeared to reveal a sky such I have never witnessed before in my life.

'We'll not sleep' Oleg said. 'Doubt if we'll ever see a night like this again.'

We brooded silently, each sunk in his own thoughts.

'Well, we've given the emergency kit a live test' Oleg began.

'Yes, we're the first to need it.'

The forest spoke to us quietly, the stars twinkled, and a little warmth reached us from the fire. Everything was just as the first people would have seen it.

The orange dawn had barely broken when the helicopter came droning in. It hovered above the pines and lowered a hawser. Oleg went up first while I gathered the flight records from the capsule. A last look at the capsule and away…it was not to blame.

Officially, the *Soyuz T8–1* completed a suborbital flight of 21 minutes, 27 seconds duration, reaching a height of 192 kilometers (115 miles) and traveling 1 574 kilometers (945 miles).

Every test leaves someone happy, someone sad. Analysing what went wrong and working on the problem make the next mission successful. That is the dialectic of the road into the unknown. The way into space will always be complex, unpredictable and dangerous.

Vasily Lazarev, Russia
Deceased 1989

*Soyuz-28 with Vladimir Remek of
Czechoslovakia aboard, ready to
launch, March 1978. He was the first
non-Russian and non-American to go
into space.*

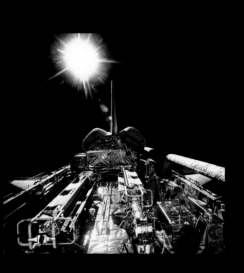

Enroute to repair the Hubble Space Telescope, *December 1993. A sunburst is captured through the aft flight deck window of* Endeavour. *This highly successful mission restored the telescope systems to meet all of its original objectives.*

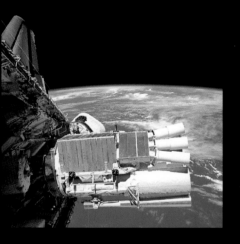

The complex Astro-1 *payload emerging from the cargo bay of* Columbia.

Spacelab J *in the cargo bay of* Endeavour. *Within* Spacelab *are scientific experiments, conducted for 8 days by Japan, the United States and the European Space Agency.*

DISCOVERY'S MISSION

On 29 September 1988, we were scheduled to resume the journey cut short by the tragedy of *Challenger.*

As I slipped into bed, it felt like the night before Christmas, my first combat flight and my first football game all rolled into one—eager anticipation for the adventure ahead, confidence in our readiness, but knowledge that there were no guarantees of the outcome. I knew I had a superb crew that had trained together for over two years, a great ground support team and a thoroughly tested machine with over 1 000 hardware and software modifications since *Challenger.* Yet, there are no guarantees.

My four crew mates and I had spent the day at Cape Kennedy reviewing procedures, listening to the weather and vehicle status briefs and relaxing at the astronaut beach house with our families. After one last kiss goodbye from my wife and daughter, I returned to the crew quarters with my crew, where we each passed the time in our own ways. I wrote to my son, who was serving as an ensign on a cruiser in the Persian Gulf, and told him how proud I was of him, how much I enjoyed what I was doing and how I looked forward to the flight. I didn't mention that there are no guarantees.

We awoke at 0500 hours to a potential launch delay, one that we had been warned about the night before. The upper level winds were unseasonably light and significantly different from those the shuttle was programed to cope with. Our programed flight path could cause excessive bending loads on the orbiter's wing. After an hour's delay we suited up and left for the pad with the conditions unimproved. The tension and introspection that usually accompany the 10-minute ride were missing—none of us expected to launch.

We arrived at the 195-foot level of the pad to a soli-

The most northern part of Somalia, often called the Horn of Africa. The point is Ros Azir. To the lower right the Island of Hafun becomes Cape Hafun due to the sandy connection. The Gulf of Aden is upper left.

tude that exists there only on launch day. We knew that millions of people around the world supported us, yet it seemed that the only humans in our world were a few support personnel and the five of us.

We paused for a few moments to view the shuttle against the beach and ocean—magnificent—the ultimate testament to engineering accomplishment. The hissing of the gases that vented from the external tank and the sight of the massive solid rocket boosters brought home the reality of what lay ahead—the firestorm about to crack this tranquility. Yet the clear visibility and beautiful weather made it difficult to believe launch winds at altitude could pose a problem. We wanted to go, today!

An entirely different scene had greeted the *Challenger* crew, when they arrived at the pad on that January day. They saw sheets of ice covering much of the structure and felt the near-freezing temperatures, yet they tarried little on their way in. Three of us had viewed the same scene on a TV monitor in an office at the Johnson Space Center. The picture had been disconcerting and troubling, for never before had the shuttle been launched in such numbing cold. Little did any of us realize that the combination of low temperatures and a fundamental design defect would create a human tragedy that would forever change the course of our nation's space program.

As our astronaut support crew helped us strap into *Discovery,* I noticed something strange. They had been in the cockpit for hours conducting checks with the launch control center and ensuring that all the switches were in the right positions. But the cockpit, which had become so familiar after thousands of hours of training, was now tilted skyward at 90° and, because of it, looked foreign. This unfamiliar attitude and the 60 pounds of flight gear and survival equipment we wore, made strap-in difficult. But once settled in our seats, a sense of orientation returned—all the switches, dials and gauges were indeed in their right locations.

For two hours we lay on our backs, a time that seemed like an eternity, and went through the motions of the countdown, still not expecting to launch. As far as we knew when we entered a hold at T minus 9 minutes, we were still no-go for launch. We squirmed to find comfortable positions, perspired profusely in the warm suits and saw a flock of birds circling overhead—buzzards! We joked, 'Do they know something we don't?'. They gave a

sense of comic relief to the seriousness of the moment, but as abruptly as they had arrived, they were gone—almost as if all America were saying, 'Go away, this time will be different'.

Prior to resuming the count at T minus 9 minutes, the launch director polled his team. As each discipline called out 'Go!', we expected to hear our friend and fellow astronaut Bob Crippen say 'No go' because of the winds at altitude. He called 'Go!'. We looked at each other and realized that we were probably going to launch—what a great way to keep the crew from getting uptight! Later, we debriefed the NASA brass that the late 'go' was a real stroke of management genius.

An engineering team had worked straight through the night to refine the data on the structural load forecasts. After checking and re-checking the results, the mission management team had concluded that *Discovery* could safely fly through the existing wind profile. That decision was finalized just an hour before launch. T–zero, launch time, marched towards us...

At T minus 5 minutes, Dick Covey started the auxiliary power units, hydrazine-fueled turbo-pumps that provide hydraulic power to our flight controls and main engine thrust vector controllers. The clock on our TV displays counted down—10, 9, 8, 7—the liquid fueled engines came alive with a roar we felt rather than heard—6, 5, 4, 3, 2, 1, IGNITION! Firing pulses were sent simultaneously to 10 different pyrotechnic initiators: 8 to fracture the 6-inch nuts that had held the 4.5 million pounds of hardware to the launch pad and 2 to the igniters at the top of each solid rocket. Like so many other functions on the vehicle, these 8 circuits all had to work. Obvious disaster resulted if they didn't.

Our massive vehicle, weighing the same as a World War II destroyer, was thrust skyward with astonishing power. The automatic roll to align us with our downrange azimuth came in, precise and smooth, and gave immediate reassurance that things were going well. Each of the three main engines throttled back to keep us from exceeding the maximum allowable aerodynamic pressure on the vehicle; a reading of 470 knots indicated airspeed in the cockpit, then returned to its nominal 104% thrust, a force of 500 000 pounds.

After two minutes, fire flashed over our windows, brief flashes from the smaller separation rockets on the

Lake Natron, on the Tanzania-Kenya border, south-west of Nairobi. The reddish color of the water changes between space flights.

solids that carried them away from the external tank after their release. There was time for only a fleeting thought of the *Challenger* explosion that had occurred at this point in the flight, a thought tempered by remembering the two years during which we had closely monitored the solid rocket redesign and become confident that the problem which had killed our seven friends had been corrected.

Like transitioning from the catapult on a carrier to becoming airborne, our ride smoothed out and gave the sensation of being propelled through silky smooth air by noiseless electric motors. The 'eyeballs in' forces slacked from 3 Gs back to slightly more than 1 G as we passed through Mach 5 and climbed through 220 000 feet. Outside, the sky turned from bright blue to dark blue to black within seconds, as we shot above Earth's atmosphere. Now free of aerodynamic drag, our booster's flight path flattened out as we accelerated toward orbital speed. The ocean and clouds 60 miles below raced by at 2 miles per second. During my first two flights, the eight and a half minutes to orbit seemed to take only half that, but on this day, it seemed to take twice as long. I thought, 'This is incredible! How can we humans put together a piece of machinery that does such amazing things?...Sure hope it holds together.' By then we had accelerated to 16 000 feet per second.

As our propellant weight decreased, our acceleration continued to increase until we approached the 3-G redline and the main engines were again throttled to prevent any higher acceleration forces on our vehicle. As we were pressed again into our seats, we felt flattened like a hamburger patty on a griddle. With our equipment, we each now weighed close to 750 pounds. It would have been possible to grab the stick or some other control or switch, but I'm glad I didn't have to. We were along for the ride.

At a speed of almost 5 miles per second, the engines throttled back to 65% to permit a safe and accurate shutdown. We floated up against our restraints. A pencil I let go floated in front of my eyes. Zero G!

Thirty minutes later, we burned our 6 000-pound thrust maneuvering engines to put us in a circular orbit 160 nautical miles above Earth. For the third time in my life, I felt that rush of excitement that came at the beginning of each space mission. We had survived the most critical—and dangerous—part of our adventure and were one step closer to accomplishing our objective.

I keyed the mike:

'Houston, this is *Discovery*. It's nice to be in orbit.'

Rick Hauck, USA

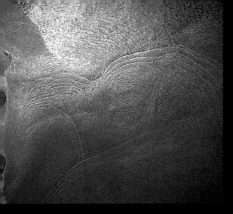

The wave system in the Gulf of Aden is accentuated by solar reflection.

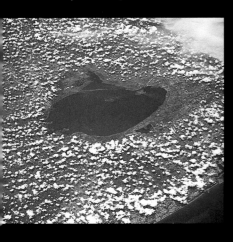

Clouds will not often form over tropical lakes and rivers. Lake Okeechobee in Florida is the largest of thousands and clouds will not usually form over its surface.

Parallel 'streets' of the clouds over the rainforest of south-east Colombia.

Right: The Earth is plastic, as this view of the Sinai Peninsula area shows. Africa on the left has moved west. The Red Sea has filled the void created between it and Asia, to the right. The Sinai Peninsula, centre, is separated on each side by the Gulf of Suez and Gulf of Aqaba. Looking north up the Rift Valley, is the blue of the Dead Sea. The Mediterranean Sea is at upper left.

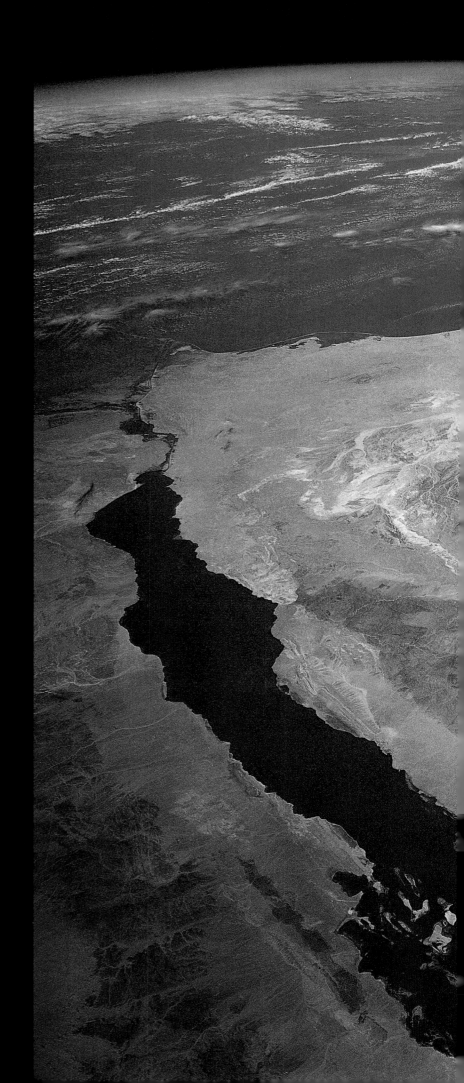

nique was to pick a couple of points on its structure, then observe their relative motion carefully in order to pick up any sideways velocity—motion left-right or up-down. At one point Vance Brand called that I was getting a little too far off to the orbiter's starboard side for his comfort. Consequently, I picked a reference line of sight, put in a left blast and waited for the effect. Nothing happened, so I repeated the procedure twice more—still with no effect. As I was about to start failure analysis and recovery procedures, it suddenly struck me that I had picked as my references the outer edge of the starboard payload bay door and one of the 'Ls' in the word *'Challenger'* painted on the wing. However, with the door fully open, its edge was only inches above the surface of the wing and resulted in a very insensitive indicator, certainly one unsuitable for my purposes. Glancing hurriedly at the vertical stabilizer, I noted happily that I was moving rapidly to my left and needed to reduce my speed immediately to avoid overshooting the desired approach corridor.

All totaled, I made the first flights on both of the MMUs, a third sortie after refueling one of them, and Bob flew two sorties as well. We accumulated significant engineering and 'night flying' data in the process.

We had been expecting a call from the President sometime, but its precise timing came as a surprise. I was making my last sortie and just about out of propellant, when we were told to take up telegenic positions. Time drifted by as the final arrangements were made for the call, and I drifted below the 'red line' on propellant. Thinking that it would be the height of disrespect to float off out of control while the President was speaking, I nulled my relative rates one last time, turned off ATTITUDE HOLD and resolved to make only the absolute minimum control inputs.

Eventually, Mr Reagan came on the line with some very nice words of congratulation and encouragement. I told him that we were opening a new frontier in what man could do in space, and were paving the way for many important operations on the coming space station. (In retrospect, I was probably too verbose in responding to an incumbent President—especially one that had just approved the space station!)

As soon as the capcom gave the 'all clear' signal at the end of Mr Reagan's call, I gave one long but very weak forward thrust command, grabbed hold of the first piece of orbiter structure that I encountered, and worked my way hand-over-hand back to the MMU support station. There I doffed a magnificent piece of equipment that had lived up to and exceeded all of its expectations—one that was also very empty!

Bruce McCandless II, USA

EVA, February 1984. Bruce McCandless II tests the manned maneuvering unit (MMU) on the first free and unattached space walk.

SPACE EXPLORATION: AN OVERVIEW

The last mission to the moon, 7–19 December 1972. Apollo 17 commander, Eugene Cernan, beside the lunar Rover.

It almost takes your breath away. The white, twisted clouds and endless shades of ocean blue make the hum of the spacecraft systems, radio chatter and even your own breathing disappear. It's more inspiring than the view from the highest mountain top. But, in a strange way, you are not part of it. You sense no wind or cold or smell to make you feel connected to Earth. You have an almost dispassionate platform—remote, Olympian—yet so moving that you can hardly believe how emotionally attached you are to those rough patterns moving steadily below.

Only a very few humans have had the privilege of seeing our planet from space. For the most part, they have been technical types, yet astronauts and cosmonauts have written books of poetry, become artists and tried almost reverently to orate or describe the experience for others. Space is now so much a part of our culture that it is hard to believe how recently a view of Earth from a window was only science fiction.

The story of humanity's foray into space is as intense and exciting as an epic poem of Arthurian adventure. It is a story of danger, risk, heroism, even death. But, perhaps more important, it is a story of reason, ingenuity, intuition, even love. It is a story of people, dedicated professionals committed to an effort.

As we celebrate the twenty-fifth anniversary of the first human on the moon, we need to realize that the world was quite different a third of a century ago. A bustling, world-leading, headstrong America was locked into a Cold War. And in space, America seemed to be losing. The *Mercury* flight on 5 May 1961 of astronaut Alan Shephard, a tremendous achievement, was overshadowed by the flight three weeks earlier of Yuri Gagarin—the first Soviet cosmonaut and the first human in space.

The Soviet lead in the 'space race', as it was known at that time, was really a product of both the Soviets' national determination and their different philosophy of technology design. The rocket technology needed for spaceflight grew out of experiments with nuclear bombs. Soviet bombs were heavy. American bombs were lighter. So the Soviets needed to develop larger boosters earlier than the USA. Shrouded in secrecy, their achievements had an almost invincible quality. Everyone knows about *Sputnik I,* but before America even orbited their first satellite, the Soviets had flown a half-ton orbiting payload with a dog aboard. They even took a fuzzy picture of the far side of the moon in 1959. Yuri Gagarin's flight was one more thorn in the side of American self-image.

But in 1961, the USA had a young President brimming with enthusiasm—John F. Kennedy. On 25 May 1961, he addressed Congress: 'I believe that this nation should commit itself to achieving the goal, before this decade is out, of landing a man on the moon and returning him safely to Earth. No single space project in this period will be more impressive to mankind, or more important in the long-range exploration of space; and none will be so difficult or expensive to accomplish.'

This decision set in motion the first step to the stars. The *Mercury* flights took on a new urgency. We needed to orbit and to see just how reliable our spacecraft and launch vehicles were. John Glenn's historic flight illustrated how difficult it can be to tame the technological beast. Plagued by delay after delay, Glenn's Atlas booster lifted the *Friendship 7* spacecraft off on a three-orbit mission on 20 February 1962. Returning from space at over 17 000 miles per hour would have incinerated Glenn and his craft, were it not for a heat shield on the blunt end of the compact *Mercury* spacecraft. But a light on the ground indicated that the heat shield might be loose. During re-entry, Glenn actually saw chunks of flaming material stream past him and he had to fly the ship himself to point it properly. Happily, the flaming chunks were part of the strapped-on retrorocket package left there to hold the heat shield in place as long as possible. The light was wrong. Glenn was all right—tired, dehydrated, overheated, severely tested, but all right. During the remaining three *Mercury* flights, the next series of spacecraft was being readied. Called *Gemini* after the constellation of the twins, Castor and Pollux, these two passenger vehicles were designed to develop and demonstrate the procedures that would get us to the moon.

How daring Kennedy's decision seemed, in view of the fact that moon trips would require the ability to endure up to two weeks of weightless flight, find and rendezvous with another spacecraft, 'space walk' outside the spacecraft with life dependent on a pressurized suit, and develop systems that functioned perfectly over a quarter-million miles from home. Moon flights would also require boosters weighing some 6 000 000 pounds and a payload (the two *Apollo* spacecraft) of 50 tons in lunar orbit. *Mercury* weighed only 3 000 pounds in Earth orbit.

The *Gemini* flights achieved every objective. Ed White stepped out of *Gemini 4* for America's first space walk. *Gemini 7,* with Frank Borman and Jim Lovell, proved humans could operate for at least two weeks in space. People may not have realized it at the time, but two weeks in a *Gemini* 'capsule', as they were often called, was like spending two weeks eating, sleeping, working and going to the bathroom stuffed in the front seat of a sports car wearing an overcoat.

While *Gemini 7* orbited, *Gemini 6,* with Wally Schirra and myself aboard, effected the first successful space rendezvous. The whole Gemini program lasted only about a year and a half, during 1965 and 1966, but it went at a furious pace and gave the USA 10 learning flights, almost 2 000 hours of orbital experience and over a dozen experienced astronauts. The Mercury and Gemini programs totaled 16 missions without loss of a flight crew though things sure were bumpy at times. America seemed to be on track for a lunar landing before the decade was out.

It's never easy losing friends and colleagues. Gus Grissom, Ed White and Roger Chaffee died in a spacecraft fire during a launch-pad test of the new *Apollo* vehicle at the Cape. This tragedy hit me especially hard since Gene Cernan, John Young and I were doing similar tests in California in a sister spacecraft at that exact moment. The Apollo program was suddenly dead in its tracks. With 36 months left to meet the original Kennedy challenge, things didn't look good.

The precise cause of the fire wasn't actually determined by the investigation board, so a massive redesign had to be undertaken. Engineers are basically organizers and problem solvers, and in the months between April 1967 and October 1968, 150 000 of them labored to examine every facet of manufacture and materials. New, ingenious materials were devised. Documentation—mountains of paper to insure the pedigree and integrity of each part—was created. The joke at the time was that the thing couldn't fly until the weight of the paperwork equaled the weight of the spacecraft. But this documentation gave NASA the confidence and information necessary to assure quality control.

Simultaneously with the spacecraft redesign, the mammoth *Saturn* boosters were being proven. It is inspiring to remember that the *Saturn 5*, still the largest rocket ever

The command and service modules, viewed from the lunar module on the first flight, March 1969. The White Sands National Monument, New Mexico, is lower left.

built—36 stories high and 6 000 000 pounds heavy, with the capacity to hurl over 50 tons to the moon—was built and used only for peaceful purposes. By November 1967, the *Saturn* was tested and ready.

On 11 October 1968, *Apollo 7* orbited Earth in the first manned test of the spacecraft and Wally Schirra became the only astronaut to ever fly in *Mercury, Gemini* and *Apollo* spacecraft. We were back in business!

The next nine months would be the most exciting period of exploration in history. A barrage of four major launches followed, missions that would awe the world. These flights were like a symphony, with mission controllers holding the baton. Most people thought the actual moon landing would take place on *Apollo 12, 13* or *14.* Only if every flight were nearly perfect could the landing occur at the earliest possible flight—*Apollo 11. Apollo 8, 9* and *10* had to verify every operation and every piece of equipment. Any major problems in men or machines, and

the decade would probably run out with Kennedy's challenge unanswered.

So, the game plan was this: *Apollo 8* would marry the giant *Saturn 5* with a crew and spacecraft. They would fly to the moon, orbit and return, checking the *Apollo* command module's ability to successfully make the trip. If *Apollo 8* were successful, *Apollo 9* would be an Earth orbital test of the lunar excursion module. If the performances of that craft and the space suits were acceptable, *Apollo 10* would be an all-up dress rehearsal to the moon with every operation performed, short of the actual landing. The *Apollo 8* mission would also provide experience for crews and controllers in working 24 hours a day at lunar distances. Mission controllers cut their teeth on round-the-clock operations on *Gemini* flights. Now they would have to work with the spacecraft more than 1 200 times farther away and with communications periodically blacked out, as the spacecraft orbited behind the moon.

David Scott, in the open hatch of the
Apollo 9 *command module.*

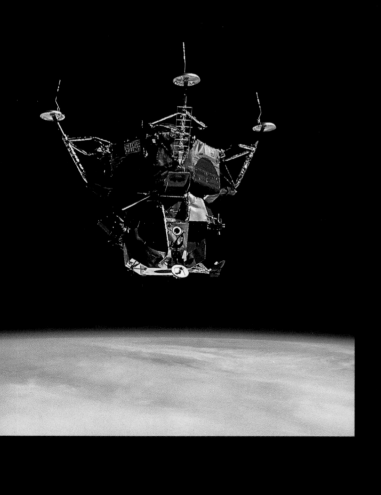

The lunar module in Earth orbit, above Africa. This is the first manned lunar module in space, March 1969. The Sahara is in the background.

Since *Apollo 7* was a nearly flawless flight, confidence ran high and *Apollo 8* was given the 'go' for lunar orbit. On 21 December 1968, the *Saturn V* roared to life. Many people had witnessed launches before. They were loud affairs with an impressive amount of smoke and flame. But few were prepared for the *Saturn V.* The ignition sequence of the five F-1 engines took about eight seconds. Blinding light flashed under the vehicle. The earth began to tremble for miles around. Then an ear-splitting roar announced humanity's supreme challenge to the 'god of gravity'. The *Saturn* rose slowly, taking what seemed an eternity to clear the tower. Its crackling, searing sound beat down as the vehicle gained speed, almost saying, 'Watch me, nothing can hold me.' Arching over the Atlantic, the bright aft end receded and 500 000 gallons of fuel were eaten in two and a half minutes!

Two hours, 27 minutes later in Earth orbit, the translunar injection burn started and *Apollo 8,* with Frank Borman, Jim Lovell and Bill Anders on board, was headed for the moon. Following NASA's policy that all communication with the spacecraft went through a capsule communicator (or capcom), it was astronaut Mike Collins who gave the crew the message that they were go for the burn. His voice was excited. He would get his chance to be on the other end of the message later. On Christmas Eve day, the craft slipped behind the moon and out of radio contact for the critical engine burn that would place them into lunar orbit. Thirty-four minutes later, applause erupted when radio confirmed that a successful lunar orbit had been achieved. That evening (Earth time) television viewers were treated to a 'live' look at their marvelous little island of life. Another view showed the barren, airless moon. Then the three astronauts took turns reading verses from the first chapter of Genesis—our first extraterrestrial message.

To understand the emotion and magic of that transmission, one has to reflect on the events of those times. 1968 was perhaps the most turbulent year in American history. The assassinations of Robert Kennedy and Martin Luther King, riots in dozens of cities, disruptions on campuses across the country and the anxiety of a nation at war, had left most of America numb. It was against this background that those pictures and words were heard. A message of hope. A sense that our species, while in turmoil, was capable of both great dreams and great deeds.

Apollo 8's critical boost out of lunar orbit, return coast back to Earth and landing were flawless. By the time it had landed, *Apollo 8* had forever changed our view of the planet and assured us that we could reach our program goal.

Next followed a full test of both the *Apollo* command module and the lunar module (LM), but in the relative safety of Earth orbit. Led by Jim McDivitt, the *Apollo 9* crew performed the major events of a full lunar mission. *Apollo 9* plucked the LM out of the *Saturn* booster and then flew it, testing both the descent and ascent engines, and the rendezvous and docking. Not since *Gemini 6* and *7* had two manned spacecraft joined in space.

However, space flight still wasn't as easy as it was beginning to look to the public.

The LM was having trouble with weight. If the craft was too heavy, it couldn't carry enough propellant to land and re-orbit the moon. So the craft was put on a diet called the Super Weight Improvement Program. The LM used for *Apollo 10* was still too heavy to actually land—a good thing that Gene Cernan and I got no closer than 47000 feet from the lunar surface.

Apollo 10 was a nearly perfect flight. Off on time and with the kind of pinpoint landing pilots like to brag about, this full dress rehearsal was very exciting, although performing the lunar orbit rendezvous was no cakewalk. Separate from John Young in the command module, the LM experienced a gyro failure, and coupled with an electrical short, the craft began to go out of control. Steadied manually, the descent stage was jettisoned early and a perfect rendezvous and docking were made. The ability to perform in spite of these problems gave the program renewed confidence in its crews and machinery.

The rest, as they say, is history. On 16 July 1969, Neil Armstrong, Buzz Aldrin and Mike Collins hurtled off the pad, strained under the 5-G stress that makes you feel like you weigh nearly half a ton, and headed for the moon. By 20 July, when a worldwide television audience saw Neil step onto the lunar surface, we all knew that our first tentative steps in space were over. There are events in history that help us fix our place, time and identity, and *Apollo 11* is one of those events. Quite appropriately, on that same morning, a note and some flowers appeared anonymously at John Kennedy's grave site on a quiet hillside in Arlington National Cemetery. The note read simply, 'Mr President, the Eagle has landed.'

The quality of the color television pictures from the moon gave a dreamlike image of the dreamlike event. The 500 000 workers on the NASA and industry teams, the whole nation in fact, reveled in those moments. As for the space race, one engineer said, 'Sometimes being first isn't everything. It may just be better to be a fast second!' Earth hadn't changed, our politics and problems hadn't changed—but our purview certainly had and our world has never been the same since.

Ultimately nine *Saturn 5*s would do their job and 10 more astronauts would explore the moon. As routine as the flights became for the public, the crews still encountered plenty of excitement. After a successful *Apollo 12* trip, the program almost got its comeuppance on *Apollo 13*. It was only an extraordinary blend of ingenuity and courage, high and low technology, that saved Jim Lovell, Jack Swigert and Fred Haise. Following a nearly perfect launch and translunar injection, the accumulation of what Lovell later called 'human errors and technical anomalies' caught up with *Apollo*. Two and a half days out, an oxygen tank in the service module exploded, leaving the command module with nothing more than battery power and the crew critically short of air. As far back as *Apollo 10,* discussions had begun about using the lunar module as a lifeboat. But the LM had life support for only 45 hours and it would take at least four days to get them around the moon and back—if it could be done at all. This was the first time the *Apollo* was not flown on a free-return trajectory. It was done to save fuel on the maneuver to brake command and service modules into lunar orbit. Thus, the first thing to do was to get *Apollo 13* back on a trajectory that would intercept Earth after swinging by the moon.

Using the LM as a lifeboat had never been done before and new procedures had to be developed and tested during the flight. Just keeping the crew alive was a major challenge. A contraption made of plastic, cardboard and tape allowed the command module's carbon dioxide scrubbers to be used in the LM. Water was cut from a normal 30 ounces a day to just 6 ounces—one small paper cupful. And the air turned cold—temperatures dropped as low as 35°F.

Using the LM descent engine, critical engine burns needed to be made. On *Apollo 13*'s trajectory at the time of the explosion, the ship would be lost. The crew had to get back to a 'free-return-to-Earth' path. Timing and alignment of the vehicles were critical for each burn, but the LM was not equipped for this kind of navigation. The crew had to rely totally on the accuracy of their wrist watches to time the precise alignment of Earth and the Sun in order to countdown the burns.

Coming home, nothing could be dumped or jettisoned overboard because doing so might disturb the trajectory. An inch of displacement could become miles of divergence back at Earth, so storage of waste became one more uncomfortable problem.

The LM *Aquarius* was separated only four hours before landing, and the command module, containing the crew and running on its last burst of battery power, landed safely. As is often the case, the problem could have been predicted based on a combination of records, reports and procedures. Some of the redesign features after the fire actually saved the mission, but the 90-day launch schedule could not continue. *Apollo 14* was delayed by almost nine months.

*Astronaut Harrison Schmitt at
'Split Rock' during* Apollo 17
EVA, December 1972.

The last four missions—*Apollo 14* through *Apollo 17*—were among the most productive scientific expeditions ever. They explored different areas of the moon and their corresponding different periods of lunar history. They used new devices and new technologies. First a cart and then lunar Rovers—electrically driven dunebuggies—were used to extend the survey areas of the landing sites. Small satellites were placed in orbit around the moon to study the lunar environment. Photo-mapping and photo-geologic surveys were also accomplished. The moon rocks turned out to be a scientific bonanza. Unlike Earth, with its atmosphere and oceans, the airless moon does not experience much erosion. So lunar materials, though pounded by meteors and solar energy, are essentially unchanged over billions of years.

The *Apollo* surveys might be compared to Lewis and Clark's journey into the American West. The picture of the moon that we now have is sufficient for planning return trips to establish lunar bases. What we have learned exploring the lunar surface should serve us well when humans eventually set foot on Mars, asteroids and perhaps the giant moons of Jupiter, Saturn, Uranus and Neptune.

The height of the Apollo lunar program was simultaneous with the buildup of American involvement in

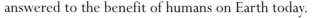

southeast Asia. Congressional and public interest waned and it was decided that *Apollo 17,* scheduled for December 1972, would be the final *Apollo* lunar mission. Unable to return to the moon, the space community turned towards other questions that needed answering, if humans were to one day live and work regularly in space. Some of these questions were critical ones. Could the loss of bone calcium observed during *Apollo* flights be retarded? Would exercise maintain the muscle tone and volume normally lost when the body no longer had to work against Earth's gravity? How long can humans work effectively in space? Many of these questions have been

answered to the benefit of humans on Earth today.

Never underestimate the creativity of the NASA people. Looking at the availability of several *Saturn 5*s and several late-model *Apollo* spacecraft and having smaller *Saturn 1-B* rockets left over because of the success of *Apollo*s 7 through to *10,* they set about economically fashioning a space station program. The result was *Skylab.*

Three crews of astronauts would ferry to and from *Skylab* using *Apollo* spacecraft and the smaller *Saturn 1-B* launch vehicles originally designed for orbital *Apollo* testing. It was a clever, cost-effective plan and a battery of scientific tests was prepared. Astronauts were to study not

Eugene Cernan, about to board the lunar Rover he and Harrison Schmitt have just assembled.

Harrison Schmitt next to the flag with a distant planet Earth in the background.

When the rear fender of the lunar Rover became detached, astronauts Cernan and Schmitt carried out a clever repair. A map was made into a fender to stop the wheel from covering them with dust.

only the sun, but Earth and its environment, the biology and physiology of long-term space flight, even the use of Buck Rogers-type jet backpacks to eventually propel individual astronauts around outside in space.

May 1973 saw preparation for two *Skylab* launches. The station was to be launched first and the crew the following day. The last *Saturn 5* flown by the USA lifted off the pad perfectly, but by the time it reached orbit, it was evident that things had gone wrong. One of the gyros had failed and the lab was overheating. One of the two solar arrays was apparently 'missing' and the other was jammed closed—there was no electrical power. If *Skylab* had been an unmanned spacecraft, the mission would have ended right there. But help was on the way.

Reminiscent of *Apollo 13*'s trip, ground and flight crews

began working around the clock. A giant parasol was fashioned to block the sun's rays and help control temperature inside the lab. It was designed, tested and built within about 72 hours. Tools were tried and procedures developed for extra vehicular activity to fix the jammed solar array. Then the first crew was launched in an attempt to salvage what they could of the program. Led by veteran Pete Conrad, they not only fixed most major problems, but stayed to complete their planned 28-day mission.

Repairs and maintenance kept *Skylab* in such good shape that two remaining missions lasted 59 and 84 days respectively. Miles of film and data tapes and weeks of active experimentation produced another scientific windfall for scientists. Owen Garriott even performed some classic physics experiments for the film camera, to

The Arabian Peninsula looking north east. Iran and Valley of the Tigris-Euphrates Rivers can be seen on the left, near the horizon and the Arabian Gulf on the right.

be used by students back on Earth.

The Apollo program was finally overtaken by history. Hardware that had been developed in response to a Cold War challenge by Soviet technology was used for the last time on a peaceful, productive, co-operative mission with those same former adversaries. The Nixon administration adopted a policy of detente with the Soviet Union. In this relaxed political environment, further co-operation in space was possible: information exchanges, participation by scientists of one country in the scientific ventures of the another country, and the jewel in the crown, a manned rendezvous between a US *Apollo* spacecraft and the Soviet *Soyuz* spacecraft.

For the first time, astronauts and cosmonauts trained together in each other's simulators. We found Soviet technology proficient and their procedures somewhat similar to ours. One difference was the amount of control the ground had over the mission. Their ground controllers really determined most of what was done, while our crews tended to fly their own mission against a predetermined plan.

Two technical problems emerged in planning. First, the Soviet spacecraft used a normal sea-level oxygen-nitrogen atmosphere at about 15 pounds per square inch pressure, while our *Apollos* used a 5 pound per square inch pure oxygen environment. It would be fine to enter the Soviet spacecraft, but returning to the lower pressure of the *Apollo*, with the nitrogen gas dissolved in the bloodstream, would produce what scuba divers call the bends —a sometimes fatal bubbling of nitrogen in the arteries, blocking blood flow. Also, the two countries had to develop an international docking mechanism for crew transfer. To solve these problems, a docking module was created, a tunnel-like affair with a decompression chamber inside and a docking apparatus on the end.

On 17 July 1975, *Apollo* chased down, found and docked with the *Soyuz* like the first orbital rendezvous between *Gemini 6* and *Gemini 7;* only six years earlier I had made the first rendezvous and dock in lunar orbit—and now we were looking straight out at a Russian craft. Deke Slayton, Vance Brand and I joined our Soviet counterparts for several days of experiments and multinational communications.

We became fast friends with our cosmonaut counterparts Alexei Leonov and Valery Kubasov. Leonov had beaten Ed White to become the first human to walk in space. He is also a fine artist who later painted the views he saw of *Apollo* out his window. The language problem we solved in a unique way. Astronauts spoke Russian, cosmonauts spoke English. When you speak a foreign language, you speak more slowly, making it easier for the native speaker to understand and respond. Only in an emergency would we be hearing information in our native language.

Two and a half years of hard work paid off with a flawless mission. When our *Apollo* splashed down, an era ended. Competition between our two countries had certainly not ended, but we did prove that we could work together in the most technical of areas.

Studying post-*Apollo* options, a late 1960s presidential task force outlined many exciting possibilities— permanent space stations, a reusable airplane-like space shuttle, lunar bases, even manned missions to Mars. But the Administration and Congress were cutting, not expanding, civilian space activity. So NASA had to choose one program and try to sell it to a not-very-interested executive and legislative audience. They selected the shuttle, which would be useful for many aspects of space exploration. It would be reusable, a necessary feature since costs for *Apollo* had been criticised. It would be used to ferry many payloads to and from Earth orbit. It would be used by the military and it would, theoretically, pay its way by selling launch services to industry and other countries. The shuttle orbiter is, of course, a hybrid: it uses three liquid-fuel rocket engines for lift-off, performs like a

Clouds and their shadows above the Indian Ocean, north-east of Madagascar.

spacecraft then de-orbits and lands like a glider.

The shuttle also carries larger crews than *Apollo*. This has allowed more work per mission to be accomplished. In addition, shuttle launches exert only a maximum of 3 Gs on payloads and the astronaut's body, instead of the 8 Gs experienced by *Gemini* astronauts. This lower stress opened space travel to any normal, healthy individual—and many more useful payloads.

During the shuttle flights to date, so many new accomplishments have taken place that they are too numerous to list in their entirety here. The first satellite to be repaired in orbit, the *Solar Maximum Mission,* is back at work. Commercial communication satellites that hadn't been able to reach their proper orbits were retrieved for reuse. The *Skylab* experimental backpacks have evolved into sophisticated manned maneuvering units that power individual astronauts around like minispacecraft. *Spacelab* modules, built by the European Space Agency, provide test beds for space science and are prototypes for future permanent space laboratory facilities on Space Station *Freedom*. The first commercial products made in the microgravity of space are already being sold. Crews are young and old, male and female, from America, Europe and elsewhere.

We have only started to tap the potential of space flight, as our whole planet becomes involved in the space enterprise. Rockets are built in Europe, Japan, China and India. Satellites are owned by dozens of countries. Fierce competition is brewing for space access and space services. Future priorities include both space stations and further use of the space shuttle. We have come a long way in a short time—but only scratched the surface.

Future generations will look back on the space shuttle as the Model T of reusable spacecraft. Our old *Apollos* are already museum pieces displayed alongside fabric-winged biplanes. Twenty-five years ago, we were challenged to go to the moon. What is our challenge today? Are the first astronauts to Mars in our grade schools now? How many of us or our children—hundreds, thousands—will look down on those white clouds and blue oceans and radio back, 'It almost takes your breath away!'?

Thomas Stafford, USA

Above: *A vertical view of a remote section of the Himalaya Range, in contrast with the moon's surface opposite.*

Right: *20 square mile portion of the moon's 'farside' surface from Apollo 8, December 1968.*

PART 2

SAVORING
THE
EXPERIENCE

The Mediterranean island of Cyprus is above the vertical stabilizer of space shuttle Endeavour. *Turkey is lower left. The flags of 15 nations are visible.*

FLYING

Lake Balkhash in Kazakhstan. Melting snow from the Tien Shan mountain range provides most of the water for this land-locked lake.

Opposite: Soyuz *booster launch with the Soyuz-TM spacecraft aboard, from Baikonur Cosmodrome in Kazakhstan.*

ONE FULL DAY ...

The events of 12 April 1961 have left an indelible mark on the minds of many boys and girls, and not only those in the Soviet Union. On that day humanity took its first step into the unknown. It disturbed something in our subconscious, yet every forward-thinking person could imagine the possibilities.

An announcer's voice came over the loudspeakers in the school playground. The faces of the children lit up with excitement. Good wishes and congratulations passed between the teachers. It would be hard to find one indifferent person, one frowning face. The whole country rejoiced. We had opened up a new era—the space era!

Our Soviet man in space was Yuri Gargarin. How did he achieve it? I considered the necessary steps, drew up

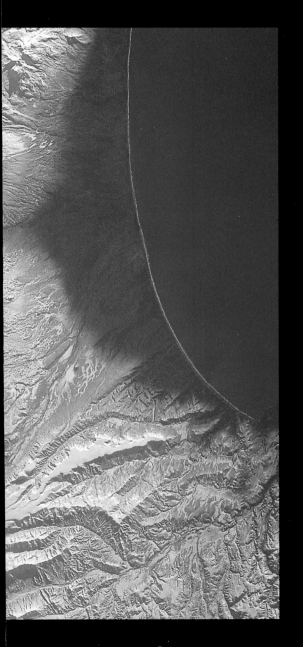

*An autumn view of the
Kamchatka Peninsula and the
Pacific Coast of Siberia.*

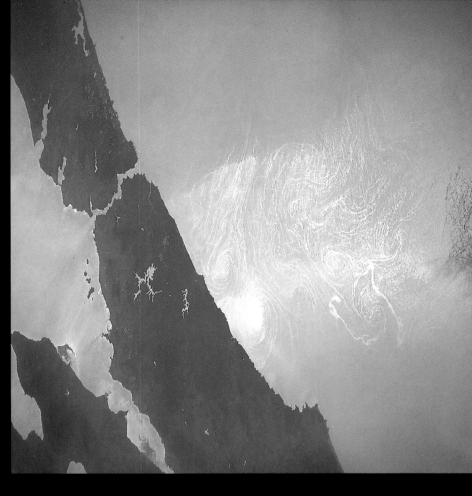

*The Black Sea at Istanbul, Turkey. The
sun's reflection off the sea also gives an
indication of the surface 'sea state'.*

EARTH EXIT

In the language of space travel 'L minus 1' means one day before launch. Until this point in my life, the calendar held good, but now L minus time begins.

A small company of people takes care of me, so my psyche can cope with the difference between the previously simulated launch and this actual one. Now my soul is also part of the program: the fact that I will leave Earth tomorrow has effects of its own.

L minus 0: 15 minutes past midnight. My eyes have to be closed, that is what someone has planned for me. Get-up time is 7:40; 9:45 is boarding time. Two and a quarter hours later, liquid hydrogen and oxygen will take us towards the stars. Twelve o'clock will be 'high noon', blast off.

10:30: the difference from anything else I know creates a sense of isolation. Apart from us eight blue-suited astronauts, there are only a few white suits still here to take care of us. Steam clouds rise from the rocket nozzles. The spaceship stands upright, ready to go. Birds take advantage of the solitude and circle around us solicitously. Loud hissing can still be heard as the vehicle strains to equalise a 280°C temperature difference between the outside and the liquid hydrogen in its gut. The tank pipes are coated with ice and from far below, flame barriers point back towards us.

White herons still sail with dignity. Everything seems to be ready to go. OK, then I must be ready, too.

11:00: I lie on my seat. You go to the stars lying down. A familiar face looks in, then a thumb stretches

upwards where we want to go. The handle on the door turns, the hatch is closed.

Take-off minus 30 minutes: the bird is coming alive. On the flight deck, hectic activity begins. Soon the wires will be cut. Where we are going, no one will be around to help. The last man outside drives the bridge away. We are on our own.

5:48 minutes: vibrations start.

2:40 minutes: gimble check—we test how our engines move. No one says 'Halt!' I hear my own breathing in my ear. Still 35 seconds to go. 'Engine start!' The gimble comes again...'Go!'

The sails are set, upright into the sky. Traveling at 162 knots, I see Earth through the window. The sky is still blue. The ride becomes calm. Our solid rockets fall away into the sea. Around us it turns black. We are now really moving away from Earth.

'Negative return!': now there is no way back to the launch site. We are six and a half minutes into flight and the engines are so quiet because their sound can no longer keep up with us. 'MECO': main engines cut off, we are free. Seats as heavy as hundredweights drift past me. We belong no more to Earth.

After one hour and 45 minutes in space, our faces are swollen. A ray of light passes from left to right. Blue, with a white edge—turquoise perhaps, no—here I also see colors another way.

My hands no longer feel part of me. When I let myself

Issyk-Kul is a large, deep, salt lake in Kirgizskaya. The Terskey Ala-Too mountains are below the lake, the Kungey Ala-Too mountains above.

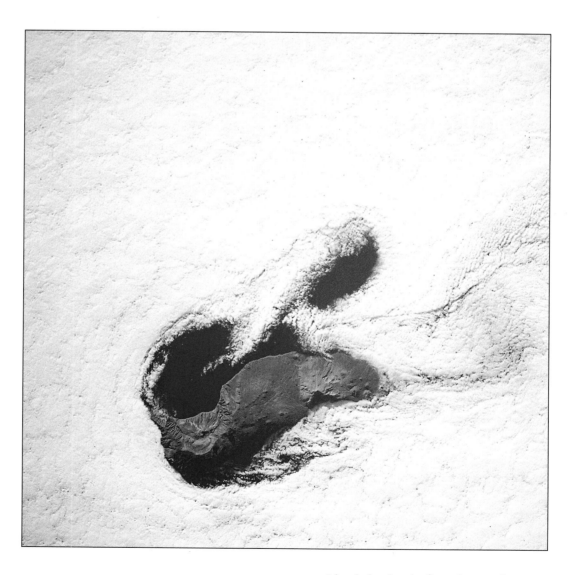

Island cloud wake formed around Guadalupe in the Pacific Ocean.

free, I first make sure these arms are mine. What remains of my earthly self? I think, and I can see. In every other way, I no longer feel like me.

Earth is still there, very beautiful, without my being able to say why. A planet, cocooned in blue and white, and yet it is strange to me. I know that the voices in my headphones come from it, and yet they hardly make sense and are not strong enough to hold me. I feel weight nowhere and nothing more demands my strength.

Only through my knowledge will I reach home. My orbit is reduced to numbers on a piece of paper, my velocity is measured on the picture that revolves in front of me. My stars have nothing more in common with the sky. They rise behind a planet and eventually I fly past them. Sometimes they also lose their place and fall. Actually, I want only to go towards them. More than anything else, I would like to abandon the last remnants of my earthly world.

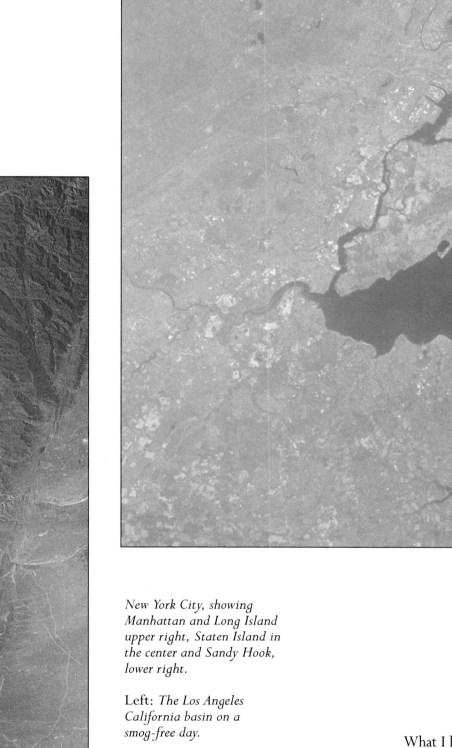

New York City, showing
Manhattan and Long Island
upper right, Staten Island in
the center and Sandy Hook,
lower right.

Left: *The Los Angeles
California basin on a
smog-free day.*

Next page: *The Bahamas.
Andros Island is upper left,
Great Abaco Island, right. The
deep waters of the Tongue of
the Ocean are dark blue.
Reefs and shallow areas are
lighter in color.*

What I have brought with me from Earth seems pointless. My feeling needs no spaceship. My world transforms
itself into points of light in empty space. Earth days are
now only a geometric consideration. Time has no content. The moon is a light that will be extinguished by
Earth.

My consciousness of circling Earth is lost; my aimless
drifting could take me with it wherever it will. Human
beings become tiny voices in my ear. My world has nothing more to do with Earth.

Reinhard Furrer, Germany

SPACE WALK

Do you want to try something you won't quickly forget? Admittedly it might be a rare opportunity, but whenever you're in Earth orbit and you have a chance to sneak outside for a space walk—do it!

It's not easy to give you an idea of what you're in for, but a comparison helps. If you're in a tall building or an aircraft and you look out a window, you'll have a good view of Earth's surface below... lots of interesting features, varied textures and vivid colors for sure. Pleasant. Relaxing.

But now step outside, look down and move away from the spacecraft. Position yourself so that all of its structure is out of view and you no longer feel a part of it. Your world is reduced to just two components: you and Earth—hundreds of miles below. Somehow, this feels different.

To get just a taste of how different, let's go back up to the top floor of our tall building, the Sears Tower or the Empire State Building will do, but this time open the window, stroll out to the end of a long diving board and have a highly motivated, steel-fisted Arnold Schwarzenegger hold you by your ankles—head down. Intellectually, you know you'll never fall. Even though you're at the same height as you were inside, maybe even a couple of feet lower, somehow it feels a bit different, doesn't it?

Yeah, can't deny it does.

On a space walk, you can have a similar feeling, just a lot more of it. As you glide over Earth, face down, at a serene 5 miles a second, you have full intellectual confidence that you're up there for sure—even though you're no longer part of any structure, even though no one is there to hold your ankles, even though you just fall and fall and fall straight down towards Earth—that Earth's perfectly curved surface is moving away at just the right speed so that you'll never catch up to it, never fall fast enough to get any closer than the height you're currently at. With full confidence that Sir Isaac Newton was right, you put away your calculator and enjoy the view. Nope, not a chance, you'll never impact Earth.

But how do you convince the gut?

After all, it's the gut that really feels the void. It's the gut that's screaming, 'Hey, couldn't that Newton guy have been just a tiny bit wrong?'. It's the gut that has your heart stroking at full bore, your lungs frozen and a big, wide grin consuming your face.

Yep, if you get a chance, do it. Don't fight it. Just look down, open yourself wide and drink.

Edward Gibson, USA

Space walk. Bruce McCandless II leans out into space, feet anchored in the mobile foot restraint.

estern union

WESTAR VI

WHAT IS IT LIKE?

What is it like in space? People always ask that same question.

When you first experience zero gravity, your body says, 'I don't need my legs.' And so the brain says, 'We don't need legs, let's shrink them.' Your legs actually do shrink about an inch in diameter very quickly.

When your legs shrink, where does the excess go? It goes right to your face, and we all had this sort of chipmunk look. It's rather uncomfortable but of short duration, because the face is telling the brain, 'I don't want this stuff either; would you get rid of it?'. And what happens is that you start to discharge it outside your body. The only problem is that there are usually several team members and only one waste management system.

Next, there's no up and no down. So you can live on any of the six surfaces. When we started out, the spacecraft was pretty cramped for all seven of us. But once we got into space, we found that you don't have to live on the floor; you can live on the ceiling, or on the wall, and the spacecraft thereby becomes spacious. I picked the ceiling for my home base.

In space you can really fly. If you want to go someplace, you don't walk, you just push with your finger and you fly over. Not everything is positive; for example, writing is difficult, but you learn to adjust to these things. The human body is a very adaptive system, and it takes only about a day or two to adjust to the space environment. From that point on you feel quite comfortable.

What do we eat in space? A typical menu would consist of dehydrated meat and vegetables. This is a meal you could eat if you had a good appetite. But in space, even if you're not sick, you often don't feel that great. So most of us didn't eat much. I brought some Chinese tea along, and that kept me going most of the time—a cup of tea and some nuts. When I came home, I had lost about four and a half pounds, and that's quite typical. (We also gain about one and a half inches in height, but only while we remain in space.) One person on our flight, however, had a great appetite. Whatever the rest of us didn't eat, he finished. And when he came back, he had actually gained five pounds. That made NASA history.

How do we eat in space? There are two ways. If you want to do it the way you would normally eat on Earth, you have to move the food towards your mouth at a very slow pace, so the food won't leave the spoon or fork and land in some undesired place. Alternatively, rather than bringing the food to your mouth, you can leave the food in mid-air and move your mouth to it. That works pretty well unless a colleague gets his mouth to your food before you.

Putting on clothes in space is also different from on Earth. You don't put on pants one foot at a time. Because the clothes spring out and take their own form, you don't really put them on at all; you just wriggle yourself in. When you sleep, you don't lie down on something—you just float. So when you're tired, you just close your eyes and go to sleep whenever you want to. It's very comfortable. The only trouble is that sometimes you float too far and drift into your friends.

But just as important as what happens in space is our teamwork with the ground. There were about 300 individuals at the Johnson Space Center in Houston supporting our flight. I had nine people just on my experiment team, working all the time I was working, even when I got to rest. I don't think they slept the entire time, to be sure of being there when I needed help.

Taylor Wang, USA

On board space shuttle Columbia. *Payload specialist Millie Hughes-Fulford at work on an experiment.*

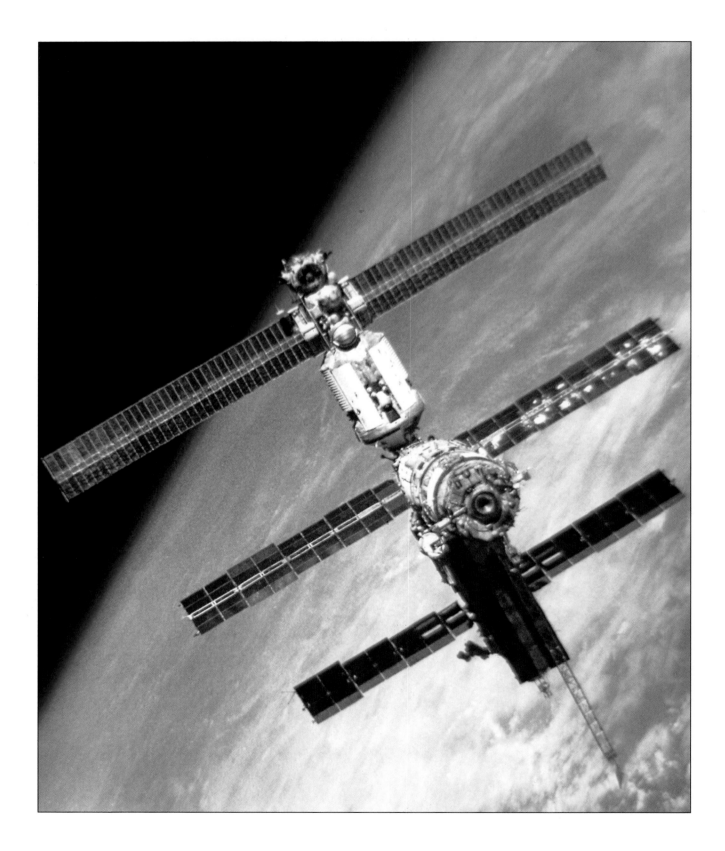

RIVER OF FIRE

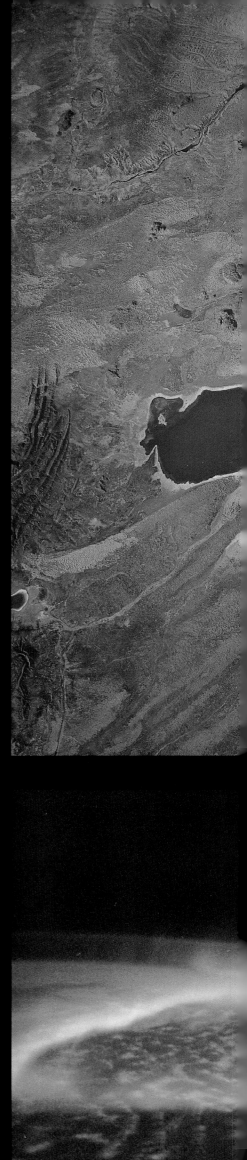

Left: *The Arabian Peninsula with urban lights at twilight. The large city at left center is Riyadh. Persian Gulf coastal cities visable are Doha at right, Kuwait, and Bahrain.*

What I saw below startled me.

It looked like a river of fire stretching from horizon to horizon, almost like a single strand of flowing lava, with utter darkness as far as I could see on either side. Following this shimmering skein up to one horizon, it bloomed in two places, as if the blazing river had spilled over its banks and inundated two large valleys. At the most distant reaches of this river, more than 1 000 miles away, it forked out and created a crescent, trying to encircle a large mountain.

I was confused.

It took me a few moments to realize that I was in fact staring at the River Nile. And instead of seeing a river of fire, I was looking at a solid string of lights from the communities that line the banks of the Nile. The lights extended less than a few miles on either side of the river bed, except further north, where first Cairo and then Alexandria blossomed.

The crescent furthest to the north was the Mediterranean Sea, defining the sweep of the African continent where it meets Eurasia, past the Suez Canal up through the Sinai into Israel and Lebanon. I was looking at the lights of civilization! What intrigued me was the starkness of the contrast of bright lights and darkness. Humanity was not a master of its environment but was bonded to the giver of life, water. Where water was plentiful, mankind flourished.

Rick Hauck, USA

Lake Poopo, Bolivia is a salt lake located in one of the earth's remotest areas.

Interaction between the atmosphere and Van Allen Radiation Belts produces the phenomena of the Southern Lights or Aurora Australis. Seen from space shuttle Discovery, May 1991.

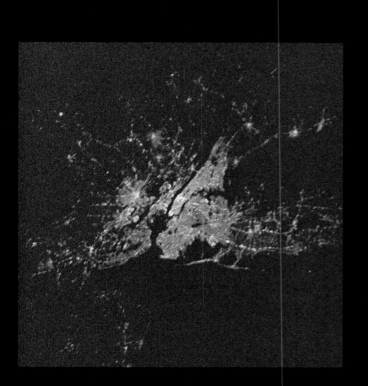

NIGHT VISION

At night the universe opens up. Darkness gives you a new perspective both on Earth and the sky. The high contrast of city lights against Earth's dark surface makes human civilization more visible at night than during the day. City lights provide excellent beacons to guide you around the human geography of our planet, all the way out to the horizon.

Flying over Baja California on a clear December night, it was easy to pick out the lights of Denver. Over Houston we could see all the way to Chicago and Toronto. The most spectacular sight was flying over the Atlantic and looking back at the entire eastern seaboard, with cities all the way from Miami to Boston, strung out like jewels on a magnificent necklace.

The sky changes dramatically at night. Astronauts often comment on how fragile the thin blue line of the atmosphere looks from space. This is a daytime view. At night, this blue line disappears entirely and is replaced by a ghostly, rustcolored halo, hovering above Earth. This glow is caused by emission from oxygen and nitrogen atoms in the atmosphere 60 miles above the ground. At first sight, you can mistake it for the horizon, until you notice the stars between it and Earth.

Once, over the Pacific Ocean, the moon was new and there were no lightning storms below and, of course, no city lights. Earth was totally dark. All I could see were the stars and the entire universe surrounding us. The Sun was gone and Earth seemed far away.

It was incredibly lonely.

Jeffrey Hoffman, USA

Jupiter rising above the air glow over Earth's horizon, with a crescent moon above. Seen from space shuttle Endeavour, *December 1993.*

Inset: *New York City at night.*

TO REALLY SEE IT, LEAVE IT

Only eight and a half thunderous minutes after launch, I was orbiting high above Earth, suddenly able to watch typhoons form, volcanoes smolder, and meteors streak through the atmosphere below.

Surprisingly, the Hawaiian Islands really do look as if that part of the world has been carpeted with a big page torn out of Rand-McNally—a surreal scene.

In orbit, racing along at 5 miles per second, the space shuttle circles Earth once every 90 minutes. If I turned my concentration away from the window for too long, I could miss an entire land mass. It's embarrassing to float up to a window, glance outside, and then have to ask a crewmate, 'What continent is this?'.

We could see smoke rising from fires that dotted the entire east coast of Africa, and in the same orbit only moments later, ice floes jostling for position in the Antarctic. We could see the Ganges River dumping its murky, sediment-laden water into the Indian Ocean and watch ominous hurricane clouds expanding and rising like biscuits in the oven of the Carribean.

Mountain ranges, volcanoes, and river deltas appeared in the salt-and-flour relief, all leading me to assume the role of novice geologist. In such moments, it was easy to imagine the dynamic upheavals that created jutting mountain ranges and the internal wrenchings that created rifts and seas. I also became an instant believer in plate tectonics; India really is crashing into Asia, and Saudi Arabia and Egypt really are pulling apart, making the Red Sea even wider. Even though their respective motion is really no more than mere inches a year, the view from overhead makes theory come alive.

One day, as I scanned the sandy expanse of Northern Africa, I couldn't find any familiar landmarks—colorful outcroppings of rock in Chad, irrigated patches of the Sahara. Then I realized they were obscured by a huge dust storm, a cloud of sand that enveloped the continent from Morocco to the Sudan.

The signatures of civilization are usually seen in straight lines (bridges or runways) or sharp delineations (abrupt transitions from desert to irrigated land, as in California's Imperial Valley). A modern city like New York doesn't leap from the canvas of its surroundings, but its straight piers and concrete runways catch the eye, and around them, the city materializes.

Part of Lake Nasser reservoir, for the Aswan Dam, Nile River, Egypt.

Water covers most of the Earth's surface, and at first glance it looks the same: blue. But with the right lighting conditions and a couple of orbits practice, it's possible to make out the intricate patterns in the oceans—eddies and spirals become visible because of the subtle differences in water color or reflectivity.

An astronaut can also see the wakes of large ships and the contrails of airplanes. When the lighting conditions are perfect, you can follow otherwise invisible oil tankers on the Persian Gulf and trace the major shipping lanes through the Mediterranean Sea. Similarly, when the atmospheric conditions allow contrail formation, the thousand-mile-long condensation trails let us trace the major air routes across the northern Pacific Ocean.

Part of every orbit takes us to the dark side of the planet. In space, night is very, very black, but that doesn't mean there's nothing to look at. The lights of cities sparkle; on nights when there was no moon, it was difficult for me to tell the Earth from the sky—the twinkling lights could be stars or they could be small cities. On one night-time pass from Cuba to Nova Scotia, the entire East Coast of the United States appeared in twinkling outline.

When the moon is full, it casts an eerie light on Earth. In its light, we see ghostly clouds and bright reflections on the water. One night, the Mississippi River flashed into view, and because of our viewing angle and orbital path, the reflected moonlight seemed to flow downstream, as if Huck Finn had tied a candle to his raft.

Of all the sights from orbit, the most spectacular may be the magnificent displays of lightning that ignite the clouds at night. Bolts of lightning are diffused by the clouds into bursting balls of light. Sometimes, when a storm extends hundreds of miles, it looks like a transcontinental brigade is tossing fireworks from cloud to cloud.

As the shuttle races around Earth, we pass from day to night and back again—hurtling into darkness, then bursting into daylight. The sun's appearance unleashes spectacular blue and orange bands along the horizon, a clockwork miracle that we witness every 90 minutes. But I really can't describe a sunset in orbit. The drama set against the black backdrop of space and the magic of materializing colors can't be captured in an astronomer's equations or an astronaut's photographs.

While it's natural to try to liken space flight to familiar experiences, it can't be brought 'down to Earth', not in the final sense. The environment is different, the perspective is different. Part of the fascination with space travel is the element of the unknown—the conviction that it's different from earthbound experiences. And it is!

Sally Ride, USA

A south-west view over New Zealand from space station Skylab *showing the lower North Island and the South Island.*

Left: *Sunrise from the* MIR *space station.*

OUR ONE AND ONLY EARTH

The station progressed in its orbit, moving in a black chasm where the stars and Earth's surface at dusk became one. Suddenly, a panorama opened up—as the bright, colored rays of the setting sun painted the Earth's surface, changed the dark and tinted the clouds, and exposed a whole network of rivers and streams, lakes and marshes. The solar panels, antennas and hull of the station lit up with golden light.

In those fleeting moments, Earth seemed so small. Then came the admiration for humanity's power of reason. It was humanity that created this unique technology that enabled us to circle Earth, to view everything on our planet.

The furtherest corner of Earth seems close from space. And after a few minutes of flying, every second becomes priceless.

Over the horizon comes the amazing sight of the forests of the Amazon River Basin—thick dark-green velvet unbroken by roads or fields. Only the thin threads of the rivers falling into the Amazon cut through the cover. The thin blue layer of our atmosphere covering the horizon depends on this oxygen factory. From this River Basin, the atmosphere spreads out and nourishes Earth.

Doubts come creeping into the consciousness about the possibility of a repetition of Earth, because of the gigantic diversity and movement opening before our eyes. The very smallest of small of this multitude below is necessary to humanity.

Vladimir Vasyutin, Russia

An Apollo-Soyuz *view of the* Amazon *rainforest taken from the* Apollo *spacecraft. The major river is the Rio Jurua at its junction with the Rio Tarauaca.*

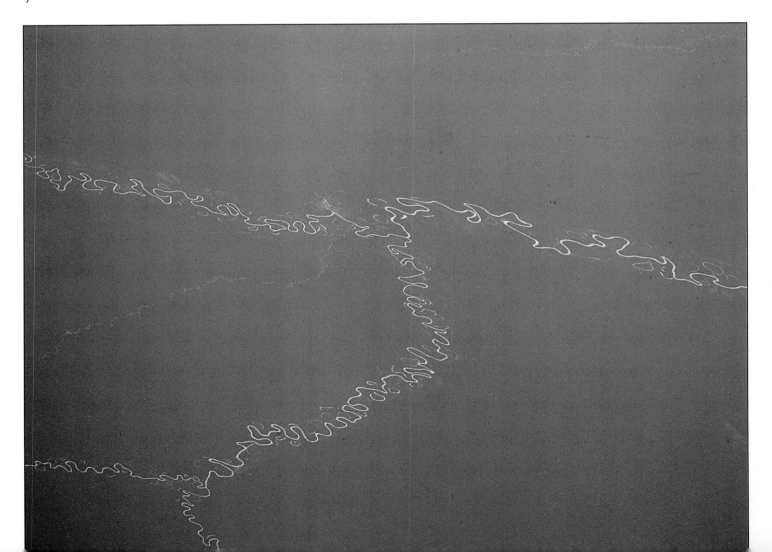

Space shuttle Atlantis *passes overhead the European Retrievable Carrier (Eureca) satellite.*

Left: *Vladimir Kovalyonok emerging from Salyut-6 to undertake EVA.*

OUR COMMON COSMIC HOME

Flying above our lovely planet, I was carried away by its beauty. I watched with ecstasy the bright colors of the Earth's horizon at sunrise and I observed the delightful, daylight, sunny side of Earth. She might be compared to an elegant bride behind a thin, tender blue veil. And unintentionally the ideas came: we must preserve her at all costs, the cradle of humanity, our common cosmic home, so that humanity can live in peace, so that space can serve peaceful purposes and promote friendship between nations.

Cosmonauts and astronauts have seen Earth from a distance, from space, in all the astonishing diversity of her beauty. Our main task, the task of all the people on Earth, is not to allow under any circumstances a thermonuclear catastrophe in our cosmic home. It is the only one we have, at the moment, in the whole universe. We must use our exceptional opportunities in space to solve international economic problems for the good and prosperity of all mankind.

I believe that reason is invincible; it will triumph forever.

Andrian Nikolayev, Russia

Right: *North-eastern Africa and the Near East. The Mediterranean Sea is at the left edge, with the Indian Ocean to the right.*

THROUGH THE WINDOW

Orbiting Earth at 17 800 miles per hour, we passed over continents within a matter of minutes. No sooner did I spot the Horn of Africa than we were over India, then China, and out over the Pacific Ocean. Yet it was amazing how much detail I could see. Crossing the isthmus of Panama, it was easy to see the plume of an erupting volcano, Masaya, in Nicaragua. The wind from the east blew the plume of smoke hundreds of miles out to sea. Lake Maracaibo in Venezuela was clearly visible.

Passing over the Persian Gulf at night, I saw bright flares of the oil wells in the desert as they burned excess gas. Looking down on the jungle-covered mountains of the Philippines, I imagined the thatched huts in the villages. I spotted the Soviet submarine base in Ethiopia, sitting at the narrow opening where the Red Sea joins the Indian Ocean, and realized how strategically situated it was. The cotton fields of Egypt, Lake Okeechobee in Florida, the trail of a jet airplane over Malaysia—all were vividly clear.

Hanging upside down with Pinky Nelson, sipping hot coffee through a straw, I saw the brilliant lights of Rio de Janeiro and wondered if any sightseers on top of Pao de Acucar—Sugarloaf Mountains—were sipping Brazilian coffee and looking up at us as we emerged from the Southern Cross constellation and streaked across the night sky.

On one night pass across the USA, I could see the extensive lights of the west coast of California, with the Los Angeles area brilliantly distinct. But the brightest lights at night in the USA were from the city of Las Vegas. On one pass across the east coast, I saw lights all the way from the tip of Florida up the eastern seaboard to Washington, DC.

Lightning storms were most spectacular and easy to spot. One night the entire eastern half of America was lit up by brilliant lightning that lasted as long as we maintained visibility. On the night side of Earth, during times of intense thunderstorm activity, thousands of square miles lit up with each flash. In one massive storm over the continent of Africa, the lightning seemed to flash in syncopated pulses, as though it were huge strobe lights hundreds of miles apart.

Surely, I thought, if some extraterrestrial beings ever do look down on us from outer space and see those magnificent electrical flashes from cloud to cloud, or cloud to surface, they will know without a doubt that there is a special energy and vitality on the planet below.

I spent little time sleeping, preferring to float at the windows looking out over Earth while the others slept. I could sleep when I got home. I did not want to miss a single detail of this unrepeatable experience.

Bill Nelson, USA

Opposite: *The Hubble Space Telescope, over Madagascar, is berthed in space shuttle* Endeavour's *cargo bay.*

A plankton bloom off the coast of New Zealand's South Island. Being in the southern hemisphere the vortex is spinning clockwise.

133

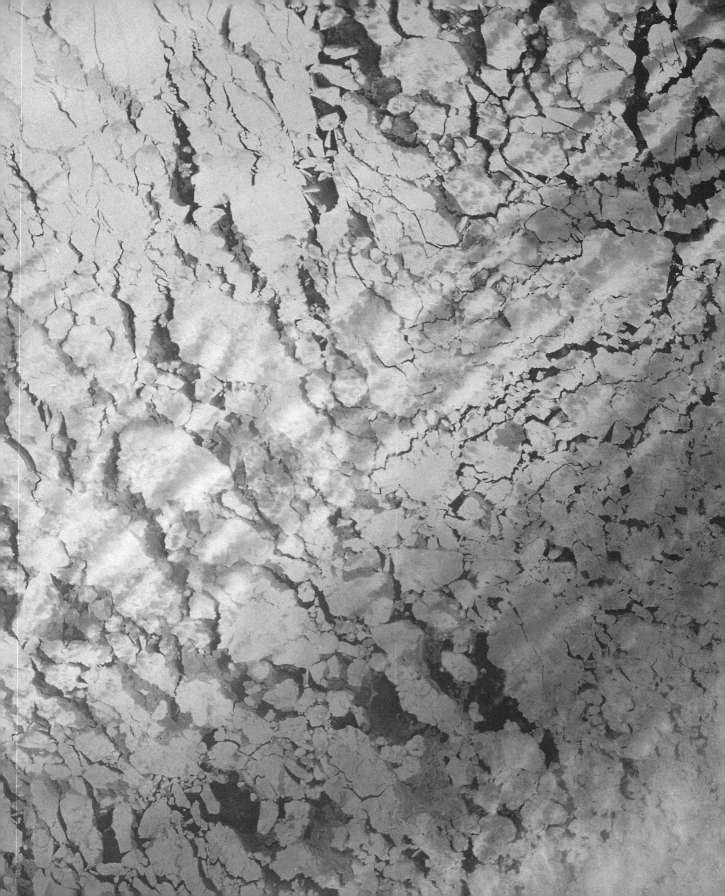

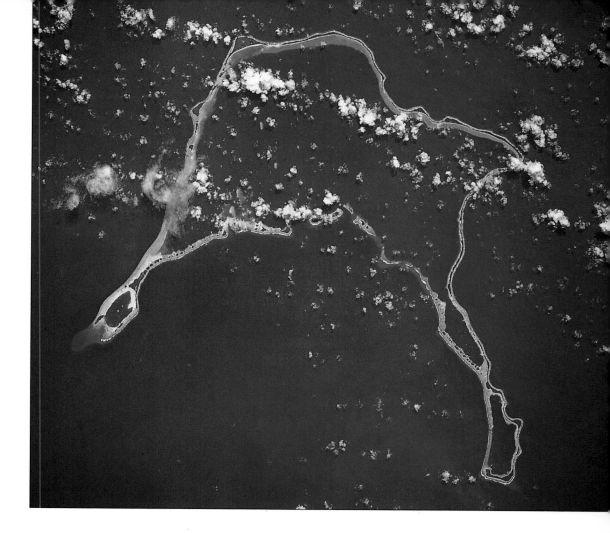

The Arno Atoll in the Marshall Islands, a complex atoll compared to 'classical' atolls.

IF EVERYBODY COULD FLY JUST ONCE

As a boy, I always dreamed of flying in space but it was hard to imagine the vast distances to celestial bodies and the speed at which one would have to travel to reach them. During the 1950s, no one had ever flown in space. I had no reason to believe that I ever would.

In November 1985, I flew on NASA's space orbiter *Atlantis.*

The flight deck was the most popular part of the spacecraft because of its 10 windows. Amazed and captivated, my six companions and I looked out whenever we could, knowing that very few humans had had the privilege of seeing our planet's beauty from this perspective. How magnificent it was! I can still see the deep blue, dotted with hundreds of white cloud spots which, from that distance, resembled tiny balls of cotton.

I wondered if there were other living creatures far away, what they might be like, or whether they had existed earlier and been absorbed by the vastness of the Universe or the infinity of time. How insignificant this one terrestrial human appeared compared to the blue planet that sustained so many millions of us through countless generations.

I marveled at the human brain's capacity to develop technology which allowed us to explore space, and wondered if, one day, we could really explore the entire Solar System, and then the galaxies around us.

I thought of the possibility, very slight but real, that we might never make it home, that perhaps the computers or the oxygen supply would fail, or that a window would break, exposing us to the vacuum of space.

But I refused to fear—that would have been pointless; I knew our mission was extremely worthwhile. Yet I still longed to return to Earth and embrace my family and friends, to enjoy Nature and help others look after it. I kept thinking how beautiful our planet is and wished that somehow everybody on Earth could fly at least once. Then they would respect our planet more, look after it and share it in peace.

Rodolfo Neri-Vela, Mexico

Fog, caused by the cold Benguela current touching the hot desert coast of Namibia is common and the only form of moisture. Rainfall is about half an inch a decade.

REFLECTING

The Mediterranean coast of France at Marseilles and Provence.

TWO MOONS

I find that my two space flights have changed my perception of Earth. Of course, *Apollo 11* also changed my perception of the moon, but I don't regard that as being nearly as important.

There seem to be two moons now, the one I see in my backyard and the one I remember from up close. Intellectually, I know they are one and the same, but emotionally they are separate entities. The small moon, the one I have known all my life, remains unchanged, except that I know it is three days away. The new one, the big one, I remember primarily for its vivid contrast with Earth.

I really didn't appreciate the first planet until I saw the second. The moon is so scarred, so desolate, so monotonous, that I cannot recall its tortured surface without thinking of the infinite variety the delightful planet Earth offers: misty waterfalls, pine forests, rose gardens, blues and greens and reds and whites that are missing entirely on the gray-tan moon.

Michael Collins, USA, from *Carrying the Fire*

137

Space Thinking

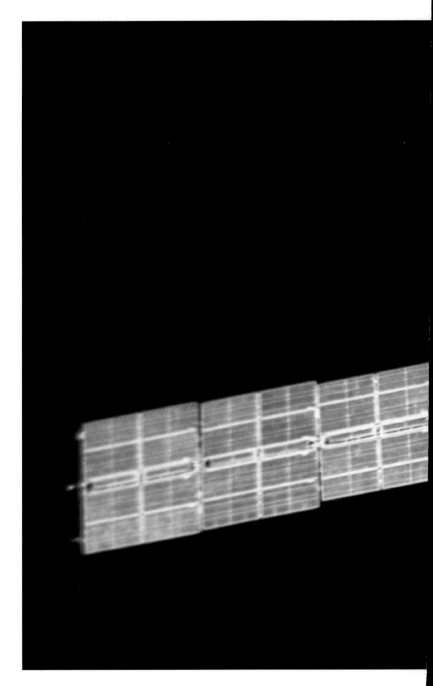

After I returned from space, my thinking changed. Simply, I felt kinder towards people. I now often feel sorry for those who are egotistical or put their small problems above all else.

In my opinion 'space thinking' results from one's own experience in space. It is the ability to think about the problems of humanity as a whole, about Earth as a single, interdependent world. We have seen the negative side of people's acts that are global in their manifestation, have glanced at the ulcers of our civilization and felt them in our hearts and minds.

I believe we can achieve mutual understanding between people through joint space flights on ships from many nations. This co-operation would have a wide attraction for all countries, both developed and developing. We should establish an International Center for Space Research and work out a unified plan for exploration of the planets. Perhaps Mars could be first.

More than 200 people have been out into space. We have a responsibility to speak about our feelings, our thoughts and conclusions, and our general and personal responsibilities towards our planet.

Who knows, maybe we really are alone in the Universe. To risk this uniqueness would be a crime!

Yuri Glazkov, Russia

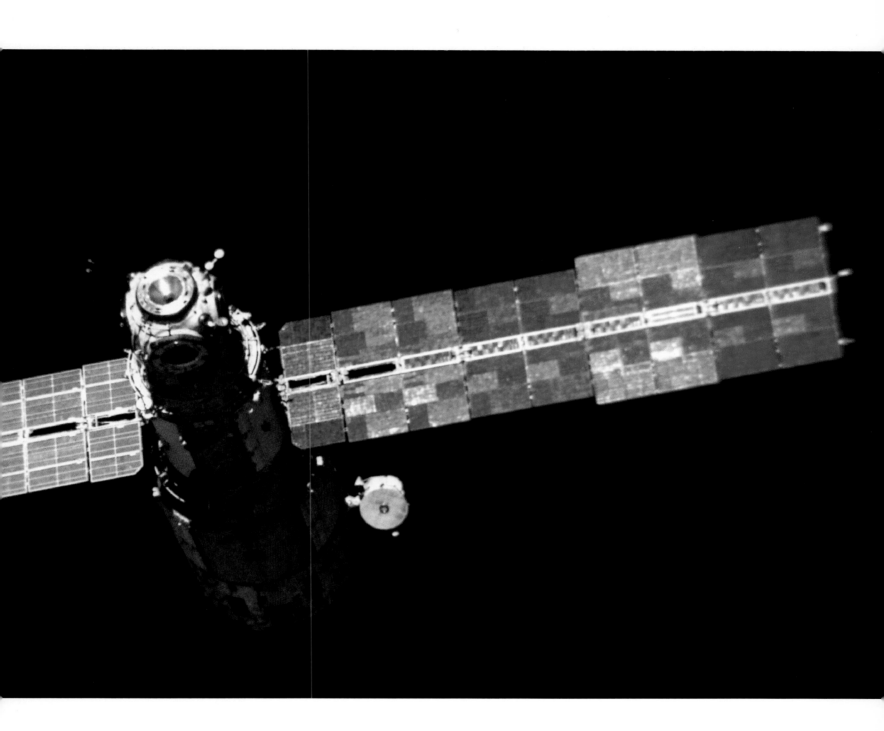

The main module of space station
MIR *during a mission in 1986.*

UNITED NATIONS

In 1986 the *Challenger* accident shattered the routine of space travel, awakening the world to the realization that such travel was still a pioneering effort that few people undertake.

Those of us who ventured into space and returned safely know that our reward is not only the contribution we make to space science, but also the special insight we gain into the world, which we must impart to those who have not shared the experience.

All of us who have gone into space since the beginning of the space age were treated to a view of our planet that no photograph or television picture can convey. The scene floods your vision, as your entire view fills with the vivid colors of mountains, oceans and land masses.

At first you are inclined to seek out your home town, state or country. For the first day, as you see the sun rise and set 16 times, you go to a window whenever possible, to seek out the different countries and to match them against what you were taught in geography class. Then without warning, you are transformed by this magical view. A special feeling evolves: you lose the urge to find boundaries between states and countries: the world becomes a globe of seven continents and seas. Soon, even the continents and great oceans of the world seem to meld into a large kaleidoscope of color and beauty. No longer do you think in terms of 'my city' or 'my country', rather you begin to sense that you are a part of something much larger. It is at this moment that astronauts gain the wisdom that could change the way people treat each other.

The insight I gained in space confirms my deep conviction that we are all part of a much larger whole, one that demands we stalwartly work toward understanding relationships between individuals and nations, compelling us to live and work together toward making our planet a better place.

Sultan Al-Saud, Saudi Arabia

Lakes of different colors are found in south-west Ethiopia. Lake Chamo has floating red algae while Lake Abaya is blue-green.

140

Clouds, shadows and solar reflections above the Indian Ocean, 1 000 miles west of Australia.

ATMOSPHERES

People are accustomed to the word 'atmosphere'. They understand it as the blue skies of our planet. In their day-to-day life, people deal with only a tiny fraction of that huge mass of air.

When we move out into space, we take our little part of Earth's atmosphere with us, to live and breath in this distant void. An orbital station or a spaceship is a miniature Earth. The life-support and heat-regulating systems never stop working as they create an acceptable temperature, composition, humidity, dust content and odor level.

Ideas come forth again and again comparing impressions of Earth and space. In this era of space exploration, we can imagine our cradle—planet Earth—as a gigantic natural spaceship flying through the Universe with billions of 'cosmonauts' on board. What is the atmosphere of this 'ship' like?

Living on Earth, we tend to forget about the enormous amount of carbon dioxide, heat, aerosols, acids, freon and nitrous components, and the accumulation of weapons that could pollute our environment and atmosphere.

Is it not up to us, the passengers, to resolve problems with the atmosphere of our spaceship? Is it not time to think about this responsibility, to help our planet, to secure our future?

Yuri Glazkov, Russia

143

SPACE: A UNITING LINK

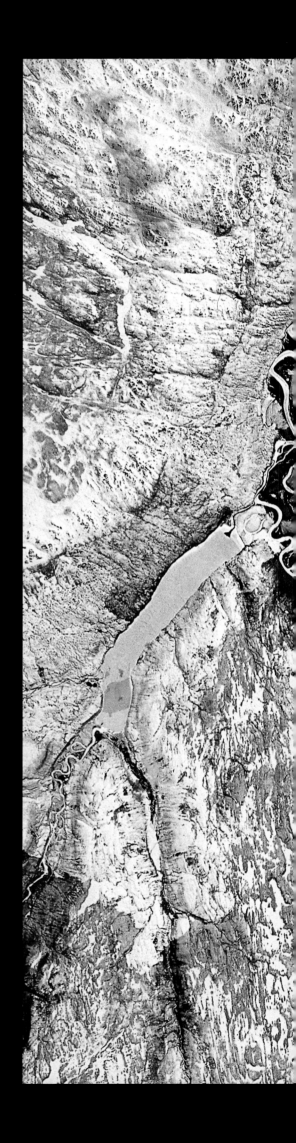

Training for space flight demands more than just physical fitness and an ability to use technology. It requires a mastery of experiment operations and a knowledge of many fields of science. One of the main attractions of this profession is its universality.

Ten years have passed since I took my place in the commander's couch in a spaceship ready for lift-off. To reach that point, I had to learn the principles of testing aeronautical technology; train to survive in a desert, wintery forest or at sea; go underwater hundreds of times; and ascend to altitude in a pressure chamber. I took part in working out ways of setting up and testing unique equipment and instruments for carrying out work in open space. I completed five space flights, four of them as commander of the crew.

Time is passing—behind me are the space flights, ahead are new tasks—yet I reflect. Space spreads out above all, and belongs to all. I would like to see the further mastering of space being carried out on an international basis so that all countries, without exception, could take part in this research for the good of humanity.

A more effective use of space flight would be to set up special programs for meteorologists, oceanologists and specialists in a wide variety of fields. Space could become a co-ordinating, uniting link for humanity in resolving many of its global problems in the same way as medicine and art.

Vladimir Vasyutin, Russia

The extreme geology of the Canadian Shield, Labrador, is accentuated by snow cover.

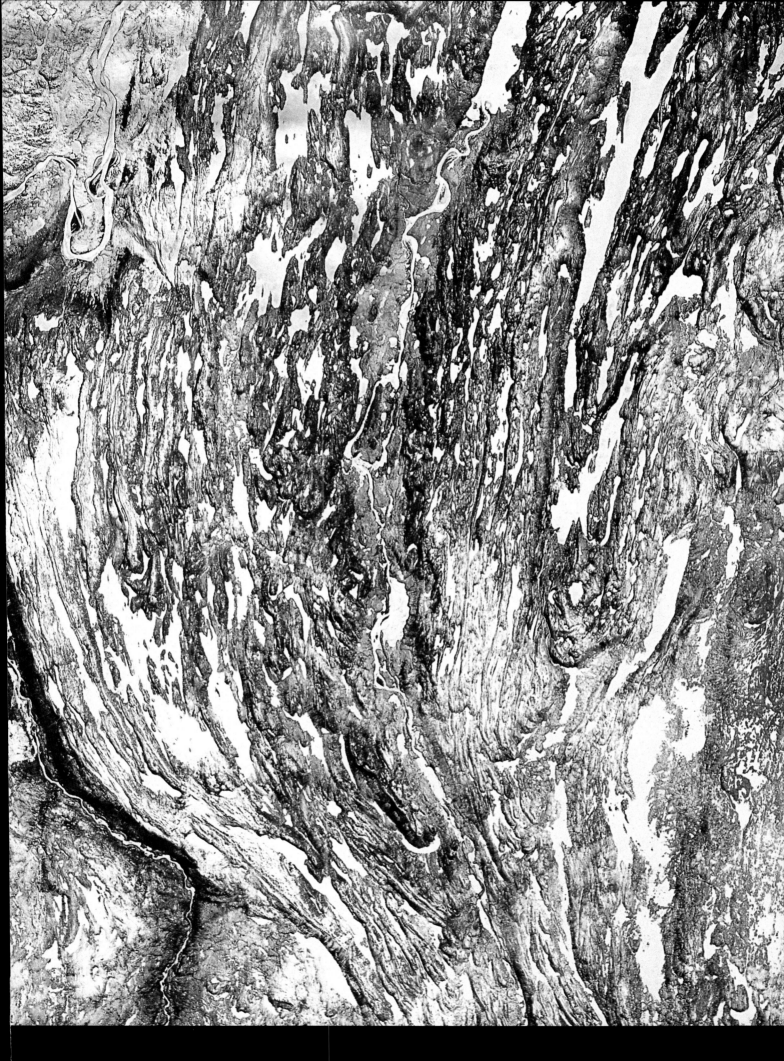

TIME TO BE HUMAN

Georgi Grechko and I were extremely busy working on experiments for several days on *Salyut-4*. How we had felt about one another at the beginning of the flight was no longer relevant. In periods of stress, what you really wanted were friendly smiles, kind looks and warm words from your friend. When the day's work was over, you wanted to have a chat about your family and friends, how you had spent your holidays, where you had been in the forest or fishing on the Black Sea rather than talking shop.

The main radio contact with Earth was always about the program. The radiograms we received were also facts, figures and instructions. It was great when people not connected with the flight spoke to us, like journalists. You wanted something new and distracting, to give a fresh emotional boost.

At the end of the shift when the experiments had all been carried out and we had some free time, we each had different ways of relaxing.

The orbiting space station
Salyut-7 *and the crew transport*
craft Soyuz T-14 *during a*
mission in 1985.

I filled my diary and puttered about with 'Tonus', an electrical muscle simulator. You place the moistened electrodes on the principal muscles of the body, the calves, hands, spine or stomach, and plug it in to the power supply. By using a variable current, 'Tonus' wakes up the muscles and they contract. The whole body begins to jerk. You can see one leg lift, an arm become smaller and curved. The action is very effective in preventing the muscles from atrophying.

On the other hand, before going to sleep, Georgi had unplanned radio sessions with the Center's duty officer. They talked about all sorts of topics. As Commander, I first decided this was out of order because unnecessary radio talk is not allowed in aviation. It is a 'choking' of the airwaves.

I explained this to Georgi, but received a negative reaction. I wondered if I was doing the right thing—I decided I was not!

I noticed Georgi glancing at me the next time he made radio contact. He obviously felt uncomfortable. Before he made contact again, I said,

'Listen, Georgi, go talk with Earth. Find out what's happening. See if there's any news from home, what sporting results they've got. I'll go about my own business. I wasn't right in what I said earlier.'

Georgi's eyes lit up as he smiled. From then on, it was also easier for me.

'Alexei, pick up the earphones and listen to what they are saying to us' said a happy Georgi.

Tensions that were about to surface were removed. There's always time to be human.

Alexei Gubarev, Russia
Deceased 1989

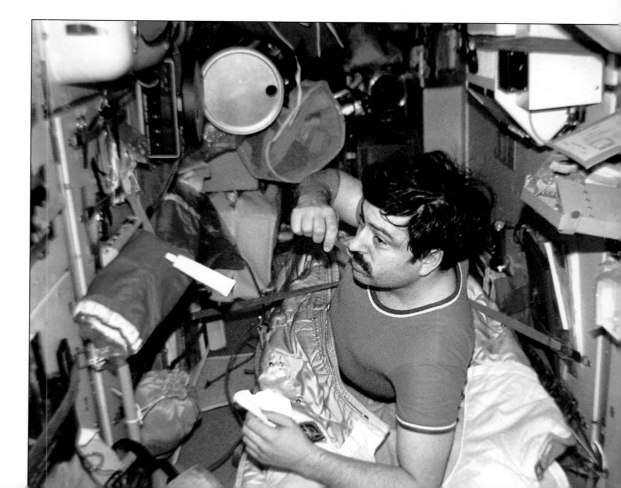

Morning on the space station MIR. Musa Manarov brushes his teeth in his sleeping compartment, while the tooth-paste floats conveniently in front of him.

THE FLAME OF ADVENTURE

Tamara Jernigan relaxes in the Spacelab.

The failures of unmanned rockets and satellites certainly have an impact on space agencies and politics, but to nowhere near the same degree as failures of manned systems. Yet, despite consequent improvements, risk remains—it cannot be reduced to zero.

The risk inherent in space flight became all too visible in the *Challenger* accident. Since then, there have been renewed efforts to ensure that astronauts do not lose their lives. These efforts do not come from human compassion alone. After all, accident victims die at a much greater rate on the roads every year without equivalent efforts. Rather, the stringent safety standards have arisen from the visability of manned space flights, the high degree of personal identification with the crews by all those left on the ground, and the intense national prestige at stake.

Risk has been an accepted companion to all great human adventures. In 1519, Ferdinand Magellan's quest to circumnavigate the globe began with 5 vessels and a crew of approximately 280. Three years later, only 1 ship and 34 crewmen returned—and without Magellan. Test pilots in the 1950s suffered a fatality rate of about one in four, as they pushed the barriers of supersonic flight. Today, some safety experts say that the probability of losing another space shuttle in the coming years is quite high. Although I believe that there will always be some risk of losing a crew, I have the feeling that the risk, being unevenly distributed between launch, on-orbit and entry, is in the order of 1%. This assessment is shared by many safety specialists in the East and West. In a very real sense, human space flight is analogous to the exploration and settlement of the New World. Hence, the term 'pioneering the space frontier' is most appropriate, and risk and sacrifice are seen as inherent.

In the face of this heritage and these realities, I believe that today we face another very real danger—the flame of adventure may flicker as we become averse to taking chances. Today, the public and politicians demand only perfection, not as a goal, but as a reality. Yet clearly, no person or program is perfect. If we can accept only success, we cannot take chances—and we will not move forward.

Thus, in this never-perfect world, it is often the astronauts themselves who must accept the responsibility for pointing to some of the more hazardous routes to take in exploration, for it is they who must accept the challenge and risk the ultimate loss.

Ernst Messerschmid, Germany

Against a background of Adelaide, South Australia, astronaut Story Musgrave, anchored on the end of the remote manipulator arm, is elevated to the top of the Hubble Space Telescope.

A FATHER AND DAUGHTER LAUNCH

Standing in front of the elevator, which would take Alexander Volkov, Toktai Aubakirov and me up to the crew hatch of the *Soyuz TM-13* spaceship, I thought of my wife, 5 000 kilometers away. She was in her ninth month of pregnancy, due to deliver in another two weeks. In the crowd that was seeing us off, I saw the Austrian TV and used the opportunity to send her regards and to wish my baby a successful start in life.

On 2 October 1991 at 7:00 a.m., we lifted off from the cosmodrome in Baikonur, Kazakhstan. Less than nine minutes later, we were in orbit.

Weightlessness—what a wonderful feeling! All systems were perfect. We were in a good mood. I enjoyed the unique view of our fascinating planet and my home country from an altitude of 300 kilometers. Then the flight control center called. My wife was going to the hospital and was doing fine. But I didn't realize what was really happening, as I prepared for my first sleep.

Apparently my daughter didn't want to miss her father's adventure in space. She was born only a few hours after launch.

The morning of the next day was definitely one of the most exciting in my life. Our spaceship was working perfectly. I still enjoyed weightlessness without any feelings of sickness. There was no doubt that our docking to the Space Station *MIR* would be successful. And most important—I'd become a father in space! Nothing could be nicer.

I was actually one of the last to know. Flight control center got the news during the night shift, and, according to the rules, could not interrupt the sleep of the cosmonauts. In the meantime, the Austrian TV and radio stations transmitted the story throughout the country and made it a sensation.

A surprise greeted me on the fourth day of our mission. Over television I saw and heard my daughter for the first time. The fascination of that moment, the excitement of becoming a father in space, will live with me forever.

Franz Viehböck, Austria

The dark blue of the Atlantic ocean, upper right, contrasts with the shallow waters of the Bahama Banks. The submerged canyon, Tongue of the Ocean is center and Andros Island, left.

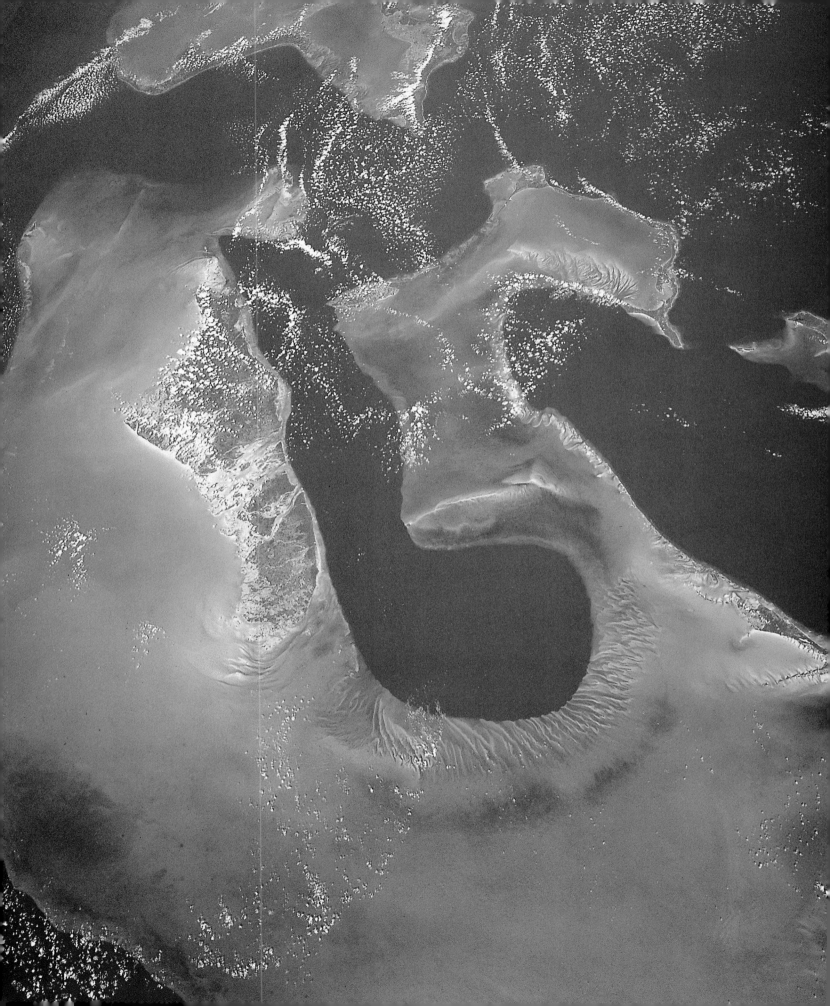

The South Island of New Zealand. The alpine fault along the western side of the Southern Alps is a distinct line and lies on the opposite side of the Pacific plate to the San Andreas fault in North America.

152

GRAVITY: DON'T TRUST IT

T minus 36 seconds and counting: automatic sequence start.

The shuttle computers have taken over the countdown, and I continue waiting...

Waiting is part of the game: two years of basic astronaut training in Houston, another three years as a backup for the first *Spacelab,* then another two years of training for this flight, the *D-1 Spacelab.* Now, 30 November 1985, I am—at last—lying inside *Challenger* hoping that nothing goes wrong, that nothing comes between me and space.

T minus 6 seconds: main engine start.

The shuttle comes alive...3...2...1...the solids go—and we go!

The force on my body from acceleration climbs to 3 Gs, three times my weight on Earth. After two minutes, the solids burn out and separate with a lurch, then nothing... almost.

Since the shuttle is nearly on a ballistic course, like that of a falling rock, we no longer feel the force of gravity. All we feel is the shuttle's acceleration along our direction of flight, which is now only 1.2 Gs, only slightly more than I felt waiting on the pad when we were standing still.

And I can't tell the difference!

We arrive in space.

Often I have tried to imagine a life without gravity. Now I feel it—it's real, and strangely different. I wonder now that I'm away from Earth and its gravity, will I think differently? The evolution of life, the evolution that produced me, all took place on Earth. The force of gravity to which we are exposed all our lives is always the same. I am struck by this new sensation of weightlessness, as if I can now see a new color that I'd not been allowed to see before—so new, so real—I have no name for it.

I think again about life on the surface of Earth. We are pulled down by an enormous force, or maybe we should say that we are accelerated up by a steady, enormous acceleration. Each second everyone is accelerated upward, moving 22 miles per hour faster in one second, 66 miles per hour faster in three seconds, 1.9 million miles per hour faster in a day, and the speed of light faster in a little less than a year! Our brains cannot accept that, of course, since the force of gravity is a constant, something so easy to ignore, and we appear stationary as we rest on Earth's surface.

But are we being tricked?

When we sit in a car, horizontal forces against our back are interpreted as a change in speed; vertical forces, as just the normal force of gravity. Thus, we develop different attitudes about the horizontal versus the vertical. A friend 100 yards away seems much closer than a friend 100 yards higher up. How striking is the difference in apparent size of the moon on the horizon versus overhead. The brain fools us—but does it also fool us about gravity? Is it a force that continually accelerates us upward?

Once the shuttle touches down, I try to stand and experience the most impressive, yet frightening, movement of my flight. I feel like I have stepped into an elevator moving up with incredible acceleration—I perceive gravity as a real acceleration!

The first few nights back on Earth, I wake several times and feel the bed accelerating me upward, upward, then switch back to feeling only force, one that binds my hands and feet. I feel suspicious, no longer able to trust the forces that I feel.

How does the continuous nature of gravity distort our view of it? What is it, really?

Wubbo Ockels, The Netherlands

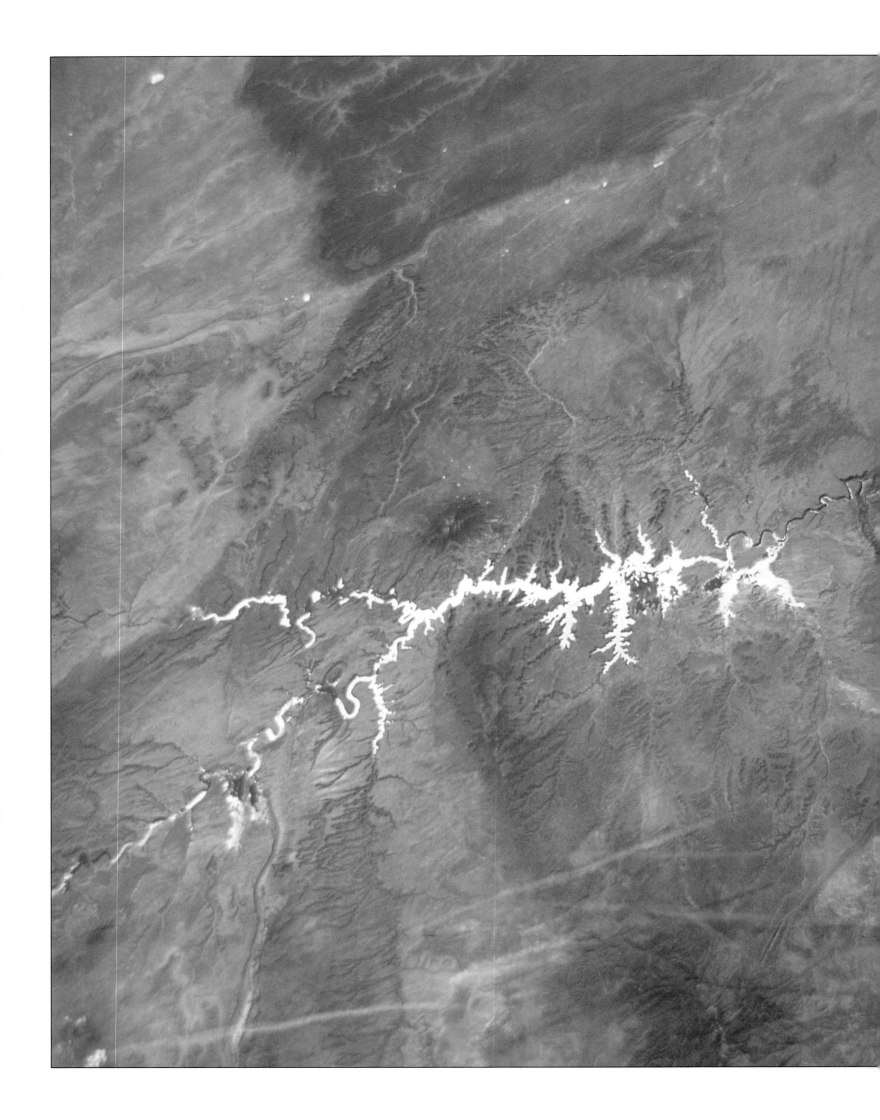

FROM BAIKONUR OR KENNEDY:
SPACE IS SPACE

The space age is now three decades old and those of us who have lived through it have witnessed incredible scientific feats. The limits set by our planet have been transcended, the highways to the stars have been opened, while rocks from the moon and images from the surface of Mars and Venus are now in laboratories all over the world.

Long-term missions on the *Salyut* space stations now seem an everyday occurrence, even ordinary. This seeming ordinariness of each flight might make one think that it has all become easy.

Not so!

True, the technology is reliable and the main systems aboard a spaceship are duplicated, but space is space. It is difficult to think of technologies more complex than those used in space systems of manned capsules and orbiting stations. Each space system about to fly has actually been tested in real life relatively few times, and the reliability of each one depends on that of its many subsystems and parts.

In space, nothing is absolutely reliable. It's all a matter of probability. Space is space.

Vasily Lazarev, Russia
Deceased 1991

The Colorado River and Lake Powell, Utah and Arizona from space station MIR.

155

CHALLENGER: ITS SPIRIT AND LEGACY

Substance of a letter written to the many con-cerned friends and supporters at the time of the *Challenger* tragedy:

The loss of our close friends has been very hard on us all. Their deaths were certainly quick—no suffering, no realization of impending disaster. Undoubtedly, they died feeling the exhilaration of adventure, the fulfilment of their efforts and of their dreams.

I would imagine 'Scobes', the mission commander, on

Tropical storms south-east of Japan. On the left typhoon Pat, on the right typhoon Odessa.

his second flight, felt confidence in the familiarity of his surroundings, in the incredible power of the two solid rocket boosters and the three liquid fueled engines accelerating the 4 500 000 pounds of hardware and human cargo through twice the speed of sound. For Mike, who as co-pilot of *Challenger* was on his first flight, the end came at the time he could have been glancing out the right window, seeing the sky changing from light to darker blue as more of the Earth's atmosphere was left below. Judy, also on her second flight, was sitting center seat as MS 2 or mission specialist number two. Her job was to survey both the commander's and co-pilot's instruments, providing continuity in the execution of the normal checklist. She was prepared to assist in the event that Scobes and Mike had to react to any shuttle problems. Undoubtedly, J.R. had just heard Mike tell Scobes 'Three at 104'—the three liquid fueled engines had just throttled back up to 104% power level as programmed. El was sitting behind Mike and to the right of J.R. As the only other crew member on the flight deck, but one with no instruments to monitor, he was prepared to provide additional data on equipment malfunctions, should the need arise. He would also have time to look out the forward windows and see 'sky' turning into 'space'.

On the lower deck, Ron, Christa and Greg had only a small window to look out. They could glance over their left shoulders to see the sky's hues change. Ron was on his second mission and the sensation of being on his back, strapped into his seat, with his feet towards the stars and head towards Earth accelerating faster and faster, would have been familiar. He knew that the rumbling and shaking generated by the solid rockets would gradually decrease as the rapidly diminishing atmosphere provided a more tenuous medium through which the thundering noise could travel. In less than 60 seconds, the solid rockets would be ejected from the liquid fuel tank and the smooth quiet ride on the liquid engines would take them into orbit. Christa and Greg, on their first flight, were certainly eagerly anticipating every new experience they were to encounter during their journey. They knew their first nine minutes of flight would be the most dynamic and stressful. They could both hear through their helmet-mounted earphones the call from the capcom in mission control: 'Go at throttle up' and Scobes reply 'Roger, go at throttle up.'

I was sitting in a meeting in Houston in the chief flight director's office discussing 'flight rules' for my upcoming flight—the next on *Challenger*. (Flight rules are an exhaustive list of 'what ifs', which provide well-reasoned responses to be acted on by the flight and ground crew, should certain systems fail during flight.) We briefly adjourned the meeting to watch the *Challenger* launch. Vicariously, I felt the exhilaration of lift-off. I had witnessed five different launches from the ground at the Kennedy Space Center in Florida and had ridden through two on board *Challenger* and *Discovery*. Without a doubt, seeing a launch in person was one of the most impressive sights in my life.

In that split second when the shuttle was engulfed in flames, it was immediately obvious that a terrible disaster had occurred. The two boosters, having broken free of their attach points, going on divergent paths with smoking bits of debris raining down, left no doubt. It was over—then—immediately. We exchanged glances silently, hardly moving. There was nothing to say. We picked up our notes and slowly left the room. Thoughts turned to the families who were on the roof of the Launch Control Center, in Florida. They had seen it all happen. We knew that the family support plan, invoked in the event of an accident, was already in motion.

There were no illusions that space flight is risk free. As one astronaut had said 'Anyone who thinks that sitting on top of rockets providing 6 000 000 pounds of thrust is routine just doesn't understand the situation'. The families of the astronauts were not oblivious to the risks. They shared the adventure of their careers, knowing that adventure means taking risks. Those whose husbands were military aviators had before shared the anguish of friends lost.

As you might expect, NASA is a very close family which, after this tragedy, has pulled together with even tighter bonds. We were not weakened by the death of our friends. The deep loss we all felt provided us with a focal point for our thoughts, our emotions, and our resolve. In visiting the wives, husbands, children and parents, we heard the same chorus: 'Keep the program going. Don't let this interrupt our efforts. They would want you to keep going.' We knew that, but it was good to hear it from those most deeply affected. We have also heard it from people all over the country.

The pride we all feel in our accomplishments is not diminished by the recognition that we aren't perfect. We will learn from this tragedy. Our space program will be stronger. The impelling reasons for sending men and women into space remain.

Rick Hauck, USA

The Kunlun
Ranges, China,
in the area where
Afghanistan,
China, Kashmir
and Tadzhikistan
all meet.

AFTER THE FLIGHT

The Cosmonaut Hotel in Baikonur on the morning of 3 October 1984. Lying on my bed, I still have difficulty convincing myself that I am now on Earth when only yesterday I was in the *Salyut* station flying in space.

Maybe these last eight months have been a dream? No, my body, arms and legs are heavy. Lucky I did not break the bed with my weight. My left shoulder is still aching from yesterday's landing. So, perhaps the eight months in orbit have not been a fantasy. Yesterday's landing was quite real. The realization that the fascinating flight, with its packed schedule, was already part of the past, leaves sadness in my soul. A space mission imposes its own tough but truly satisfying routine. Afterwards, you still feel a captive of that tight schedule, but the doctors say, 'Take a rest, guy... and a medical examination'.

An apt line comes from the poet Zabolotsky, 'Don't allow your soul to get lazy'.

Back at the Bauman Technical College in Moscow, my teachers took great pains to give us a wise life principle: set yourself a task and deal with it; once the task is over, set yourself a new one, and so on, for this is what progress is about. Time flies swiftly and there are few fields of science or technology which are developing as rapidly as cosmonautics. All you accomplished yesterday rapidly becomes just stuff for reports, textbooks and archives. You cannot mark time, for then, unwittingly, you turn into a mothball and drop out of the race. Others are rapidly moving forward and gradually they cease to recognize you or gaze at you as if at a loss to comprehend how you can go on like this. Time is racing away.

A meeting at the chief designer's has just ended. The work on a new station is in full swing. What next?

Vladimir Solovyov, Russia

160

THE FANTASY

Imagine training for three years, travelling 250 000 miles to the moon, then watching your two friends descend the last 60 miles to the surface while you stay behind. Six humans have experienced this frustration.

When assigned as the backup crew for *Apollo 9* we were excited. Three missions later we'd be the prime crew and have the ultimate adventure in any profession —we'd make one of the first moon landings!

Pete Conrad, the most experienced, was designated the commander, Dick Gordon, the next most experienced, was assigned to take care of the command module, our ticket home. This left me, a rookie, with a prize assignment, I'd accompany Pete down to the moon.

As Pete and I trained for placing experiments on the lunar surface, gathering rocks and making observations, our excitement mounted day after day. And Dick, as he trained right along side us, demonstrated an unwavering discipline and strength of character. Never once did he say, 'It's not fair, I wish I would walk on the moon too.'

Pete and I often fantasized that Dick would join us down there. But, of course, that was not to be.

Yet now as an artist, I can make it happen in a painting as we dreamed it had in real life—finally, our best friend has come the last 60 miles!

Alan Bean, USA

56 day, 4 PSI chamber simulation called *Skylab Medical Experiments Altitude Test* (SMEAT).

   After many delays Bob Crippen, Karol Bobko and I started our unbroken diet of *Skylab* food and water. Iced urine and fecal collection (in bright anodized boxes) were carried with us wherever we went for over four months! Daily improvisation was needed to cope with multiple failures and unexpected results, all of which was excellent training for mission support. Most troublesome for me was the repeated bursting of unrefrigerated urine collection bags and the resulting clean up of the urine volume measuring system, with its multiple sharp edges and points. There were numerous other failures such as the

*The high remote plateaux and
ranges of central Tibet, about
300 miles west of Lhasa.*

cycle ergometer and our diet—I lost 18 pounds and developed a loathing for the prescribed supplement of sugar drops and cookies.

Many essential changes were made during testing, including total redesign of the urine collection system, but other changes were not made; for example, there was no augmentation of exercise devices or change to our diet. I obtained permission to make pre- and post-strength measurements and used discarded equipment for the task.

Launch of the unmanned *Skylab* by a two-stage *Saturn 5* rocket produced sound, sight and power of a magnitude no longer seen. However, there was soon doom and gloom as insulation and a solar array tore away before it reached orbit. Much hectic improvisation followed. Some days later, in the wee hours, I flew a T-38 across the Gulf of Mexico with the last element of a hurriedly improvised solar umbrella to be taken up by the *Skylab* crew that morning—the first of three crews to visit the space laboratory.

Action-packed days followed in which the crew—Pete Conrad, Joseph Kerwin and Paul Weitz—cleared debris, extended a solar panel, entered the sun-baked vehicle for brief periods and erected the solar umbrella. In a remarkably short time, operations and science observations began. The learning curve was still steep. Change was the order of the day and an unprecedented flow of new information was gathered about Earth, the sun and the human body in a new environment. For eight hours I cap-commed, and for another eight I analyzed data from my experiments. Just prior to return, the flight director approved my request for the crew to take unscheduled mug shots of themselves. These photos clearly showed the effects of massive fluid shifts from the legs into the upper body and thus began an enhancement of data return through simple ad hoc studies.

When the first crew returned after 28 days, many modifications were made to the next flight, including food and exercise. The second crew to visit *Skylab*—Alan Bean, Owen Garriott and Jack Lousma—capitalized on the experience of the first crew and offered to expand their activities! Between and on capcom shifts, I was able to formulate a number of studies in anthropometrics and fluid shift using on-board gear. After 56 days, the crew returned on their feet but showed the effects of weightlessness which, without better counter measures, promised to literally force future crews to their knees on return. Many adjustments were needed, but weight was now considered crucial and only 5 pounds were available for a crude locomotor exercise device that I constructed.

The third and final flight culminated in a tremendous return of data, not only that originally scheduled but other, equally important, material based on flight results which greatly extended the planned data return. Increased diet and improved exercise allowed the crew—Gerald Carr, Ed Gibson and Bill Pogue—to walk off with virtually no weight loss after 84 days in flight, and to strut through the next day's examination. America now owned all endurance records, a mass of unique data and a remarkable lab vehicle still in orbit with two spares on the ground.

At the end of *Skylab,* some of us had learned enough to understand the basic effects of weightlessness on humans: fluid shifts; bone, muscle and other losses; neurological adaptations; and what would be required to return people to Earth in functional state after 84 or 168 days of flight. We knew enough to ask the right questions and get the answers for much longer flights. It is hard now to appreciate the expense and hullabaloo surrounding preparations to fly astronauts for 18 days, after having been a part of these aggressive flights lasting 28, 56 and 84 days.

We all would have benefited greatly if *Skylab* had continued. The backup *Skylab* could have been upgraded, launched and revisited time and time again. In fact, if only the existing *Skylab* space station had been maintained, expanded and kept in continuous service, we would now be ready to plan lunar and Mars missions with far more confidence, to say nothing of the unknown scientific returns that would have resulted.

Continuation of *Skylab* would also have yielded additional and valuable 'lessons learned', a continuation of those that did result when *Skylab's* limited resources were applied with vigor, determination and imagination.

William Thornton, USA

BOMBS OVER DUBROVNIK

Although being busy with experiments on board the space station *MIR,* I used every opportunity to enjoy the view of our magnificent planet. Because of our high orbital inclination (51.6 degrees), we could see most of the countries of the world. When we went over Europe, I saw many familiar places that I had visited as an ordinary Earth inhabitant.

During one orbit, which was going over the Adriatic sea, I had a live television connection with my wife and emotionally described how Austria, and her home country, Croatia, looked from space. I saw the beautiful bright islands in the dark blue sea and recognized Krk, the island where we have a house on the beach. The bay in front of the house and even the bridge from the mainland to the island could be seen. With emotion and the best words I could find, I transmitted my impressions.

Coastal areas of Croatia, Bosnia-Herzegovina, Montenegro and Albania from Split in the north, to Tirane, in the south. Under smoke drifting out over the Adriatic Sea lies Dubrovnik.

Right: *Unimak Island, and the snow-covered volcano Shishaldin.*

Below: *The Croatian coastline looking toward the Istra Peninsula. The island close to the coast is Krk. The island of Cres lies beyond.*

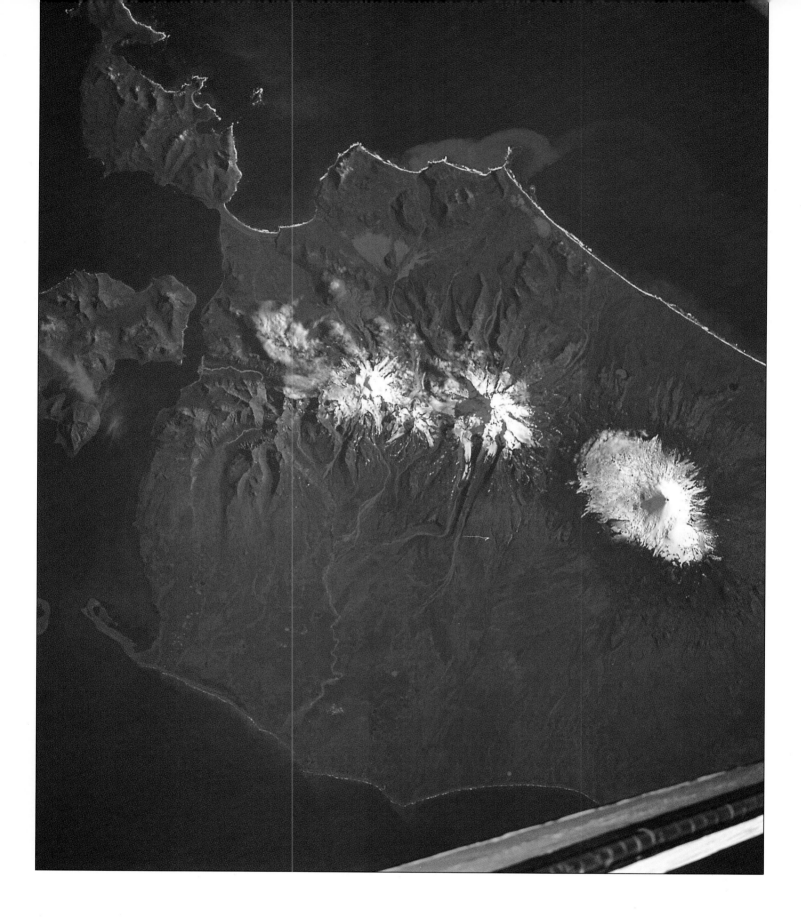

My wife quietly listened, then asked if I could also see the smoke from the bombing of Dubrovnik, which was taking place at that very time. Her question jolted me back to reality. I could see Dubrovnik but not any smoke. But I could see Italy, Austria, Hungary, Slowenia, Croatia and the whole Balkan area. There were no artificial borders evident. Everything looked peaceful and in total harmony.

I simply could not accept the existence of war within this incredible beauty! There was only land and water . . . beautiful land and water that should belong to all humans, disregarding color, religion or nationality.

Franz Viehböck, Austria

THE GAMMA RAY OBSERVATORY

It was Day 3 of our 5-day mission—the big day—we would release the Gamma Ray Observatory (GRO). The launch of GRO was the second of NASA's 'Great Observatories' and everyone wanted it to work perfectly. After having our launch delayed a year, we made every effort to capitalize on the additional time by adding many extra simulations to practise.

So far it appeared the preparations had paid off, as everything was going exactly on time and according to plan. Linda grappled the GRO, a 35 000 pound satellite, with the remote arm and moved it slowly out of the payload bay with assistance from her backup, Ken. This was no small feat, as the GRO was the most massive object ever moved by the shuttle arm.

Both of the GRO's solar arrays were successfully unlatched and deployed. I maneuvered the *Atlantis* so that the arrays could catch the full sun and begin to charge GRO's batteries. Its wingspan was 70 feet, almost the same as the orbiter. We were all impressed by its beauty and the size of this huge observatory suspended above the crew cabin.

The mood was now jovial—we all had worried about the possibility of the solar arrays giving problems during deployment but they worked as planned. And the high gain antenna was so mechanically straightforward—what could possibly go wrong with it? Once it was deployed, we would simply wait a few hours while the batteries came up to full charge and ground control finished their commanding. Then we would release the GRO to begin its 8–10 year mission of celestial observation.

Right: *The Defence Support Payload is pointed skyward from* Atlantis *during an experiment.*

Above Mauritania, space shuttle Atlantis *is about to place the Gamma Ray Observatory into orbit.*

I placed the *Atlantis* in free drift so that the ground could send the command to unlatch the high gain antenna. When the latches were released, we would see the high gain slowly spring out a couple of feet due to the stored energy in the system.

Minutes passed and nothing happened. Jay, Linda and Ken were on the aft flight deck watching, while Jerry and I occupied the pilot and commander seats. As more time passed, it became obvious to everyone that the antenna was going nowhere.

The first part of our troubleshooting plan called for additional commanding from the ground. We attempted to shake the GRO by firing the large primary attitude control thrusters, first in roll, then in pitch, all to no avail. The remote arm was used to move the GRO at maximum rate in one direction and reverse maximum rate in the opposite direction. Because the GRO is so

massive, these efforts imparted very little motion to the observatory and had no beneficial effects at all.

Jerry and I agreed that a spacewalk was necessary. A few minutes later our Houston capcom, Marsha Ivins, called us to confirm that it was time for 'the Jay and Jerry show'. As a tribute to the excellent training we received from NASA I must say that this entire day felt like another simulation and that we had been there before—because we had. At the same time, the knot in my stomach was a lot tighter than in any simulation. There was a $617 million satellite hanging on the end of that arm, and none of us was sure that the EVA would fix the problem.

After suiting up and prebreathing for 40 minutes, Jerry and Jay depressurized the airlock and moved out into the bay. Linda had moved the GRO down very close to the bay so our guys could climb onto it. It was night and the scene was illuminated by the floodlights in the bay. Jay collected some tools and translated down the port side of the orbiter, while Jerry moved down the starboard side from where he climbed onto the GRO.

Once on the observatory, Jerry gingerly moved from handhold to handhold, working his way to the high gain antenna. A cursory examination revealed nothing obvious that would cause it to bind. Jerry then found that by holding onto a docking trunnion with his right hand, he was able to grab the antenna boom with his left. After regaining ground contact and receiving approval from Houston, he began shaking the boom, first with small in-and-out motions, then with more force until it began to move. 'It's free! It's free!' he exclaimed. In only 17 minutes, from the beginning of the EVA, the problem was solved. This action changed the mission from possible failure to success.

Jerry then translated to the other side of the GRO and, with Jay's assistance, manually deployed the antenna boom and locked it into place. A few hours later and only three orbits late, we released the GRO with all appendages deployed and all systems operating normally. The GRO continues to function exceptionally well with all instruments on line and taking data.

The GRO deploy mission would have been quite exciting even without any problems—but the successful EVA release of the stuck antenna made the ending all the sweeter. I believe that there are two important lessons to be learned from this experience. First, the excellent training that we had for the mission allowed us to feel confident in carrying out the contingency plan in a high pressure environment, with the whole world looking over our shoulders. Those who would advocate cutting back on crew training to save time and money should take a look at this mission and think twice. Second, the GRO mission stands out as an excellent example of the good relationship that can exist between the manned and unmanned elements of the space program and how each one can benefit the other. The government/contractor team assembled for this mission worked together extremely well both before and during the flight. Had the GRO been launched on an expendable rocket instead of the manned space shuttle, the end of this story would have been totally different. As it turned out, we have a fully functional observatory in orbit which will provide a wealth of additional knowledge of the universe in which we live.

Steve Nagel, USA

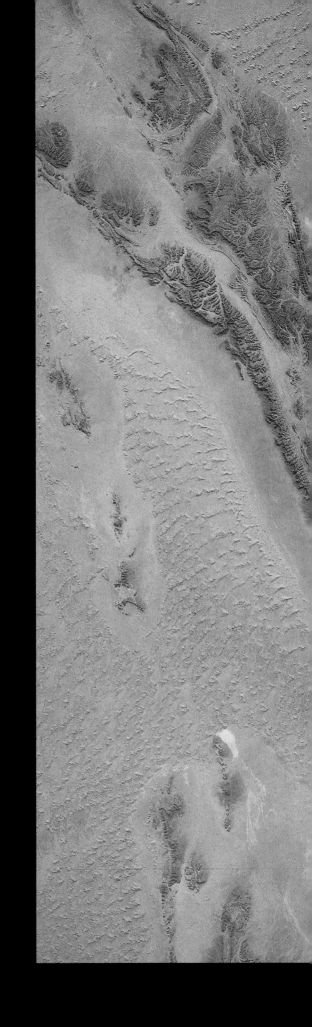

The Sahara Desert in Algeria is a contrast between mountains and basins of sand. This region is part of the Grand Erg Occidental west of Adrar.

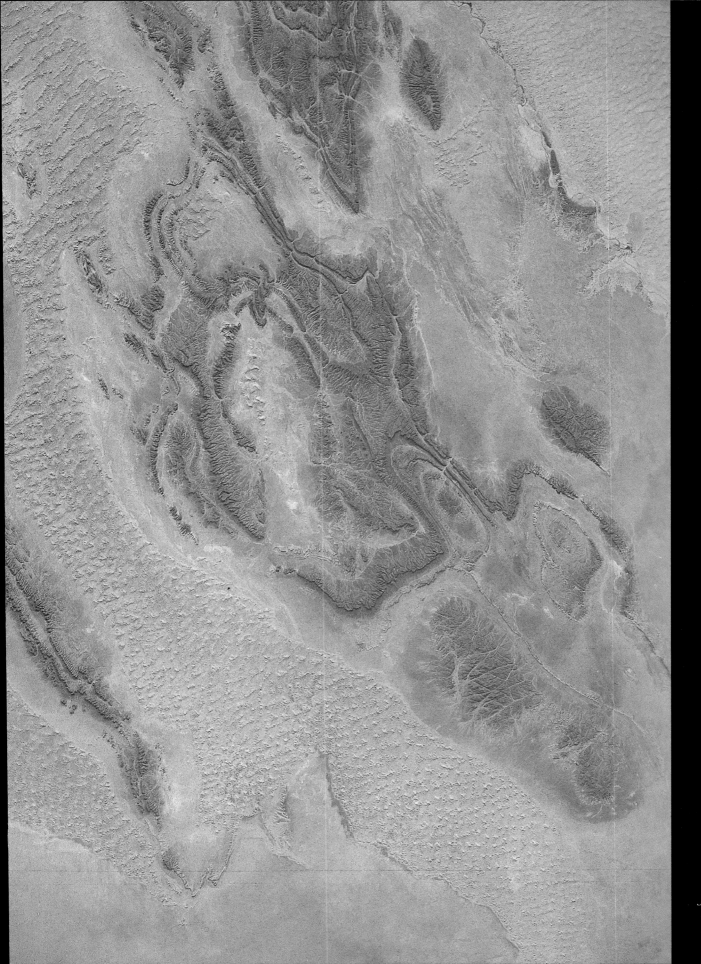

Next page: A
volocano sprouts
from the salt bed of
Lake Coipasa,
Bolivia. Chile and
the spine of the
Andes are lower left.

Parallel mountain ridges cause unique cloud formations in the Szechwan province of China, north of Chungking.

Snow capped volcanoes Mauna Kea, top and Mauna Loa bottom, on the Island of Hawaii.

DREADED FAILURE

They say it is always darkest before dawn. From our perspective in orbit in February 1984, it got pretty dark.

Our first inkling that something might be amiss came at dinner time on the first day, when mission control, with a low-keyed question, asked us to confirm that the earlier deployment of the *Westar* satellite, owned by Western Union and equipped with a payload assist module (PAM), had actually occurred uneventfully. We confirmed it. A few moments later came an apologetic request: 'We know that you are in the middle of dinner, but could you play back the videotape of the deployment now, instead of waiting for the scheduled time?'.

Since all air-to-ground conversations are released directly to the press, a code of silence has evolved—don't say things that aren't required; don't ask questions that the control center hasn't brought up but must know are on your mind. So we waited—and wondered. Some hours later came the news: after several unsuccessful attempts, *Westar* had been located—in a 160 by 600 nautical mile orbit, far short of the 160 by 22 300 mile orbit that it should have been in!

In order to provide time for further analysis, the deployment of the nearly identical *Palapa* satellite was postponed until the fourth day at the latest, with the return of the *Palapa,* still in the payload bay of the orbiter, a distinct possibility. The deployment of the integrated rendezvous target (IRT), a self-inflating 6 foot-diameter reflective balloon, was moved ahead to fill the void in our timeline. We hadn't been deeply involved in the development of this item, since it was scheduled to fly first on a previous classified mission, which was cancelled for some never-to-be-divulged reason.

With cameras of all ilk in operation—video, motion picture and still—I threw the switches and the IRT came up and out of its canister trailing its two lanyards. After 60 seconds, the two protective 'staves' would separate and the balloon would inflate. Time passed. The canister moved away. More time passed. The canister moved further away. Conversations with the ground ensued—the IRT had four lanyards, and they were *all* supposed to stay in the deployment canister.

Then it exploded! Pieces of white painted plastic film shot off in various directions, and the titanium ballast weight could not be located. This ballast represented a deadly hazard should it hit the orbiter, so we were committed to maneuvering the orbiter away from the remnants of the explosion, taking what data we could

relax. The responsiveness to each command reassured me that this machine was going to take me exactly where I wanted, precisely in the manner for which simulators back on Earth had prepared me. From then on, the flight was 'comfortably exciting'.

Like flyers of aircraft and spacecraft, I worried about running out of fuel. The nitrogen gas which propels the MMU is stored in two scubalike tanks whose pressures are displayed on two small gauges visible to the pilot. As nitrogen is used up, the gauge pressure decreases, giving some feel for consumption rate as well as fuel remaining. Because of concerns about thruster gas impinging upon the *Westar 6* satellite and disturbing its orientation, I purposely flew the MMU in a control mode which prevented thruster firings toward the satellite. Unfortunately, this mode turned the MMU into a gas hog.

A minute or so from docking, I glanced at the gauges. I was already close to the reading which would require me to return immediately to the shuttle. I would have loved to pull up to a self-service gas pump! I began to conserve gas with even more vigor than previously. It paid off, for at the end of the flight I stowed the MMU with both gas gauges right at the minimum reading.

Most astronauts experience fear during space flight, but it is usually fear of failure or error, not fear for their lives or well-being. In the case of the shuttle, the astronauts are key players in a multihundred-million dollar mission aboard a several-billion dollar spaceship being watched, directly or indirectly, by most of the inhabitants of this planet. Not a good time to mess up!

During my MMU flight, I put myself in this situation. After docking with the *Westar 6* and stopping its spin using a device fitted in front of the MMU called the 'stinger', procedures called for me to disconnect the stinger tip, leaving it stuck in the satellite. I would then fly back to the payload bay where Joe Allen would remove the bulky remainder of the stinger from the front of my MMU. We had trained countless times to do this.

Owing to equipment problems on our first space walk, however, we changed our plans for the disconnect procedure. Now I was to disconnect the MMU entirely from the stinger, leaving the total device attached to the satellite because Joe was not available to remove it—he was on the end of the shuttle's robot arm holding the satellite in his hands!

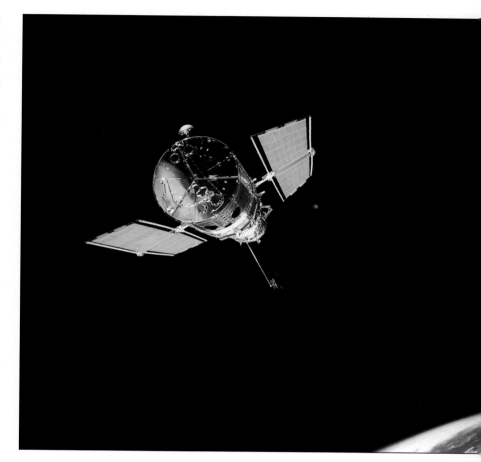

The Hubble Space Telescope begins separation from space shuttle Endeavour, *after repairs, September 1993.*

When it was time to disconnect from the satellite, I entered my Pavlov-dog mode and did exactly what I had trained to do—pulled the normal disconnect handle. Within a few seconds I realized that I had made a mistake. A sinking feeling followed.

As I flew back to the payload bay, with the stinger still attached to the MMU, I came up with a way to remove it by myself all the while flying the MMU in a hover in the payload bay. It sounded like a four-handed job, but weightlessness and the stable flying qualities of the MMU made it possible. In the payload bay, I put the MMU into an 'attitude hold', so that it wouldn't rotate while I took my hands off the control sticks, and carefully disconnected the stinger. Using a tether stored on my suit, I tied the stinger to a fixture in the bay.

Occasionally, I had to reach down to the MMU controller to move back into position, but it ended up being a relatively simple task. Later, after I had doffed and stowed the MMU, I returned to the stinger and properly stored it. As you might suspect, I did not choose to make a big deal of this episode during the post-flight debriefings, and NASA was kind enough not to ask too many questions!

Before I flew out to the *Westar 6* satellite and attached to it, I had little opportunity to observe Earth, *Discovery*, or the vast blackness around me. However, once attached to the satellite and having stopped its rotation, I had an unforgettable opportunity to relax and absorb the universe. Not attempting to hold any particular orientation with respect to *Discovery*, I eventually rotated to a position where I saw only space. Over the radio in my space suit, I could hear my fellow astronauts and the folks at Houston. I put those discussions into the background and felt that it would take only an exceedingly small leap of imagination to believe that I was alone in the cosmos.

This feeling was not disconcerting or frightening but rather calming. At first I thought it was the result of having just completed a difficult task, combined with the knowledge that the shuttle was really out there someplace and would come to get me. But somehow I knew that was not the answer. Nor was it a spiritual or religious response. The explanation that seemed to fit best was that I was not in a strange or forbidding place at all, but in a place where I—as a member of the human race—was meant to be.

I thought of those who claim that human beings should not fly because they were not given wings. Those same critics conjured up, I am sure, similar analogies for space travel. As I looked at my space suit and the MMU, however, I knew that we are meant to travel away from Earth because we have been given the curiosity, the intelligence and the will to devise the means and build the wonderful machines that permit such adventures!

I was pulled from my thoughts and the vista surrounding me when I heard a voice over the radio: 'Dale, we're in position to take the satellite. Give me a slow pitch up now on the MMU and stop it on my call.' It was time to go back to work.

Dale Gardner, USA

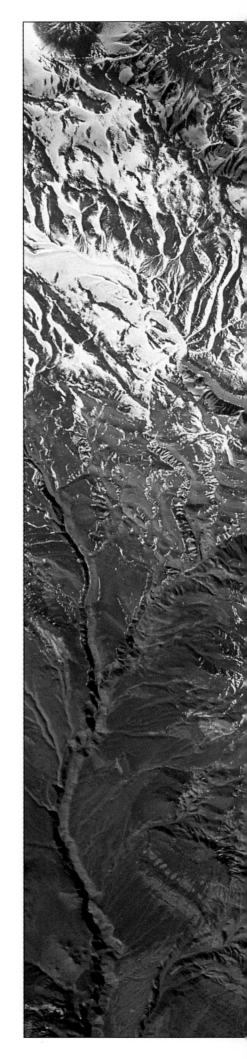

The Argentina-Chile frontier of the Altiplano is known as the Puna De Atacama, located about 190 miles south-east of Antofagasta.

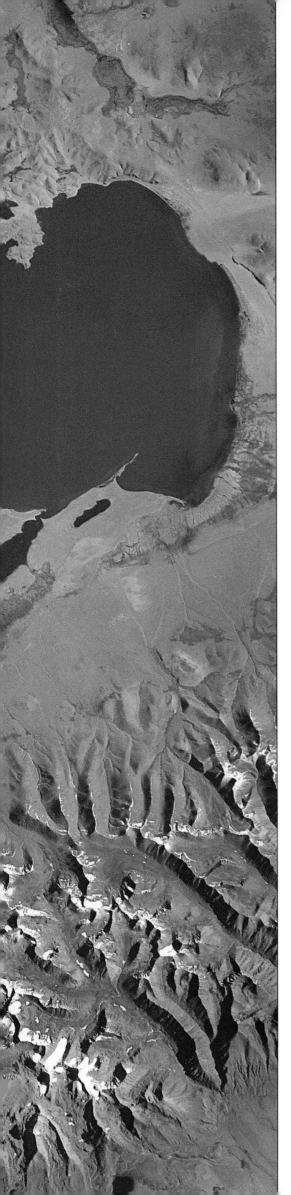

Lake Nam in Tibet is about 95 miles north of the city of Lhasa. The Nyenchen Tanglha Range is below.

EXPERIMENTS IN SPACE

Scientists have one fatal flaw. They're obsessed with their experiments. I'm no exception. I went to where I could find something not available anywhere else—the extended zero gravity of space.

The particular experiments I wanted to perform were called 'equilibrium shapes of the dynamics of a rotating and oscillating drop'. They require about 30 minutes of zero gravity because everything has to move very slowly so that it is always in a state of near-equilibrium.

In one experiment, I investigated the equilibrium shapes of a rotating spheroid, a very old experiment going back 300 years. Sir Isaac Newton, looking at the equilibrium shape of Earth, was the first to pose this question. Many calculations have been made since but there hasn't been a single, definitive experiment to verify the theory. In a second experiment, I investigated large-amplitude oscillations of drops, the related calculations being about 100 years old. Both these experiments require an extended gravity-free environment.

When you rotate a liquid perfect sphere, it first goes to an axysymmetric shape, a little flat at both poles. Once you get to a certain point, the so-called bifurcation point, the axysymmetric shape is no longer stable, and it goes to a nonaxysymmetric shape. We are trying to understand what this bifurcation point is. Everybody accepts it because almost every mathematician at one time or another has done some calculations on it. So the point itself is very well defined. Our questions involve the stability of various shapes, how they behave relative to one another, and how they behave dynamically.

The blue of the Gulf of St Lawrence, Canada contrasts with the snow covered eastern tip of Anticosti Island. Floating ice shows the surface currents of the Gulf.

In the large-amplitude oscillation experiment, we stimulate a droplet and it goes into various oscillation modes. If you introduce a larger amplitude, the drop not only oscillates but it undergoes a fission process. Now, you may ask, if this is a containerless experiment (you're not touching it), how do you stimulate the drop? There are many ways you can do it, including the use of electric or magnetic fields. We use acoustic waves, which causes less perturbation to the droplet. We create an energy field, which is almost like a bag to hold the drop. Since we can control the acoustical frequency, beating, modulation and amplitude, I can make the drop do what I tell it to—rotate, oscillate, change its shape, move around, or sit still—all without touching it.

After NASA accepted our proposal in 1974, we developed the experimental hardware, which we finished in 1980. During all that time, it never occurred to me that I might actually conduct the experiment in person. But in 1982 NASA asked: 'Is it better to train a career astronaut as a scientist or a career scientist as an astronaut?' They finally opted for the latter since our *Spacelab 3* mission would be primarily science orientated. I was selected.

It didn't take too long to adjust to zero gravity, and we entered *Spacelab* ready to start work. Everything performed well except one thing—my experiment! On the second day when I turned on the instrument, it didn't work. Normally when that happens, you have to forfeit the experiment because it's very difficult to repair them in space. You have no place to put components once you take them apart, few tools (all I had was a voltmeter and

a couple of screwdrivers) and no supply depot to pick up replacement parts. Because we had a payload specialist (me) on board, we were given the opportunity to try.

Since I could not take the experiment out, I had to go inside it. I lived inside the instrument for two and a half days. All my colleagues could see of my anatomy was my legs. I took the whole instrument apart from the back, troubleshooting line by line, point by point. Although there wasn't a high probability of fixing it, with good support from my team on the ground we were able to discover the problem and find a way around it. Perhaps this provided a justification for NASA's decision to train scientists as astronauts; when experiments don't work as expected, a trained scientist/technician may be the best one to solve the problem.

Clearly, the best time of the flight for me was when I did my experiment. Normally, we are supposed to work only 12 hours a day, but in reality we worked 15–16 hours. The experiment would spin out a drop, bifurcate, and then become axysymmetric again, then bifurcate again, and so on, again and again to confirm the theory as expected. And in the axysymmetric shape region, it also behaved very nicely. But when we took it further to the fission point, we found that it agrees with theory but the shapes are quite different. Now, I always like this sort of outcome because I can tell my theoretician friends that they're not really as good as they think they are!

Taylor Wang, USA

188

*Large internal waves northwest of
Borneo in the South China Sea.*

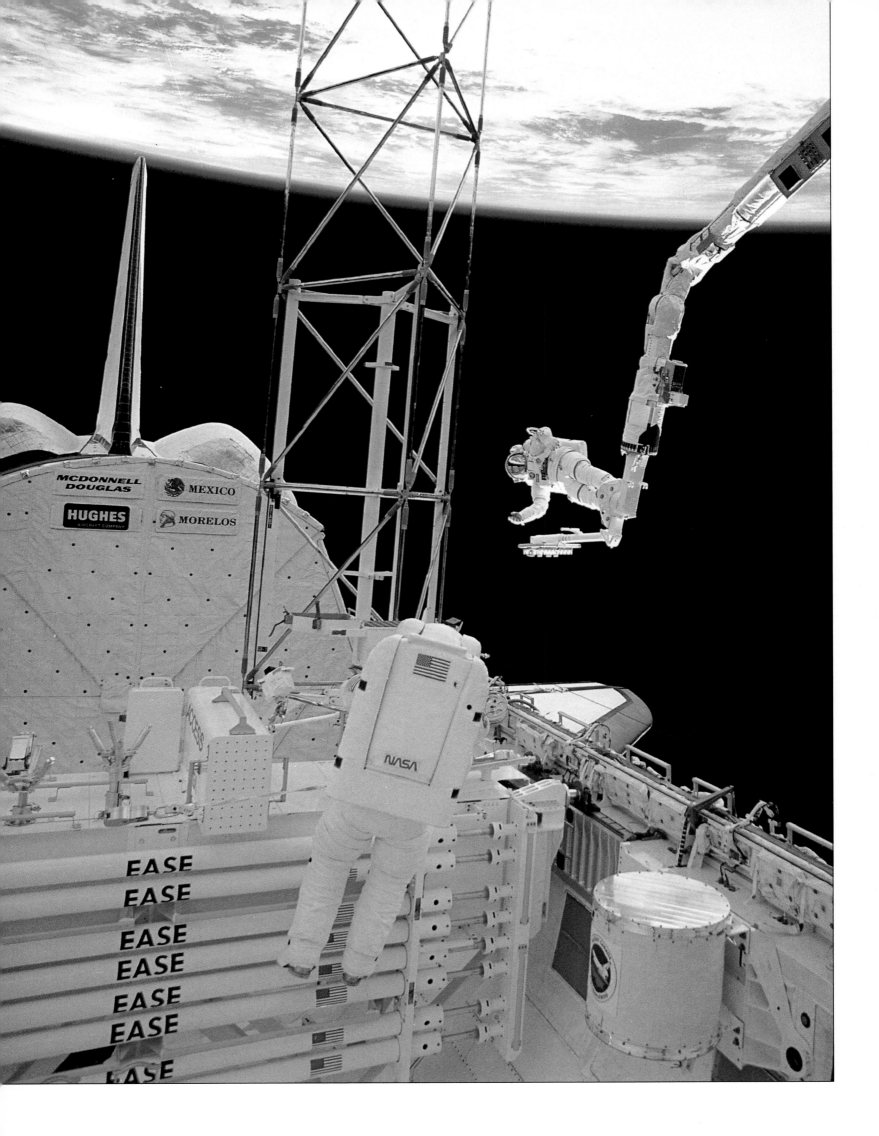

200

STEPPING STONES INTO THE UNIVERSE

Early explorers of the sky not only went into space and became the eyes and minds of billions of other explorers on the starship Earth, they also began the long process of transplanting civilization into space. As this fundamental change in the course of history occurred, humans also gained new insight into themselves and their home. With the conclusion of the *Apollo 17* mission and the Apollo program in December 1972, humankind reached the 'end of the beginning' of its movement into the universe.

Space, the environment and education are closely linked to our children's future, so we must begin to make irrevocable commitments in these critical fields of endeavor. Our generation's commitment could be embodied in a project focused on the start of the third millennium. This unique milestone looms less than seven years away, and the potential has grown for a millennium project that will match society's vision, needs and capabilities.

An appropriate, affordable and self-sustaining project combines ventures to the moon and to Mars. Primary objectives are both the human settlement of Mars by 2010 and the provision of abundant, environmentally acceptable energy for Earth.

Energy resources on the moon, specifically a light isotope of helium known as helium 3, provide the link between these seemingly unrelated objectives. Fusion power plants on Earth, fueled by lunar helium 3, could provide essentially unlimited and environmentally acceptable electrical power for an ever increasing population. By-products from the production of helium 3 on the moon would provide the oxygen, water and other consumable materials critical to sustaining early settlers of the moon and Mars.

To manage the sustained international commitment required to undertake this plan, we should consider a participant-based treaty for international co-operation.

'Intermars' would be an appropriate name for the managing organization. The Intermars Charter would create a relationship between nations, users and investors, modeled on the successful INTELSAT Agreements, but structured to recognize the special legal and technical considerations involved in the implementation of the plan. As envisioned by provisions of the 1967 Outer Space Treaty, organizational mechanisms for the co-operative use of

2 000 feet deep and 20 miles in diameter, this depression, called Richat, is located in the Sahara Desert of Mauritania, North West Africa. It was once thought to be the result of a meteor impact but space photography has shown it to be caused by wind erosion.

lunar resources and the sharing of economic and environmental benefits derived from those resources ought to be included within the Intermars Charter.

With vision, humankind could be standing on the threshold of another series of great adventures in education, science, civilization and evolution.

Education will be able to provide greater learning choices for young people as new skills are required to work and live in space.

Science will enable us to search for fossilized life forms that may have evolved three and a half billion years ago, contemporaneously with early single-celled life on Earth. If found on Mars, such fossils could answer one of the most perplexing philosophical questions—whether or not life on Earth is only a cosmic accident.

Civilization will be tested and re-inforced by the challenge of new frontiers in space.

The great adventure in human evolution will be the establishment of self-sufficient enclaves of human beings on the first stepping stones into the universe. These planetary harbors could lead to permanence as a species.

Space is exciting! Like dinosaurs, space is vast, mysterious, packed with action. It challenges us to use extraordinary technology. With improved education, all the issues and challenges of our future, from food and water supply to health preservation, care and the quality of life, can be addressed more successfully by future generations.

Harrison Schmitt, USA

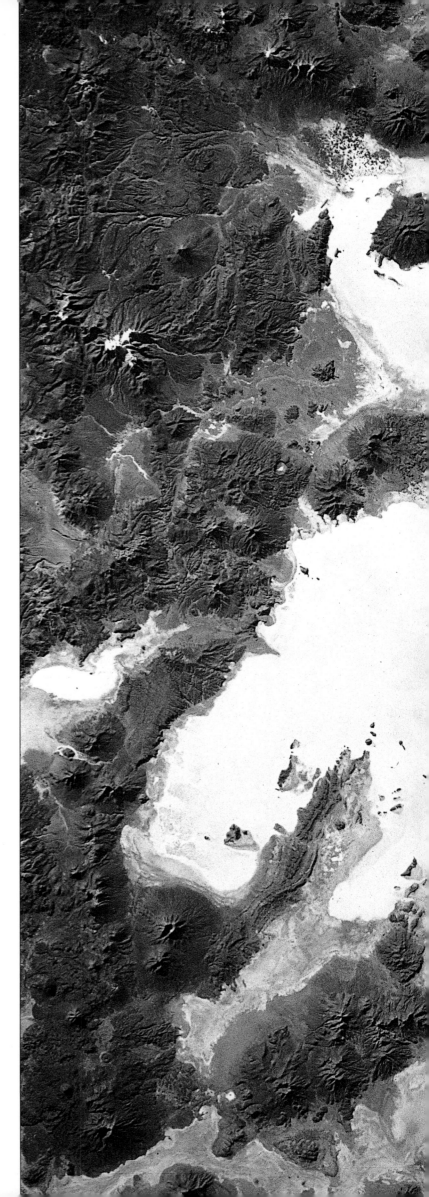

The great salt desert of Salar De Uyuni and Lake Poopo in the remote Bolivian Andes range.

206

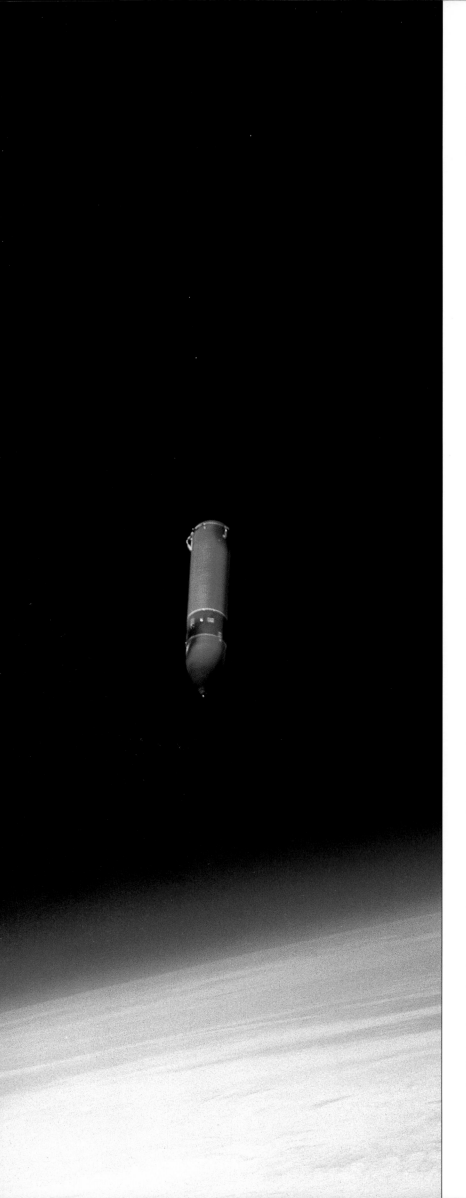

After a space shuttle is launched and the solid rocket boosters are expended, they are jettisoned. Just prior to achieving orbit, the liquid-fuel external tank is also jettisoned.

MUCH ROAD BEHIND, FAR MORE AHEAD

I am 63 years old, and the doctors have closed the road to the heavens on me. Now my main work is passing on my experience to the younger generation—those special aspects you cannot learn from books that I absorbed in many long years of 'wandering' in space.

My work is vitally important, for I help my students become professionals, true explorers of the unknown. They are attacking new engineering problems several years down the track compared to those we, the explorers of the '80s, addressed.

Attempts are now being made to create artificial gravity. If successful, it would do away with the present necessity of daily, exhausting, physical training and would allow us to live and work quietly without the problems of food consumption in zero gravity and without heavy suits to stress our bodies. With a more natural atmosphere, the problems of spending long periods in space would decrease as the body would be living in conditions closer to those on Earth.

In the future, I can see many scientists and other specialists of our international community working in large complexes, hundreds of metres long in near-Earth and lunar orbits. The first small orbital factories for the production of pure medical preparations, unique metallurgical alloys and special optics might make their appearance along with other types of manned ships.

Perhaps by this time humans would also be visiting other planets relatively close by. There could be construction of an intermediate lift-off base on the moon, an international program undertaken by the many countries involved in space exploration.

Greece, the Peloponnesian Peninsular and Cyclades Islands. Crete is centre and the North African coast is on the horizon.

The work of the pilot-cosmonaut would become similar to that of an international airline pilot, only their destination would be an orbital space station to ferry up personnel, equipment, fuel and other cargo, then return the products and other results of the work done in space, along with teams of specialists.

This vision can become a reality only if the production of weapons of mass destruction ceases. We must recycle the material from massed armaments to improve the quality of life on Earth and achieve new and peaceful discoveries in space.

Alexander Volkov, Russia

Next page: *This view from space shuttle* Atlantis, *in May 1992, shows clearly how the earth appears blue from space due to water covering most of its surface.*

215

100 000 Out ...

I really believe that if the political leaders of the world could see their planet from a distance of, let's say, 100 000 miles, their outlook could be fundamentally changed. That all-important border would be invisible, that noisy argument suddenly silenced. The tiny globe would continue to turn, serenely ignoring its subdivisions, presenting a unified facade that would cry out for unified understanding, for homogeneous treatment. Earth must become as it appears: blue and white, not capitalist or communist; blue and white, not rich or poor; blue and white, not envious or envied.

I am not a naive man. I don't believe that a glance from 100 000 miles out would cause a Prime Minister to scurry back to his parliament with a disarmament plan, but I do think it would plant a seed that ultimately could grow into such concrete action. Just because borders are invisible from space doesn't mean they are not real—they are and I like them. I feel just as thankful today that I live in the USA as I did before flying in space, and I have no desire for this country to merge into a United States of the World.

What I am saying, however, is that all countries must begin thinking of solutions to their problems which benefit the entire globe, not simply their own national interest. The smoke from the Saar Valley may pollute half a dozen other countries depending on the direction of the wind. We all know that, but it must be seen to make an indelible impression, to produce an emotional impact that makes one argue for long-term virtues at the expense of short-term gains.

I think the view from 100 000 miles could be invaluable in getting people together to work out joint solutions, by causing them to realize that the planet we share unites us in a way far more basic and far more important than differences in skin color or religion or economic system. The pity of it is that so far, the view from 100 000 miles has been the exclusive property of a handful of test pilots, rather than the world leaders who need this new perspective, or the poets who might communicate it to them.

Of course, we could always pass out whole-earth photographs and have everyone study them and, if there is any truth in my 100 000 mile premise, the results would be the same. Unfortunately, it doesn't work that way. Seeing Earth on an 8-by-10-inch piece of paper, or ringed by the plastic border of a television screen, is not only not the same as the real view, but even worse—it is a pseudo-sight that denies the reality of the matter. To actually be 100 000 miles out, to look out four windows and find nothing but black infinity, to finally locate the blue-and-white golf ball in the fifth window, to know how fortunate we are to be able to return to it—all these things are required, in addition to merely guaging its size and color. While the proliferation of photos constantly reminds us of Earth's dimensions, the photos deceive us as well, for they transfer the emphasis from one Earth to the multiplicity of reproduced images. There is but one Earth, tiny and fragile, and one must get 100 000 miles away to appreciate fully one's good fortune in living on it.

The Sahara, including mostly Libya and parts of Chad, Niger, Sudan, Algeria and Egypt.

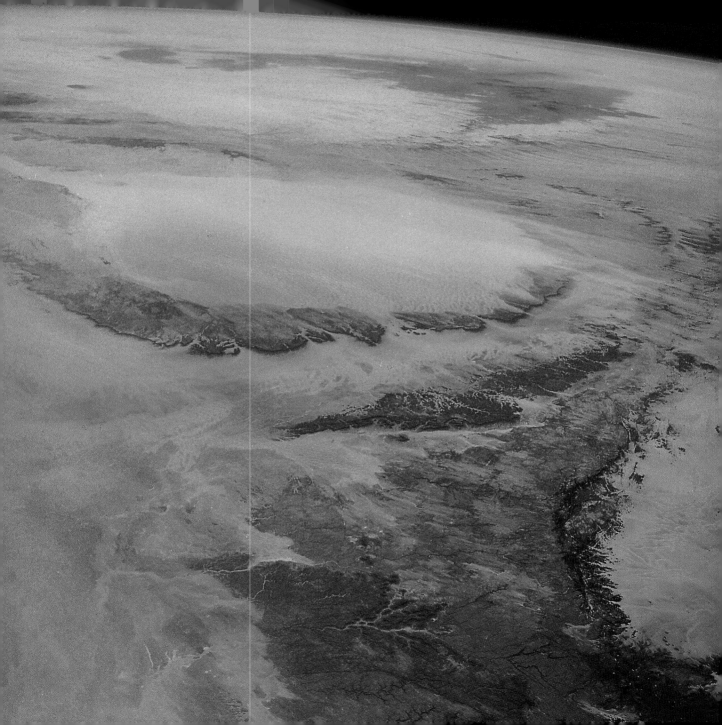

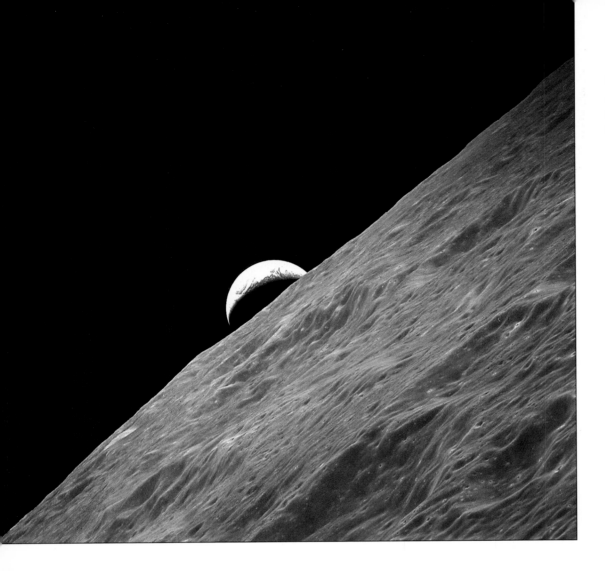

Earthrise viewed from Apollo 17. A crescent Earth is rising above the lunar horizon.

November 1984, space shuttle Discovery *lifts off on a duel mission to launch and salvage satellites.*

If I could use only one word to describe Earth as seen from the moon, I would ignore both its size and color and search for a more elemental quality, that of fragility. Earth appears 'fragile' above all else. I don't know why, but it does. As we walk its surface, it seems solid and substantial enough, almost infinite as it extends flatly in all directions. But from space there is no hint of ruggedness to it; smooth as a billiard ball, it seems delicately poised in its circular journey around the sun and, above all, it seems fragile.

Once this concept of the apparent Earthly fragility is introduced, one questions whether it is real or imagined and that leads inexorably to an examination of its surface. There we find things are very fragile indeed. Is the sea water clean enough to pour over your head, or is there a glaze of oil on its surface? Is the sky blue and the clouds white, or are they both obscured by the yellow-brown airborne filth? Is the riverbank a delight or an obscenity? The difference between a blue-and-white planet and a black-and-brown one is delicate indeed.

We rush about like busy ants, bringing immense quantities of subsurface solids, liquids and gases up from their hiding places, and converting them into quickly discarded solids, liquids and waste gases which lie on or just above the surface as unholy evidence of our collective insanity. The entropy of the planet, its unavailable energy, is increasing at an alarming rate; the burning of fossil fuels is an irreversible process and can only be slowed down. At the same time, the sun shines on us whether we like it or not; yet we are making but feeble efforts to focus this energy for our use. For that matter, the sun's energy, which is produced by converting hydrogen into helium, can probably be duplicated by creating our own little thermonuclear reactors here on Earth, if we ever put enough effort into the attempt.

These problems and their solutions are becoming increasingly well known, and I'm sure they would have been recognized had there been no space program. But anyone who has ever viewed our planet from afar can only cry out in pain at the knowledge that the pristine blue and white one can still close one's eyes and see, is an illusion masking an ever more senseless ugliness below.

The beauty of the planet from 100 000 miles out should be a goal for all of us, to help in our struggle to make it as it appears to be.

Michael Collins, USA from *Carrying the Fire*

GLOSSARY

ACA Out of Detent—the action that disengages the Attitude Control Assembly so that the hand controller in the lunar module crew cabin is no longer active after landing.

Anthropometrics—that part of anthropology having to do with physical measurements of the human body.

Attitude—the direction an object, such as a spacecraft, is pointing.

Capcom—the member of the team in mission control responsible for talking directly with the crew. It originates from the Mercury program where the capsule communicator talked with the crew in the *Mercury* capsule.

Cooling Sublimator—a device that supplies cooling by sublimating water into a vacuum.

CRT—a cathode ray tube (TV tube).

Cryo Tank—a tank that holds cryogenics (low temperature liquids and gases).

CST—Central Standard Time.

Downrange Azimuth—the angle between north and the direction downrange or the direction of spacecraft motion.

Drogue Chutes—small parachutes that are deployed to stabilize the spacecraft and pull out the main parachute.

Elapsed Time—the time elapsed from some event such as liftoff, beginning of re-entry, etc.

EMU—Extra-vehicular mobility unit; i.e., space suit.

EVA—Extra-vehicular activity; i.e., space walk.

Footpad Probe—probe that hangs down from the footpad of the lunar module to indicate ground contact during landing.

Gantry—a vertical structure used to assemble or service rocket boosters.

G Force—the force experienced by a body due to its acceleration measured in units of the force felt by gravity; i.e. the force equivalent to a body's weight would be a G force of 1.0.

Gimbal—the action or mechanism that causes something to swivel; e.g. the swiveling or mechanism that causes the swiveling of a rocket engine to steer the rocket.

High Gain Antenna—an antenna that has a narrow focus and gives a high gain (multiplication) to the signal received or sent.

Hypergolic Propellants—propellants that ignite upon contact.

Libration Points—points around a rotating system of two or more bodies where the force on an additional body (relatively small) is zero.

Main B Electrical Bus—a main line that supplies electricity distinct from other lines designated A, C, D, etc.

MECO—Main Engine Cutoff.

Mode Controls—controls for the mode of operation of equipment or systems.

MET—Mission Elapsed Time.

MMU—Manned Maneuvering Unit; i.e. jet pack used to rotate and propel an astronaut in space.

Nulled—reduced to zero.

Payload—that which is carried into orbit to be used on orbit.

Payload bay—the 60' long by 15' diameter bay used to hold and support payloads during launch, on-orbit activities and/or re-entry.

PDI—Powered Descent Initiate; the firing of rocket engines that starts the lunar module on its descent towards the lunar surface.

Roll, Pitch and Yaw—rotation about the forward, sideways and vertical axes.

S-Band Antenna—antenna that sends and receives signals in the S-band of the radio spectrum.

Solar Arrays—arrays of material that generate electricity when impacted by sunlight.

Telemetry—the automatic measurement and transmission of data from a distant source to a receiving station.

Timing Lanyard—line or chord connected to a piece of released equipment that starts a timer when the line reaches its full length.

Trans-Lunar Injection—the rocket engine burn that starts an *Apollo* spacecraft on its way towards the moon.